ROGER CA
TREASURY OF GREAT
CAT
STORIES

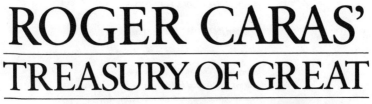

ROGER CARAS'
TREASURY OF GREAT

CAT STORIES

TRUMAN TALLEY BOOKS
E. P. DUTTON
NEW YORK

This paperback edition of Roger Caras' Treasury of Great Cat Stories
first published in 1988 by E. P. Dutton

Copyright © 1987 by Roger Caras

All rights reserved. Printed in the U.S.A.

Published in the United States by
Truman Talley Books • *E. P. Dutton,*
a division of NAL Penguin Inc.,
2 Park Avenue, New York, N.Y. 10016.

Published simultaneously in Canada
by Fitzhenry and Whiteside, Limited, Toronto.

Library of Congress Cataloging-in-Publication Data
Caras, Roger A.
Roger Caras' treasury of great cat stories.
"Truman Talley books."
1. Cats—Fiction. 2. Short stories, English.
3. Short stories, American. I. Title. II. Title:
Treasury of great cat stories.
PR1309.C36C37   1987   823'.01'0836   86-2200
ISBN: 0-525-48427-2

Designed by Earl Tidwell

1   3   5   7   9   10   8   6   4   2

Grateful acknowledgment is made to the following for permission to reprint copyright material:

Joan Aiken: "The Cat Who Lived in a Drainpipe." Copyright © 1977 by Joan Aiken Enterprises Ltd. From *The Faithless Lollybird* by Joan Aiken. Reprinted by permission of Doubleday & Company, Inc.

Stephen Vincent Benét: "The King of the Cats." From *The Selected Works of Stephen Vincent Benét,* published by Holt, Rinehart & Winston, Inc. Copyright 1933 by Stephen Vincent Benét. Copyright renewed © 1963 by Thomas C. Benét, Stephanie B. Mahin, and Rachel Benét Lewis. Reprinted by permission of Brandt & Brandt Literary Agents Inc.

CONTENTS

Contents

CONTENTS

Contents

Roger Caras

INTRODUCTION

Domestic cats emerged in Egypt between 1700 and 1600 B.C., not at all coincidentally at the same time the Egyptians invented the silo and began to store grain. For virtually their entire history our tabbies and their kin have had an arcane relationship with us. We have worshiped them, feared them, made them demigods and the familiars of devils and witches. They have foretold happiness and despair and been the agent of both. We have painted them, sculpted them, etched them, incorporated them into our architecture, used them as trademarks, eye-catchers, mousers, and most important, as companions.

Now, in our time, as the industrial revolution has just about completed its work of urbanizing and suburbanizing formerly rural man, the cat, that ultimate companion animal, is coming into its own to a greater degree and at a faster rate than ever before. Well over half the homes in America have cats now, and the number is increasing.

Another factor that has helped make the cat even more popular now than in the past is style. We live in a time of high fashion, exotic makeup, and very expensive gewgaws. Cats, inherently gemlike as they are, lend themselves to this hedonistic-materialist element in the human condition. The Russian blue with its satiny blue coat and emerald eyes, copper-colored Persians with amber eyes, and the newly emerging varieties of Siamese and Burmese cats are all gems waiting to be mounted in some very aesthetically sophisticated life-style. Cats like these go well with CD digital recordings, VCRs, and BMWs, just as they always have with Ming vases and needlepoint pillows. Cats are luxurious and they make us feel luxurious. We love to look at them and we love to read about them. Perhaps they are symbols of man's ineffable artistic longings.

Why are companion cats surpassing dogs in numbers? There are enough inherent wonders in the personality and style of the cat to explain it, but add convenience and you have the winning combination. Cats are not only lovely to behold and dear to have as friends, but they are ideal in size, do not not require exercise at a time when a great many people just don't like to walk around at night, and they are not expensive to feed. You don't have to cook for your cat now. The seven-billion-dollar-a-year pet food and accessory business has made it all very easy. Some supermarkets earn between two and five percent of their gross in the pet food department. What used to cover a few shelves now occupies an entire aisle, both sides.

While our finest artists were sculpting cats sacred and

profane and painting them as part of the normal household scene in culture after culture, those artists who work with language were equally bewitched. In Japan and Italy, France and England, the United States, China, Africa, everywhere one might turn the literature of the cat has grown and spread and been embraced by the greatest writers of their time. Ponder for a moment this spread: Rudyard Kipling ("The Cat That Walked by Himself"), Edgar Allan Poe ("The Black Cat"), Mark Twain ("Dick Baker's Cat"), Paul Gallico, Stephen Vincent Benét, and P. G. Wodehouse. These master storytellers were so taken with the cat that they turned away at least temporarily from the thousands of other things they might have written about and wrote about the soft one on four paws. Note as well, and this is most important, they did not write children's literature, at least not in the works assembled here. For some people assume that if a story is about a cat or a cat and human beings it has to be for youngsters. Nothing, as the pages that follow will demonstrate, could be further from the truth.

With the help of Martin Greenberg, the most knowledgeable anthologist in the English language, I have tried to select some of the best cat tales and to put them together in one place, a feline wonder book to which some of the greatest writers we know of have contributed their own sense of wonder and their own praise of beauty.

July 6, 1986
East Hampton, Long Island

Rudyard Kipling

THE CAT THAT WALKED BY HIMSELF

This befell and behappened and became and was, O, my Best Beloved, when the tame animals were wild. The Dog was wild, and the Horse was wild, and the Cow was wild, and the Sheep was wild, and the Pig was wild—as wild as could be—and they walked in the wet wild woods by their wild lones, but the wildest of all the wild animals was the Cat. He walked by himself, and all places were alike to him.

Of course the Man was wild too. He was dreadfully wild. He didn't even begin to be tame till he met the Woman and she did not like living in his wild ways. She picked out a nice dry cave, instead of a heap of wet leaves, to lie down in, and she strewed clean sand on the floor, and she lit a nice fire of wood at the back of the cave, and she hung a dried Wild Horse skin, tail down, across the opening of the cave, and she said: "Wipe your feet when you come in, and now we'll keep house."

That night, Best Beloved, they ate Wild Sheep roasted on the hot stones and flavored with wild garlic and wild pepper, and Wild Duck stuffed with wild rice, and wild fenugreek and wild coriander, and marrowbones of Wild Oxen, and wild cherries and wild granadillas. Then the Man went to sleep in front of the fire ever so happy, but the Woman sat up, combing. She took the bone of the shoulder of mutton, the big flat blade bone, and she looked at the wonderful marks on it, and she threw more wood on the fire and she made a magic. She made the first Singing Magic in the world.

Out in the wet wild woods all the wild animals gathered together where they could see the light of the fire a long way off, and they wondered what it meant.

Then Wild Horse stamped with his foot and said: "O, my friends and my enemies, why have the Man and the Woman made that great light in that great cave, and what harm will it do us?"

Wild Dog lifted up his nose and smelled the smell of the roast mutton and said: "I will go up and see and look and stay: for I think it is good. Cat, come with me."

"Nenni," said the Cat. "I am the Cat who walks by himself, and all places are alike to me. I will not come."

"Then we will never be friends again," said Wild Dog, and he trotted off to the cave.

But when he had gone a little way, the Cat said to himself: "All places are alike to me. Why should I not go too and see and look and come away?" So he slipped after Wild Dog softly, very softly, and hid himself where he could hear everything.

When Wild Dog reached the mouth of the cave he lifted up the dried Horse skin with his nose a little bit and sniffed the beautiful smell of the roast mutton, and the Woman heard him and laughed and said: "Here comes the first wild thing out of the wild woods. What do you want?"

Wild Dog said: "O, my enemy and wife of my enemy, what is this that smells so good in the wild woods?"

Then the Woman picked up a roasted mutton bone and threw it to Wild Dog and said: "Wild thing out of the wild woods, taste and try." Wild Dog gnawed the bone and it was more delicious than anything he had ever tasted, and he said: "O, my enemy and wife of my enemy, give me another."

The Woman said: "Wild thing out of the wild woods, help my Man to hunt through the day and guard this cave at night and I will give you as many roast bones as you need."

"Ah!" said the Cat listening, "this is a very wise Woman, but she is not so wise as I am."

Wild Dog crawled into the cave and laid his head on the Woman's lap and said: "O, my friend and wife of my friend, I will help your Man to hunt through the day, and at night I will guard your cave."

"Ah!" said the Cat listening, "that is a very foolish Dog." And he went back through the wet wild woods waving his tail and walking by his wild lone. But he never told anybody.

When the Man woke up he said: "What is Wild Dog doing here?" And the Woman said: "His name is not Wild Dog anymore, but the First Friend because he will be our friend for always and always and always. Take him with you when you go hunting."

Next night the Woman cut great green armfuls of fresh grass from the water meadows and dried it before the fire so that it smelled like new-mown hay, and she sat at the mouth of the cave and plaited a halter out of horsehide, and she looked at the shoulder of mutton bone—at the big broad blade bone— and she made a magic. She made the second Singing Magic in the world.

Out in the wild woods all the wild animals wondered what had happened to Wild Dog, and at last Wild Horse stamped with his foot and said: "I will go and see why Wild Dog has not returned. Cat, come with me."

"Nenni," said the Cat. "I am the Cat who walks by himself, and all places are alike to me. I will not come." But all the same he followed Wild Horse softly, very softly, and hid himself where he could hear everything.

When the Woman heard Wild Horse tripping and stumbling on his long mane she laughed and said: "Here comes the second wild thing out of the wild woods. What do you want?"

Wild Horse said: "O, my enemy and wife of my enemy, where is Wild Dog?"

The Woman laughed and picked up the blade bone and looked at it and said: "Wild thing out of the wild woods, you did not come here for Wild Dog, but for the sake of this good grass."

And Wild Horse, tripping and stumbling on his long mane, said: "That is true, give it to me to eat."

The Woman said: "Wild thing out of the wild woods, bend your wild head and wear what I give you and you shall eat the wonderful grass three times a day."

"Ah," said the Cat listening, "this is a clever Woman, but she is not so clever as I am."

Wild Horse bent his wild head and the Woman slipped the plaited hide halter over it, and Wild Horse breathed on the woman's feet and said: "O, my mistress and wife of my master, I will be your servant for the sake of the wonderful grass."

"Ah," said the Cat listening, "that is a very foolish Horse." And he went back through the wet wild woods, waving his wild tail and walking by his wild lone.

When the Man and the Dog came back from hunting, the Man said: "What is Wild Horse doing here?" And the Woman said: "His name is not Wild Horse anymore, but the First Servant because he will carry us from place to place for always and always and always. Take him with you when you go hunting."

Next day, holding her wild head high that her wild horns should not catch in the wild trees, Wild Cow came up to the cave, and the Cat followed and hid himself just the same as before; and everything happened just the same as before; and the Cat said the same things as before, and when Wild Cow had promised to give her milk to the Woman every day in exchange for the wonderful grass, the Cat went back through the wet wild woods walking by his lone just the same as before.

And when the Man and the Horse and the Dog came home from hunting and asked the same questions, same as before, the Woman said: "Her name is not Wild Cow anymore, but the Giver of Good Things. She will give us the warm white milk for always and always and always, and I will take care of her while you three go hunting."

Next day the Cat waited to see if any other wild thing would go up to the cave, but no one moved, so the Cat walked there by himself, and he saw the Woman milking the Cow, and he saw the light of the fire in the cave, and he smelled the smell of the warm white milk.

Cat said: "O, my enemy and wife of my enemy, where did Wild Cow go?"

The Woman laughed and said: "Wild thing out of the wild woods, go back to the woods again, for I have braided

5

up my hair and I have put away the blade bone, and we have no more need of either friends or servants in our cave."

Cat said: "I am not a friend and I am not a servant. I am the Cat who walks by himself and I want to come into your cave."

The Woman said: "Then why did you not come with First Friend on the first night?"

Cat grew very angry and said: "Has Wild Dog told tales of me?"

Then the Woman laughed and said: "You are the Cat who walks by himself and all places are alike to you. You are neither a friend nor a servant. You have said it yourself. Go away and walk by yourself in all places alike."

Then the Cat pretended to be sorry and said: "Must I never come into the cave? Must I never sit by the warm fire? Must I never drink the warm white milk? You are very wise and very beautiful. You should not be cruel even to a Cat."

Then the Woman said: "I knew I was wise but I did not know I was beautiful. So I will make a bargain with you. If ever I say one word in your praise you may come into the cave."

"And if you say two words in my praise?" said the Cat.

"I never shall," said the Woman, "but if I say two words you may sit by the fire in the cave."

"And if you say three words?" said the Cat.

"I never shall," said the Woman, "but if I do you may drink the warm white milk three times a day for always and always and always."

Then the Cat arched his back and said: "Now let the curtain at the mouth of the cave, and the fire at the back of the cave, and the milk pots that stand beside the fire remember what my enemy and the wife of my enemy has said." And he went away through the wet wild woods waving his wild tail and walking by his wild lone.

That night when the Man and the Horse and the Dog

came home from hunting, the Woman did not tell them of the bargain that she had made because she was afraid that they might not like it.

Cat went far and far away and hid himself in the wet wild woods by his wild lone for a long time till the Woman forgot all about him. Only the Bat—the little upside-down Bat—that hung inside the cave knew where Cat hid, and every evening he would fly to Cat with the news.

One evening the Bat said: "There is a Baby in the cave. He is new and pink and fat and small, and the Woman is very fond of him."

"Ah," said the Cat listening, "but what is the Baby fond of?"

"He is fond of things that are soft and tickle," said the Bat. "He is fond of warm things to hold in his arms when he goes to sleep. He is fond of being played with. He is fond of all those things."

"Ah," said the Cat, "then my time has come."

Next night Cat walked through the wet wild woods and hid very near the cave till morning time. The woman was very busy cooking, and the Baby cried and interrupted; so she carried him outside the cave and gave him a handful of pebbles to play with. But still the Baby cried.

Then the Cat put out his paddy-paw and patted the Baby on the cheek, and it cooed; and the Cat rubbed against its fat knees and tickled it under its fat chin with his tail. And the Baby laughed; and the Woman heard him and smiled.

Then the Bat—the little upside-down Bat—that hung in the mouth of the cave said: "O, my hostess and wife of my host and mother of my host, a wild thing from the wild woods is most beautifully playing with your Baby."

"A blessing on that wild thing whoever he may be," said the Woman straightening her back, "for I was a busy Woman this morning and he has done me a service."

7

That very minute and second, Best Beloved, the dried horse-skin curtain that was stretched tail-down at the mouth of the cave fell down—*So!*—because it remembered the bargain, and when the Woman went to pick it up—lo and behold! —the Cat was sitting quite comfy inside the cave.

"O, my enemy and wife of my enemy and mother of my enemy," said the Cat, "it is I, for you have spoken a word in my praise, and now I can sit within the cave for always and always and always. But still I am the Cat who walks by himself and all places are alike to me."

The Woman was very angry and shut her lips tight and took up her spinning wheel and began to spin.

But the Baby cried because the Cat had gone away, and the Woman could not hush him for he struggled and kicked and grew black in the face.

"O, my enemy and wife of my enemy and mother of my enemy," said the Cat, "take a strand of the thread that you are spinning and tie it to your spindle wheel and drag it on the floor and I will show you a magic that shall make your Baby laugh as loudly as he is now crying."

"I will do so," said the Woman, "because I am at my wits' end, but I will not thank you for it."

She tied the thread to the little pot spindle wheel and drew it across the floor and the Cat ran after it and patted it with his paws, and rolled head over heels, and tossed it backward over his shoulder, and chased it between his hind legs, and pretended to lose it, and pounced down upon it again till the Baby laughed as loudly as he had been crying, and scrambled after the Cat and frolicked all over the cave till he grew tired and settled down to sleep with the Cat in his arms.

"Now," said the Cat, "I will sing the Baby a song that shall keep him asleep for an hour." And he began to purr loud and low, low and loud, till the Baby fell fast asleep. The

Woman smiled as she looked down upon the two of them and said: "That was wonderfully done. Surely you are very clever, O, Cat."

That very minute and second, Best Beloved, the smoke of the fire at the back of the cave came down in clouds from the roof because it remembered the bargain, and when it had cleared away—lo and behold!—the Cat was sitting, quite comfy, close to the fire.

"O, my enemy and wife of my enemy and mother of my enemy," said the Cat, "it is I, for you have spoken a second word in my praise, and now I can sit by the warm fire at the back of the cave for always and always and always. But still I am the Cat who walks by himself and all places are alike to me."

Then the Woman was very, very angry and let down her hair and put more wood on the fire and brought out the broad blade bone of the shoulder of mutton and began to make a magic that should prevent her from saying a third word in praise of the Cat. It was not a Singing Magic, Best Beloved, it was a Still Magic; and by and by the cave grew so still that a little we-wee Mouse crept out of a corner and ran across the floor.

"O, my enemy and wife of my enemy and mother of my enemy," said the Cat, "is that little Mouse part of your magic?"

"No," said the Woman, and she dropped the blade bone and jumped upon a footstool in front of the fire and braided up her hair very quick for fear that the Mouse should run up it.

"Ah," said the Cat listening, "then the Mouse will do me no harm if I eat it?"

"No," said the Woman, braiding up her hair; "eat it quick and I will always be grateful to you."

Cat made one jump and caught the little Mouse, and the Woman said: "A hundred thanks to you, O, Cat. Even the

9

First Friend is not quick enough to catch little Mice as you have done. You must be very wise."

That very moment and second, O, Best Beloved, the milk pot that stood by the fire cracked in two pieces—*So!*—because it remembered the bargain, and when the Woman jumped down from the footstool—lo and behold!—the Cat was lapping up the warm white milk that lay in one of the broken pieces.

"O, my enemy and wife of my enemy and mother of my enemy," said the Cat, "it is I, for you have spoken three words in my praise, and now I can drink the warm white milk three times a day for always and always and always. But *still* I am the Cat who walks by himself and all places are alike to me."

Then the Woman laughed and set him a bowl of the warm white milk and said: "O, Cat, you are as clever as a Man, but remember that the bargain was not made with the Man or the Dog, and I do not know what they will do when they come home."

"What is that to me?" said the Cat. "If I have my place by the fire and my milk three times a day I do not care what the Man or the Dog can do."

That evening when the Man and the Dog came into the cave the Woman told them all the story of the bargain, and the Man said: "Yes, but he has not made a bargain with me or with all proper Men after me." And he took off his two leather boots and he took up his little stone ax (that makes three) and he fetched a piece of wood and a hatchet (that is five altogether), and he set them out in a row and he said: "Now we will make a bargain. If you do not catch Mice when you are in the cave, for always and always and always, I will throw these five things at you whenever I see you, and so shall all proper Men do after me."

"Ah," said the Woman listening. "This is a very clever Cat, but he is not so clever as my Man."

The Cat counted the five things (and they looked very knobby) and he said: "I will catch Mice when I am in the cave for always and always and always: but still I am the Cat that walks by himself and all places are alike to me."

"Not when I am near," said the Man. "If you had not said that I would have put all these things away (for always and always and always), but now I am going to throw my two boots and my little stone ax (that makes three) at you whenever I meet you, and so shall all proper Men do after me."

Then the Dog said: "Wait a minute. He has not made a bargain with me." And he sat down and growled dreadfully and showed all his teeth and said: "If you are not kind to the Baby while I am in the cave for always and always and always I will chase you till I catch you, and when I catch you I will bite you, and so shall all proper Dogs do after me."

"Ah," said the Woman listening. "This is a very clever Cat, but he is not so clever as the Dog."

Cat counted the Dog's teeth (and they looked very pointed) and he said: "I will be kind to the Baby while I am in the cave as long as he does not pull my tail too hard for always and always and always. But still I am the Cat that walks by himself and all places are alike to me."

"Not when I am near," said the Dog. "If you had not said that I would have shut my mouth for always and always and always, but now I am going to chase you up a tree whenever I meet you, and so shall all proper Dogs do after me."

Then the Man threw his two boots and his little stone ax (that makes three) at the Cat, and the Cat ran out of the cave and the Dog chased him up a tree, and from that day to this, Best Beloved, three proper Men out of five will always throw things at a Cat whenever they meet him, and all proper Dogs will chase him up a tree. But the Cat keeps his side of the bargain too. He will kill Mice and he will be kind to Babies when he is in the house, as long as they do not pull his tail too hard. But when he has done that, and between times, he is the Cat that walks by himself and all places are alike to him, and if you look out at nights you can see him waving his wild tail and walking by his wild lone—just the same as before.

Leigh Hunt

THE CAT BY THE FIRE

A blazing fire, a warm rug, candles lit and curtains drawn, the kettle on for tea (nor do the "first circles" despise the preference of a kettle to an urn, as the third or fourth may do), and, finally, the cat before you, attracting your attention—it is a scene which everybody likes unless he has a morbid aversion to cats; which is not common. There are some nice inquirers, it is true, who are apt to make uneasy comparisons of cats with dogs—to say they are not so loving, that they prefer the house to the man, et cetera. But agreeably to the good old maxim, that "comparisons are odious," our readers, we hope, will continue to like what is likable in anything, for its own sake, without trying to render it unlikable from its inferiority to something else—a process by which we might ingeniously contrive to put soot into every dish that is set before us, and to reject one thing after another, till we were pleased with nothing. Here is a good fireside, and a cat to it; and it would be our own fault, if, in removing to another house and another fireside, we did not take care that the cat removed with us. Cats cannot look to the moving of goods, as men do. If we would have creatures considerate toward us, we must be so toward them. It is not to be expected of everybody, quadruped or biped, that they should stick to us in spite of our want of merit, like a dog or a benevolent sage. Besides, stories have been told of cats very much to the credit of their benignity; such as their following a master about like a dog, waiting at a gentleman's door to thank him for some obligation overnight, et cetera. And our readers may remember the history of the famous Godolphin Arabian, upon whose grave a cat that had lived with him in the stable went and stretched itself, and died.

The cat purrs, as if it applauded our consideration—and gently moves its tail. What an odd expression of the power to be irritable and the will to be pleased there is in its face, as it looks up at us! We must own that we do not prefer a cat in the act of purring, or of looking in that manner. It reminds us of the sort of smile, or simmer (*simper* is too weak and fleeting a word) that is apt to be in the faces of irritable people when they are pleased to be in a state of satisfaction. We prefer, for a general expression, the cat in a quiet, unpretending state, and the human countenance with a look indicative of habitual grace and composure, as if it were not necessary to take any violent steps to prove its amiability—the "smile without a smile," as the poet beautifully calls it.

Furthermore (in order to get rid at once of all that may be objected to poor Pussy, as boys at school get down their bad dumpling as fast as possible before the meat comes), we own we have an objection to the way in which a cat sports with a mouse before she kills it, tossing and jerking it about like a ball, and letting it go, in order to pounce upon it with the greater relish. And yet what right have we to apply human measures of cruelty to the inferior reflectability of a cat? Perhaps she has no idea of the mouse's being alive, in the sense that we have—most likely she looks upon it as a pleasant movable toy, made to be eaten—a sort of lively pudding, that oddly jumps hither and thither. It would be hard to beat into the head of a country squire of the old class that there is any cruelty in hunting a hare; and most assuredly it would be still harder to beat mouse-sparing into the head of a cat. You might read the most pungent essay on the subject into her ear, and she would only sneeze at it.

As to the unnatural cruelties which we sometimes read of, committed by cats upon their offspring, they are exceptions to the common and beautiful rules of nature, and accordingly we have nothing to do with them. They are traceable to some unnatural circumstances of breeding or position. Enormities as monstrous are to be found among human beings, and argue nothing against the general character of the species. Even dogs are not always immaculate; and sages have made slips. Dr. Franklin cut off his son with a shilling for differing with him in politics.

But cats resemble tigers? They are tigers in miniature? Well—and very pretty miniatures they are. And what has the tiger himself done, that he has not a right to eat his dinner as well as Jones? A tiger treats a man much as a cat does a mouse—granted; but we have no reason to suppose that he is aware of the man's sufferings, or means anything but to satisfy his hunger; and what have the butcher and poulterer been about meanwhile? The tiger, it is true, lays about him a little superfluously sometimes, when he gets into a sheepfold, and kills more than he eats; but does not the squire or the marquis do pretty much like him in the month of September? Nay, do we not hear of venerable judges that would not hurt a fly going about in that refreshing month, seeking whom they may lame? See the effect of habit and education! And you can educate the tiger in no other way than by attending to his stomach. Fill that, and he will want no men to eat, probably not even to lame. On the other hand, deprive Jones of his dinner for a day or two, and see what a state he will be in, especially if he is by nature irascible. Nay, keep him from it for a half an hour, and observe the tiger propensities of his stomach and fingers—how worthy of killing he thinks the cook, and what boxes of the ear he feels inclined to give the footboy.

Animals, by the nature of things, in their present state dispose of one another into their respective stomachs, without ill will on any side. They keep down the several populations of their neighbors, till time may come when superfluous population of any kind need not exist, and predatory appearances may vanish from the earth, as the wolves have done from England. But whether they may or not is not a question by a hundred times so important to moral inquirers as into the possibilities of human education and the nonsense of ill will. Show the nonentity of that, and we may all get our dinners as jovially as we can, sure of these three undoubted facts—that life is long, death short, and the world beautiful. And so we bring our thoughts back again to the fireside, and look at the cat.

Poor Pussy! She looks up at us again, as if she thanked us for those vindications of dinner; and symbolically gives a twist of a yawn and a lick to her whiskers. Now she proceeds to clean herself all over, having a just sense of the demands of her elegant person—beginning judiciously with her paws, and fetching amazing tongues at her hind hips. Anon, she scratches her neck with a foot of rapid delight, leaning her head toward it, and shutting her eyes, half to accommodate the action of the skin, and half to enjoy the luxury. She then rewards her paws with a few more touches—look at the action of her head and neck, how pleasing it is, the ears pointed forward, and the neck gently arching to and fro. Finally, she gives a sneeze and another twist of mouth and whiskers, and then, curling her tail toward her front claws, settles herself on her hindquarters, in an attitude of bland meditation.

What does she think of? Of her saucer of milk at breakfast? Or of the thump she got yesterday in the kitchen for stealing the meat? Or of her own meat, the Tartar's dish, noble horseflesh? Or of her friend the cat next door, the most impassioned of serenaders? Or of her little ones, some of whom are now large, and all of them gone? Is *that* among her recollections when she looks pensive? Does she taste of the noble prerogative sorrows of man?

She is a sprightly cat, hardly past her youth; so, happening to move the fringe of the rug a little with our foot, she darts out a paw, and begins plucking it and inquiring into the matter, as if it were a challenge to play, or something lively enough to be eaten. What a graceful action of that foot of hers, between delicacy and petulance—combining something of a thrust out, a beat, and a scratch. There seems even something of a little bit of fear in it, as if just enough to provoke her courage, and give her the excitement of a sense of hazard. We remember being much amused with seeing a kitten manifestly making a series of experiments upon the patience of its mother—trying how far the latter would put up with positive bites and thumps. The kitten ran at her every moment, gave her a knock or a bite of the tail; and then ran back again, to recommence the assault. The mother sat looking at her, as if betwixt tolerance and admiration, to see how far the spirit of the family was inherited or improved by her sprightly offspring. At length, however, the "little Pickle" presumed too far, and the mother, lifting up her paw, and meeting her at the very nick of the moment, gave her one of the most unsophisticated boxes of the ear we ever beheld. It sent her rolling half over the room, and made her come to a most ludicrous pause, with the oddest little look of premature and wincing meditation.

The lapping of the milk out of the saucer is what one's human thirst cannot sympathize with. It seems as if there could be no satisfaction in such a series of atoms of drink. Yet the saucer is soon emptied; and there is a refreshment to one's ears in that sound of plashing with which the action is accompanied and which seems indicative of a like comfort to Pussy's mouth. Her tongue is thin and can make a spoon of itself. This, however, is common to other quadrupeds with the cat, and does not, therefore, more particularly belong to our feline consideration. Not so the electricity of its coat, which gives out sparks under the hand; its passion for the herb valerian (Did the reader ever see one roll in it? It is a mad sight) and other singular delicacies of nature, among which, perhaps, is to be reckoned its taste for fish, a creature with whose element it has so little to do that it is supposed even to abhor it; though lately we read somewhere of a swimming cat that used to fish for itself. And this reminds us of an exquisite anecdote of dear, dogmatic, diseased, thoughtful, surly, charitable Johnson, who would go out of doors himself and buy oysters for his cat, because his black servant was too proud to do it! Not that we condemn the black, in those enslaving, unliberating days. He had a right to the mistake, though we should have thought better of him had he seen further, and subjected his pride to affection for such a master. But Johnson's true practical delicacy in the matter is beautiful. Be assured that he thought nothing of "condescension" in it, or of being eccentric. He was singular in some things, because he could not help it. But he hated eccentricity. No, in his best moments he felt himself simply to be a man, and a good man too, though a frail—one that in virtue as well as humility, and in a knowledge of his ignorance as well as his wisdom, was desirous of being a Christian philosopher; and accordingly he went out, and bought food for his hungry cat, because his poor Negro was too proud to do it, and there was nobody else in the way whom he had a right to ask. What must anybody that saw him have thought as he turned up Bolt Court! But doubtless he went as secretly as possible—that is to say, if he considered the thing at all. His friend Garrick could not have done as much! He was too grand, and on the great "stage" of life. Goldsmith could, but he would hardly have thought of it. Beauclerc might, but he would have thought it necessary to excuse it with a jest or a wager, or some such thing. Sir Joshua Reynolds, with his fashionable, fine-lady-painting hand, would certainly have shrunk from it. Burke would have reasoned himself into its propriety, but he would have reasoned himself out again. Gibbon! Imagine its being put into the head of Gibbon!! He and his bagwig would have started with all the horror of a gentleman usher; and he would have rung the bell for the cook's-deputy's-under-assistant-errand-boy.

Cats at firesides live luxuriously and are the picture of comfort; but lest they should not bear their portion of trouble in this world, they have the drawbacks of being liable to be shut out of doors on cold nights, beatings from the "aggravated" cooks, overpettings of children (how should we like to be squeezed and pulled about in that manner by some great patronizing giants?), and last, not least, horrible merciless tramples of unconscious human feet and unfeeling legs of chairs. Elegance, comfort, and security seem the order of the day on all sides, and you are going to sit down to dinner, or to music, or to take tea, when all of a sudden the cat gives a squall as if she were mashed; and you are not sure that the fact is otherwise. Yet she gets in the way again, as before, and dares all the feet and mahogany in the room. Beautiful present sufficingness of a cat's imagination! Confined to the snug circle of her own sides, and the two next inches of rug or carpet.

W. W. Jacobs

THE WHITE CAT

The traveler stood looking from the taproom window of the Cauliflower at the falling rain. The village street below was empty, and everything was quiet with the exception of the garrulous old man smoking with much enjoyment on the settle behind him.

"It'll do a power o' good," said the ancient, craning his neck round the edge of the settle and turning a bleared eye on the window. "I ain't like some folk; I never did mind a drop o' rain."

The traveler grunted and, returning to the settle opposite the old man, fell to lazily stroking a cat which had strolled in attracted by the warmth of the small fire which smoldered in the grate.

"He's a good mouser," said the old man, "but I expect that Smith the landlord would sell 'im to anybody for arf a crown; but we 'ad a cat in Claybury once that you couldn't ha' bought for a hundred golden sovereigns."

The traveler continued to caress the cat.

"A white cat, with one yaller eye, and one blue one," continued the old man. "It sounds queer, but it's as true as I sit 'ere wishing that I 'ad another mug o' ale as good as the last you gave me."

The traveler, with a start that upset the cat's nerves, finished his own mug, and then ordered both to be refilled. He stirred the fire into a blaze and, lighting his pipe and putting one foot onto the hob, prepared to listen.

It used to belong to old man Clark, young Joe Clark's uncle, said the ancient, smacking his lips delicately over the ale and extending a tremulous claw to the tobacco pouch pushed toward him; and he was never tired of showing it off to people. He used to call it 'is blue-eyed darling, and the fuss 'e made o' that cat was sinful.

Young Joe Clark couldn't bear it, but being down in 'is uncle's will for five cottages and a bit o' land bringing in about forty pounds a year, he 'ad to 'ide his feelings and pretend as he loved it. He used to take it little drops o' cream and tidbits o' meat, and old Clark was so pleased that 'e promised 'im that he should 'ave the cat along with all the other property when 'e was dead.

Young Joe said he couldn't thank 'im enough, and the old man, who 'ad been ailing a long time, made 'im come up every day to teach 'im 'ow to cook its meat and then chop it up fine; 'ow it liked a clean saucer every time for its milk; and 'ow he wasn't to make a noise when it was asleep.

"Take care your children don't worry it, Joe," he sez one

day, very sharp. 'One o' your boys was pulling its tail this morning, and I want you to clump his 'ead for 'im."

"Which one was it?" sez Joe.

"The slobbery-nosed one," says old Clark.

"I'll give 'im a clout as soon as I get 'ome," sez Joe, who was very fond of 'is children.

"Go and fetch 'im and do it 'ere," sez the old man, "that'll teach 'im to love animals."

Joe went off 'ome to fetch the boy, and arter his mother 'ad washed his face, and wiped his nose, an' put a clean pinneyfore on 'im, he took 'im to 'is uncle's and clouted his 'ead for 'im. Arter that Joe and 'is wife 'ad words all night long, and next morning old Clark, coming in from the garden, was just in time to see 'im kick the cat right acrost the kitchen.

He could 'ardly speak for a minute, and when 'e could, Joe see plain wot a fool he'd been. Fust of all 'e called Joe every name he could think of—which took 'im a long time—and then he ordered 'im out of 'is house.

"You shall 'ave my money when your betters have done with it," he sez, "and not afore. That's all you've done for yourself."

Joe Clark didn't know what he meant at the time, but when old Clark died three months arterward 'e found out. His uncle 'ad made a new will and left everything to old George Barstow for as long as the cat lived, providing that he took care of it. When the cat was dead the property was to go to Joe.

The cat was only two years old at the time, and George Barstow, who was 'arf crazy with joy, said it shouldn't be 'is fault if it didn't live another twenty years.

The funny thing was the quiet way Joe Clark took it. He didn't seem to be at all cut up about it, and when Henery Walker said it was a shame, 'e said he didn't mind, and that George Barstow was a old man, and he was quite welcome to 'ave the property as long as the cat lived.

"It must come to me by the time I'm an old man," he sez, "and that's all I care about."

Henery Walker went off, and as 'e passed the cottage where old Clark used to live, and which George Barstow 'ad moved into, 'e spoke to the old man over the palings and told 'im wot Joe Clark 'ad said. George Barstow only grunted and went on stooping and prying over 'is front garden.

"Bin and lost something?" sez Henery Walker, watching 'im.

"No, I'm finding," sez George Barstow, very fierce, and picking up something. "That's the fifth bit o' powdered liver I've found in my garden this morning."

Henery Walker went off whistling, and the opinion he'd 'ad o' Joe Clark began to improve. He spoke to Joe about it that arternoon, and Joe said that if 'e ever accused 'im o' such a thing again he'd knock 'is 'ead off. He said that he 'oped the cat 'ud live to be a hundred, and that 'e'd no more think of giving it poisoned meat than Henery Walker would of paying for 'is drink so long as 'e could get anybody else to do it for 'im.

They 'ad bets up at this 'ere Cauliflower public 'ouse that evening as to 'ow long that cat 'ud live. Nobody gave it more than a month, and Bill Chambers sat and thought o' so many ways o' killing it on the sly that it was wunnerful to hear 'im.

George Barstow took fright when he 'eard of them, and the care 'e took o' that cat was wunnerful to behold. 'Arf its time it was shut up in the back bedroom, and the other 'arf George Barstow was fussing arter it till that cat got to hate 'im like pison. Instead o' giving up work as he'd thought to do, 'e told Henery Walker that 'e'd never worked so hard in his life.

"Wot about fresh air and exercise for it?" sez Henery.

"Wot about Joe Clark?" sez George Barstow. "I'm tied 'and and foot. I dursen't leave the house for a moment. I ain't been to the Cauliflower since I've 'ad it, and three times I got out o' bed last night to see if it was safe."

"Mark my words," sez Henery Walker, "if that cat don't 'ave exercise, you'll lose it."

"I shall lose it if it does 'ave exercise," sez George Barstow, "that I know."

He sat down thinking arter Henery Walker 'ad gone, and then he 'ad a little collar and chain made for it and took it out for a walk. Pretty nearly every dog in Claybury went with 'em, and the cat was in such a state o' mind afore they got 'ome he couldn't do anything with it. It 'ad a fit as soon as they got indoors, and George Barstow, who 'ad read about children's fits in the almanac, gave it a warm bath. It brought it round immediate, and then it began to tear around the room and up and downstairs till George Barstow was afraid to go near it.

It was so bad that evening, sneezing, that George Barstow went for Bill Chambers, who'd got a good name for doctoring animals, and asked 'im to give it something. Bill said he'd got some powders at 'ome that would cure it at once, and he went and fetched 'em and mixed one up with a bit o' butter.

"That's the way to give a cat medicine," he sez, "smear it with the butter and then it'll lick it off, powder and all."

He was just going to rub it on the cat when George Barstow caught 'old of 'is arm and stopped 'im.

"How do I know it ain't pison?" he sez. "You're a friend o' Joe Clark's, and for all I know he may ha' paid you to pison it."

"I wouldn't do such a thing," sez Bill. "You ought to know me better than that."

"All right," sez George Barstow, "you eat it then, and I'll give you two shillings instead o' one. You can easy mix some more."

"Not me," sez Bill Chambers, making a face.

"Well, three shillings, then," sez George Barstow, getting more and more suspicious like. "Four shillings—five shillings."

Bill Chambers shook his 'ead, and George Barstow, more and more certain that he 'ad caught 'im trying to kill 'is cat and that 'e wouldn't eat the stuff, rose 'im up to ten shillings.

Bill looked at the butter and then 'e looked at the ten shillings on the table, and at last he shut 'is eyes and gulped it down and put the money in 'is pocket.

"You see, I 'ave to be careful, Bill," sez George Barstow, rather upset.

Bill Chambers didn't answer 'im. He sat there as white as a sheet, and making such extraordinary faces that George was 'arf afraid of 'im.

"Anything wrong, Bill?" he sez at last.

Bill sat staring at 'im, and then all of a sudden he clapped 'is 'andkerchief to 'is mouth and, getting up from 'is chair, opened the door and rushed out. George Barstow thought at fust that he 'ad eaten pison for the sake o' the ten shillings, but when 'e remembered that Bill Chambers 'ad got the most delikit stummock in Claybury he altered 'is mind.

The cat was better next morning, but George Barstow 'ad 'ad such a fright about it 'e wouldn't let it go out of 'is sight, and Joe Clark began to think that 'e would 'ave to wait longer for that property than 'e had thought, arter all. To 'ear 'im talk anybody'd ha' thought that 'e loved that cat. We didn't pay much attention to it up at the Cauliflower 'ere, except maybe to wink at 'im—a thing he couldn't a-bear—but at 'ome, o' course, his young 'uns thought as everything he said was Gospel; and one day, coming 'ome from work, as he was passing George Barstow's he was paid out for his deceitfulness.

"I've wronged you, Joe Clark," sez George Barstow, coming to the door, "and I'm sorry for it."

"Oh!" sez Joe staring.

"Give that to your little Jimmy," sez George Barstow, giving 'im a shilling. "I've give 'im one, but I thought arterward it wasn't enough."

"What for?" sez Joe, staring at 'im again.

"For bringing my cat 'ome," sez George Barstow. " 'Ow it got out I can't think, but I lost it for three hours, and I'd about given it up when your little Jimmy brought it to me in 'is arms. He's a fine little chap and 'e does you credit."

Joe Clark tried to speak, but he couldn't get a word out, and Henery Walker, wot 'ad just come up and 'eard wot passed, took hold of 'is arm and helped 'im home. He walked like a man in a dream, but 'arfway he stopped and cut a stick from the hedge to take 'ome to little Jimmy. He said the boy 'ad been asking him for a stick for some time, but up till then 'e'd always forgotten it.

At the end o' the fust year that cat was still alive, to everybody's surprise; but George Barstow took such care of it 'e never let it out of 'is sight. Every time 'e went out he took it with 'im in a hamper, and, to prevent its being pisoned, he paid Isaac Sawyer, who 'ad the biggest family in Claybury, sixpence a week to let one of 'is boys taste its milk before it had it.

The second year it was ill twice, but the horse doctor that George Barstow got for it said that it was as 'ard as nails, and with care it might live to be twenty. He said that it wanted more fresh air and exercise; but when he 'eard 'ow George Barstow came by it he said that p'r'aps it would live longer indoors arter all.

At last one day, when George Barstow 'ad been living on the fat o' the land for nearly three years, that cat got out again. George 'ad raised the front-room winder two or three inches to throw something outside, and, afore he knew wot was 'appening, the cat was outside and going up the road about twenty miles an hour.

George Barstow went after it, but he might as well ha' tried to catch the wind. The cat was 'arf wild with joy at getting out again, and he couldn't get within 'arf a mile of it.

He stayed out all day without food or drink, follering it about until it came on dark, and then, o' course, he lost sight of it, and hoping against 'ope that it would come 'ome for its food, he went 'ome and waited for it. He sat up all night dozing in a chair in the front room with the door left open, but it was all no use; and arter thinking for a long time wot was best to do, he went out and told some o' the folks it was lost and offered a reward of five pounds for it.

You never saw such a hunt then in all your life. Nearly every man, woman, and child in Claybury left their work or school and went to try to earn that five pounds. By the arternoon George Barstow made it ten pounds, provided the cat was brought 'ome safe and sound, and people as was too old to walk stood at their cottage doors to snap it up as it came by.

Joe Clark was hunting for it 'igh and low, and so was 'is wife and the boys. In fact, I b'lieve that everybody in Claybury excepting the parson and Bob Pretty was trying to get that ten pounds.

O' course, we could understand the parson—'is pride wouldn't let 'im; but a low, poaching, thieving rascal like Bob Pretty turning up 'is nose at ten pounds was more than we could make out. Even on the second day, when George Barstow made it ten pounds down and a shilling a week for a year besides, he didn't offer to stir; all he did was to try and make fun o' them as was looking for it.

"Have you looked everywhere you can think of for it, Bill?" he sez to Bill Chambers.

"Yes, I 'ave," sez Bill.

"Well, then, you want to look everywhere else," sez Bob Pretty. "I know where I should look if I wanted to find it."

"Why don't you find it, then," sez Bill.

" 'Cos I don't want to make mischief," sez Bob Pretty.

"I don't want to be unneighborly to Joe Clark by interfering at all."

"Not for all that money?" sez Bill.

"Not for fifty pounds," sez Bob Pretty. "You ought to know me better than that, Bill Chambers."

"It's my belief that you know more about where that cat is than you ought to," sez Joe Gubbins.

"You go on looking for it, Joe," sez Bob Pretty, grinning. "It's good exercise for you, and you've only lost two days' work."

"I'll give you 'arf a crown if you let me search your 'ouse, Bob," sez Bill Chambers, looking at 'im very 'ard.

"I couldn't do it at the price, Bill," sez Bob Pretty, shaking his 'ead. "I'm a pore man, but I'm very partikler who I 'ave come into my 'ouse."

O' course, everybody left off looking at once when they heard about Bob—not that they believed that he'd be such a fool as to keep the cat in his 'ouse; and that evening, as soon as it was dark, Joe Clark went round to see 'im.

"Don't tell me as that cat's found, Joe," sez Bob Pretty, as Joe opened the door.

"Not as I've 'eard of," said Joe, stepping inside. "I wanted to speak to you about it; the sooner it's found the better I shall be pleased."

"It does you credit, Joe Clark," sez Bob Pretty.

"It's my belief that it's dead," sez Joe, looking at 'im very 'ard, "but I want to make sure afore taking over the property."

Bob Pretty looked at 'im and then he gave a little cough. "Oh, you want it to be found dead," he sez. "Now, I wonder whether that cat's worth more dead or alive."

Joe Clark coughed then. "Dead, I should think," he sez at last.

"George Barstow's just 'ad bills printed offering fifteen pounds for it," sez Bob Pretty.

"I'll give that or more when I come into the property," sez Joe Clark.

"There's nothing like ready money, though, is there?" sez Bob.

"I'll promise it to you in writing, Bob," sez Joe, trembling.

"There's some things that don't look well in writing, Joe," says Bob Pretty, considering. "Besides, why should you promise it to *me*?"

"O' course, I meant if you found it," sez Joe.

"Well, I'll do my best, Joe," sez Bob Pretty, "and none of us can do no more than that, can they?"

They sat talking and argufying over it for over an hour, and twice Bob Pretty got up and said 'e was going to see whether George Barstow wouldn't offer more. By the time they parted they was as thick as thieves, and next morning Bob Pretty was wearing Joe Clark's watch and chain, and Mrs. Pretty was up at Joe's 'ouse to see whether there was any of 'is furniture as she 'ad a fancy for.

She didn't seem to be able to make up 'er mind at fust between a chest o' drawers that 'ad belonged to Joe's mother and a grandfather clock. She walked from one to the other for about ten minutes, and then Bob, who 'ad come in to 'elp her, told 'er to 'ave both.

"You're quite welcome," he sez. "Ain't she, Joe?"

Joe Clark said "Yes," and arter he 'ad helped them carry 'em 'ome the Prettys went back and took the best bedstead to pieces, 'cos Bob said as it was easier to carry that way. Mrs. Clark 'ad to go and sit down at the bottom o' the garden with the neck of 'er dress undone to give herself air, but when she saw the little Prettys each walking 'ome with one of 'er best chairs on their 'eads she got and walked up and down like a mad thing.

"I'm sure I don't know where we are to put it all," sez Bob Pretty to Joe Gubbins, wot was looking on with other folks, "but Joe Clark is that generous he won't 'ear of our leaving anything."

"Has 'e gorn mad?" sez Bill Chambers, staring at 'im.

"Not as I knows on," sez Bob Pretty. "It's 'is good'artedness, that's all. He feels sure that that cat's dead, and that he'll 'ave George Barstow's cottage and furniture. I told 'im he'd better wait till he'd made sure, but 'e wouldn't."

Before they'd finished the Prettys 'ad picked that 'ouse as clean as a bone and Joe Clark 'ad to go and get clean straw for his wife and children to sleep on; not that Mrs. Clark 'ad any sleep that night, nor Joe neither.

Henery Walker was the fust to see what it really meant, and he went rushing off as fast as 'e could run to tell George Barstow. George couldn't believe 'im at fust, but when 'e did he swore that if a 'air of that cat's head was harmed 'e'd have the law o' Bob Pretty, and arter Henery Walker 'ad gone 'e walked round to tell 'im so.

"You're not yourself, George Barstow, else you wouldn't try and take away my character like that," sez Bob Pretty.

"Wot did Joe Clark give you all them things for?" sez George, pointing to the furniture.

"Took a fancy to me, I s'pose," sez Bob. "People do sometimes. There's something about me at times that makes 'em like me."

"He gave 'em to you to kill my cat," sez George Barstow. "It's plain enough for anybody to see."

Bob Pretty smiled. "I expect it'll turn up safe and sound one o' these days," he sez, "and then you'll come round and beg my pardon. P'r'aps—"

"P'r'aps wot?" sez George Barstow, arter waiting a bit.

"P'r'aps somebody 'as got it and is keeping it till you've drawed the fifteen pounds out o' the bank," sez Bob, looking at 'im very hard.

"I've taken it out o' the bank," sez George, starting. "If

that cat's alive, Bob, and you've got it, there's fifteen pounds the moment you 'and it over."

"Wot d'ye mean—me got it?" sez Bob Pretty. "You be careful o' my character."

"I mean if you know where it is," sez George Barstow, trembling all over.

"I don't say I couldn't find it, if that's wot you mean," sez Bob. "I can gin'rally find things when I want to."

"You find me that cat, alive and well, and the money's yours, Bob," sez George, 'ardly able to speak, now that 'e fancied the cat was still alive.

Bob Pretty shook his 'ead. "No, that won't do," he sez. "S'pose I did 'ave the luck to find that pore animal, you'd say I'd had it all the time and refuse to pay."

"I swear I wouldn't, Bob," sez George Barstow, jumping up.

"Best thing you can do if you want me to try and find that cat," says Bob Pretty, "is to give me the fifteen pounds now, and I'll go and look for it at once. I can't trust you, George Barstow."

"And I can't trust you," sez George Barstow.

"Very good," sez Bob, getting up, "there's no 'arm done. P'r'aps Joe Clark'll find the cat is dead and p'r'aps you'll find it's alive. It's all one to me."

George Barstow walked off 'ome, but he was in such a state o' mind 'e didn't know wot to do. Bob Pretty turning up 'is nose at fifteen pounds like that made 'im think that Joe Clark 'ad promised to pay 'im more if the cat was dead; and at last, arter worrying about it for a couple of hours, 'e came up to this 'ere Cauliflower and offered Bob the fifteen pounds.

"Wot's this for?" sez Bob.

"For finding my cat," sez George.

"Look here," sez Bob, handing it back. "I've 'ad enough o' your insults; I don't know where your cat is."

"I mean for trying to find it, Bob," sez George Barstow.

"Oh, well, I don't mind that," sez Bob, taking it. "I'm a 'ardworking man, and I've got to be paid for my time; it's only fair to my wife and children. I'll start now."

He finished up 'is beer, and while the other chaps was telling George Barstow wot a fool he was, Joe Clark slipped out arter Bob Pretty and began to call 'im all the names he could think of.

"Don't you worry," sez Bob. "The cat ain't found yet.'

"Is it dead?" sez Joe Clark, 'ardly able to speak.

" 'Ow should I know?" sez Bob. "That's wot I got to try and find out. That's wot you gave me your furniture for, and what George Barstow gave me the fifteen pounds for, ain't it? Now, don't you stop me now, 'cos I'm goin' to begin looking."

He started looking there and then, and for the next two or three days George Barstow and Joe Clark see 'im walking up and down with his 'ands in 'is pockets looking over garden fences and calling "Puss." He asked everybody 'e see whether they 'ad seen a white cat with one blue eye and one yaller one, and every time 'e came into the Cauliflower he puts his 'ead over the bar and called "Puss," 'cos, as 'e said, it was as likely to be there as anywhere else.

It was about a week after the cat 'ad disappeared that George Barstow was standing at 'is door talking to Joe Clark, who was saying the cat must be dead and 'e wanted 'is property, when he sees a man coming up the road carrying a basket stop and speak to Bill Chambers. Just as 'e got near them an awful "meow" come from the basket and George Barstow and Joe Clark started as if they'd been shot.

"He's found it?" shouts Bill Chambers, pointing to the man.

"It's been living with me over at Ling for a week pretty nearly," sez the man. "I tried to drive it away several times, not knowing that there was fifteen pounds offered for it."

George Barstow tried to take 'old of the basket.

"I want that fifteen pounds fust," sez the man.

"That's on'y right and fair, George," sez Bob Pretty, who 'ad just come up. "You've got all the luck, mate. We've been hunting 'igh and low for that cat for a week."

Then George Barstow tried to explain to the man and call Bob Pretty names at the same time; but it was all no good. The man said it 'ad nothing to do with 'im wot he 'ad paid to Bob Pretty; and at last they fetched Policeman White over from Cudford, and George Barstow signed a paper to pay five shillings a week till the reward was paid.

George Barstow 'ad the cat for five years arter that, but he never let it get away again. They got to like each other in time and died within a fortnight of each other, so that Joe Clark got 'is property arter all.

Edgar Allan Poe

THE BLACK CAT

For the most wild, yet most homely narrative which I am about to pen, I neither expect nor solicit belief. Mad indeed would I be to expect it in a case where my very senses reject their own evidence. Yet mad am I not—and very surely do I not dream. But tomorrow I die, and today I would unburden my soul. My immediate purpose is to place before the world, plainly, succinctly, and without comment, a series of mere household events. In their consequences, these events have terrified—have tortured—have destroyed me. Yet I will not attempt to expound them. To me, they have presented little but horror; to many they will seem less terrible than baroques. Hereafter, perhaps, some intellect may be found which will reduce my phantasm to the commonplace: some intellect more calm, more logical, and far less excitable than my own, which will perceive, in the circumstances I detail with awe, nothing more than an ordinary succession of very natural causes and effects.

From my infancy I was noted for the docility and humanity of my disposition. My tenderness of heart was even so conspicuous as to make me the jest of my companions. I was especially fond of animals, and was indulged by my parents with a great variety of pets. With these I spent most of my time, and never was so happy as when feeding and caressing them. This peculiarity of character grew with my growth, and in my manhood I derived from it one of my principal sources of pleasure. To those who have cherished an affection for a faithful and sagacious dog, I need hardly be at the trouble of explaining the nature or the intensity of the gratification thus derivable. There is something in the unselfish and self-sacrificing love of a brute which goes directly to the heart of him who has had frequent occasion to test the paltry friendship and gossamer fidelity of mere Man.

I married early, and was happy to find in my wife a disposition not uncongenial with my own. Observing my partiality for domestic pets, she lost no opportunity of procuring those of the most agreeable kind. We had birds, goldfish, a fine dog, rabbits, a small monkey, and *a cat.*

This latter was a remarkably large and beautiful animal, entirely black, and sagacious to an astonishing degree. In speaking of his intelligence, my wife, who at heart was not a little tinctured with superstition, made frequent allusion to the ancient popular notion which regarded all black cats as witches in disguise. Not that she was ever *serious* upon this point—and I mention the matter at all for no better reason than that it happens, just now, to be remembered.

Pluto—this was the cat's name—was my favorite pet and

playmate. I alone fed him, and he attended me wherever I went about the house. It was even with difficulty that I could prevent him from following me through the streets.

Our friendship lasted, in this manner, for several years, during which my general temperament and character, through the instrumentality of the Fiend Intemperance, had (I blush to confess it) experienced a radical alteration for the worse. I grew, day by day, more moody, more irritable, more regardless of the feelings of others. I suffered myself to use intemperate language to my wife. At length, I even offered her personal violence. My pets, of course, were made to feel the change in my disposition. I not only neglected but ill-used them. For Pluto, however, I still retained sufficient regard to restrain me from maltreating him, as I made no scruple of maltreating the rabbits, the monkey, or even the dog, when by accident, or through affection, they came in my way. But my disease grew upon me—for what disease is like Alcohol! —and at length even Pluto, who was now becoming old, and consequently somewhat peevish—even Pluto began to experience the effects of my ill temper.

One night, returning home, much intoxicated, from one of my haunts about town, I fancied that the cat avoided my presence. I seized him; when, in his fright at my violence, he inflicted a slight wound upon my hand with his teeth. The fury of a demon instantly possessed me. I knew myself no longer. My original soul seemed, at once, to take its flight from my body; and a more than fiendish malevolence, gin-nurtured, thrilled every fiber of my frame. I took from my waistcoat pocket a penknife, opened it, grasped the poor beast by the throat, and deliberately cut one of its eyes from the socket! I blush, I burn, I shudder, while I pen the damnable atrocity.

When reason returned with the morning—when I had slept off the fumes of the night's debauch—I experienced a sentiment half of horror, half of remorse, for the crime of which I had been guilty; but it was, at best, a feeble and equivocal feeling, and the soul remained untouched. I again plunged into excess, and soon drowned in wine all memory of the deed.

In the meantime the cat slowly recovered. The socket of the lost eye presented, it is true, a frightful appearance, but he no longer appeared to suffer any pain. He went about the house as usual, but, as might be expected, fled in extreme terror at my approach. I had so much of my old heart left, as to be at first grieved by this evident dislike on the part of a creature which had once so loved me. But this feeling soon gave place to irritation. And then came, as if to my final and irrevocable overthrow, the spirit of Perverseness. Of this spirit philosophy takes no account. Yet I am not more sure that my soul lives than I am that perverseness is one of the primitive impulses of the human heart—one of the indivisible primary faculties, or sentiments, which give direction to the character of Man. Who has not, a hundred times, found himself committing a vile or a silly action, for no other reason than because he knows he should *not?* Have we not a perpetual inclination, in the teeth of our best judgment, to violate that which is Law, merely because we understand it to be such? This spirit of perverseness, I say, came to my final overthrow. It was this unfathomable longing of the soul *to vex itself*—to offer violence to its own nature; to do wrong for the wrong's sake only—that urged me to continue and finally to consummate the injury I had inflicted upon the unoffending brute. One morning, in cold blood, I slipped a noose about its neck and hung it to the limb of a tree; hung it with the tears streaming from my eyes, and with the bitterest remorse at my heart; hung it *because* I knew that it had loved me, and *because* I felt it had given me no reason of offense; hung it *because* I knew that in so doing I was committing a sin—a deadly sin that would so jeopardize my immortal soul as to place it, if such a thing were possible, even beyond the reach of the infinite mercy of the Most Merciful and Most Terrible God.

On the night of the day on which this cruel deed was done, I was aroused from sleep by the cry of fire. The curtains of my bed were in flames. The whole house was blazing. It was with great difficulty that my wife, a servant, and myself made our escape from the conflagration. The destruction was complete. My entire worldly wealth was swallowed up, and I resigned myself thenceforward to despair.

I am above the weakness of seeking to establish a sequence of cause and effect between the disaster and the atrocity. But I am detailing a chain of facts, and wish not to leave even a possible link imperfect. On the day succeeding the fire, I visited the ruins. The walls, with one exception, had fallen in. This exception was found in a compartment wall, not very thick, which stood about the middle of the house, and against which had rested the head of my bed. The plastering had here, in great measure, resisted the action of the fire—a fact which I attributed to its having been recently spread. About this wall a dense crowd were collected, and many persons seemed to be examining a particular portion of it with very minute and eager attention. The words "Strange!" "Singular!" and other similar expressions excited my curiosity. I approached and saw, as if graven in bas-relief upon the white surface, the figure of a gigantic cat. The impression was given with an accuracy truly marvelous. There was a rope about the animal's neck.

When I first beheld this apparition—for I could scarcely regard it as less—my wonder and my terror were extreme. But at length reflection came to my aid. The cat, I remembered, had been hung in a garden adjacent to the house. Upon the alarm of fire, this garden had been immediately filled by the crowd—by some one of whom the animal must have been cut from the tree and thrown, through an open window, into my chamber. This had probably been done with the view of arousing me from sleep. The falling of other walls had compressed the victim of my cruelty into the substance of the freshly spread plaster; the lime of which, with the flames, and the ammonia from the carcass, had then accomplished the portraiture as I saw it.

Although I thus readily accounted to my reason, if not altogether to my conscience, for the startling fact just detailed, it did not the less fail to make a deep impression upon my fancy. For months I could not rid myself of the phantasm of the cat; and during this period there came back into my spirit a half sentiment that seemed, but was not, remorse. I went so far as to regret the loss of the animal, and to look about me, among the vile haunts which I now habitually frequented, for another pet of the same species, and of somewhat similar appearance, with which to supply its place.

One night as I sat, half stupefied, in a den of more than infamy, my attention was suddenly drawn to some black object, reposing upon the head of one of the immense hogsheads of gin, or of rum, which constituted the chief furniture of the apartment. I had been looking steadily at the top of this hogshead for some minutes, and what now caused me surprise was the fact that I had not sooner perceived the object thereupon. I approached it, and touched it with my hand. It was a black cat—a very large one—fully as large as Pluto, and closely resembling him in every respect but one: Pluto had not a white hair upon any portion of his body; but this cat had a large, although indefinite, splotch of white, covering nearly the whole region of the breast.

Upon my touching him, he immediately arose, purred loudly, rubbed against my hand, and appeared delighted with my notice. This, then, was the very creature of which I was in search. I at once offered to purchase it of the landlord; but this person made no claim to it—knew nothing of it—had never seen it before.

I continued my caresses, and when I prepared to go home, the animal evinced a disposition to accompany me. I permitted it to do so; occasionally stooping and patting it as

I proceeded. When it reached the house, it domesticated itself at once and became immediately a great favorite with my wife.

For my own part, I soon found a dislike to it arising within me. This was just the reverse of what I had anticipated; but—I know not how or why it was—its evident fondness for myself rather disgusted and annoyed. By slow degrees these feelings of disgust and annoyance rose into the bitterness of hatred. I avoided the creature—a certain sense of shame, and the remembrance of my former deed of cruelty, preventing me from physically abusing it. I did not, for some weeks, strike, or otherwise violently ill use it; but gradually—very gradually—I came to look upon it with unutterable loathing, and to flee silently from its odious presence, as from the breath of a pestilence.

What added, no doubt, to my hatred of the beast, was the discovery, on the morning after I brought it home, that, like Pluto, it also had been deprived of one of its eyes. This circumstance, however, only endeared it to my wife, who, as I have already said, possessed, in a high degree, that humanity of feeling which had once been my distinguishing trait, and the source of many of my simplest and purest pleasures.

With my aversion to this cat, however, its partiality for myself seemed to increase. It followed my footsteps with a pertinacity which it would be difficult to make the reader comprehend. Wherever I sat, it would crouch beneath my chair, or spring upon my knees, covering me with its loathsome caresses. If I arose to walk it would get between my feet and thus nearly throw me down, or, fastening its long and sharp claws in my dress, clamber, in this manner, to my breast. At such times, although I longed to destroy it with a blow, I was yet withheld from so doing, partly by a memory of my former crime, but chiefly—let me confess it at once—by absolute *dread* of the beast.

This dread was not exactly a dread of physical evil—and

yet I should be at a loss how otherwise to define it. I am almost ashamed to own—yes, even in this felon's cell, I am almost ashamed to own—that the terror and horror with which the animal inspired me had been heightened by one of the merest chimeras it would be possible to conceive. My wife had called my attention, more than once, to the character of the mark of white hair, of which I have spoken, and which constituted the sole visible difference between the strange beast and the one I had destroyed. The reader will remember that this mark, although large, had been originally very indefinite; but, by slow degrees—degrees nearly imperceptible, and which for a long time my reason struggled to reject as fanciful—it had, at length, assumed a rigorous distinctness of outline. It was now the representation of an object that I shudder to name—and for this, above all, I loathed, and dreaded, and would have rid myself of the monster *had I dared*—it was now, I say, the image of a hideous—of a ghastly thing—of the Gallows!—oh, mournful and terrible engine of Horror and of Crime, of Agony and of Death!

And now was I indeed wretched beyond the wretchedness of mere Humanity. And a brute beast—whose fellow I had contemptuously destroyed—*a brute beast* to work out for *me*—for me, a man fashioned in the image of the High God —so much of insufferable woe! Alas! neither by day nor by night knew I the blessing of rest anymore! During the former the creature left me no moment alone, and in the latter I started hourly from dreams of unutterable fear to find the hot breath of *the thing* upon my face, and its vast weight—an incarnate nightmare that I had no power to shake off—incumbent eternally upon my heart!

Beneath the pressure of torments such as these the feeble remnant of the good within me succumbed. Evil thoughts became my sole intimates—the darkest and most evil of thoughts. The moodiness of my usual temper increased to hatred of all things and of all mankind; while from the sudden, frequent, and ungovernable outbursts of a fury to which I now blindly abandoned myself, my uncomplaining wife, alas! was the most usual and the most patient of sufferers.

One day she accompanied me, upon some household errand, into the cellar of the old building which our poverty compelled us to inhabit. The cat followed me down the steep stairs, and, nearly throwing me headlong, exasperated me to madness. Uplifting an ax, and forgetting in my wrath the childish dread which had hitherto stayed my hand, I aimed a blow at the animal, which, of course, would have proved instantly fatal had it descended as I wished. But this blow was arrested by the hand of my wife. Goaded by the interference into a rage more than demoniacal, I withdrew my arm from her grasp and buried the ax in her brain. She fell dead upon the spot, without a groan.

This hideous murder accomplished, I set myself forthwith, and with entire deliberation, to the task of concealing the body. I knew that I could not remove it from the house, either by day or by night, without the risk of being observed by the neighbors. Many projects entered my mind. At one period I thought of cutting the corpse into minute fragments, and destroying them by fire. At another, I resolved to dig a grave for it in the floor of the cellar. Again, I deliberated about casting it in the well in the yard—about packing it in a box, as if merchandise, with the usual arrangements, and so getting a porter to take it from the house. Finally I hit upon what I considered a far better expedient than either of these. I determined to wall it up in the cellar, as the monks of the Middle Ages are recorded to have walled up their victims.

For a purpose such as this the cellar was well adapted. Its walls were loosely constructed, and had lately been plastered throughout with a rough plaster, which the dampness of the atmosphere had prevented from hardening. Moreover, in one of the walls was a projection, caused by a false chimney, or fireplace, that had been filled up and made to resemble the rest of the cellar. I made no doubt that I could readily displace the bricks at this point, insert the corpse, and wall the whole up as before, so that no eye could detect anything suspicious.

And in this calculation I was not deceived. By means of a crowbar I easily dislodged the bricks, and, having carefully deposited the body against the inner wall, I propped it in that position, while with little trouble I relaid the whole structure as it originally stood. Having procured mortar, sand, and hair, with every possible precaution, I prepared a plaster which could not be distinguished from the old, and with this I very carefully went over the new brickwork. When I had finished, I felt satisfied that all was right. The wall did not present the slightest appearance of having been disturbed. The rubbish on the floor was picked up with the minutest care. I looked around triumphantly, and said to myself: "Here at least, then, my labor has not been in vain."

My next step was to look for the beast which had been the cause of so much wretchedness; for I had, at length, firmly resolved to put it to death. Had I been able to meet with it at the moment, there could have been no doubt of its fate; but it appeared that the crafty animal had been alarmed at the violence of my previous anger, and forbore to present itself in my present mood. It is impossible to describe or to imagine the deep, the blissful sense of relief which the absence of the detested creature occasioned in my bosom. It did not make its appearance during the night; and thus for one night, at least, since its introduction into the house, I soundly and tranquilly slept; aye, *slept* even with the burden of murder upon my soul!

The second and the third day passed, and still my tormentor came not. Once again I breathed as a free man. The monster, in terror, had fled the premises forever! I should behold it no more! My happiness was supreme! The guilt of my dark deed disturbed me but little. Some few inquiries had been made, but these had been readily answered. Even a search had been instituted—but of course nothing was to be discovered. I looked upon my future felicity as secured.

Upon the fourth day of the assassination, a party of the police came, very unexpectedly, into the house, and proceeded again to make rigorous investigation of the premises. Secure, however, in the inscrutability of my place of concealment, I felt no embarrassment whatever. The officers bade me accompany them in their search. They left no nook or corner unexplored. At length, for the third or fourth time, they descended into the cellar. I quivered not in a muscle. My heart beat calmly as that of one who slumbers in innocence. I walked the cellar from end to end. I folded my arms upon my bosom, and roamed easily to and fro. The police were thoroughly satisfied and prepared to depart. The glee at my heart was too strong to be restrained. I burned to say if but one word, by way of triumph, and to render doubly sure their assurance of my guiltlessness.

"Gentlemen," I said at last, as the party ascended the steps, "I delight to have allayed your suspicions. I wish you all health and a little more courtesy. By the bye, gentlemen, this—this is a very well-constructed house" (in the rabid desire to say something easily, I scarcely knew what I uttered at all)—"I may say an *excellently* well-constructed house. These walls—are you going, gentlemen?—these walls are solidly put together"; and here, through the mere frenzy of bravado, I rapped heavily with a cane which I held in my hand, upon that very portion of the brickwork behind which stood the corpse of the wife of my bosom.

But may God shield and deliver me from the fangs of the Archfiend! No sooner had the reverberation of my blows sunk into silence than I was answered by a voice from within the tomb!—by a cry, at first muffled and broken, like the sobbing of a child, and then quickly swelling into one long, loud, and continuous scream, utterly anomalous and inhuman —a howl—a wailing shriek, half of horror and half of triumph, such as might have arisen only out of hell, conjointly from the throats of the damned in their agony and of the demons that exult in the damnation.

Of my own thoughts it is folly to speak. Swooning, I staggered to the opposite wall. For one instant the party on the stairs remained motionless, through extremity of terror and of awe. In the next, a dozen stout arms were toiling at the wall. It fell bodily. The corpse, already greatly decayed and clotted with gore, stood erect before the eyes of the spectators. Upon its head, with red extended mouth and solitary eye of fire, sat the hideous beast whose craft had seduced me into murder and whose informing voice had consigned me to the hangman. I had walled the monster up within the tomb!

Philip Gilbert Hamerton

CATS

One evening before dinner-time the present writer had occasion to go into a dining room where the cloth was already laid, the glasses all in their places on the sideboard and table, and the lamp and candles lighted. A cat, which was a favorite in the house, finding the door ajar, entered softly after me, and began to make a little exploration after his manner. I have a fancy for watching animals when they think they are not observed, so I affected to be entirely absorbed in the occupation which detained me there, but took note of the cat's proceedings without in any way interrupting them. The first thing he did was to jump upon a chair, and thence upon the sideboard. There was a good deal of glass and plate upon that piece of furniture, but nothing as yet which, in the cat's opinion, was worth purloining; so he brought all his paws together on the very edge of the board, the two forepaws in the middle, the others on both sides, and sat balancing himself in that attitude for a minute or two, whilst he contemplated the long glittering vista of the table. As yet there was not an atom of anything eatable upon it, but the cat probably thought he might as well ascertain whether this were so or not by a closer inspection, for with a single spring he cleared the abyss and alighted noiselessly on the tablecloth. He walked all over it and left no trace; he passed amongst the slender glasses, fragile-stemmed, like air bubbles cut in half and balanced on spears of ice; yet he disturbed nothing, broke nothing, anywhere. When his inspection was over he slipped out of sight, having been perfectly inaudible from the beginning, so that a blind person could only have suspected his visit by that mysterious sense which makes the blind aware of the presence of another creature.

This little scene reveals one remarkable characteristic of the feline nature, the innate and exquisite refinement of its behavior. It would be infinitely difficult, probably even impossible, to communicate a delicacy of this kind to any animal by teaching. The cat is a creature of most refined and subtle perceptions naturally. Why should she tread so carefully? It is not from fear of offending her master and incurring punishment, but because to do so is in conformity with her own ideal of behavior; exactly as a lady would feel vexed with herself if she broke anything in her own drawing room, though no one would blame her *maladresse* and she would never feel the loss.

The contrast in this respect between cats and other animals is very striking. I will not wrong the noble canine nature so far as to say that it has no delicacy, but its delicacy is not of this kind, not in actual touch, as the cat's is. The motions of the cat, being always governed by the most refined sense of touch in the animal world, are typical in quite a perfect way of what we call tact in the human world. And as a man who has tact exercises it on all occasions for his own satisfaction, even when there is no positive need for it, so a cat will walk daintily and observantly everywhere, whether amongst the glasses on a dinner table or the rubbish in a farmyard.

It is easy to detract from the admirableness of this delicate quality in the cat by a reference to the necessities of her life in a wild state. Anyone not much disposed to enter into imaginative sentimentalities about animals might say to us, "What you admire so much as a proof of ladylike civilization in the cat is rather an evidence that she has retained her savage habits. When she so carefully avoids the glasses on the dinner table she is not thinking of her behavior as a dependent on civilized man, but acting in obedience to hereditary habits of caution in the stealthy chase, which is the natural accomplishment of her species. She will stir no branch of a shrub lest her fated bird escape her, and her feet are noiseless that the mouse may not know of her coming." This, no doubt, would be a probable account of the origin of that fineness of touch and movement which belongs to cats, but the fact of that fineness remains. In all the domestic animals, and in man himself, there are instincts and qualities still more or less distinctly traceable to a savage state, and these qualities are often the very basis of civilization itself. That which in the wild cat is but the stealthy cunning of the hunter is refined in the tame one into a habitual gentleness often very agreeable to ladies, who dislike the boisterous demonstrations of the dog and his incorrigible carelessness.

This quality of extreme caution, which makes the cat avoid obstacles that a dog would dash through without a thought, makes her at the same time somewhat reserved and suspicious in all the relations of her life. If a cat has been allowed to run half wild this suspicion can never be overcome. There was a numerous population of cats in this half-wild state for some years in the garrets of my house. Some of these were exceedingly fine, handsome animals, and I very much wished to get them into the rooms we inhabited and so domesticate them; but all my blandishments were useless. The nearest approach to success was in the case of a superb white-and-black animal, who, at last, would come to me occasionally and permit me to caress his head, because I scratched him behind the ears. Encouraged by this measure of confidence, I went so far on one occasion as to lift him a few inches from the ground; on which he behaved himself very much like a wild-cat just trapped in the woods, and for some days after it was impossible even to get near him. He never came downstairs in a regular way, but communicated with the outer world by means of roofs and trees, like the other untamable creatures in the garrets. On returning home after an absence I sought him vainly, and have never encountered him since.

This individual lived on the confines of civilization, and it is possible that his tendency to friendliness might have been developed into a feeling more completely trustful by greater delicacy and care. I happened to mention him to a hotel-keeper who was unusually fond of animals, and unusually successful in winning their affections. He told me that his own cats were remarkable for their uncommon tameness, being very much petted and caressed and constantly in the habit of seeing numbers of people who came to the hotel, and he advised me to try a kitten of his breed. This kitten, from hereditary civilization, behaved with the utmost confidence from the beginning and, with the exception of occasional absences for his own purposes, has lived with me regularly enough. In winter he generally sleeps upon my dog, who submits in patience; and I have often found him on horseback in the stable, not from any taste for equestrianism, but simply because a horse cloth is a perpetual warmer when there is a living horse beneath it.

All who have written on cats are unanimous in the opinion that their caressing ways bear reference simply to themselves. My cat loves the dog and horse exactly with the tender sentiment we have for foot warmers and railway rugs during a journey in the depth of winter, nor have I ever been able to detect any worthier feeling toward his master. Ladies are often fond of cats, and pleasantly encourage the illusion that they are affectionate; it is said too that very intellectual men have often a liking for the same animal. In both these cases the attachment seems to be due more to certain other qualities of the cat than to any strength of sentiment on his part. Of all animals that we can have in a room with us, the cat is the least disturbing. Dogs bring so much dirt into houses that many ladies have a positive horror of them; squirrels leap about in a manner highly dangerous to the ornaments of a drawing room; whilst monkeys are so incorrigibly mischievous that it is impossible to tolerate them, notwithstanding the nearness of the relationship. But you may have a cat in the room with you without anxiety about anything except eatables. He will rob a dish if he can get at it, but he will not, except by the rarest of accidents, displace a sheet of paper or upset an inkstand. The presence of a cat is positively soothing to a student, as the presence of a quiet nurse is soothing to the irritability of an invalid. It is agreeable to feel that you are not absolutely alone, and it seems to you, as you work, as if the cat took care that all her movements should be noiseless, purely out of consideration for your comfort. Then, if you have time to caress her, you know that there will be purring responses, and why inquire too closely into the sincerity of her gratitude? There have been instances of people who surrounded themselves with cats; old maids have this fancy sometimes, which is intelligible, because old maids delight in having objects on which to lavish their inexhaustible kindness, and their love of neatness and comfort is in harmony with the neat habits of these comfort-appreciating creatures. A dog on velvet is evidently out of place—he would be as happy on clean straw—

but a cat on velvet does not awaken any sense of the incongruous. It is more difficult to understand how men of business ever take to cats. A well-known French politician, who certainly betrayed nothing feminine in his speeches, was so fond of cats that it was impossible to dine peaceably at his house on account of four licensed feline marauders which promenaded upon the dinner table, helping themselves to everything, and jumping about the shoulders of the guests. . . .

There has always been a feeling that a black cat was not altogether "canny." Many of us, if we were quite sincere, would confess to a superstition about black cats. They seem to know too much, and is it not written that their ancestors were the companions and accomplices of witches in the times of old? Who can tell what baleful secrets may not have been transmitted through their generations? There can be no doubt that cats know a great deal more than they choose to tell us, though occasionally they may let a secret out in some unguarded moment. Shelley, the poet, who had an intense sense of the supernatural, narrates the following history, as he heard it from Mr. G. Lewis:

> A gentleman on a visit to a friend who lived on the skirts of an extensive forest on the east of Germany lost his way. He wandered for some hours among the trees, when he saw a light at a distance. On approaching it, he was surprised to observe that it proceeded from the interior of a ruined monastery. Before he knocked, he thought it prudent to look through the window. He saw a multitude of cats assembled round a small grave, four of whom were letting down a coffin with a crown upon it. The gentleman, startled at this unusual sight, and imagining that he had arrived among the retreats of fiends or witches, mounted his horse and rode away with the utmost precipitation. He arrived at his friend's house at a late hour, who had sat up for him. On his arrival, his friend questioned as to the cause of the traces of trouble visible on his

face. He began to recount his adventure, after much difficulty, knowing that it was scarcely possible that his friends should give faith to his relation. No sooner had he mentioned the coffin with a crown upon it, than his friend's cat, who seemed to have been lying asleep before the fire, leaped up, saying, "Then I am the King of the Cats!" and scrambled up the chimney and was seen no more.

Now, is not that a remarkable story, proving, at the same time, the attention cats pay to human conversation even when they outwardly seem perfectly indifferent to it, and the monarchical character of their political organization, which without this incident might have remained forever unknown to us? This happened, we are told, in eastern Germany; but in our own island, less than a hundred years ago, there remained at least one cat fit to be the ministrant of a sorceress. When Sir Walter Scott visited the Black Dwarf, "Bowed Davie Ritchie," the Dwarf said, "Man, hae ye ony poo'r?" meaning power of a supernatural kind, and he added solemnly, pointing to a large black cat whose fiery eyes shone in a dark corner of the cottage, "*He* has poo'r!" In Scott's place any imaginative person would have more than half believed Davie, as indeed did his illustrious visitor. The ancient Egyptians, who knew as much about magic as the wisest of the moderns, certainly believed that the cat had *poo'r,* or they would not have mummified him with such painstaking conscientiousness. It may easily be imagined that, in times when science did not exist, a creature whose fur emitted lightnings when anybody rubbed it in the dark must have inspired great awe, and there is really an air of mystery about cats which considerably exercises the imagination. This impression would be intensified in the case of people born with a physical antipathy to cats, and there are such persons. A Captain Logan, of Knockshinnock in Ayrshire, is mentioned in one of the early numbers of *Chambers' Journal* as having this antipathy in the strongest form. He simply could not endure the sight of cat or kitten, and though a tall, strong man, would do anything to escape from the objects of his instinctive and uncontrollable horror, climbing upon chairs if a cat entered the room and not daring to come down till the creature was removed from his presence. These mysterious repugnances are outside the domain of reason. Many people, not without courage, are seized with involuntary shudderings when they see a snake or a toad; others could not bring themselves to touch a rat, though the rat is one of the cleanliest of animals—not, certainly, as to his food, but his person. It may be presumed that one Mrs. Griggs, who lived, I believe, in Edinburgh, did not share Captain Logan's antipathy, for she kept in her house no less than eighty-six living cats, and had, besides, twenty-eight dead ones in glass cases, immortalized by the art of the taxidermist. If it is true, and it certainly is so in a great measure, that those who love most know most, then Mrs. Griggs would have been a much more competent person to write on cats than the colder-minded author of these chapters. It is wonderful to think how much that good lady must have known of the *lovableness* of cats, of those recondite qualities which may endear them to the human heart!

What a difference in knowledge and feeling concerning cats between Mrs. Griggs and a gamekeeper! The gamekeeper knows a good deal about them too, but it is not exactly affection which has given keenness to *his* observation. He does not see a "dear sweet pet" in every cat that crosses his woodland paths, but the most destructive of poachers, the worst of "vermin." And there can be no doubt that from his point of view the gamekeeper is quite right, even as good Mrs. Griggs may have been from hers. If cats killed game from hunger only, there would be a limit to their depredations, but unfortunately they have the instinct of sport, which sportsmen consider a very admirable quality in themselves, but regard with the strongest disapprobation in other animals. Mr. Frank Buckland says that when once a cat has acquired the passion for hunting, it becomes so strong that it is impossible to break him of it. He knew a cat which had been condemned to death, but the owner begged its life on condition that it should be shut up every night and well fed. The very first night of its incarceration it escaped up the chimney and was found the next morning, black with soot, in one of the gamekeeper's traps. The keeper easily determines what kind of animal has been committing depredations in his absence.

Every animal has his own way of killing and eating his prey. The cat always turns the skin *inside out,* leaving the same reversed like a glove. The weasel and stoat will eat the brain and nibble about the head and suck the blood. The fox will always leave the legs and hinder parts of a hare or a rabbit; the dog tears his prey to pieces, and eats it "anyhow—all over the place"; the crows and magpies always peck at the eyes before they touch any part of the body.

Again, let the believer in the innocence of Mrs. Puss listen to the crow of the startled pheasant; he will hear him "tree," as the keeper calls it, and from his safe perch up in a branch again crow as if to summon his protector to his aid. No second summons does the keeper want; he at once runs to the spot, and there, stealing with erect ears, glaring eyes, and limbs collected together, and at a high state of tension, ready for the fatal spring, he sees—what?—the cat, of course, caught in the very attitude of premeditated poaching.

This love of sport might perhaps be turned to account if cats were trained as larger felines are trained for the princes of India. A fisherman of Portsmouth, called "Robinson Crusoe," made famous by Mr. Buckland, had a cat called Puddles, which overcame the horror of water characteristic of his race and employed his piscatorial talents in the service of his master:

He was the wonderfullest water-cat as ever came out of Portsmouth Harbor was Puddles, and he used to go out a-fishing with me every night. On cold nights he would sit in my lap while I was a-fishing and poke his head out every now and then, or else I would wrap him up in a sail, and make him lay quiet. He'd lay down on me when I was asleep, and if anybody come he'd swear a good one, and have the face off on 'em if they went to touch me; and he'd never touch a fish, not even a little teeny pout, if you did not give it him. I was obligated to take him out a-fishing, for else he would stand and yowl and marr till I went back and catched him by the poll and shied him into the boat, and then he was quite happy. When it was fine he used to stick up at the bows of the boat and sit a-watching the dogs (*i.e.,* dogfish). The dogs used to come alongside by thousands at a time, and when they was thick all about he would dive in and fetch them out, jammed in his mouth as fast as may be, just as if they was a parcel of rats, and he did not tremble with the cold half as much as a Newfoundland dog; he was used to it. He looked terrible wild about the head when he came up out of the water with the dogfish. I larnt him the water myself. One day, when he was a kitten, I took him down to the sea to wash and brush the fleas out of him, and in a week he could swim after a feather or a cork.

Mary E. Wilkins Freeman

THE CAT

The snow was falling, and the Cat's fur was stiffly pointed with it, but he was imperturbable. He sat crouched, ready for the death spring, as he had sat for hours. It was night—but that made no difference—all times were as one to the Cat when he was in wait for prey. Then, too, he was under no constraint of human will, for he was living alone that winter. Nowhere in the world was any voice calling him; on no hearth was there a waiting dish. He was quite free except for his own desires, which tyrannized over him when unsatisfied as now. The Cat was very hungry—almost famished, in fact. For days the weather had been very bitter, and all the feebler wild things that were his prey by inheritance, the born serfs to his family, had kept, for the most part, in their burrows and nests, and the Cat's long hunt had availed him nothing. But he waited with the inconceivable patience and persistency of his race; besides, he was certain.

The Cat was a creature of absolute convictions, and his faith in his deductions never wavered. The rabbit had gone in there between those low-hung pine boughs. Now her little doorway had before it a shaggy curtain of snow, but in there she was. The Cat had seen her enter, so like a swift gray shadow that even his sharp and practiced eyes had glanced back for the substance following, and then she was gone. So he sat down and waited, and he waited still in the white night, listening angrily to the north wind starting in the upper heights of the mountains with distant screams, then swelling into an awful crescendo of rage, and swooping down with furious white wings of snow like a flock of fierce eagles into the valleys and ravines.

The Cat was on the side of a mountain, on a wooded terrace. Above him a few feet away towered the rock ascent as steep as the wall of a cathedral. The Cat had never climbed it; trees were the ladders to his heights of life. He had often looked with wonder at the rock and meowed bitterly and resentfully as man does in the face of a forbidding Providence. At his left was the sheer precipice. Behind him, with a short stretch of woody growth between, was the frozen perpendicular wall of a mountain stream. Before him was the way to his home. When the rabbit came out she was trapped; her little cloven feet could not scale such unbroken steeps.

So the Cat waited. The place in which he was looked like a maelstrom of the wood. The tangle of trees and bushes clinging to the mountainside with a stern clutch of roots, the prostrate trunks and branches, the vines embracing everything with strong knots and coils of growth, had a curious effect, as of things that had whirled for ages in a current of raging water; only it was not water, but wind, that had disposed everything in circling lines of yielding to its fiercest points of onset. And now over all this whirl of wood and rock and dead trunks and branches and vines descended the snow. It blew down like smoke over the rock crest above; it stood in a gyrating column like some death wraith of nature, on the level; then it broke over the edge of the precipice, and the Cat cowered before the fierce backward set of it. It was as if ice needles pricked his skin through his beautiful, thick fur, but he never faltered and never once cried. He had nothing to gain from crying, and everything to lose; the rabbit would hear him cry and know he was waiting.

It grew darker and darker, with a strange white smother, instead of the natural blackness of night. It was a night of storm and death superadded to the night of nature. The mountains were all hidden, wrapped about, overawed, and tumultuously overborne by it, but in the midst of it waited, quite unconquered, this little, unswerving, living patience and power under a little coat of gray fur.

A fiercer blast swept over the rock, spun on one mighty foot of whirlwind athwart the level, then was over the precipice.

At that moment the Cat saw two eyes luminous with terror, frantic with the impulse of flight. He saw a little, quivering, dilating nose, he saw two pointing ears, and he kept still, with every one of his fine nerves and muscles strained like wires. Then the rabbit was out—there was one long line of incarnate flight and terror—and the Cat had her.

Finally the Cat went home, trailing his prey through the snow.

The Cat lived in the house that his master had built, as rudely as a child's blockhouse, but staunchly enough. The snow was heavy on the low slant of its roof, but it would not settle under it. The two windows and the door were made fast, but the Cat knew a way in. Up a pine tree behind the house he scuttled, though it was hard work with his heavy rabbit, and was in his little window under the eaves, then down through the trap to the room below, and on his master's bed with a spring and a great cry of triumph, rabbit and all. But his master was not there; he had been gone since early fall and it was now February. He would not return until spring, for he was an old man, and the cruel cold of the mountains clutched at his vitals like a panther, and he had gone to the village to winter. The Cat had known for a long time that his master was gone, but his reasoning was always sequential and circuitous; always for him what had been would be, and the more easily for his marvelous waiting powers so he always came home expecting to find his master.

When he saw that he was still gone, he dragged the rabbit off the rude couch that was the bed to the floor, put one little paw on the carcass to keep it steady, and began gnawing with head to one side to bring his strongest teeth to bear.

It was darker in the house than it had been in the wood, and the cold was as deadly, though not so fierce. If the Cat had not received his fur coat unquestioningly of Providence, he would have been thankful that he had it. It was a mottled gray, white on the face and breast, and thick as fur could grow.

The wind drove the snow on the windows with such force that it rattled like sleet, and the house trembled a little. All at once the Cat heard a noise and stopped gnawing his rabbit and listened, his shining green eyes fixed upon a window. Then he heard a hoarse shout, a halloo of despair and entreaty. But he knew it was not his master come home, and he waited, one paw still on the rabbit. The halloo came again, and then the Cat answered. He said all that was essential quite plainly to his own comprehension. There was in his cry of response inquiry, information, warning, terror, and finally the offer of comradeship, but the man outside did not hear him because of the howling of the storm.

Then there was a great battering pound at the door, then

another, and another. The Cat dragged his rabbit under the bed. The blows came thicker and faster. It was a weak arm that gave them, but it was nerved by desperation. Finally the lock yielded, and the stranger came in. Then the Cat, peering from under the bed, blinked with a sudden light, and his green eyes narrowed. The stranger struck a match and looked about. The Cat saw a face wild and blue with hunger and cold, and a man who looked poorer and older than his poor old master, who was an outcast among men for his poverty and lowly mystery of antecedents, and he heard a muttered, unintelligible voicing of distress from the harsh piteous mouth. There was in it both profanity and prayer, but the Cat knew nothing of that.

The stranger braced the door that he had forced, got some wood from the stock in the corner, and kindled a fire in the old stove as quickly as his half-frozen hands would allow. He shook so pitiably as he worked that the Cat under the bed felt the tremor of it. Then the man, who was small and feeble and marked with the scars of suffering that he had pulled down upon his own head, sat down in one of the old chairs and crouched over the fire as if it were the one love and desire of his soul, holding out his yellow hands like yellow claws, and he groaned. The Cat came out from under the bed and leaped up on his lap with the rabbit. The man gave a great shout and start of terror, and sprang. The Cat slid clawing to the floor, the rabbit fell inertly, and the man leaned, gasping with fright, and ghastly, against the wall. The Cat grabbed the rabbit by the slack of its neck and dragged it to the man's feet. Then he raised his shrill, insistent cry and arched his back high, his tail a splendid waving plume. He rubbed against the man's feet, which were bursting out of their torn shoes.

The man pushed the Cat away, gently enough, and began searching about the little cabin. He even painfully climbed the ladder to the loft, lit a match, and peered up in the darkness with straining eyes. He feared lest there might be a man, since there was a cat. His experience with men had not been pleasant, and neither had the experience of men been pleasant with him. He was an old wandering Ishmael among his kind; he had stumbled upon the house of a brother, and the brother was not at home, and he was glad.

He returned to the Cat, stooped stiffly, and stroked his back, which the animal arched like the spring of a bow.

Then he took up the rabbit and looked at it eagerly by the firelight. His jaws worked. He could almost have devoured it raw. He fumbled—the Cat close at his heels—around some rude shelves and a table, and found, with a grunt of self-gratulation, a lamp with oil in it. That he lighted; then he found a frying pan and a knife, skinned the rabbit, and prepared it for cooking, the Cat always at his feet.

When the odor of the cooking flesh filled the cabin, both the man and the Cat looked wolfish. The man turned the rabbit with one hand and stooped to pat the Cat with the other. The Cat thought him a fine man. He loved him with all his heart, though he had known him such a short time, and though the man had a face both pitiful and sharply set at variance with the best of things.

It was a face with the grimy grizzle of age upon it, with fever hollows in the cheeks, and the memories of wrong in the dim eyes, but the Cat accepted the man unquestioningly and loved him. When the rabbit was half cooked, neither the man nor the Cat would wait any longer. The man took it from the fire, divided it exactly in halves, gave the Cat one, and took the other himself. Then they ate.

At last the man blew out the light, called the Cat to him, got on the bed, drew up the ragged coverings, and fell asleep with the Cat in his bosom.

The man was the Cat's guest all the rest of the winter, and winter is long in the mountains. The rightful owner of the little hut did not return until May. All that time the Cat toiled hard, and he grew rather thin himself, for he shared everything except mice with his guest. Sometimes game was wary, and the fruit of patience of days was very little for two. The man was ill and weak, however, and unable to eat much, which was fortunate, since he could not hunt for himself. All day long he lay on the bed or else sat crouched over the fire. It was a good thing that firewood was ready at hand for the picking up, not a stone's throw from the door, for that he had to attend to himself.

The Cat foraged tirelessly. Sometimes he was gone for days together, and at first the man used to be terrified, thinking he would never return. Then he would hear the familiar cry at the door, stumble to his feet, and let him in. Afterward the two would dine together, sharing equally; the Cat would rest and purr and finally sleep in the man's arms.

Toward spring the game grew plentiful; more wild little quarry were tempted out of their homes, in search of love as well as food. One day the Cat had luck—a rabbit, a partridge, and a mouse. He could not carry them all at once, but finally he had them together at the house door. Then he cried, but no one answered. All the mountain streams were loosened, and the air was full of the gurgle of many waters, occasionally pierced by a bird whistle. The trees rustled with a new sound to the spring wind; there was a flush of rose and gold-green on the breasting surface of a distant mountain seen through an opening in the wood. The tips of the bushes were swollen and glistening red, and now and then there was a flower, but the Cat had nothing to do with flowers. He stood beside his booty at the house door and cried and cried with his insistent triumph and complaint and pleading, but no one came to let him in. Then the Cat left his little treasures at the door, went around to the back of the house to the pine tree, was up the trunk with a wild scramble, in through his little window, and down through the trap to the room, and the man was gone.

The Cat cried again, that cry of the animal for human companionship that is one of the sad notes of the world; he looked in all the corners; he sprang to the chair at the window and looked out. But no one came. The man was gone, and he never came again.

The Cat ate his mouse out on the turf beside the house; the rabbit and the partridge he carried painfully into the house. But the man did not come to share them. Finally, in the course of a day or two, he ate them up himself; then he slept a long time on the bed, and when he waked the man was not there.

Then the Cat went forth to his hunting grounds again and came home at night with a plump bird, reasoning with his tireless persistency in expectancy that the man would be there, and there was a light in the window. When he cried, his old master opened the door and let him in.

His master had strong comradeship with the Cat, but not affection. He never patted him like that gentler outcast, but he had a pride in him and an anxiety for his welfare, though he had left him alone all winter without scruple. He feared lest some misfortune might have come to the Cat, though he was so large of his kind and a mighty hunter. Therefore, when he saw him at the door in all the glory of his glossy winter coat, his white breast and face shining like snow in the sun, his own face lit up with welcome, and the Cat embraced his feet with his sinuous body vibrant with rejoicing purrs.

The Cat had his bird to himself, for his master had his own supper already cooking on the stove. After supper the Cat's master took his pipe and sought a small store of tobacco that he had left in his hut over winter. He had thought often of it; that and the Cat seemed something to come home to in the spring. But the tobacco was gone, not a dust left. The man swore a little in a grim monotone, which made the profanity lose its customary effect. He had been, and was, a hard drinker; he had knocked about the world until the marks of its sharp corners were on his very soul, which was thereby calloused until his very sensibility to loss was dulled. He was a very old man.

He searched for the tobacco with a sort of dull combat-
iveness of persistency; then he stared with stupid wonder
around the room. Suddenly many features struck him as being
changed. Another stove lid was broken; an old piece of carpet
was tacked up over a window to keep out the cold; his firewood was gone. He looked and there was no oil left in his can.
He looked at the coverings on his bed; he took them up, and
again he made that strange remonstrant noise in his throat.
Then he looked again for his tobacco.

Finally he gave it up. He sat down beside the fire, for
May in the mountains is cold; he held his empty pipe in his
mouth, his rough forehead knitted, and he and the Cat looked
at each other across that impassable barrier of silence that has
been set between man and beast from the creation of the
world.

Charles Dudley Warner

CALVIN, THE CAT

Calvin is dead. His life, long to him, but short for the rest of us, was not marked by startling adventures, but his character was so uncommon and his qualities were so worthy of imitation that I have been asked by those who personally knew him to set down my recollections of his career.

His origin and ancestry were shrouded in mystery; even his age was a matter of pure conjecture. Although he was of the Maltese race, I have reason to suppose that he was American by birth as he certainly was in sympathy. Calvin was given to me eight years ago by Mrs. Stowe, but she knew nothing of his age or origin. He walked into her house one day out of the great unknown and became at once at home, as if he had been always a friend of the family. He appeared to have artistic and literary tastes, and it was as if he had inquired at the door if that was the residence of the author of *Uncle Tom's Cabin,* and, upon being assured that it was, had decided to dwell there. This is, of course, fanciful, for his antecedents were wholly unknown, but in his time he could hardly have been in any household where he would not have heard *Uncle Tom's Cabin* talked about. When he came to Mrs. Stowe, he was as large as he ever was, and apparently as old as he ever became. Yet there was in him no appearance of age; he was in the happy maturity of all his powers, and you would rather have said in that maturity he had found the secret of perpetual youth. And it was as difficult to believe that he would ever be aged as it was to imagine that he had ever been in immature youth. There was in him a mysterious perpetuity.

After some years, when Mrs. Stowe made her winter home in Florida, Calvin came to live with us. From the first moment, he fell into the ways of the house and assumed a recognized position in the family—I say recognized, because after he became known he was always inquired for by visitors, and in the letters to the other members of the family he always received a message. Although the least obtrusive of beings, his individuality always made itself felt.

His personal appearance had much to do with this, for he was of royal mold, and had an air of high breeding. He was large, but he had nothing of the fat grossness of the celebrated Angora family; though powerful, he was exquisitely proportioned, and as graceful in every movement as a young leopard. When he stood up to open a door—he opened all the doors with old-fashioned latches—he was portentously tall, and when he stretched on the rug before the fire he seemed too long for this world—as indeed he was. His coat was the finest and softest I have ever seen, a shade of quiet Maltese;

and from his throat downward, underneath, to the white tips of his feet, he wore the whitest and most delicate ermine; and no person was ever more fastidiously neat. In his finely formed head you saw something of his aristocratic character; the ears were small and cleanly cut, there was a tinge of pink in the nostrils, his face was handsome, and the expression of his countenance exceedingly intelligent—I should call it even a sweet expression if the term were not inconsistent with his look of alertness and sagacity.

It is difficult to convey a just idea of his gaiety in connection with his dignity and gravity, which his name expressed. As we know nothing of his family, of course it will be understood that Calvin was his Christian name. He had times of relaxation into utter playfulness, delighting in a ball of yarn, catching sportively at stray ribbons when his mistress was at her toilet, and pursuing his own tail, with hilarity, for lack of anything better. He could amuse himself by the hour, and he did not care for children; perhaps something in his past was present to his memory. He had absolutely no bad habits, and his disposition was perfect. I never saw him exactly angry, though I have seen his tail grow to an enormous size when a strange cat appeared upon his lawn. He disliked cats, evidently regarding them as feline and treacherous, and he had no association with them. Occasionally there would be heard a night concert in the shrubbery. Calvin would ask to have the door opened, and then you would hear a rush and a "Pestzt," and the concert would explode, and Calvin would quietly come in and resume his seat on the hearth. There was no trace of anger in his manner, but he wouldn't have any of that about the house. He had the rare virtue of magnanimity. Although he had fixed notions about his own rights, and extraordinary persistency in getting them, he never showed temper at a repulse; he simply and firmly persisted till he had what he wanted. His diet was one point; his idea was that of the scholars about dictionaries—to "get the best." He knew as well as anyone what was in the house, and would refuse beef if turkey was to be had; and if there were oysters, he would wait over the turkey to see if the oysters would not be forthcoming. And yet he was not a gross gourmand; he would eat bread if he saw me eating it, and thought he was not being imposed on. His habits of feeding, also, were refined; he never used a knife, and he would put up his hand and draw the fork down to his mouth as gracefully as a grown person. Unless necessity compelled, he would not eat in the kitchen, but insisted upon his meals in the dining room, and would wait patiently, unless a stranger were present; and then he was sure to importune the visitor, hoping that the latter was ignorant of the rule of the house, and would give him something. They used to say that he preferred as his tablecloth on the floor a certain well-known Church journal; but this was said by an Episcopalian. So far as I know, he had no religious prejudices, except that he did not like the association with Romanists. He tolerated the servants, because they belonged to the house, and would sometimes linger by the kitchen stove; but the moment visitors came in he arose, opened the door, and marched into the drawing room. Yet he enjoyed the company of his equals, and never withdrew, no matter how many callers—whom he recognized as of his society— might come into the drawing room. Calvin was fond of company, but he wanted to choose it; and I have no doubt that his was an aristocratic fastidiousness rather than one of faith. It was so with most people.

The intelligence of Calvin was something phenomenal, in his rank of life. He established a method of communicating his wants, and even some of his sentiments; and he could help himself in many things. There was a furnace register in a retired room, where he used to go when he wished to be alone, that he always opened when he desired more heat; but never shut it, any more than he shut the door after himself. He could do almost everything but speak; and you would declare sometimes that you could see a pathetic longing to do that in his intelligent face. I have no desire to overdraw his qualities, but if there was one thing in him more noticeable than another, it was his fondness for nature. He could content himself for hours at a low window, looking into the ravine and at the great trees, noting the smallest stir there; he delighted, above all things, to accompany me walking about the garden, hearing the birds, getting the smell of the fresh earth, and rejoicing in the sunshine. He followed me and gamboled like a dog, rolling over on the turf and exhibiting his delight in a hundred ways. If I worked, he sat and watched me, or looked off over the bank, and kept his ear open to the twitter in the cherry trees. When it stormed, he was sure to sit at the window, keenly watching the rain or the snow, glancing up and down at its falling; and a winter tempest always delighted him. I think he was genuinely fond of birds, but, so far as I know, he usually confined himself to one a day; he never killed, as some sportsmen do, for the sake of killing, but only as civilized people do—from necessity. He was intimate with the flying squirrels who dwelt in the chestnut trees—too intimate, for almost every day in the summer he would bring in one, until he nearly discouraged them. He was, indeed, a superb hunter, and would have been a devastating one if his bump of destructiveness had not been offset by a bump of moderation. There was very little of the brutality of the lower animals about him; I don't think he enjoyed rats for themselves, but he knew his business, and for the first few months of his residence with us he waged an awful campaign against the horde, and after that his simple presence was sufficient to deter them from coming on the premises. Mice amused him, but he usually considered them too small game to be taken seriously; I have seen him play for an hour with a mouse, and then let him go with a royal condescension. In this whole matter of "getting a living," Calvin was a great contrast to the rapacity of the age in which he lived.

I hesitate to speak of his capacity for friendship and the affectionateness of his nature, for I know from his own reserve that he would not care to have it much talked about. We understood each other perfectly, but we never made any fuss about it; when I spoke his name and snapped my fingers, he came to me; when I returned home at night, he was pretty sure to be waiting for me near the gate, and would rise and saunter along the walk, as if his being there were purely accidental—so shy was he commonly of showing feeling; and when I opened the door he never rushed in, like a cat, but loitered, and lounged, as if he had had no intention of going in, but he would condescend to. And yet, the fact was, he knew dinner was ready, and he was bound to be there. He kept the run of dinnertime. It happened sometimes, during our absence in the summer, that dinner would be early, and Calvin, walking about the grounds, missed it and came in late. But he never made a mistake the second day. There was one thing he never did—he never rushed through an open doorway. He never forgot his dignity. If he had asked to have the door opened, and was eager to go out, he always went deliberately; I can see him now, standing on the sill, looking about at the sky as if he was thinking whether it were worthwhile to take an umbrella, until he was near having his tail shut in.

His friendship was rather constant than demonstrative. When we returned from an absence of nearly two years, Calvin welcomed us with evident pleasure, but showed his satisfaction rather by tranquil happiness than by fuming about. He had the faculty of making us glad to get home. It was his constancy that was so attractive. He liked companionship, but he wouldn't be petted, or fussed over, or sit in anyone's lap a moment; he always extricated himself from such familiarity with dignity and with no show of temper. If there was any petting to be done, however, he chose to do it. Often he would sit looking at me, and then, moved by a delicate affection, come and pull at my coat and sleeve until he could touch my face with his nose, and then go away contented. He had a habit of coming to my study in the morning, sitting quietly by my side or on the table for hours, watching the pen run over the paper, occasionally swinging his tail round for a blotter, and then going to sleep among the papers by the inkstand. Or, more rarely, he would watch the writing from a perch on my shoulder. Writing always interested him, and, until he understood it, he wanted to hold the pen.

He always held himself in a kind of reserve with his friend, as if he had said, "Let us respect our personality, and not make a 'mess' of friendship." He saw, with Emerson, the risk of degrading it to trivial conveniency. "Why insist on rash personal relations with your friends? Leave this touching and clawing." Yet I would not give an unfair notion of his aloofness, his fine sense of the sacredness of the me and the not-me. And, at the risk of not being believed, I will relate an incident, which was often repeated. Calvin had the practice of passing a portion of the night in the contemplation of its beauties, and would come into our chamber over the roof of the conservatory through the open window, summer and winter, and go to sleep at the foot of my bed. He would do this always exactly in this way; he never was content to stay in the chamber if we compelled him to go upstairs and through the door. He had the obstinacy of General Grant. But this is by the way. In the morning he performed his toilet and went down to breakfast with the rest of the family. Now, when the mistress was absent from home, and at no other time, Calvin would come in the morning, when the bell rang, to the head of the bed, put up his feet and look into my face, follow me about when I rose, "assist" at the dressing, and in many purring ways show his fondness, as if he had plainly said, "I know that she has gone away, but I am here." Such was Calvin in rare moments.

He had his limitations. Whatever passion he had for nature, he had no conception of art. There was sent to him once a fine and very expressive cat's head in bronze, by

Frémiet. I placed it on the floor. He regarded it intently, approached it cautiously and crouchingly, touched it with his nose, perceived the fraud, turned away abruptly, and never would notice it afterward. On the whole, his life was not only a successful one, but a happy one. He never had but one fear, so far as I know: he had a mortal and a reasonable terror of plumbers. He would never stay in the house when they were here. No coaxing could quiet him. Of course, he didn't share our fear about their charges, but he must have had some dreadful experience with them in that portion of his life which is unknown to us. A plumber was to him the devil, and I have no doubt that, in his scheme, plumbers were foreordained to do him mischief.

In speaking of his worth, it has never occurred to me to estimate Calvin by the worldly standard. I know that it is customary now, when anyone dies, to ask how much he was worth, and that no obituary in the newspapers is considered complete without such an estimate. The plumbers in our house were one day overheard to say that, "They say that *she* says that *he* says that he wouldn't take a hundred dollars for him." It is unnecessary to say that I never made such a remark, and that, so far as Calvin was concerned, there was no purchase in money.

As I look back upon it, Calvin's life seems to me a fortunate one, for it was natural and unforced. He ate when he was hungry, slept when he was sleepy, and enjoyed existence to the very tips of his toes and the end of his expressive and slow-moving tail. He delighted to roam about the garden, and stroll among the trees, and to lie on the green grass and luxuriate in all the sweet influences of summer. You could never accuse him of idleness, and yet he knew the secret of repose. The poet who wrote so prettily of him that his little life was rounded with a sleep, understated his felicity; it was rounded with a good many. His conscience never seemed to interfere with his slumbers. In fact, he had good habits and a contented mind. I can see him now walk in at the study door, sit down by my chair, bring his tail artistically about his feet, and look up at me with unspeakable happiness in his handsome face. I often thought that he felt the dumb limitation which denied him the power of language. But since he was denied speech, he scorned the inarticulate mouthings of the lower animals. The vulgar mewing and yowling of the cat species was beneath him; he sometimes uttered a sort of articulate and well-bred ejaculation when he wished to call attention to something that he considered remarkable or to some want of his, but he never went whining about. He would sit for hours at a closed window, when he desired to enter, without a murmur, and when it was opened he never admitted that he had been impatient by bolting in. Though speech he had not, and the unpleasant kind of utterance given to his race he would not use, he had a mighty power of purr to express his measureless content with congenial society. There was in him a musical organ with stops of varied power and expression, upon which I have no doubt he could have performed Scarlatti's celebrated cat's fugue.

Whether Calvin died of old age, or was carried off by one of the diseases incident to youth, it is impossible to say; for his departure was as quiet as his advent was mysterious. I only know that he appeared to us in this world in his perfect stature and beauty, and that after a time, like Lohengrin, he withdrew. In his illness there was nothing more to be regretted than in all his blameless life. I suppose there never was an illness that had more dignity and sweetness and resignation in it. It came on gradually, in a kind of listlessness and want of appetite. An alarming symptom was his preference for the warmth of a furnace register to the lively sparkle of the open wood fire. Whatever pain he suffered, he bore it in silence, and seemed only anxious not to obtrude his malady. We tempted him with the delicacies of the season, but it soon became impossible for him to eat, and for two weeks he ate or drank scarcely anything. Sometimes he made an effort to take something, but it was evident that he made the effort to please us. The neighbors—and I am convinced that the advice of neighbors is never good for anything—suggested catnip. He wouldn't even smell it. We had the attendance of an amateur practitioner of medicine, whose real office was the cure of souls, but nothing touched his case. He took what was offered, but it was with the air of one to whom the time for pellets was past. He sat or lay day after day almost motionless, never once making a display of those vulgar convulsions or contortions of pain which are so disagreeable to society. His favorite place was on the brightest spot of a Smyrna rug by the conservatory, where the sunlight fell and he could hear the fountain play. If we went to him and exhibited our interest in his condition, he always purred in recognition of our sympathy. And when I spoke his name, he looked up with an expression that said, "I understand it, old fellow, but it's no use." He was to all who came to visit him a model of calmness and patience in affliction.

I was absent from home at the last, but heard by daily postal card of his failing condition; and never again saw him alive. One sunny morning he rose from his rug, went into the conservatory (he was very thin then), walked around it deliberately, looking at all the plants he knew, and then went to the bay window in the dining room, and stood a long time looking out upon the little field, now brown and sere, and toward the garden, where perhaps the happiest hours of his life had been spent. It was a last look. He turned and walked away, laid himself down upon the bright spot in the rug, and quietly died.

It is not too much to say that a little shock went through the neighborhood when it was known that Calvin was dead, so marked with his individuality; and his friends, one after another, came in to see him. There was no sentimental nonsense about his obsequies; it was felt that any parade would have been distasteful to him. John, who acted as undertaker, prepared a candlebox for him, and I believe assumed a professional decorum; but there may have been the usual levity underneath, for I heard that he remarked in the kitchen that it was the "driest wake he ever attended." Everybody, however, felt a fondness for Calvin, and regarded him with a certain respect. Between him and Bertha there existed a great friendship, and she apprehended his nature; she used to say that sometimes she was afraid of him, he looked at her so intelligently; she was never certain that he was what he appeared to be.

When I returned, they had laid Calvin on a table in an upper chamber by an open window. It was February. He reposed in a candlebox, lined about the edge with evergreen, and at his head stood a little wineglass with flowers. He lay with his head tucked down in his arms—a favorite position of his before the fire—as if asleep in the comfort of his soft and exquisite fur. It was the involuntary exclamation of those who saw him, "How natural he looks!" As for myself, I said nothing. John buried him under the twin hawthorn trees—one white and the other pink—in a spot where Calvin was fond of lying and listening to the hum of summer insects and the twitter of birds.

Perhaps I have failed to make appear the individuality of character that was so evident to those who knew him. At any rate, I have set down nothing concerning him but the literal truth. He was always a mystery. I did not know whence he came; I do not know whither he has gone. I would not weave one spray of falsehood in the wreath I lay upon his grave.

Samuel Lover

YE MARVELOUS LEGEND OF TOM CONNOR'S CAT

There was a man in these parts, sir, you must know, called Tom Connor, and he had a cat that was equal to any dozen of rat traps, and he was proud of the baste, and with rayson; for she was worth her weight in goold to him in saving his sacks of meal from the thievery of the rats and mice; for Tom was an extensive dealer in corn, and influenced the rise and fall of that article in the market, to the extent of a full dozen of sacks at a time, which he either kept or sold, as the spirit of free trade or monopoly came over him. Indeed, at one time, Tom had serious thoughts of applying to the government for a military force to protect his granary when there was a threatened famine in the country."

"Pooh pooh, sir!" said the matter-of-fact little man. "As if a dozen sacks could be of the smallest consequence in a whole country—pooh pooh!"

"Well, sir," said Murtough, "I can't help you if you don't believe; but it's truth what I'm telling you, and pray don't interrupt me, though you may not believe; by the time the story's done you'll have heard more wonderful things than *that*—and besides, remember you're a stranger in these parts, and have no notion of the extraordinary things, physical, metaphysical, and magical, which constitute the idiosyncrasy of rural destiny."

The little man did not know the meaning of Murtough's last sentence—nor Murtough either; but, having stopped the little man's throat with big words, he proceeded:

"This cat, sir, you must know, was a great pet, and was so up to everything, that Tom swore she was a'most like a Christian, only she couldn't speak, and had so sensible a look in her eyes, that he was sartin sure the cat knew every word that was said to her. Well, she used to set by him at breakfast every morning, and the eloquent cock of her tail, as she used to rub against his leg, said: 'Give me some milk, Tom Connor,' as plain as print, and the plentitude of her purr afterward spoke a gratitude beyond language. Well, one morning, Tom was going to the neighboring town to market, and he had promised the wife to bring home shoes to the childre' out o' the price of the corn; and sure enough before he sat down to breakfast, there was Tom taking the measure of the children's feet, by cutting notches on a bit of stick; and the wife gave him so many cautions about getting a 'nate fit' for 'Billy's purty feet,' that Tom, in his anxiety to nick the closest possible measure, cut off the child's toe. This disturbed the harmony of the party, and Tom was obliged to breakfast alone, while the mother was endeavoring to cure Billy; in short, trying to make a *heal* of his *toe*. Well, sir, all the time Tom was taking measure for the shoes, the cat was observing him with that luminous peculiarity of eye for which her tribe is remarkable; and when Tom sat down to breakfast the cat rubbed up against him more vigorously than usual; but Tom being bewildered, between his expected gain in corn and the positive loss of his child's toe, kept never minding her, until the cat, with a sort of caterwauling growl, gave Tom a dab of her claws, that went clean through his leathers, and a little further. 'Wow!' says Tom, with a jump, clapping his hand on the part, and rubbing it. 'By this and that, you drew the blood out o' me,' says Tom. 'You wicked divil—tish!—go along!' says he, making a kick at her. With that the cat gave a reproachful look at him, and her eyes glared just like a pair of mail-coach lamps in a fog. With that, sir, the cat, with a mysterious 'meow,' fixed a most penetrating glance on Tom, and distinctly uttered his name.

"Tom felt every hair on his head as stiff as a pump handle; and scarcely crediting his ears, he returned a searching look at the cat, who very quietly proceeded in a sort of nasal twang:

" 'Tom Connor,' says she.

" 'The Lord be good to me!' says Tom. 'If it isn't spakin' she is!'

" 'Tom Connor,' says she again.

" 'Yes, ma'am,' says Tom.

" 'Come here,' says she. 'Whisper—I want to talk to you, Tom,' says she, 'the laste taste in private,' says she—rising on her hams and beckoning him with her paw out o' the door, with a wink and a toss o' the head aiqual to a milliner.

"Well, as you may suppose, Tom didn't know whether he was on his head or his heels, but he followed the cat, and off she went and squatted herself under the hedge of a little paddock at the back of Tom's house; and as he came round the corner, she held up her paw again, and laid it on her mouth, as much as to say 'Be cautious, Tom.' Well, divil a word Tom could say at all, with the fright, so up he goes to the cat, and says she:

" 'Tom,' says she, 'I have a great respect for you, and there's something I must tell you, because you're losing character with your neighbors,' says she, 'by your goin's on,' says she, 'and it's out o' the respect that I have for you, that I must tell you,' says she.

" 'Thank you, ma'am,' says Tom.

" 'You're going off to the town,' says she, 'to buy shoes for the childre',' says she, 'and never thought o' getting me a pair.'

" 'You!' says Tom.

" 'Yis, me, Tom Connor,' says she, 'and the neighbors wondhers that a respectable man like you allows your cat to go about the counthry barefutted,' says she.

" 'Is it a cat to ware shoes?' says Tom.

" 'Why not?' says she. 'Doesn't horses ware shoes? And I have a prettier foot than a horse, I hope,' says she with a toss of her head.

" 'Faix, she spakes like a woman; so proud of her feet,' says Tom to himself, astonished, as you may suppose, but pretending never to think it remarkable all the time; and so he went on discoursin'; and says he: 'It's thrue for you, ma'am,' says he, 'that horses ware shoes—but that stands to rayson, ma'am, you see—seeing the hardship their feet has to go through on the hard roads.'

" 'And how do you know what hardship my feet has to go through?' says the cat, mighty sharp.

" 'But, ma'am,' says Tom, 'I don't well see how you could fasten a shoe on you,' says he.

" 'Lave that to me,' says the cat.

" 'Did anyone ever stick walnut shells on you, pussy?' says Tom, with a grin.

" 'Don't be disrespectful, Tom Connor,' says the cat, with a frown.

" 'I ax your pard'n, ma'am,' said he, 'but as for the horses you wor spakin' about warin' shoes, you know their shoes is fastened on with nails, and how would your shoes be fastened on?'

" 'Ah, you stupid thief!' says she, 'haven't I illigant nails o' my own?' and with that she gave him a dab of her claw, that made him roar.

" 'Ow! murdher!' says he.

" 'Now no more of your palaver, Misther Connor,' says the cat. 'Just be off and get me the shoes.'

" 'Tare and ouns!' says Tom. 'What'll become o' me if I'm to get shoes for my cats?' says he. 'For you increase your family four times a year, and you have six or seven every time,' says he; 'and then you must all have two pair apiece—wirra! wirra!—I'll be ruined in shoeleather,' says Tom.

" 'No more o' your stuff,' says the cat; 'don't be standin' here undher the hedge talkin' or we'll lose our characters—for I've remarked your wife is jealous, Tom.'

" ''Pon my sowl, that's thrue,' says Tom, with a smirk.

" 'More fool she,' says the cat, 'for 'pon my conscience, Tom, you're as ugly as if you wor bespoke.'

"Off ran the cat with these words, leaving Tom in amazement. He said nothing to the family, for fear of fright'ning them, and off he went to the town, as he pretended—for he saw the cat watching him through a hole in the hedge; but when he came to a turn at the end of the road, the dickings a mind he minded the market, good or bad, but went off to Squire Botherum's, the magisthrit, to swear examinations agen the cat."

"Pooh pooh—nonsense!" broke in the little man, who had listened thus far to Murtough with an expression of mingled wonder and contempt, while the rest of the party willingly gave up the reins to nonsense, and enjoyed Murtough's legend and their companion's more absurd common sense.

"Don't interrupt him, Coggins," said Mr. Wiggins.

"How can you listen to such nonsense!" returned Coggins. "Swear examinations against a cat, indeed! Pooh pooh!"

"My dear sir," said Murtough, "remember this is a fairy story, and that the country all round here is full of enchantment. As I was telling you, Tom went off to swear examinations."

"Ay, ay!" shouted all but Coggins. "Go on with the story."

"And when Tom was asked to relate the events of the morning, which brought him before Squire Botherum, his brain was so bewildered between his corn, and his cat, and his child's toe, that he made a very confused account of it.

" 'Begin your story from the beginning,' said the magistrate to Tom.

" 'Well, your honor,' says Tom, 'I was goin' to market this mornin', to sell the child's corn—I beg your pard'n—my own toes, I mane, sir.'

" 'Sell your toes!' said the Squire.

" 'No, sir, takin' the cat to market, I mane—'

" 'Take a cat to market!' said the Squire. 'You're drunk, man.'

" 'No, your honor, only confused a little; for when the toes began to spake to me—the cat, I mane—I was bothered clane—'

" 'The cat speak to you!' said the Squire. 'Phew! Worse than before. You're drunk, Tom.'

" 'No, your honor; it's on the strength of the cat I come to spake to you—'

" 'I think it's on the strength of a pint of whiskey, Tom.'

" 'By the vartue o' my oath, your honor, it's nothin' but the cat.' And so Tom then told him all about the affair, and the Squire was regularly astonished. Just then the bishop of the diocese and the priest of the parish happened to call in, and heard the story; and the bishop and the priest had a tough argument for two hours on the subject: the former swearing she must be a witch; but the priest denying *that,* and maintaining she was *only* enchanted, and that part of the argument was afterward referred to the primate, and subsequently to the conclave at Rome; but the Pope declined interfering about cats, saying he had quite enough to do minding his own bulls.

" 'In the meantime, what are we to do with the cat?' says Botherum.

" 'Burn her,' says the bishop. 'She's a witch.'

" '*Only* enchanted,' said the priest, 'and the ecclesiastical court maintains that—'

" 'Bother the ecclesiastical court!' said the magistrate; 'I can only proceed on the statutes'; and with that he pulled down all the lawbooks in his library, and hunted the laws from Queen Elizabeth down, and he found that they made laws against everything in Ireland, *except a cat.* The divil a thing escaped them but a cat, which did *not* come within the meaning of any Act of Parliament—*the cats only had escaped.*

" 'There's the alien act, to be sure,' said the magistrate, 'and perhaps she's a French spy in disguise.'

" 'She spakes like a French spy, sure enough,' says Tom, 'and she was missin', I remember, all last Spy Wednesday.'

" 'That's suspicious,' says the Squire, 'but conviction might be difficult; and I have a fresh idea,' says Botherum.

" 'Faith, it won't keep fresh long, this hot weather,' says Tom, 'so your honor had betther make use of it at wanst.'

" 'Right,' says Botherum. 'We'll make her a subject to the game laws; we'll hunt her,' says he.

" 'Ow! Elegant!' says Tom; 'we'll have a brave run out of her.'

" 'Meet me at the crossroads,' says the Squire, 'in the morning, and I'll have the hounds ready.'

"Well, off Tom went home; and he was racking his brain what excuse he could make to the cat for not bringing the shoes; and at last he hit one off, just as he saw her cantering up to him, half a mile before he got home.

" 'Where's the shoes, Tom?' says she.

" 'I have not got them today, ma'am,' says he.

" 'Is that the way you keep your promise, Tom?' says she. 'I'll tell you what it is, Tom—I'll tare the eyes out o' the childre' if you don't get me those shoes.'

" 'Whist, whist!' says Tom, frightened out his life for his children's eyes. 'Don't be in a passion, pussy. The shoemaker said he had not a shoe in his shop, nor a last that would make one to fit you; and he says I must bring you into the town for him to take your measure.'

" 'And when am I to go?' says the cat, looking savage.

" 'Tomorrow,' says Tom.

" 'It's well you said that, Tom,' said the cat, 'or the devil an eye I'd leave in your family this night,' and off she hopped.

"Tom thrimbled at the wicked look she gave.

" 'Remember!' says she, over the hedge, with a bitter caterwaul.

" 'Never fear,' says Tom.

"Well, sure enough, the next mornin' there was the cat at cockcrow, licking herself as nate as a new pin, to go into the town, and out came Tom with a bag undher his arm and the cat after him.

" 'Now git into this, and I'll carry you into the town,' says Tom, opening the bag.

" 'Sure, I can walk with you,' says the cat.

" 'Oh, that wouldn't do,' says Tom. 'The people in the town is curious and slandherous people, and sure it would rise ugly remarks if I was seen with a cat afther me—a dog is a man's companion by nature, but cats does not stand to rayson.'

"Well, the cat, seeing there was no use in argument, got into the bag, and off Tom set to the crossroads with the bag over his shoulder, and he came up, quite innocent-like, to the corner, where the Squire, and his huntsman, and the hounds, and a pack of people were waitin'. Out came the Squire on a sudden, just as if it was all by accident.

" 'God save you, Tom,' says he.

" 'God save you kindly, sir,' says Tom.

" 'What's that bag you have at your back?' says the Squire.

" 'Oh, nothin' at all, sir,' says Tom, makin' a face all the time, as much as to say, I have her safe.

" 'Oh, there's something in that bag, I think,' says the Squire. 'You must let me see it.'

" 'If you bethray me, Tom Connor,' says the cat, in a low voice, 'by this and that I'll never spake to you again!'

" ''Pon my honor, sir,' says Tom, with a wink and a twitch of his thumb toward the bag, 'I haven't anything in it.'

" 'I have been missing my praties of late,' says the Squire, 'and I'd just like to examine that bag,' says he.

" 'Is it doubting my character you'd be, sir?' says Tom, pretending to be in a passion.

" 'Tom, your sowl!' says the voice in the sack. 'If you let the cat out of the bag, I'll murther you.'

" 'An honest man would make no objection to be sarched,' said the Squire, 'and I insist on it,' says he, laying hold o' the bag, and Tom purtending to fight all the time; but, my jewel! before two minutes, they shook the cat out o' the bag, sure enough, and off she went, with her tail as big as a sweeping brush, and the Squire, with a thundering view halloo after her, clapped the dogs at her heels, and away they went for the bare life. Never was there seen such running as that day—the cat made for a shaking bog, the loneliest place in the whole country, and there the riders were all thrown out, barrin' the huntsman, who had a web-footed horse on purpose for soft places, and the priest, whose horse could go anywhere by reason of the priest's blessing; and, sure enough, the huntsman and his riverence stuck to the hunt like wax; and just as the cat got on the border of the bog, they saw her give a twist as the foremost dog closed with her, for he gave her a nip in the flank. Still she went on, however, and headed them well, toward an old mud cabin in the middle of the bog, and there they saw her jump in at the window, and up came the dogs the next minit, and gathered round the house, with the most horrid howling ever was heard. The huntsman alighted, and went into the house to turn the cat out again, when what should he see but an old hag lying in bed in the corner!

" 'Did you see a cat come in here?' says he.

" 'Oh, no-o-o-o!' squealed the old hag in a trembling voice. 'There's no cat here,' says she.

" 'Yelp, yelp, yelp!' went the dogs outside.

" 'Oh, keep the dogs out of this,' says the old hag—'oh-o-o-o!' and the huntsman saw her eyes glare under the blanket, just like a cat's.

" 'Hillo!' says the huntsman, pulling down the blanket—and what should he see but the old hag's flank all in a gore of blood.

" 'Ow, ow! you old divil—is it you? You old cat!' says he, opening the door.

"In rushed the dogs. Up jumped the old hag and, changing into a cat before their eyes, out she darted through the window again, and made another run for it; but she couldn't escape, and the dogs gobbled her while you could say 'Jack Robinson.' But the most remarkable part of this extraordinary story, gentlemen, is that the pack was ruined from that day out; for after having eaten the enchanted cat, *the devil a thing they would ever hunt afterward but mice.*"

Mark Twain

DICK BAKER'S CAT

One of my comrades there—
another of those victims of eighteen years of unrequited toil
and blighted hopes—was one of the gentlest spirits that ever
bore its patient cross in a weary exile; grave and simple Dick
Baker, pocket miner of Dead-Horse Gulch. He was forty-six,
gray as a rat, earnest, thoughtful, slenderly educated, slouch-
ily dressed, and clay-soiled, but his heart was finer metal than
any gold his shovel ever brought to light—than any, indeed,
that ever was mined or minted.

Whenever he was out of luck and a little downhearted,
he would fall to mourning over the loss of a wonderful cat he

used to own (for where women and children are not, men of kindly impulses take up with pets, for they must love something). And he always spoke of the strange sagacity of that cat with the air of a man who believed in his secret heart that there was something human about it—maybe even supernatural.

I heard him talking about this animal once. He said: "Gentlemen, I used to have a cat here, by the name of Tom Quartz, which you'd 'a' took an interest in, I reckon—most anybody would. I had him here eight year—and he was the remarkablest cat *I* ever see. He was a large gray one of the Tom specie, an' he had more hard, natchral sense than any man in this camp—'n' a *power* of dignity—he wouldn't let the Gov'ner of Californy be familiar with him. He never ketched a rat in his life—'peared to be above it. He never cared for nothing but mining. He knowed more about mining, that cat did, than any man *I* ever, ever see. You couldn't tell *him* noth'n' 'bout placer-diggin's—'n' as for pocket mining, why he was just born for it. He would dig out after me an' Jim when we went over the hills prospect'n', and he would trot along behind us for as much as five mile, if we went so fur. An' he had the best judgment about mining ground—why, you never see anything like it. When we went to work, he'd scatter a glance round, 'n' if he didn't think much of the indications, he would give a look as much as to say, 'Well, I'll have to get you to excuse *me'*—'n' without another word he'd hyste his nose in the air 'n' shove for home. But if the ground suited him, he would lay low 'n' keep dark till the first pan was washed, 'n' then he would sidle up 'n' take a look, an' if there was about six or seven grains of gold *he* was satisfied— he didn't want no better prospect 'n' that—'n' then he would lay down on our coats and snore like a steamboat till we'd struck the pocket, an' then get up 'n' superintend. He was nearly lightnin' on superintending.

"Well, by an' by, up comes this yer quartz excitement.

Everybody was into it—everybody was pick'n' 'n' blast'n' instead of shovelin' dirt on the hillside—everybody was putt'n' down a shaft instead of scrapin' the surface. Noth'n' would do Jim, but *we* must tackle the ledges, too, 'n' so we did. We commenced putt'n' down a shaft, 'n' Tom Quartz he begin to wonder what in the dickens it was all about. *He* hadn't ever seen any mining like that before, 'n' he was all upset, as you may say—he couldn't come to a right understanding of it no way—it was too many for *him.* He was down on it too, you bet you—he was down on it powerful—'n' always appeared to consider it the cussedest foolishness out. But that cat, you know, was *always* agin' newfangled arrangements—somehow he never could abide 'em. *You* know how it is with old habits. But by and by Tom Quartz begin to git sort of reconciled a little though he never *could* altogether understand that eternal sinkin' of a shaft an' never pannin' out anything. At last he got to comin' down in the shaft, hisself, to try to cipher it out. An' when he'd git the blues, 'n' feel kind o' scruffy, 'n' aggravated 'n' disgusted—knowin' as he did, that the bills was runnin' up all the time an' we warn't makin' a cent—he would curl up on a gunnysack in the corner an' go to sleep. Well, one day when the shaft was down about eight foot, the rock got so hard that we had to put in a blast—the first blast'n' we'd ever done since Tom Quartz was born. An' then we lit the fuse 'n' clumb out 'n' got off 'bout fifty yards—'n' forgot 'n' left Tom Quartz sound asleep on the gunnysack. In 'bout a minute we seen a puff of smoke bust up out of the hole, 'n' then everything let go with an awful crash, 'n' about four million ton of rocks 'n' dirt 'n' smoke 'n' splinters shot up 'bout a mile an' a half into the air, an' by George, right in the dead center of it was old Tom Quartz a-goin' end over end, an' a-snortin' an' a-sneezin', an' a-clawin' an' a-reach'n' for things like all possessed. But it warn't no use, you know, it warn't no use. An' that was the last we see of *him* for about two minutes 'n' a half, an' then all of a sudden it begin to rain rocks and rubbage an' directly he come down ker-whoop about ten foot off f'm where we stood. Well, I reckon he was p'r'aps the orneriest-lookin' beast you ever see. One ear was sot back on his neck, 'n' his tail was stove up, 'n' his eye-winkers was singed off, 'n' he was all blacked up with powder an' smoke, an' all sloppy with mud 'n' slush f'm one end to the other. Well, sir, it warn't no use to try to apologize —we couldn't say a word. He took a sort of disgusted look at himself, 'n' then he looked at us—an' it was just exactly the same as if he had said—'Gents, maybe *you* think it's smart to take advantage of a cat that ain't had no experience of quartz minin', but *I* think different'—an' then he turned on his heel 'n' marched off home without ever saying another word.

"That was jest his style. An' maybe you won't believe it, but after that you never see a cat so prejudiced agin' quartz mining as what he was. An' by an' by when he *did* get to goin' down in the shaft agin', you'd 'a' been astonished at his sagacity. The minute we'd tetch off a blast 'n' the fuse'd begin to sizzle, he'd give a look as much as to say, 'Well, I'll have to git you to excuse *me,*' an' it was surpris'n' the way he'd shin out of that hole 'n' go f'r a tree. Sagacity? It ain't no name for it. 'Twas inspiration!"

I said, "Well, Mr. Baker, his prejudice against quartz mining *was* remarkable, considering how he came by it. Couldn't you ever cure him of it?"

"*Cure him!* No! When Tom Quartz was sot once, he was *always* sot—and you might 'a' blowed him up as much as three million times 'n' you'd never 'a' broken him of his cussed prejudice agin' quartz mining."

Agnes A. Sandham

THE CONSCIENTIOUS CAT

It was a curious place for a cat —the lonely Hydraulic Mines, on the crest of the Sierra Nevada Mountains in California. Where she came from, no one could tell. My acquaintance with her was made in a singular and altogether startling manner. It was in this wise: I was visiting the mines, and, under the guidance of the superintendent, had just passed over the brow of a great hill crowned with a thick growth of magnificent sugar pines, when suddenly we came upon the Hydraulic Mines—so lonely, so dreary, so utterly uninviting in appearance and situation, that

I could not help asking, "Could anything but a gold-hunting man be induced to live in such a place?"

"Wait and see," replied the superintendent as he walked in the direction of a rough shanty used by the miners as a place of shelter.

Just then I was startled at seeing a white cat come dashing toward us at full speed, her tail puffed out to an enormous size, and apparently pursued by a number of men armed with picks and crowbars.

Full of sympathy for the poor cat making such a wild race for her life, I glanced toward the shanty which must be her only refuge. As I did so a dog's head was thrust cautiously out —only the head—and then stopped. Round the corner of the hut dashed the flying cat, and, before the dog's head could be drawn in, there came a violent collision, and a perfect storm of howls and hisses which marked the meeting of the angry cat and the much astonished dog. In spite of my sympathy, I could not help laughing heartily at this ludicrous collision— and my laugh was echoed by the cruel men who, as I supposed, were chasing poor Pussy with murderous designs. But my laughter was suddenly cut short as I saw what seemed to be the great mountain sliding directly upon me, and, following the example of the cat, I turned and fled for shelter to the hut, while the men redoubled their laughter.

"What under the sun is the matter?" I asked, perplexed alike by the cat, the rushing men, and the moving mountain.

And then, with many jokes and much laughter, the whole matter was explained.

It appears that one cold and stormy night, about a year before my visit to the mines, the men were startled by a pitiful mewing outside the camp. One of the miners, following up the sound of distress, soon returned with a most forlorn and miserable-looking kitten, more dead than alive. How she came to that desolate camp and where she came from was a mystery, but the miners, naturally tenderhearted, and welcoming any-thing that brought a change in the monotony of their daily life, took pity on the foundling and at once adopted her. Perhaps, too, the sight of such a homebody as a cat, away off in that desolate spot, brought back memories of their boyhood and the old homes far to the east in Maine woods or on New Hampshire hills, and called up, for all of them, a picture of the happy childhood days before the fever of adventure had led them so far from the dear old home in the mad race for gold.

Well, whatever their thoughts, they adopted the cat and made her so warm and comfortable, with plenty of milk to drink and a warm fire to curl before, that Pussy was soon purring away as contentedly as if she had never been a home-less wanderer.

There is no such thing as stopping work in the mines. Day and night the work goes on, and the men are divided into day and night gangs, each of which works for a certain length of time, relieving the other at regular intervals. So it hap-pened that Pussy, dozing before the fire, was aroused by a stir in the room, and glancing up saw the miner who had rescued and cared for her preparing to go out to his work. Deter-mined not to lose sight of her preserver, she jumped up and followed him. When the men arrived at their destination, Pussy at once took up her position near her friend and care-fully watched the proceedings.

A hydraulic mine is one in which water is made to take the part of pick and shovel. A tremendous pressure forces the water through a great iron pipe three or four feet in diameter, and sends it in a torrent against the bank of dirt in which the gold is hidden. This mighty stream of water washes away the bank and brings it caving and tumbling down, while it sepa-rates the gold from the gravel, and with the occasional assis-tance of blasting powder does a vast amount of mining work.

It was at one of these hydraulic mines that the fugitive cat had found friends; and as after several visits she lay watching their operations, she seemed to reason it all out in her own mind that as soon as the great dirt bank opposite her showed signs of giving way under the action of the water forced against it, the men would rush for shelter to the shanty nearby, to which, of course, she too would scamper to escape the falling earth. So, reasoned Pussy, if these kind friends of mine are always in danger from these tumbling-down banks, why cannot I, in return for their kindness, watch the dirt banks and give them proper warning?

Now, as you all know, there is nothing a cat dislikes so much as water; just watch your kitty shake her paws daintily when she steps into a puddle, and see how disgusted she is if a drop of water falls on her nose or back. But this Sierra Nevada pussy was a most conscientious cat. She felt that it was her duty to make some sacrifice for her friends, and so, after thinking it all over, she took her place right on top of the nozzle of the "monitor" (as the big iron pipe through which the water is forced is called), and here, in spite of occasional and most unwelcome shower baths, she would watch for the first movement of the falling bank, when away she would go like a flash with all the miners at her heels, until they all reached the shelter of the hut. So faithfully did she perform her self-imposed task that, in a little while, the men gave up their precaution of keeping one eye on the dangerous slide and waited for Puss to give the signal. As soon as they saw her spring down from the comfortable bed which the miners had made for her on the monitor, they would all cry, "The cat, the cat!" and start on a run for the shanty. And it was at just such a moment that I came to the mine and encountered this most conscientious cat leading her friends to safety.

She soon learned also to distinguish between the various phases of hydraulic mining; and when the monitor was being used simply for washing the gold or for general cleaning-up purposes, she knew that there was no danger, and would serenely close her eyes and take a comfortable nap on her cushion, regardless of what was going on around her, until by some strange instinct she knew that the monitor was turned upon the bank again, and was awake and watchful in an instant. Her very color, too, was a help to her friends, as, being a white cat, she served on dark nights as a guide to the men who came to relieve the gang to which Pussy belonged, and which no consideration would induce her to desert.

Now, it happened that about the time of Pussy's appearance at the mine a very unprepossessing mongrel pup had been left at the camp, as not worth taking away, and so he too was adopted by the kindhearted miners. But alas! The dog proved as great a coward as the cat was a heroine. His only thought was to look out for number one, and he did that so thoroughly that when he too had learned that a sudden move on the part of the men meant danger, he would scud into the hut in an agony of fear, and, like the dastardly dog he was, retreat into the farthest corner with his tail between his legs. Evidently, when I first made his acquaintance, he had not heard them rushing toward the hut and had thus been caught napping, and hence the collision I had witnessed. He was such a good-for-nothing that the men called him "Tailings"—which also means the refuse gravel and dirt out of which every speck of gold has been taken. And in such awe did he stand of Pussy that, though they took their meals together, Tailings always waited until Pussy had finished before he presumed to take a bite, wagging his tail until the ground was swept clean, and whining meanwhile with hunger and impatience. Once, and once only, he endeavored to assert himself and take a bite before his betters. Pussy stopped eating, looked the culprit sternly in the eye, and then, slowly lifting her paw, brought it down with a sudden blow exactly in the center of the dog's nose. Tailings gave such a howl that the miners thought the whole mountain was caving in, and rushed out to see what was the matter. Pussy went on calmly finishing her dinner, and Tailings never again presumed to eat at the first table, to rebel against Pussy's rules.

Julian Ralph

HE WROTE
TO THE RATS

Our suspicions were first aroused by the disappearance of a whole beefsteak. Before that we did not know we were entertaining any rats in our cellar. When we made the discovery, we were at a loss to know how to act; but one day there came to the house a poor old woman who lives mysteriously by offering needles, and thread, and pencils, and candy of sizes and kinds that nobody likes and nobody buys. At our house she gets a cup of tea and ten cents, and, to ease her conscience, she leaves a peppermint stick for the little ones. The kitchen girl told her of the loss of the steak.

"Well," said the mysterious old woman, "I would write a letter to the rats and they will go away. That is what we used to do when I lived at home in Germany."

Fancy the surprise of the kitchen maid! She thought the old woman had lost her mind.

The rats became an intolerable nuisance, and the news of what the old woman had recommended was brought to me. The children were anxious to have the experiment tried.

"It can do no harm," I said, and at once drew up the following letter:

> To the Boss Rat: Get out of our cellar at once. We hired this house for ourselves, and you have no business to make yourselves at home, living here and stealing our provisions. If you do not heed this warning we will keep a terrier and make it very lively for you.
>
> Yours angrily,
> The People of This House.

I quite prided myself on this missive. I thought it was at once logical in its argument, firm in tone, and very generous, inasmuch as the rats could see that we might have hired a terrier first and written the letter afterward. I at first put the letter in an envelope; but we all agreed afterward that even if rats could read they might not know anything about envelopes, and so I tore the cover off and laid the letter on the cellar floor with its written side up.

We then waited to see what effect it would have. Alas! The rats behaved worse than ever and robbed us of everything that suited their tastes. Then the poor old German woman came again on her rounds, and the children saw her and informed her of the failure.

"Read the letter to me," said she.

It was read to her.

"Oh, dear, dear, dear!" she exclaimed. "What an impudent letter to send to the rats! It is a mercy they haven't attacked some of the people in the house and bitten them in their beds. I could not sleep a wink in a house where such a letter had been sent to the rats."

She spoke very gravely and with evident alarm. I inquired very particularly about her manner afterward and was told that it seemed far from a mere pretense of being vexed.

"Why!" she exclaimed. "Rats are *kings,* in their way. At least they are in Germany. They must be treated very politely. Tell your parents to write another letter at once and let it be soft and gentle and very respectful. Call them 'Dear rats' or 'Dear friends,' and find no fault with what they do—only be sure to recommend some other place for them to go to, for it is a rule that rats will never leave a home unless they are told of a better place close by, to which they can go. Oh, dear, dear, dear! I wonder you are not afraid to stay in the house after such a letter."

When I reached home I thought, as before, that there could be no harm in doing as the old woman said; and I confess I felt guilty of some stupidity in not having known, as everyone ought to know, that politeness is always better than rudeness. There is a wealth of wisdom in the homely saying, "More flies are caught with syrup than with vinegar." It costs nothing to be kind and courteous, and as we know that more can be done among men and women by gentleness than by anger, why might not the same be true with regard to rats? Thus I reflected, and therefore I wrote this letter:

Dear Rats: We have discovered signs of your presence in our cellar. Perhaps you mean to honor us and pay us a compliment in coming to this particular cellar in a city where there are a hundred thousand such resorts. It may be news to you that there lives not far away a French family, much given to rich gravies, sweetmeats, delightful pastries, rare and high-scented imported cheese, and various other luxuries of which we know you to be fond.

If you should go there, you would fare better than in our cellar. Of course, we should miss you, but we feel certain we could bear it.

Believing, from what we see of your activity and appetites, that you are all very well and happy and that you have been benefited by our having the plumbing attended to the other day, we beg the right to sign ourselves,

Yours politely,
The People of This House.

That touch about the plumbing was my own; but the phrase, "yours politely," was dictated by the children, who assured me that the word "polite" must be somewhere in the letter, in some form or other. It really took me a long while to make up my mind where to tell the rats to go, and I felt no little ashamed when at last the thought of the rich gravies and pastries led me to recommend my neighbors, the French folks. To be sure, I do not know them, and no one will ever tell them what I did; but I must confess I never would have been guilty of such an unneighborly act had I really believed the rats would have paid any attention to the letter.

They did not. They grew more and more at home, and even became so noisy that the ladies more than once thought that burglars had broken in downstairs. "Master Fitz," our tomcat, was sent into the cellar to drive them out; but after the first encounter he bounded back into the kitchen, bleeding on one cheek and one leg; and if ever a cat said anything, he plainly spoke, and very indignantly, too. "I am a tremendous mouser," was what he meant to convey, "but when it comes to eating up rats that are bigger than I am, I must beg to be excused!"

We all waited for the old woman, and when she came the children eagerly informed her of the failure of even the most polite letter writing where rats are concerned.

She is a shrewd old woman. She did not like to admit she

was wrong, so she said she was sure that if we hadn't written that very rude first letter the rats would have gone.

"I know they would if they were German rats," she said, "but I never wrote to American rats, and perhaps they are different."

The four-footed robbers are still at home in our cellar, and not even the children believe it worthwhile to write to them again.

Saki

THE PHILANTHROPIST
AND
THE HAPPY CAT

Jocantha Bessbury was in the mood to be serenely and graciously happy. Her world was a pleasant place, and it was wearing one of its pleasantest aspects. Gregory had managed to get home for a hurried lunch and a smoke afterward in the little snuggery; the lunch had been a good one, and there was just time to do justice to the coffee and cigarettes. Both were excellent in their way, and Gregory was, in his way, an excellent husband. Jocantha rather suspected herself of making him a very charming wife, and more than suspected herself of having a first-rate dressmaker.

"I don't suppose a more thoroughly contented personality is to be found in all Chelsea," observed Jocantha in allusion to herself, "except perhaps Attab," she continued, glancing toward the large tabby-marked cat that lay in considerable ease in a corner of the divan. "He lies there, purring and dreaming, shifting his limbs now and then in an ecstasy of cushioned comfort. He seems the incarnation of everything soft and silky and velvety, without a sharp edge in his composition, a dreamer whose philosophy is sleep and let sleep; and then, as evening draws on, he goes out into the garden with a red glint in his eyes and slays a drowsy sparrow."

"As every pair of sparrows hatches out ten or more young ones in the year, while their food supply remains stationary, it is just as well that the Attabs of the community should have that idea of how to pass an amusing afternoon," said Gregory. Having delivered himself of this sage comment he lit another cigarette, bade Jocantha a playfully affectionate good-bye, and departed into the outer world.

"Remember, dinner's a wee bit earlier tonight, as we're going to the Haymarket," she called after him.

Left to herself, Jocantha continued the process of looking at her life with placid, introspective eyes. If she had not everything she wanted in this world, at least she was very well pleased with what she had got. She was very well pleased, for instance, with the snuggery, which contrived somehow to be cozy and dainty and expensive all at once. The porcelain was rare and beautiful, the Chinese enamels took on wonderful tints in the firelight, the rugs and hangings led the eye through sumptuous harmonies of coloring. It was a room in which one might have suitably entertained an ambassador or an archbishop, but it was also a room in which one could cut out pictures for a scrapbook without feeling that one was scandalizing the deities of the place with one's litter. And as with the snuggery, so with the rest of the house, and as with the house, so with the other departments of Jocantha's life;

she really had good reason for being one of the most contented women in Chelsea.

From being in a mood of simmering satisfaction with her lot she passed to the phase of being generously commiserating for those thousands around her whose lives and circumstances were dull, cheap, pleasureless, and empty. Work girls, shop assistants, and so forth, the class that have neither the happy-go-lucky freedom of the poor nor the leisured freedom of the rich, came specially within the range of her sympathy. It was sad to think that there were young people who, after a long day's work, had to sit alone in chill, dreary bedrooms because they could not afford the price of a cup of coffee and a sandwich in a restaurant, still less a shilling for a theater gallery.

Jocantha's mind was still dwelling on this theme when she started forth on an afternoon campaign of desultory shopping; it would be rather a comforting thing, she told herself, if she could do something, on the spur of the moment, to bring a gleam of pleasure and interest into the life of even one or two wistful-hearted, empty-pocketed workers; it would add a good deal to her sense of enjoyment at the theater that night. She would get two upper-circle tickets for a popular play, make her way into some cheap tea shop, and present the tickets to the first couple of interesting work girls with whom she could casually drop into conversation. She could explain matters by saying that she was unable to use the tickets herself and did not want them to be wasted, and, on the other hand, did not want the trouble of sending them back. On further reflection she decided that it might be better to get only one ticket and give it to some lonely-looking girl sitting eating her frugal meal by herself; the girl might scrape acquaintance with her next-seat neighbor at the theater and lay the foundations of a lasting friendship.

With the fairy-godmother impulse strong upon her, Jocantha marched into a ticket agency and selected with immense care an upper-circle seat for the *Yellow Peacock,* a play that was attracting a considerable amount of discussion and criticism. Then she went forth in search of a tea shop and philanthropic adventure, at about the same time that Attab sauntered into the garden with a mind attuned to sparrow stalking. In a corner of an A.B.C. shop she found an unoccupied table, whereat she promptly installed herself, impelled by the fact that at the next table was sitting a young girl, rather plain of feature, with tired, listless eyes and a general air of uncomplaining forlornness. Her dress was of poor material, but aimed at being in the fashion, her hair was pretty, and her complexion bad; she was finishing a modest meal of tea and scone, and she was not very different in her way from thousands of other girls who were finishing, or beginning, or continuing their teas in London tea shops at that exact moment. The odds were enormously in favor of the supposition that she had never seen the *Yellow Peacock;* obviously she supplied excellent material for Jocantha's first experiment in haphazard benefaction.

Jocantha ordered some tea and a muffin, and then turned a friendly scrutiny on her neighbor with a view to catching her eye. At that precise moment the girl's face lit up with sudden pleasure, her eyes sparkled, a flush came into her cheeks, and she looked almost pretty. A young man, whom she greeted with an affectionate "Hullo, Bertie," came up to her table and took his seat in a chair facing her. Jocantha looked hard at the newcomer; he was in appearance a few years younger than herself, very much better looking than Gregory, rather better looking, in fact, than any of the young men of her set. She guessed him to be a well-mannered young clerk in some wholesale warehouse, existing and amusing himself as best he might on a tiny salary, and commanding a holiday of about two weeks in the year. He was aware, of course, of his good looks, but with shy self-consciousness, not blatant complacency. He was obviously on terms of friendly intimacy with the girl he was talking to, probably they were drifting toward a formal engagement. Jocantha pictured the boy's home, in a rather narrow circle, with a tiresome mother who always wanted to know how and where he spent his evenings. He would exchange that humdrum thralldom in due course for a home of his own, dominated by a chronic scarcity of pounds, shillings, and pence, and a dearth of most of the things that made life attractive or comfortable. Jocantha felt extremely sorry for him. She wondered if he had seen the *Yellow Peacock;* the odds were enormously in favor of the supposition that he had not. The girl had finished her tea, and would shortly be going back to her work; when the boy was alone it would be quite easy for Jocantha to say: "My husband has made other arrangements for me this evening; would you care to make use of this ticket, which would otherwise be wasted?" Then she could come there again one afternoon for tea, and, if she saw him, ask him how he liked the play. If he was a nice boy and improved on acquaintance he could be given more theater tickets and perhaps asked to come one Sunday to tea at Chelsea. Jocantha made up her mind that he would improve on acquaintance, and that Gregory would like him, and that the fairy-godmother business would prove far more entertaining than she had originally anticipated. The boy was distinctly presentable; he knew how to brush his hair, which was possibly an imitative faculty; he knew what color of tie suited him, which might be intuition; he was exactly the type that Jocantha admired, which of course was accident. Altogether she was rather pleased when the girl looked at the clock and bade a friendly but hurried farewell to her companion. Bertie nodded "good-bye," gulped down a mouthful of tea, and then produced from his overcoat pocket a paper-covered book bearing the title *Sepoy and Sahib, a Tale of the Great Mutiny.*

The laws of tea-shop etiquette forbid that you should offer theater tickets to a stranger without having first caught the stranger's eye. It is even better if you can ask to have a sugar basin passed to you, having previously concealed the fact that you have a large and well-filled sugar basin on your own table; this is not difficult to manage, as the printed menu is generally nearly as large as the table, and can be made to stand on end. Jocantha set to work hopefully; she had a long and rather high-pitched discussion with the waitress concerning alleged defects in an altogether blameless muffin, she made loud and plaintive inquiries about the tube service to some impossibly remote suburb, she talked with brilliant insincerity to the tea-shop kitten, and as a last resort she upset a milk jug and swore at it daintily. Altogether she attracted a good deal of attention, but never for a moment did she attract the attention of the boy with the beautifully brushed hair, who was some thousands of miles away in the baking plains of Hindustan, amid deserted bungalows, seething bazaars, and riotous barrack squares, listening to the throbbing of tomtoms and the distant rattle of musketry.

Jocantha went back to her house in Chelsea, which struck her for the first time as looking dull and overfurnished. She had a resentful conviction that Gregory would be uninteresting at dinner, and that the play would be stupid after dinner. On the whole her frame of mind showed a marked divergence from the purring complacency of Attab, who was again curled up in his corner of the divan with a great peace radiating from every curve of his body.

But then, he had killed his sparrow.

Saki

TOBERMORY

It was a chill, rain-washed afternoon of a late August day, that indefinite season when partridges are still in security or cold storage, and there is nothing to hunt—unless one is bounded on the north by the Bristol Channel, in which case one may lawfully gallop after fat red stags. Lady Blemley's house party was not bounded on the north by the Bristol Channel, hence there was a full gathering of her guests round the tea table on this particular afternoon. And, in spite of the blankness of the season and the triteness of the occasion, there was no trace in the company of that fatigued restlessness which means a dread of the pianola and a subdued hankering for auction bridge. The undisguised openmouthed attention of the entire party was fixed on the homely negative personality of Mr. Cornelius Appin. Of all her guests, he was the one who had come to Lady Blemley with the vaguest reputation. Someone had said he was "clever," and he had gotten his invitation in the moderate expectation, on the part of his hostess, that some portion at least of his cleverness would be contributed to the general entertainment. Until teatime that day she had been unable to discover in what direction, if any, his cleverness lay. He was neither a wit nor a croquet champion, a hypnotic force nor a begetter of amateur theatricals. Neither did his exterior suggest the sort of man in whom women are willing to pardon a generous measure of mental deficiency. He had subsided into mere Mr. Appin, and the Cornelius seemed a piece of transparent baptismal bluff. And now he was claiming to have launched on the world a discovery beside which the invention of gunpowder, of the printing press, and of steam locomotion were inconsiderable trifles. Science had made bewildering strides in many directions during recent decades, but this thing seemed to belong to the domain of miracle rather than to scientific achievement.

"And do you really ask us to believe," Sir Wilfrid was saying, "that you have discovered a means for instructing animals in the art of human speech, and that dear old Tobermory has proved your first successful pupil?"

"It is a problem at which I have worked for the last seventeen years," said Mr. Appin, "but only during the last eight or nine months have I been rewarded with glimmerings of success. Of course I have experimented with thousands of animals, but latterly only with cats, those wonderful creatures which have assimilated themselves so marvelously with our civilization while retaining all their highly developed feral instincts. Here and there among cats one comes across an outstanding superior intellect, just as one does among the ruck of human beings, and when I made the acquaintance of Tobermory a week ago I saw at once that I was in contact with a 'Beyond-cat' of extraordinary intelligence. I had gone far along the road to success in recent experiments; with Tobermory, as you call him, I have reached the goal."

Mr. Appin concluded his remarkable statement in a voice which he strove to divest of a triumphant inflection. No one said "Rats," though Clovis's lips moved in a monosyllabic contortion which probably invoked those rodents of disbelief.

"And do you mean to say," asked Miss Resker, after a slight pause, "that you have taught Tobermory to say and understand easy sentences of one syllable?"

"My dear Miss Resker," said the wonder-worker patiently, "one teaches little children and savages and backward adults in that piecemeal fashion; when one has once solved the problem of making a beginning with an animal of highly developed intelligence one has no need for those halting methods. Tobermory can speak our language with perfect correctness."

This time Clovis very distinctly said, "Beyond-rats!" Sir Wilfrid was more polite, but equally skeptical.

"Hadn't we better have the cat in and judge for ourselves?" suggested Lady Blemley.

Sir Wilfrid went in search of the animal, and the company settled themselves down to the languid expectation of witnessing some more or less adroit drawing-room ventriloquism.

In a minute Sir Wilfrid was back in the room, his face white beneath its tan and his eyes dilated with excitement. "By Gad, it's true!"

His agitation was unmistakably genuine, and his hearers started forward in a thrill of awakened interest.

Collapsing into an armchair he continued breathlessly: "I found him dozing in the smoking room, and called out to him to come for his tea. He blinked at me in his usual way, and I said, 'Come on, Toby; don't keep us waiting'; and, by Gad!

he drawled out in a most horribly natural voice that he'd come when he dashed well pleased! I nearly jumped out of my skin!"

Appin had preached to absolutely incredulous hearers; Sir Wilfrid's statement carried instant conviction. A Babel-like chorus of startled exclamation arose, amid which the scientist sat mutely enjoying the first fruit of his stupendous discovery.

In the midst of the clamor Tobermory entered the room and made his way with velvet tread and studied unconcern across to the group seated round the tea table.

A sudden hush of awkwardness and constraint fell on the company. Somehow there seemed an element of embarrassment in addressing on equal terms a domestic cat of acknowledged dental ability.

"Will you have some milk, Tobermory?" asked Lady Blemley in a rather strained voice.

"I don't mind if I do," was the response, couched in a tone of even indifference. A shiver of suppressed excitement went through the listeners, and Lady Blemley might be excused for pouring out the saucerful of milk rather unsteadily.

"I'm afraid I've spilled a good deal of it," she said apologetically.

"After all, it's not my Axminster," was Tobermory's rejoinder.

Another silence fell on the group, and then Miss Resker, in her best district-visitor manner, asked if the human language had been difficult to learn. Tobermory looked squarely at her for a moment and then fixed his gaze serenely on the middle distance. It was obvious that boring questions lay outside his scheme of life.

"What do you think of human intelligence?" asked Mavis Pellington lamely.

"Of whose intelligence in particular?" asked Tobermory coldly.

"Oh, well, mine for instance," said Mavis, with a feeble laugh.

"You put me in an embarrassing position," said Tobermory, whose tone and attitude certainly did not suggest a shred of embarrassment. "When your inclusion in this house party was suggested Sir Wilfrid protested that you were the most brainless woman of his acquaintance, and that there was a wide distinction between hospitality and the care of the feebleminded. Lady Blemley replied that your lack of brain power was the precise quality which had earned you your invitation, as you were the only person she could think of who might be idiotic enough to buy their old car. You know, the one they call 'The Envy of Sisyphus,' because it goes quite nicely uphill if you push it."

Lady Blemley's protestations would have had greater effect if she had not casually suggested to Mavis only that morning that the car in question would be just the thing for her down at her Devonshire home.

Major Barfield plunged in heavily to effect a diversion.

"How about your carryings-on with the tortoiseshell puss up at the stables, eh?"

The moment he had said it everyone realized the blunder.

"One does not usually discuss these matters in public," said Tobermory frigidly. "From a slight observation of your ways since you've been in this house I should imagine you'd find it inconvenient if I were to shift the conversation on to your own little affairs."

The panic which ensued was not confined to the major.

"Would you like to go and see if cook has got your dinner ready?" suggested Lady Blemley hurriedly, affecting to ignore the fact that it wanted at least two hours to Tobermory's dinnertime.

"Thanks," said Tobermory, "not quite so soon after my tea. I don't want to die of indigestion."

"Cats have nine lives, you know," said Sir Wilfrid heartily.

"Possibly," answered Tobermory; "but only one liver."

"Adelaide!" said Mrs. Cornett, "do you mean to encourage that cat to go out and gossip about us in the servants' hall?"

The panic had indeed become general. A narrow ornamental balustrade ran in front of most of the bedroom windows at the Towers, and it was recalled with dismay that this had formed a favorite promenade for Tobermory at all hours, whence he could watch the pigeons—and heaven knew what else besides. If he intended to become reminiscent in his present outspoken strain, the effect would be something more than disconcerting. Mrs. Cornett, who spent much time at her toilet table, and whose complexion was reputed to be of a nomadic though punctual disposition, looked as ill at ease as the major. Miss Scrawen, who wrote fiercely sensuous poetry and led a blameless life, merely displayed irritation; if you are methodical and virtuous in private you don't necessarily want everyone to know it. Bertie van Tahn, who was so depraved at seventeen that he had long ago given up trying to be any worse, turned a dull shade of gardenia white, but he did not commit the error of dashing out of the room like Odo Finsberry, a young gentleman who was understood to be reading for the Church and who was possibly disturbed at the thought of scandals he might hear concerning other people. Clovis had the presence of mind to maintain a composed exterior; privately he was calculating how long it would take to procure a box of fancy mice through the agency of the Exchange and Mart as a species of hush money.

Even in a delicate situation like the present, Agnes Resker could not endure to remain too long in the background.

"Why did I ever come down here?" she asked dramatically.

Tobermory immediately accepted the opening.

"Judging by what you said to Mrs. Cornett on the cro-quet lawn yesterday, you were out for food. You described the Blemleys as the dullest people to stay with that you knew, but said they were clever enough to employ a first-rate cook; otherwise they'd find it difficult to get anyone to come down a second time."

"There's not a word of truth in it! I appeal to Mrs. Cornett—" exclaimed the discomfited Agnes.

"Mrs. Cornett repeated your remark afterwards to Bertie van Tahn," continued Tobermory, "and said, 'That woman is a regular Hunger Marcher; she'd go anywhere for four square meals a day,' and Bertie van Tahn said—"

At this point the chronicle mercifully ceased. Tobermory had caught a glimpse of the big yellow tom from the rectory working his way through the shrubbery toward the stable wing. In a flash he had vanished through the open French window.

With the disappearance of his too brilliant pupil Cor-nelius Appin found himself beset by a hurricane of bitter upbraiding, anxious inquiry, and frightened entreaty. The responsibility for the situation lay with him, and he must prevent matters from becoming worse. Could Tobermory impart his dangerous gift to other cats? was the first question he had to answer. It was possible, he replied, that he might have initiated his intimate friend the stable puss into his new accomplishment, but it was unlikely that his teaching could have taken a wider range as yet.

"Then," said Mrs. Cornett, "Tobermory may be a valu-able cat and a great pet; but I'm sure you'll agree, Adelaide, that both he and the stable cat must be done away with with-out delay."

"You don't suppose I've enjoyed the last quarter of an hour, do you?" said Lady Blemley bitterly. "My husband and I are very fond of Tobermory—at least, we were before this horrible accomplishment was infused into him; but now, of course, the only thing is to have him destroyed as soon as possible."

"We can put some strychnine in the scraps he always gets at dinnertime," said Sir Wilfrid, "and I will go and drown the stable cat myself. The coachman will be very sore at losing his pet, but I'll say a very catching form of mange has broken out in both cats and we're afraid of it spreading to the kennels."

"But my great discovery!" expostulated Mr. Appin. "After all my years of research and experiment—"

"You can go and experiment on the shorthorns at the farm, who are under proper control," said Mrs. Cornett, "or the elephants at the Zoological Gardens. They're said to be highly intelligent, and they have this recommendation, that they don't come creeping about our bedrooms and under chairs, and so forth."

An archangel ecstatically proclaiming the millennium, and then finding that it clashed unpardonably with Henley and would have to be indefinitely postponed, could hardly have felt more crestfallen than Cornelius Appin at the reception of his wonderful achievement. Public opinion, however, was against him; in fact, had the general voice been consulted on the subject it is probable that a strong minority vote would have been in favor of including him in the strychnine diet.

Defective train arrangements and a nervous desire to see matters brought to a finish prevented an immediate dispersal of the party, but dinner that evening was not a social success. Sir Wilfrid had had rather a trying time with the stable cat and subsequently with the coachman. Agnes Resker ostentatiously limited her repast to a morsel of dry toast, which she bit as though it were a personal enemy; while Mavis Pellington maintained a vindictive silence throughout the meal. Lady Blemley kept up a flow of what she hoped was conversation, but her attention was fixed on the doorway. A plateful of carefully dosed fish scraps was in readiness on the sideboard, but sweets and savory and dessert went their way, and no Tobermory appeared either in the dining room or kitchen.

The sepulchral dinner was cheerful compared with the subsequent vigil in the smoking room. Eating and drinking had at least supplied a distraction and cloak to the prevailing embarrassment. Bridge was out of the question in the general tension of nerves and tempers, and after Odo Finsberry had given a lugubrious rendering of "Mélisande in the Wood" to a frigid audience, music was tacitly avoided. At eleven the servants went to bed, announcing that the small window in the pantry had been left open as usual for Tobermory's private use. The guests read steadily through the current batch of magazines, and fell back gradually on the Badminton Library and bound volumes of *Punch.* Lady Blemley made periodic visits to the pantry, returning each time with an expression of listless depression which forestalled questioning.

At two o'clock Clovis broke the dominating silence.

"He won't turn up tonight. He's probably in the local newspaper office at the present moment, dictating the first installment of his reminiscences. Lady What's-her-name's book won't be in it. It will be the event of the day."

Having made this contribution to the general cheerfulness, Clovis went to bed. At long intervals the various members of the house party followed his example.

The servants taking round the early tea made a uniform announcement in reply to a uniform question. Tobermory had not returned.

Breakfast was, if anything, a more unpleasant function than dinner had been, but before its conclusion the situation was relieved. Tobermory's corpse was brought in from the shrubbery, where a gardener had just discovered it. From the bites on his throat and the yellow fur which coated his claws it was evident that he had fallen in unequal combat with the big tom from the rectory.

By midday most of the guests had quitted the Towers,

and after lunch Lady Blemley had sufficiently recovered her spirits to write an extremely nasty letter to the rectory about the loss of her valuable pet.

Tobermory had been Appin's one successful pupil, and he was destined to have no successor. A few weeks later an elephant in the Dresden Zoological Garden, which had shown no previous signs of irritability, broke loose and killed an Englishman who had apparently been teasing it. The victim's name was variously reported in the papers as Oppin and Eppelin, but his front name was faithfully rendered Cornelius.

"If he was trying German irregular verbs on the poor beast," said Clovis, "he deserved all he got."

John Coleman Adams

MIDSHIPMAN, THE CAT

This is a true story about a real cat who, for aught I know, is still alive and following the sea for a living. I hope to be excused if I use the pronouns "who" and "he" instead of "which" and "it," in speaking of this particular cat; because although I know very well that the grammars all tell us that "he" and "who" apply to persons, while "it" and "which" apply to things, yet this cat of mine always seemed to us who knew him to be so much like a human being that I find it unsatisfactory to speak of him in any other way. There are some animals of whom you prefer to say "he," just as there are persons whom you sometimes feel like calling "it."

The way we met this cat was after this fashion: It was back somewhere in the seventies, and a party of us were cruising east from Boston in the little schooner-yacht *Eyvor*. We had dropped into Marblehead for a day and a night, and some of the boys had gone ashore in the tender. As they landed on the wharf, they found a group of small boys running sticks into a woodpile, evidently on a hunt for something inside.

"What have you in there?" asked one of the yachtsmen.

"Nothin' but a cat," said the boys.

"Well, what are you doing to him?"

"Oh, pokin' him up! When he comes out we'll rock him," was the answer, in good Marblehead dialect.

"Well, don't do it anymore. What's the use of tormenting a poor cat? Why don't you take somebody of your size?"

The boys slowly moved off, a little ashamed and a little afraid of the big yachtsman who spoke; and when they were well out of sight the yachtsmen went on, too, and thought no more about the cat they had befriended. But when they had wandered about the tangled streets of the town for a little while, and paid the visits which all good yachtsmen pay, to the grocery and the post office and the apothecary's soda fountain, they returned to the wharf and found their boat. And behold, there in the stern sheets sat the little gray-and-white cat of the woodpile! He had crawled out of his retreat and made straight for the boat of his champions. He seemed in no wise disturbed or disposed to move when they jumped on board, nor did he show anything but pleasure when they stroked and patted him. But when one of the boys started to put him ashore, the plucky little fellow showed his claws; and no sooner was he set on his feet at the edge of the wharf than he turned about and jumped straight back into the boat.

"He wants to go yachting," said one of the party, whom we called "the Bos'n."

"Ye might as wal take the cat," said a grizzly old fisherman standing on the wharf. "He doesn't belong to anybody, and ef he stays here the boys'll worry him t'death."

"Let's take him aboard," said the yachtsmen. "It's good luck to have a cat on board ship."

Whether it was good luck to the ship or not, it was very clear that pussy saw it meant good luck to him, and curled himself down in the bottom of the boat, with a look that meant business. Evidently he had thought the matter all over and made up his mind that this was the sort of people he wanted to live with; and, being a Marblehead cat, it made no difference to him whether they lived afloat or ashore; he was going where they went, whether they wanted him or not. He had heard the conversation from his place in the woodpile, and had decided to show his gratitude by going to sea with these protectors of his. By casting in his lot with theirs he was paying them the highest compliment of which a cat is capable. It would have been the height of impoliteness not to recognize his distinguished appreciation. So he was allowed to remain in the boat, and was taken off to the yacht.

Upon his arrival there, a council was held, and it was unanimously decided that the cat should be received as a member of the crew; and as we were a company of amateur sailors, sailing our own boat, each man having his particular duties, it was decided that the cat should be appointed midshipman, and should be named after his position. So he was at once and ever after known as "Middy." Everybody took a great interest in him, and he took an impartial interest in everybody—though there were two people on board to whom he made himself particularly agreeable. One was the quiet, kindly professor, the captain of the *Eyvor;* the other was Charlie, our cook and only hired hand. Middy, you see, had a seaman's true instinct as to the official persons with whom it was his interest to stand well.

It was surprising to see how quickly Middy made himself at home. He acted as if he had always been at sea. He was never seasick, no matter how rough it was or how uncomfortable any of the rest of us were. He roamed wherever he wanted to, all over the boat. At mealtimes he came to the table with the rest, sat up on a valise, and lapped his milk and took what bits of food were given him, as if he had eaten that way all his life. When the sails were hoisted it was his especial joke to jump upon the main gaff and be hoisted with it; and once he stayed on his perch till the sail was at the masthead. One of us had to go aloft and bring him down. When we had come to anchor and everything was snug for the night, he would come on deck and scamper out on the main boom, and race from there to the bowsprit end as fast as he could gallop, then climb, monkey-fashion, halfway up the masts, and drop back to the deck or dive down into the cabin and run riot among the berths.

One day, as we were jogging along, under a pleasant southwest wind, and everybody was lounging and dozing after dinner, we heard the Bos'n call out, "Stop that, you fellows!" and a moment after, "I tell you, quit! Or I'll come up and make you!"

We opened our lazy eyes to see what was the matter, and there sat the Bos'n, down in the cabin, close to the companionway, the tassel of his knitted cap coming nearly up to the combings of the hatch; and on the deck outside sat Middy, digging his claws into the tempting yarn, and occasionally going deep enough to scratch the Bos'n's scalp.

When night came and we were all settled down in bed, it was Middy's almost invariable custom to go the rounds of all the berths, to see if we were properly tucked in, and to end his inspection by jumping into the captain's bed, treading himself a comfortable nest there among the blankets, and curling himself down to sleep. It was his own idea to select the captain's berth as the only proper place in which to turn in.

But the most interesting trait in Middy's character did not appear until he had been a week or so on board. Then he gave us a surprise. It was when we were lying in Camden Harbor. Everybody was going ashore to take a tramp among the hills, and Charlie, the cook, was coming too, to row the boat back to the yacht.

Middy discovered that he was somehow "getting left." Being a prompt and very decided cat, it did not take him long to make up his mind what to do. He ran to the low rail of the yacht, put his forepaws on it, and gave us a long, anxious look. Then as the boat was shoved off he raised his voice in a plaintive mew. We waved him a good-bye, chaffed him pleasantly, and told him to mind the anchor, and have dinner ready when we got back.

That was too much for his temper. As quick as a flash he had dived overboard, and was swimming like a water spaniel, after the dinghy!

That was the strangest thing we had ever seen in all our lives! We were quite used to elephants that could play at seesaw, and horses that could fire cannon, to learned pigs and to educated dogs; but a cat that of his own accord would take to the water like a full-blooded Newfoundland was a little beyond anything we had ever heard of. Of course the boat was stopped, and Middy was taken aboard drenched and shivering, but perfectly happy to be once more with the crew. He had been ignored and slighted; but he had insisted on his rights, and as soon as they were recognized he was quite contented.

Of course, after that we were quite prepared for anything that Middy might do. And yet he always managed to surprise us by his bold and independent behavior. Perhaps his most brilliant performance was a visit he paid a few days after his swim in Camden Harbor.

We were lying becalmed in a lull of the wind off the entrance to Southwest Harbor. Near us, perhaps a cable's-length away, lay another small yacht, a schooner hailing from Lynn. As we drifted along on the tide, we noticed that Middy was growing very restless; and presently we found him running along the rail and looking eagerly toward the other yacht. What did he see—or smell—over there which interested him? It could not be the dinner, for they were not then cooking. Did he recognize any of his old chums from Marblehead? Perhaps there were some cat friends of his on the other craft. Ah, that was it! There they were on the deck, playing and frisking together—two kittens! Middy had spied them, and was longing to take a nearer look. He ran up and down the deck, mewing and snuffing the air. He stood up in his favorite position when on lookout, with his forepaws on the rail. Then, before we realized what he was doing, he had plunged overboard again, and was making for the other boat as fast as he could swim! He had attracted the attention of her company, and no sooner did he come up alongside than they prepared to welcome him. A fender was lowered, and when Middy saw it he swam toward it, caught it with his forepaws, clambered along it to the gunwale, and in a twinkling was over the side and on the deck scraping acquaintance with the strange kittens.

How they received him I hardly know, for by that time our boat was alongside to claim the runaway. And we were quite of the mind of the skipper of the *Winnie L.,* who said, as he handed our bold midshipman over the side, "Well, that beats all *my* going a-fishing!"

Only a day or two later Middy was very disobedient when we were washing decks one morning. He trotted about in the wet till his feet were drenched, and then retired to dry them on the white spreads of the berths below. That was quite too much for the captain's patience. Middy was summoned aft, and, after a sound rating, was hustled into the dinghy which was moored astern, and shoved off to the full length of her painter. The punishment was a severe one for Middy, who could bear anything better than exile from his beloved ship-mates. So of course he began to exercise his ingenious little brain to see how he could escape. Well under the overhang of the yacht he spied, just about four inches out of water, a little shoulder of the rudder. That was enough for him. He did not stop to think whether he would be any better off there. It was a part of the yacht, and that was home. So overboard he went, swam for the rudder, scrambled on to it, and began howling piteously to be taken on deck again; and, being a spoiled and much-indulged cat, he was soon rescued from his uncomfortable roosting place and restored to favor.

I suppose I shall tax your powers of belief if I tell you many more of Middy's doings. But truly he was a strange cat, and you may as well be patient, for you will not soon hear of his equal. The captain was much given to rifle practice, and used to love to go ashore and shoot at a mark. On one of his trips he allowed Middy to accompany him, for the simple reason, I suppose, that Middy decided to go, and got on board the dinghy when the captain did. Once ashore, the marksman selected a fine large rock as a rest for his rifle, and opened fire upon his target. At the first shot or two Middy seemed a little surprised, but showed no disposition to run away. After the first few rounds, however, he seemed to have made up his mind that since the captain was making all that racket it must be entirely right and proper, and nothing about which a cat need bother his head in the least. So, as if to show how entirely he confided in the captain's judgment and good inten-tions, that imperturbable cat calmly lay down, curled up, and went to sleep in the shade of the rock over which the captain's rifle was blazing and cracking about once in two minutes. If anybody was ever acquainted with a cooler or more self-possessed cat I should be pleased to hear the particulars.

I wish that this chronicle could be confined to nothing

but our shipmate's feats of daring and nerve. But, unfortunately, he was not always blameless in his conduct. When he got hungry he was apt to forget his position as midshipman, and to behave just like any cat with an empty stomach. Or perhaps he may have done just what any hungry midshipman does under the circumstances; I do not quite know what a midshipman does under all circumstances and so I cannot say. But here is one of this cat midshipman's exploits. One afternoon, on our way home, we were working along with a head wind and sea toward Wood Island, a haven for many of the small yachts between Portland and the Shoals. The wind was light and we were a little late in making port. But as we were all agreed that it would be pleasanter to postpone our dinner till we were at anchor, the cook was told to keep things warm and wait till we were inside the port before he set the table. Now, his main dish that day was to be a fine piece of baked fish; and, unfortunately, it was nearly done when we gave orders to hold back the dinner. So he had closed the drafts of his little stove, left the door of the oven open, and turned into his bunk for a quiet doze—a thing which every good sailor does on all possible occasions; for a seafaring life is very uncertain in the matter of sleep, and one never quite knows when he will lose some, nor how much he will lose. So it is well to lay in a good stock of it whenever you can.

It seems that Middy was on watch, and when he saw Charlie fast asleep he undertook to secure a little early dinner for himself. He evidently reasoned with himself that it was very uncertain when we should have dinner and he'd better get his while he could. He quietly slipped down to the stove, walked coolly up to the oven, and began to help himself to baked haddock.

He must have missed his aim or made some mistake in his management of the business, and, by some lucky chance for the rest of us, waked the cook. For, the first we knew, Middy came flying up the cabin companionway, followed by a volley of shoes and spoons and pieces of coal, while we could hear Charlie, who was rather given to unseemly language when he was excited, using the strongest words in his dictionary about "that thief of a cat!"

"What's the matter?" we all shouted at once.

"Matter enough, sir!" growled Charlie. "That little cat's eaten up half the fish! It's a chance if you get any dinner tonight, sir."

You may be very sure that Middy got a sound wigging for that trick, but I am afraid the captain forgot to deprive him of his rations as he threatened. He was much too kindhearted.

The very next evening Middy startled us again by a most remarkable display of coolness and courage. After a weary thrash to windward all day, under a provokingly light breeze, we found ourselves under the lee of the little promontory at Cape Neddick, where we cast anchor for the night. Our supply of water had run very low, and so, just after sunset, two of the party rowed ashore in the tender to replenish our water keg, and by special permission Middy went with them.

It took some time to find a well, and by the time the jugs were filled it had grown quite dark. In launching the boat for the return to the yacht, by some ill luck a breaker caught her and threw her back upon the beach. There she capsized and spilled out the boys, together with their precious cargo. In the confusion of the moment, and the hurry of setting matters to rights, Middy was entirely forgotten, and when the boat again was launched, nobody thought to look for the cat. This time everything went well, and in a few minutes the yacht was sighted through the dusk. Then somebody happened to think of Middy! He was nowhere to be seen. Neither man remembered anything about him after the capsize. There was consternation in the hearts of those unlucky wights. To lose Middy was almost like losing one of the crew.

But it was too late and too dark to go back and risk another landing on the beach. There was nothing to be done but to leave poor Middy to his fate, or at least to wait until morning before searching for him.

But just as the prow of the boat bumped against the fender on the yacht's quarter, out from under the stern sheets came a wet, bedraggled, shivering cat, who leaped on board the yacht and hurried below into the warm cabin. In that moist adventure in the surf, Middy had taken care of himself, rescued himself from a watery grave, got on board the boat as soon as she was ready, and sheltered himself in the warmest corner. All this he had done without the least outcry, and without asking any help whatever. His self-reliance and courage were extraordinary.

Well, the pleasant month of cruising drew to a close, and it became a question what should be done with Middy. We could not think of turning him adrift in the cold world, although we had no fears but that so bright and plucky a cat would make a living anywhere. But we wanted to watch over his fortunes, and perhaps take him on the next cruise with us when he should have become a more settled and dignified Thomas. Finally, it was decided that he should be boarded for the winter with an artist, Miss Susan H——, a friend of one of our party. She wanted a studio cat, and would be particularly pleased to receive so accomplished and traveled a character as Middy. So when the yacht was moored to the little wharf at Annisquam, where she always ended her cruises, and we were packed and ready for our journey to Boston, Middy was tucked into a basket and taken to the train. He bore the confinement with the same good sense which had marked all his life with us, though I think his feelings were hurt at the lack of confidence we showed in him. And, in truth, we were a little ashamed of it ourselves, and when once we were on the cars somebody suggested that he be released from his prison just to see how he would behave. We might have known he would do himself credit. For when he had looked over his surroundings, peeped above the back of the seat at the passengers, taken a good look at the conductor, and counted the rest of the party to see that none of us was missing, Middy snuggled down upon the seat, laid his head upon the captain's knee, and slept all the way to Boston.

That was the last time I ever saw Middy. He was taken to his new boarding place in Boylston Street, where he lived very pleasantly for a few months, and made many friends by his pleasing manners and unruffled temper. But I suppose he found it a little dull in Boston. He was not quite at home in his aesthetic surroundings. I have always believed he sighed for the freedom of a sailor's life. He loved to sit by the open window when the wind was east, and seemed to be dreaming of faraway scenes. One day he disappeared. No trace of him was ever found. A great many things may have happened to him. But I never could get rid of the feeling that he went down to the wharves and the ships and the sailors, trying to find his old friends, looking everywhere for the stanch little *Eyvor;* and, not finding her, I am convinced that he shipped on some East Indiaman and is now a sailor cat on the high seas.

W. W. Jacobs

A BLACK AFFAIR

I didn't want to bring it," said Captain Gubson, regarding somewhat unfavorably a gray parrot whose cage was hanging against the mainmast, "but my old uncle was so set on it I had to. He said a sea voyage would set its 'elth up."

"It seems to be all right at present," said the mate, who was tenderly sucking his forefinger. "Best of spirits, I should say."

"It's playful," assented the skipper. "The old man thinks a rare lot of it. I think I shall have a little bit in that quarter, so keep your eye on the beggar."

"Scratch Poll!" said the parrot, giving its bill a preliminary strop on its perch. "Scratch poor Polly!"

It bent its head against the bars, and waited patiently to play off what it had always regarded as the most consummate practical joke in existence. The first doubt it had ever had about it occurred when the mate came forward and obligingly scratched it with the stem of his pipe. It was a wholly unforeseen development, and the parrot ruffling its feathers, edged along its perch and brooded darkly at the other end of it.

Opinion before the mast was also against the new arrival, the general view being that the wild jealousy which raged in the bosom of the ship's cat would sooner or later lead to mischief.

"Old Satan don't like it," said the cook, shaking his head. "The blessed bird hadn't been aboard ten minutes before Satan was prowling around. The blooming image waited till he was about a foot off the cage, and then he did the perlite and asked him whether he'd like a glass o' beer. *I* never see a cat so took aback in all my life. Never."

"There'll be trouble between 'em," said old Sam, who was the cat's special protector, "mark my words."

"I'd put my money on the parrot," said one of the men confidently. "It's 'ad a crool bit out of the mate's finger. Where 'ud the cat be agin that beak?"

"Well, you'd lose your money," said Sam. "If you want to do the cat a kindness, every time you see him near that cage cuff his 'ed."

The crew being much attached to the cat, which had been presented to them when a kitten by the mate's wife, acted upon the advice with so much zest that for the next two days the indignant animal was like to have been killed with kindness. On the third day, however, the parrot's cage being on the cabin table, the cat stole furtively down, and, at the pressing request of the occupant itself, scratched its head for it.

The skipper was the first to discover the mischief, and he came on deck and published the news in a voice which struck a chill to all hearts.

"Where's that black devil got to?" he yelled.

"Anything wrong, sir?" asked Sam anxiously.

"Come and look here," said the skipper. He led the way to the cabin, where the mate and one of the crew were already standing, shaking their heads over the parrot.

"What do you make of that?" demanded the skipper fiercely.

"Too much dry food, sir," said Sam, after due deliberation.

"Too much what?" bellowed the skipper.

"Too much dry food," repeated Sam firmly. "A parrot —a gray parrot—wants plenty o' sop. If it don't get it, it molts."

"It's had too much *cat,*" said the skipper fiercely, "and you know it, and overboard it goes."

"I don't believe it was the cat, sir," interposed the other man. "It's too softhearted to do a thing like that."

"You can shut your jaw," said the skipper, reddening. "Who asked you to come down here at all?"

"Nobody saw the cat do it," urged the mate.

The skipper said nothing, but, stooping down, picked up a tail feather from the floor, and laid it on the table. He then went on deck, followed by the others, and began calling, in seductive tones, for the cat. No reply forthcoming from the sagacious animal, which had gone into hiding, he turned to Sam, and bade him call it.

"No, sir, I won't 'ave no 'and in it," said the old man. "Putting aside my liking for the animal, *I'm* not going to 'ave anything to do with the killing of a black cat."

"Rubbish!" said the skipper.

"Very good, sir," said Sam, shrugging his shoulders. "You know best, o' course. You're eddicated and I'm not, an' p'r'aps you can afford to make a laugh o' such things. I knew one man who killed a black cat an' he went mad. There's something very pecooliar about that cat o' ours."

"It knows more than we do," said one of the crew, shaking his head. "That time you—I mean we—ran the smack down, that cat was expecting of it 'ours before. It was like a wild thing."

"Look at the weather we've 'ad—look at the trips we've made since he's been aboard," said the old man. "Tell me it's chance if you like, but I *know* better."

The skipper hesitated. He was a superstitious man even for a sailor, and his weakness was so well known that he had become a sympathetic receptacle for every ghost story which, by reason of its crudeness or lack of corroboration, had been rejected by other experts. He was a perfect reference library for omens, and his interpretations of dreams had gained for him a widespread reputation.

"That's all nonsense," he said, pausing uneasily. "Still, I only want to be just. There's nothing vindictive about me, and I'll have no hand in it myself. Joe, just tie a lump of coal to that cat and heave it overboard."

"Not me," said the cook, following Sam's lead, and working up a shudder. "Not for fifty pun in gold. I don't want to be haunted."

"The parrot's a little better now, sir," said one of the men, taking advantage of his hesitation. "He's opened one eye."

"Well, I only want to be just," repeated the skipper. "I won't do anything in a hurry, but, mark my words, if the parrot dies that cat goes overboard."

Contrary to expectations, the bird was still alive when London was reached, though the cook, who from his connection with the cabin had suddenly reached a position of unusual importance, reported great loss of strength and irritability of temper. It was still alive, but failing fast on the day they were put to sea again; and the fo'c'sle, in preparation for the worst, stowed their pet away in the paint locker, and discussed the situation.

Their council was interrupted by the mysterious behavior of the cook, who, having gone out to lay in a stock of bread, suddenly broke in upon them more in the manner of a member of a secret society than a humble but useful unit of a ship's company.

"Where's the cap'n?" he asked in a hoarse whisper, as he took a seat on the locker with the sack of bread between his knees.

"In the cabin," said Sam, regarding his antics with some disfavor. "What's wrong, cookie?"

"What d' yer think I've got in here?" asked the cook, patting the bag.

The obvious reply to this question was, of course, bread; but as it was known that the cook had departed specially to buy some, and that he could hardly ask a question involving such a simple answer, nobody gave it.

"It come to me all of a sudden," said the cook, in a thrilling whisper. "I'd just bought the bread and left the shop, when I see a big black cat, the very image of ours, sitting on a doorstep. I just stooped down to stroke its 'ed, when it come to me."

"They will sometimes," said one of the seamen.

"I don't mean that," said the cook, with the contempt of genius. "I mean the idea did. Says I to myself, 'You might be old Satan's brother by the look of you; an' if the cap'n wants to kill a cat, let it be you,' I says. And with that, before it could say Jack Robinson, I picked it up by the scruff o' the neck and shoved it in the bag."

"What, all in along of our bread?" said the previous interrupter, in a pained voice.

"Some of yer are 'ard ter please," said the cook, deeply offended.

"Don't mind him, cook," said the admiring Sam. "You're a masterpiece, that's what you are."

"Of course, if any of you've got a better plan—" said the cook generously.

"Don't talk rubbish, cook," said Sam. "Fetch the two cats out and put 'em together."

"Don't mix 'em," said the cook warningly, "for you'll never know which is which agin if you do."

He cautiously opened the top of the sack and produced his captive, and Satan having been relieved from his prison, the two animals were carefully compared.

"They're as like as two lumps o' coal," said Sam slowly. "Lord, what a joke on the old man. I must tell the mate o' this; he'll enjoy it."

"It'll be all right if the parrot don't die," said the dainty pessimist, still harping on his pet theme. "All that bread spoilt, and two cats aboard."

"Don't mind what he says," said Sam; "you're a brick, that's what you are. I'll just make a few holes on the lid o' the boy's chest, and pop old Satan in. You don't mind, do you, Billy?"

"Of course he don't," said the other men indignantly.

Matters being thus agreeably arranged, Sam got a gimlet, and prepared the chest for the reception of its tenant, who, convinced that he was being put out of the way to make room for a rival, made a frantic fight for freedom.

"Now get something 'eavy and put on the top of it," said Sam, having convinced himself that the lock was broken; "and, Billy, put the new cat in the paint locker till we start; it's homesick."

The boy obeyed, and the understudy was kept in durance vile until they were off Limehouse, when he came on deck and nearly ended his career there and then by attempting to jump over the bulwark into the next garden. For some time he paced the deck in a perturbed fashion, and then, leaping on the stern, mewed plaintively as his native city receded farther and farther from his view.

"What's the matter with old Satan?" said the mate, who had been let into the secret. "He seems to have something on his mind."

"He'll have something round his neck presently," said the skipper grimly.

The prophecy was fulfilled some three hours later, when he came up on deck ruefully regarding the remains of a bird whose vocabulary had once been the pride of its native town. He threw it on board without a word, and then, seizing the innocent cat, who had followed him under the impression that it was about to lunch, produced half a brick attached to a string, and tied it round his neck. The crew, who were enjoying the joke immensely, raised a howl of protest.

"The *Skylark*'ll never have another like it, sir," said Sam solemnly. "That cat was the luck of the ship."

"I don't want any of your old woman's yarns," said the skipper brutally. "If you want the cat, go and fetch it."

He stepped aft as he spoke, and sent the gentle stranger hurtling through the air. There was a "plomp" as it reached the water, a bubble or two came to the surface, and all was over.

"That's the last o' that," he said, turning away.

The old man shook his head. "You can't kill a black cat for nothing," said he, "mark my words!"

The skipper, who was in a temper at the time, thought little of them, but they recurred to him vividly the next day. The wind had freshened during the night, and rain was falling heavily. On deck the crew stood about in oilskins, while below, the boy, in his new capacity of gaoler, was ministering to the wants of an ungrateful prisoner, when the cook, happening to glance that way, was horrified to see the animal emerge from the fo'c'sle. It eluded easily the frantic clutch of the boy as he sprang up the ladder after it, and walked leisurely along the deck in the direction of the cabin. Just as the crew had given it up for lost it encountered Sam, and the next moment, despite its cries, was caught up and huddled away beneath his stiff clammy oilskins. At the noise the skipper, who was talking to the mate, turned as though he had been shot, and gazed wildly round him.

"Dick," said he, "can you hear a cat?"

"Cat!" said the mate, in accents of great astonishment.

"I thought I heard it," said the puzzled skipper.

"Fancy, sir," said Dick firmly, as a mewing, appalling in its wrath, came from beneath Sam's coat.

"Did you hear it, Sam?" called the skipper, as the old man was moving off.

"Hear what, sir?" inquired Sam respectfully, without turning round.

"Nothing," said the skipper, collecting himself. "Nothing. All right."

The old man, hardly able to believe in his good fortune, made his way forward, and, seizing a favorable opportunity, handed his ungrateful burden back to the boy.

"Fancy you heard a cat just now?" inquired the mate casually.

"Well, between you an' me, Dick," said the skipper, in a mysterious voice, "I did, and it wasn't fancy neither. I heard that cat as plain as if it was alive."

"Well, I've heard of such things," said the other, "but I don't believe 'em. What a lark if the old cat comes back climbing up over the side out of the sea tonight, with the brick hanging round its neck."

The skipper stared at him for some time without speaking. "If that's your idea of a lark," he said at length, in a voice which betrayed traces of some emotion. "It ain't mine."

"Well, if you hear it again," said the mate cordially, "you might let me know. I'm rather interested in such things."

The skipper, hearing no more of it that day, tried hard

to persuade himself that he was the victim of imagination, but, in spite of this, he was pleased at night, as he stood at the wheel, to reflect on the sense of companionship afforded by the lookout in the bows. On his part the lookout was quite charmed with the unwonted affability of the skipper, as he yelled out to him two or three times on matters only faintly connected with the progress of the schooner.

The night, which had been dirty, cleared somewhat, and the bright crescent of the moon appeared above a heavy bank of clouds as the cat, which had by dint of using its back as a lever at length got free from that cursed chest, licked its shapely limbs, and came up on deck. After its stifling prison, the air was simply delicious.

"Bob!" yelled the skipper suddenly.

"Ay, ay, sir!" said the lookout, in a startled voice.

"Did you mew?" inquired the skipper.

"Did I *wot*, sir?" cried the astonished Bob.

"Mew," said the skipper sharply, "like a cat?"

"No, sir," said the offended seaman. "What 'ud I want to do that for?"

"I don't know what you want to for," said the skipper, looking round him uneasily. "There's some more rain coming, Bob."

"Ay, ay, sir," said Bob.

"Lot o' rain we've had this summer," said the skipper, in a meditative bawl.

"Ay, ay, sir," said Bob. "Sailing ship on the port bow, sir."

The conversation dropped, the skipper, anxious to divert his thoughts, watching the dark mass of sail as it came plunging out of the darkness into the moonlight until it was abreast of his own craft. His eyes followed it as it passed his quarter, so that he saw not the stealthy approach of the cat which came from behind the companion, and sat down close by him. For over thirty hours the animal had been subjected to the grossest indignities at the hands of every man on board the ship except one. That one was the skipper, and there is no doubt but that its subsequent behavior was a direct recognition of that fact. It rose to its feet, and crossing over to the unconscious skipper, rubbed its head affectionately and vigorously against his leg.

From simple causes great events do spring. The skipper sprang four yards, and let off a screech which was the subject of much comment on the bark which had just passed. When Bob, who came shuffling up at the double, reached him he was leaning against the side, incapable of speech, and shaking all over.

"Anything wrong, sir?" inquired the seaman anxiously, as he ran to the wheel.

The skipper pulled himself together a bit, and got closer to his companion.

"Believe me or not, Bob," he said at length, in trembling accents, "just as you please, but the ghost of that—cat, I mean the ghost of that poor affectionate animal which I drowned, and which I wish I hadn't, came and rubbed itself up against my leg."

"Which leg?" inquired Bob, who was ever careful about details.

"What the blazes does it matter which leg?" demanded the skipper, whose nerves were in a terrible state. "Ah, look —look there!"

The seaman followed his outstretched finger, and his heart failed him as he saw the cat, with its back arched, gingerly picking its way along the side of the vessel.

"I can't see nothing," he said doggedly.

"I don't suppose you can, Bob," said the skipper in a melancholy voice, as the cat vanished in the bows. "It's evidently only meant for me to see. What it means I don't know. I'm going down to turn in. I ain't fit for duty. You don't mind being left alone till the mate comes up, do you?"

"I ain't afraid," said Bob.

His superior officer disappeared below, and, shaking the sleepy mate, who protested strongly against the proceedings, narrated in trembling tones his horrible experiences.

"If I were you—" said the mate.

"Yes?" said the skipper, waiting a bit. Then he shook him again, roughly.

"What were you going to say?" he inquired.

"Say?" said the mate, rubbing his eyes. "Nothing."

"About the cat?" suggested the skipper.

"Cat?" said the mate, nestling lovingly down in the blankets again. "Wha' ca'—goo'ni'—"

Then the skipper drew the blankets from the mate's sleepy clutches, and, rolling him backward and forward in the bunk, patiently explained to him that he was very unwell, that he was going to have a drop of whiskey neat, and turn in, and that he, the mate, was to take the watch. From this moment the joke lost much of its savor for the mate.

"You can have a nip too, Dick," said the skipper, proffering him the whiskey, as the other sullenly dressed himself.

"It's all rot," said the mate, tossing the spirits down his throat, "and it's no use either; you can't run away from a ghost; it's just as likely to be in your bed as anywhere else. Good night."

He left the skipper pondering over his last words, and dubiously eyeing the piece of furniture in question. Nor did he retire until he had subjected it to an analysis of the most searching description, and then, leaving the lamp burning, he sprang hastily in, and forgot his troubles in sleep.

It was day when he awoke, and went on deck to find a heavy sea running, and just sufficient sail set to keep the schooner's head before the wind as she bobbed about on the waters. An exclamation from the skipper, as a wave broke against the side and flung a cloud of spray over him, brought the mate's head round.

"Why, you ain't going to get up?" he said, in tones of insincere surprise.

"Why not?" inquired the other gruffly.

"You go and lay down agin," said the mate, "and have a cup o' nice hot tea an' some toast."

"Clear out," said the skipper, making a dash for the wheel, and reaching it as the wet deck suddenly changed its angle. "I know you didn't like being woke up, Dick; but I got the horrors last night. Go below and turn in."

"All right," said the mollified mate.

"You didn't see anything?" inquired the skipper, as he took the wheel from him.

"Nothing at all," said the other.

The skipper shook his head thoughtfully, then shook it again vigorously, as another shower bath put its head over the side and saluted him.

"I wish I hadn't drowned that cat, Dick," he said.

"You won't see it agin," said Dick, with the confidence of a man who had taken every possible precaution to render the prophecy a safe one.

He went below, leaving the skipper at the wheel idly watching the cook as he performed marvelous feats of jugglery, between the galley and the fo'c'sle, with the men's breakfast.

A little while later, leaving the wheel to Sam, he went below himself and had his own, talking freely, to the discomfort of the conscience-stricken cook, about his weird experiences of the night before.

"You won't see it no more, sir, I don't expect," he said faintly. "I believe it come and rubbed itself up agin your leg to show it forgave you."

"Well, I hope it knows it's understood," said the other. "I don't want it to take any more trouble."

He finished the breakfast in silence, and then went on deck again. It was still blowing hard, and he went over to superintend the men who were attempting to lash together some empties which were rolling about in all directions amidships. A violent roll set them free again, and at the same time separated two chests in the fo'c'sle, which were standing one on top of the other. This enabled Satan, who was crouching in the lower one, half crazed with terror, to come flying madly up on deck and give his feelings full vent. Three times in full view of the horrified skipper he circled the deck at racing speed, and had just started on the fourth when a heavy packing case, which had been temporarily set on end and abandoned by the men at his sudden appearance, fell over and caught him by the tail. Sam rushed to the rescue.

"Stop!" yelled the skipper.

"Won't I put it up, sir?" inquired Sam.

"Do you see what's beneath it?" said the skipper, in a husky voice.

"Beneath it, sir?" said Sam, whose ideas were in a whirl.

"The cat, can't you see the cat?" said the skipper, whose eyes had been riveted on the animal since its first appearance on deck.

Sam hesitated a moment, and then shook his head.

"The case has fallen on the cat," said the skipper, "I can see it distinctly."

He might have said "heard it," too, for Satan was making frenzied appeals to his sympathetic friends for assistance.

"Let me put the case back, sir," said one of the men, "then p'r'aps the wision'll disappear."

"No, stop where you are," said the skipper. "I can stand it better by daylight. It's the most wonderful and extraordinary thing I've ever seen. Do you mean to say you can't see anything, Sam?"

"I can see a case, sir," said Sam, speaking slowly and carefully, "with a bit of rusty iron band sticking out from it. That's what you're mistaking for the cat, p'r'aps, sir."

"Can't you see anything, cook?" demanded the skipper.

"It may be fancy, sir," faltered the cook, lowering his eyes, "but it does seem to me as though I can see a little misty sort o' thing there. Ah, now it's gone."

"No, it ain't," said the skipper. "The ghost of Satan's sitting there. The case seems to have fallen on its tail. It appears to be howling something dreadful."

The men made a desperate effort to display the astonishment suitable to such a marvel, while Satan, who was trying all he knew to get his tail out, cursed freely. How long the superstitious captain of the *Skylark* would have let him remain there will never be known for just then the mate came on deck and caught sight of it before he was quite aware of the part he was expected to play.

"Why the devil don't you lift the thing off the poor brute," he yelled, hurrying up toward the case.

"What, can *you* see it, Dick?" said the skipper impressively, laying his hand on his arm.

"*See* it?" retorted the mate, "D'ye think I'm blind? Listen to the poor brute. I should—oh!"

He became conscious of the concentrated significant gaze of the crew. Five pairs of eyes speaking as one, all saying "idiot" plainly, the boy's eyes conveying an expression too great to be translated.

Turning, the skipper saw the byplay, and a light slowly dawned upon him. But he wanted more, and he wheeled suddenly to the cook for the required illumination.

The cook said it was a lark. Then he corrected himself and said it wasn't a lark, then he corrected himself again and became incoherent. Meantime the skipper eyed him stonily, while the mate released the cat and good-naturedly helped to straighten its tail.

It took fully five minutes of unwilling explanation before the skipper could grasp the situation. He did not appear to fairly understand it until he was shown the chest with the ventilated lid; then his countenance cleared, and, taking the unhappy Billy by the collar, he called sternly for a piece of rope.

By this statesmanlike handling of the subject a question of much delicacy and difficulty was solved, discipline was preserved, and a practical illustration of the perils of deceit afforded to a youngster who was at an age best suited to receive such impressions. That he should exhaust the resources of a youthful but powerful vocabulary upon the crew in general, and Sam in particular, was only to be expected. They bore him no malice for it, but, when he showed signs of going beyond his years, held a hasty consultation, and then stopped his mouth with sixpence-halfpenny and a broken jack-knife.

Paul Gallico

"WHEN IN DOUBT —
WASH!"

When in doubt—any kind of doubt—*wash!* That is rule number one," said Jennie. She now sat primly and a little stiffly, with her tail wrapped around her feet, near the head of the big bed beneath the Napoleon Initial and Crown, rather like a schoolmistress. But it was obvious that the role of teacher and the respectful attention Peter bestowed upon her were not unendurable, because she had a pleased expression and her eyes were again gleaming brightly.

The sun had reached its noon zenith in the sky in the

world that lay outside the dark and grimy warehouse, and coming in slantwise through the small window sent a dusty shaft that fell like a theatrical spotlight about Jennie's head and shoulders as she lectured.

"If you have committed any kind of an error and anyone scolds you—wash," she was saying. "If you slip and fall off something and somebody laughs at you—wash. If you are getting the worst of an argument and want to break off hostilities until you have composed yourself, start washing. Remember, *every* cat respects another cat at her toilet. That's our first rule of social deportment, and you must also observe it.

"Whatever the situation, whatever difficulty you may be in, you can't go wrong if you wash. If you come into a room full of people you do not know, and who are confusing to you, sit right down in the midst of them and start washing. They'll end up by quieting down and watching you. Some noise frightens *you* into a jump, and somebody you know saw you were frightened—begin washing immediately.

"If somebody calls you and you don't care to come and still you don't wish to make it a direct insult—wash. If you've started off to go somewhere and suddenly can't remember where it was you wanted to go, sit right down and begin brushing up a little. It will come back to you. Something hurt you? Wash it. Tired of playing with someone who has been kind enough to take time and trouble and you want to break off without hurting his or her feelings—start washing.

"Oh, there are dozens of things! Door closed and you're burning up because no one will open it for you—have yourself a little wash and forget it. Somebody petting another cat or dog in the same room, and you are annoyed over *that*—be nonchalant; wash. Feel sad—wash away your blues. Been picked up by somebody you don't particularly fancy and who didn't smell good—wash him off immediately and pointedly where he can see you do it. Overcome by emotion—a wash will help you to get a grip on yourself again. Anytime, anyhow, in any manner, for whatever purpose, wherever you are, whenever and why ever that you want to clear the air, or get a moment's respite or think things over—*wash!*

"And," concluded Jennie, drawing a long breath, "of course you also wash to get clean and to keep clean."

"Goodness!" said Peter, quite worried. "I don't see how I could possibly remember them all."

"You don't have to remember any of it, actually," Jennie explained. "All that you have to remember is rule one: When in doubt—*wash!*"

Peter, who, like all boys, had no objection to being reasonably clean, but not *too* clean, saw the problem of washing looming up large and threatening to occupy all of his time. "It's true, I remember, you always do seem to be washing," he protested to Jennie. "I mean, all cats I've seen, but I don't see why. Why do cats spend so much of their time at it?"

Jennie considered his question for a moment, and then replied: "Because it feels so good to be clean."

"Well, at any rate I shall never be capable of doing it," Peter remarked, "because I won't be able to reach places now that I am a cat and cannot use my hands. And even when I was a boy, Nanny used to have to wash my back for me. . . ."

"Nothing of the kind," said Jennie. "The first thing you will learn is that there isn't an inch of herself or himself that a cat cannot reach to wash. If you had ever owned one of us, you would know. Now watch me. We'll begin with the back. I'll do it first, and then you come over here alongside of me and do as I do."

And thereupon sitting upright, she turned her head around over her shoulder with a wonderful ease and grace, using little short strokes of her tongue and keeping her chin down close to her body, she began to wash over and around her left shoulder-blade, gradually increasing the amount of turn and the length of the stroking movement of her head until her rough, pink tongue was traveling smoothly and firmly along the region of her upper spine.

"Oh, I never could," cried Peter, "because I cannot twist my head around as far as you can. I never know what is going on behind me unless I turn right around."

"Try," was all Jennie replied.

Peter did, and to his astonishment found that whereas when he had been a boy he had been unable to turn his head more left and right than barely to be able to look over his shoulders, now he could swivel it quite around on his neck so that he was actually gazing out behind him. And when he stuck out his tongue and moved his head in small circles as he had seen Jennie do, there he was washing around his left shoulder.

"Oh, bravo! Splendid!" applauded Jennie. "There, you see! Well done, Peter. Now turn a little more—you're bound to be a bit stiff at first—and down the spine you go!"

And indeed, down the spine, about halfway from below his neck to the middle of his back, Peter went. He was so delighted that he tried to purr and wash at the same time, and actually achieved it.

"Now," Jennie coached, "for the rest of the way down, you can help yourself and make it easier—like this. Curve your body around and go a little lower so that you are half-sitting, half-lying. That's it! Brace yourself against your right paw and pull your left paw in a little closer to you so that it is out of the way. There . . . Now, you see, that brings the rest of you nicely around in a curve where you can get at it. Finish off the left side of your back and hindquarters and then shift around and do the other side."

Peter did so, and was amazed to find with what little effort the whole of his spine and hindquarters was brought within ample reach of his busy tongue. He even essayed to have a go at his tail from this position, but found this a more elusive customer. It would keep squirming away.

Jennie smiled. "Try putting a paw on it to hold it down. The right one. You can still brace yourself with it. That's it. We'll get at the underside of it later on."

Peter was so enchanted with what he had learned that he would have gone on washing and washing the two sides of his back and his flanks and quarters if Jennie hadn't said: "There, that's enough of that. There's still plenty left, you know. Now you must do your front and the stomach and the inside of your paws and quarters."

The front limbs and paws, of course, proved easy for Peter, for they were quite close, but when he attempted to tackle his chest, it was something else.

"Try lying down first," Jennie suggested. "After a while you'll get so supple you will be able to wash your chest sitting up just by sticking your tongue out a little more and bobbing your head. But it's easier lying down on your side. Here, like this," and she suited the action to the word, and soon Peter found that he actually was succeeding in washing his chest fur just beneath his chin.

"But I can't get at my middle," he complained, for indeed the underside of his belly defied his clumsy attempts to reach it, bend and twist as he would.

Jennie smiled. " '*Can't* catches no mice,' " she quoted. "That is more difficult. Watch me now. You won't do it lying on your side. Sit up a bit and rock on your tail. That's it, get your tail right under you. You can brace with either of your forepaws, or both. Now, you see, that bends you right around again and brings your stomach within reach. You'll get it with practice. It's all curves. That's why we were made that way."

Peter found it more awkward to balance than in the other position and fell over several times, but soon found that he was getting better at it and that each portion of his person that was thus made accessible to him through Jennie's knowledge, experience, and teaching brought him a new enjoyment and pleasure of accomplishment. And, of course, Jennie's approval made him very proud.

He was forging ahead so rapidly with his lesson that she decided to see whether he could go and learn by himself. "Now how would you go about doing the inside of the hindquarter?" she asked.

"Oh, that's easy," Peter cried. But it wasn't at all. In fact, the more he tried and strained and reached and curved, the farther away did his hind leg seem to go. He tried first the right and then the left, and finally got himself tangled in such a heap of legs, paws, and tail that he fell right over in a manner that Jennie had to take a few quick dabs at herself to keep from laughing.

"I can't—I mean, I don't see how . . . ," wailed Peter, "there isn't any way."

Jenny was contrite at once and hoped Peter had not seen she had been amused. "Oh, I'm sorry," she declared. "That wasn't fair of me. There is, but it's most difficult, and you have to know how. It took me the longest time when my mother tried to show me. Here, does this suggest anything to you— leg of mutton? I'm sure you've seen it dozens of times," and she assumed an odd position with her right leg sticking straight up in the air and somehow close to her head, almost like the contortionist that Peter had seen at the circus at Olympia who had twisted himself right around so that his head came down between his legs. He was sure that he could never do it.

Peter tried to imitate Jennie, but only succeeded in winding himself into a worse knot. Jennie came to his rescue once more. "See here," she said, "let's try it by counts, one stage at a time. Once you've done it, you know, you'll never forget it. Now:

147

"One—rock on your tail." Peter rocked.

"Two—brace yourself with your left forepaw." Peter braced.

"Three—half-sit, and bend your back." Peter managed that, and made himself into the letter *C.*

"Four—stretch out the left leg all the way. That will keep you from falling over the other side and provide a balance for the paw to push against." This, too, worked out exactly as Jennie described it when Peter tried it.

"Five—swing your right leg from the hip—you'll find it will go—with the foot pointing straight up into the air. Yes, like that, but *outside,* not inside the right forepaw." It went better this time. Peter got it almost up.

"Six—*now* you've got it. Hold yourself steady by bracing the right front forepaw. *So!*"

Peter felt like shouting with joy. For there he was, actually sitting, leg of mutton, his hindquarter shooting up right past his cheek and the whole inside of his leg exposed. He felt that he was really doubled back on himself like the contortionist, and he wished that Nanny were there so that he could show her.

By twisting and turning a little, there was no part of him underneath that he could not reach, and he first washed one side and then, without any further instruction from Jennie, managed to reverse the position and get the left leg up, which drew forth an admiring: "Oh, you are clever!" from Jennie. "It took me just ages to learn to work the left side. It all depends whether you are left or right pawed, but you caught onto it immediately. Now there's only one thing more. The back of the neck, the ears, and the face."

In a rush to earn more praise Peter went nearly cross-eyed trying to get his tongue out and around to reach behind him and on top of him, and of course it wouldn't work. He cried: "Oh, dear, *that* must be the most complicated of all."

"On the contrary," smiled Jennie, "it's quite the simplest. Wet the side of your front paw." Peter did so. "Now rub it around over your ears and the back of your neck."

Now it was Peter's turn to laugh at himself. "How stupid I am," he said. "That part is just the way I do it at home. Except I use a flannel, and Nanny stands there watching to make certain I go behind the ears."

"Well," said Jennie, "*I'm* watching you now. . . ."

So Peter completed his bath by wetting one paw and then the other, on the side and in the middle on the pads, and washing first his ears, then both sides of his face, the back of his neck, his whiskers, and even a little under his chin, and over his nose and eyes.

And now he found that having washed himself all over, from head to foot, the most wonderful feeling of comfort and relaxation had come over him. It was quite a different sensation from the time that Jennie had washed him and which had somehow taken him back to the days when he was very little and his mother was looking after him.

This time he felt a kind of glow in his skin and a sense of well-being in his muscles, as though every one of them had been properly used and stretched. In the light from the last of the shaft of the sun that was just passing from the window of the storehouse he could see how his white fur glistened from the treatment he had given it, as smooth as silk and as soft.

Peter felt a delicious drowsiness. His eyes began to close, and as from a distance he heard Jennie say: "It's good to take a nap after washing. I always do. You've earned it."

Just before he dropped off to sleep, Peter felt her curl up against him, her back touching his, warm and secure, and the next moment he was off in sweet and dreamless slumber.

"I'm awfully thirsty, Jennie," Peter whispered.

They had been crouching there around the bend of the warehouse corridor for the better part of an hour waiting for the men to finish the work of carrying out the furniture from the storage bin.

Jennie flattened herself and peered around the corner. "Soon," she said. "There are only a few pieces left."

"How I wish I had a tall, cool glass of milk," Peter said.

Jennie turned her head and looked at him. "Dish of milk, you mean. You wouldn't be able to drink it out of a glass. And as for milk—do you know how long it is since I have seen or tasted milk? In our kind of life, I mean, cut off from humans, there isn't any milk. If you're thirsty you find some rainwater or some slops in the gutter or in a pail left out, or you can go down the stone steps to the river landings when they are deserted at night, if you don't mind your water a little oily and brackish."

Peter was not at all pleased with the prospect and he had not yet got used to the fact that he was no longer a boy, with a home and family, but a white cat with no home at all and no one to befriend him but another scrawny stray.

He was so desperately thirsty and the picture drawn by Jennie so gloomy and unpleasant that he could not help bursting into tears and crying. "But I'm *used* to milk! I like it, and Nanny gives me some every day. . . ."

"Sshhh!" cautioned Jennie, "they'll hear you." Then she added: "There's nobody goes about setting out dishes of milk for strays. You'll get used to not having it eventually."

But Peter didn't think so, and continued to cry softly to himself while Jennie Baldrin watched him with growing concern and bewilderment. She seemed to be trying to make up her mind about something which apparently she did not very much wish to do. But finally, when it appeared that she could bear his unhappiness no longer, she whispered to him: "Come, now . . . don't take on so! I know a place where I think I can get you a dish of milk. We'll go there."

The thought caused Peter to stop crying and brighten up immediately. "Yes?" he said. "Where?"

"There's an old watchman lives in a shack down by the tea docks," Jennie told him. "He's lonely, likes cats, and is always good for a tidbit, especially for me. He's been after me to come and live with him for months. Of course, I wouldn't dream of it."

"But," said Peter, not wishing to argue himself out of milk but only desiring to understand clearly the terms under which they were to have it, "that *is* taking it from people, isn't it?"

"It's taking, but not *giving* anything," Jennie said, with that strange, unhappy intenseness that came over her whenever she discussed anything to do with human beings. "We'll *have it* and then walk out on him."

"Would that be right?" Peter asked. It slipped out almost before he was aware of it, for he very much wanted the milk and he equally did not wish to offend Jennie. But it was just that he had been taught certain ways of behavior, or felt them to be so by instinct, and this seemed a poor way of repaying a kindness. Clearly he had somewhat put Jennie out, for she stiffened slightly and with the nearest thing to a cold look she had bestowed upon him since they had met, said: "You can't have it both ways, Peter. If you want to live my kind of life, and I can't see where you have very much choice at the moment—"

"But of course I do!" Peter hastened to explain, "it's just that I'm not yet quite familiar with the different way cats feel than the way people feel. And I will do as you say, and I do want to learn. . . ."

From her expression, Jennie did not appear to be too pleased with this speech either, but before she could remark upon it there came a loud call from the movers: "That's the lot, then," and another voice replied: "Righty-ho!" Jennie peered around the corner and said: "They've finished. We'll wait a few minutes to make sure they don't come back, and then we'll start."

When they were certain that the aisle was quite deserted again, they set off, Jennie leading, past the empty bin and down the corridor in the direction the men had taken, but before they had gone very far Jennie branched off to the right on a new track until she came to a bin close to the outside wall of the warehouse, filled with horrible new modern kind of furniture, chrome-bound leather and overstuffed plush. She led Peter to the back where there was a good-sized hole in the baseboard. It looked dark and forbidding inside.

"Don't be afraid," Jennie said. "Just follow me. We go to the right and then to the left, but it gets light very quickly."

She slipped in with Peter after her, and it soon grew pitch black. Peter now discovered that he was feeling through the ends of his whiskers, rather than seeing where Jennie was, and he had no difficulty in following her, particularly inasmuch as it soon became bright enough to see that they were in a tunnel through which a large iron pipe more than a foot in diameter was running. Then Peter saw where the light was coming from. There was a hole in the pipe where it had rusted through a few feet from where it gave exit to the street.

Apparently the pipe was used as some kind of air intake, or had something to do with the ventilation of the warehouse, for it had once had a grating over the end of it, but the fastenings of that had long since rusted and it had fallen away, and there was nothing to bar their way out.

Peter was so pleased and excited at the prospect of seeing the sun and being out of doors again that he hurried past Jennie and would have rushed out into the street had not the alarm in her warning cry checked him just before he emerged from the opening.

"Peter! Wait!" she cried. "Not like that! Cats never, *never* rush out from places. Don't you know about Pausing on the Threshold, or Lingering on the Sill? But then, of course, you wouldn't. Oh, dear, I don't mean always to be telling you what to do and what not to do, but this is really Important.

It's almost lesson number two. You never hurry out of any-place, and particularly not outdoors."

Peter saw that Jennie had quite recovered her good na-ture and apparently had forgotten that she had been upset with him. He was curious to find out the reasons for her warning. He said: "I don't quite understand, Jennie. You mean, I'm not to stop before coming in, but I am whenever I go out?"

"Of course. What else?" replied Jennie, sitting down quite calmly in the mouth of the exit and showing not the slightest disposition to go through it and into the street. "You know what's inside because you come from there. You don't know what's outside because you haven't been there. That's common ordinary sense for anyone, I should think."

"Yes, but what is there outside to be afraid of, really?" inquired Peter. "I mean, after all, if you know where you live and the street and houses and all which don't change—"

"Oh, my goodness," said Jennie. "I couldn't try to tell you them all. To begin with—dogs, people, moving vehicles, the weather and changes in temperature, the condition of the street, is it wet or dry, clean or dirty, what has been left lying about, what is parked at the curb, and whether anybody is coming along, on which side of the street and in how much of a hurry.

"And it isn't that you're actually afraid. It's just that you want to *know*. And you ought to know, if you have your wits about you, everything your eyes, your ears, your nose, and the ends of your whiskers can tell you. And so you stop, look, listen, and *feel*. We have a saying: 'Heaven is overcrowded with kittens who rushed out of doors without first stopping and "receiving" a little.'

"There might be another cat in the vicinity, bent on mischief, or looking for a fight. You'd certainly want to know about that before you stepped out into something you weren't prepared for. Then you'd want to know all about the weather, not only what it's like at the moment, but what it's going to be doing later, say an hour from then. If it's going to come on to rain or thunder, you wouldn't want to be too far from home. Your whiskers and your skin tell you that.

"And then, anyway," Jennie concluded, "it's a good idea on general principles not to rush into things. When you go out, there are very few places to go to that won't be there just the same five minutes later, and the chances of your getting there will be ever so much better. Come here and squat down beside me and we'll just have a look."

Peter did as she suggested and lay down directly in the opening with his paws tucked under him, and felt quite natural doing it, and suddenly he was glad that Jennie had stopped him and that he hadn't gone charging out into goodness knows what.

Feet went by at intervals. By observation he got to know something about the size of the shoes, which were mostly the heavy boots belonging to workmen, their speed, and how near they came to the wall of the warehouse. The wheeled traffic was of the heavy type—huge horse-drawn wagons, and motor trucks that rumbled past ominously loud, and the horses' feet, huge things with big, shaggy fetlocks, were another danger. Far in the distance, Peter heard Big Ben strike four. The sound would not have reached him as a human being, perhaps, but it traveled all the distance from the Houses of Parliament to his cat's ears and informed him of the time.

Now he used his nostrils and sniffed the scents that came to his nose and tried to understand what they told him. There was a strong smell of tea and a queer odor that he could not identify, he just knew he didn't like it. He recognized dry goods, machinery, musk, and spices, and horses and burned gasoline, exhaust gases, tar, and soft coal smoke, the kind that comes from railway engines.

Jennie had got up now and was standing on the edge of

the opening with only her head out, whiskers extended forward, quivering a little, and making small wrinkly movements with her nose. After a moment or so of this she turned to Peter quite relaxed and said: "All clear. We can go now. No cats around. There's a dog been by, but only a mangy cur probably scared of his own shadow. There's a tea boat just docked. That's good. The watchman won't really have any responsibilities until she's unloaded. Rain's all cleared away. Probably won't rain for at least another forty-eight hours. Goods train just gone down into the docks area. That's fine. Means the gates'll be open, and besides, we can use the wagons for cover."

"Goodness!" Peter marveled. "I don't see how you can tell all that from just one tiny sniff around. Do you suppose I'll ever—?"

"Of course you will," Jennie laughed, and with a bit of a purr added: "It's only a matter of getting used to it and looking at things the way a cat would. It's really nothing." And here she gave herself two or three self-conscious licks, for, truth to tell, she was just a trifle vain and nothing delighted her so much as to appear clever in Peter's eyes, which was only feline.

"Well, I don't understand . . . ," Peter began, saying just the right thing and giving her the lead which she was quick to take up.

"It's really quite simple," she explained. "For instance, you can smell the tea. Well, that wasn't around last time I was outside. Means a tea boat has come in and they've opened the hatches. No cats about—I don't get any signals on my receiver, at least not hostile ones. The dog that went by, well, goodness knows, you can smell *him.* If he had any class or self-respect that might lead him to chase cats, he'd be clean, and a clean dog smells different. This one was filthy, and that's why I say he's nothing to worry about. He'll be slinking along down back alleys and glad to be left alone. And as for the goods train that went by, after you get to know the neighborhood it'll be easy for you too. You see, the smoke smell comes from the left, down where the docks are, so of course it went that way. And you know it was a goods train, because you can smell everything that was in the wagons. There, you see how easy it is?"

Peter again said the right thing, for he was learning how to please Jennie. "I think you're *enormously* clever," he told her. Her purr almost drowned out the sound of a passing horse-drawn wagon. Then she cried to him gaily: "Come along, Peter! We're off!" and the two friends went out into the cobbled street.

Paul Gallico

JENNIE'S LESSONS TO PETER ON HOW TO BEHAVE LIKE A CAT

Once aboard, Jennie's experience and knowledge of ships stood her in good stead. She called for the point-to-point method of procedure again, for she was particularly anxious not to encounter any human beings before the ship had cast off, and while she herself could melt and blend with the shadows in corners and behind things, she was worried over the conspicuousness of Peter's snow-white coat. But she followed her nose and her instincts as well as her memory of the other steamships on which she had served and soon was leading Peter down a narrow companionway that led to a small dining saloon and thence to the galley.

Tea was long since over, all of the crew and officers were on deck engaged with the cargo and preparations for leaving, and Jennie counted on finding that part of the ship deserted. She was right. The galley fires were out and there was no immediate sign of cook or sculleryman. Also no doors were shut anywhere, which gave Jennie further indication of what kind of craft it was, and she led him from the galley through the pantry to the small storeroom where the immediate supplies were kept. At the end of this room was a doorway and a narrow iron staircase that descended to another passageway on one side of which was the refrigeration room and on the other a large dry-stores enclosure where the ship's supplies in bulk were kept—sacks of flour and beans and dried peas, tins of fruit and vegetables, boxes of biscuits, tea, coffee, and so on.

The slatted door to this also stood wide open. It was dark, but an electric light burning far down the passageway shed sufficient light so that with their acute vision they soon accustomed themselves and could see their way about the boxes and cartons and barrels as well as though it were broad daylight.

And it was there in the storeroom, well concealed behind a case of tinned tomatoes, that Peter saw and missed his first mouse, revealing what might have been a fatal weakness in their plans. It had never dawned on him, and Jennie too had quite neglected to think about it and take into consideration that, for all his looking like and appearing to be a cat and learning to behave like one, Peter had not the faintest idea how to go about the difficult and important business of catching a mouse. Indeed, it was only through a lucky break that at the last moment more cargo arrived and the *Countess of Greenock* did not sail that night, nor the next night either, and that they were able to remedy their deficiency at least partly, for, superstition or no, a cat that proved itself wholly unable to catch marauding rodents might have received short shrift aboard such a craft.

The awkward discovery came when Jennie called Peter's attention to a little scratching, nibbling sort of noise from the other side of the storeroom, whispering: "Sh! Mouse! There he is over by the biscuit box. Let's see you get him."

Peter concentrated, staring through the gloom, and there indeed he was, just edging round the corner of the large tin marked HUNTLEY & PALMER LTD., READING, a long, grayish chap with a greedy face, impertinent whiskers, and beady black eyes.

Peter was so anxious to show off to Jennie what he could do as a cat if given the chance that he hardly even set himself to spring, or paused to measure the distance, the obstacles, and the possible avenues of escape open to the mouse. Without a moment's thought or plan, he launched himself through the air in one terrific pounce, paws spread wide, jaws open to snatch him.

There was of course no mouse there when Peter landed.

And not only that, but his teeth clicked together on empty air, there was nothing beneath his paws, and in addition, having miscalculated his distance, or rather not having calculated it at all, he gave himself a nasty knock on the head against the side of the tin box, all of which did not help the feeling that he had made a perfect fool of himself.

But while the mouse had saved itself momentarily, it also committed a fatal error by failing to dodge back behind the tin. Instead, gripped by panic, it emitted a squeak and went the other way, and the next instant, like a streak of furred lightning, Jennie had hurled herself through the air, her front paws, talons bared and extended, striking from side to side in a series of short, sharp, stunning hooks, even while she was in passage. The blows, as she landed, caught the mouse, knocking him first to one side, then back to the other, dazed and bewildered, then tossed him up in the air and batted him a couple before he came down, at which point Jennie seized him in her mouth; and it was all over before Peter had even so much as recovered his balance as well as from his confusion.

"Oh dear," Jennie said, dropping the mouse. "I hadn't thought of that. Of course you wouldn't know how. Why should you? But we *shall* be in a pretty pickle if we're caught here before you know something about it. And I don't know how much time we shall have. Still—"

Peter at last found his tongue and emitted a cry of anger and mortification. "Goodness," he said, "isn't there *anything* I can do? Does *everything* have to be learned?"

"It's practice really," Jennie explained. "Even *we* have to keep practicing constantly. That, and while I hate to use the expression—know-how. It's like everything else. You find there's a right way and a wrong way. The right way is to catch them with your paws, not your mouth, and of course the preparation is *everything*. Look here, I'll show you what I mean."

Here she crouched down a few feet away from the dead mouse and then began a slow waggling of her hindquarters from side to side, gradually increasing the speed and shortening the distance of the waggle. *"That's* what you must try, to begin with," she explained. "We don't do that for fun, or because we're nervous, but to give ourselves motion. It's ever so much harder and less accurate to spring from a standing start than from a moving one. Try it now and see how much easier it is to take off than the other way."

Peter's rear-end waggle was awkward at first, but he soon began to find the rhythm of it—it was almost like the "One to get set, two to make ready, and *three* to go" in footracing, except that this was even better because he found that what Jennie said was quite true and that the slight bit of motion did start him off the mark like an arrow.

Next he had to learn to move his paws so that, as he flew

through the air and landed, they were striking left, right, with incredible speed, a feat that was much more difficult than it sounds since he could not use his paws to land on, but had to bring up his hind part in time while lashing out with the front.

His second mouse he missed by a hair's breadth due to overanxiousness, but Jennie praised his paw work and spring, criticizing only his judgment of distance and haste. "You rarely lose a mouse by waiting just a little longer," she explained, "because a mouse has a one-track mind and will keep on doing what it started out to do provided it isn't disturbed; and if it is disturbed, it will just sit there and quake, so that you have all the time in the world really. . . ."

But his third mouse Peter caught and killed, one-two-three, just like that. Jennie said that she could not have done it better herself, and when Peter made her a present of it she accepted it graciously and with evident pleasure and ate it. But the others they saved because Jennie said that when they came to be discovered, it would be a good thing to have some samples of their type of work about them.

And so, for the rest, Peter practiced and hunted busily, and Jennie advised him to keep the mouse alive and in the air as long as possible, not to torture it, but to gain in skill and accuracy and train his muscles to react swiftly at the slightest movement.

It was the second night before they sailed that Peter awoke to an uncomfortable feeling. There was a new and unpleasant odor in the storeroom, one that tended to make him a little sick. And suddenly from a far corner he saw glowing two evil-looking red eyes. Before he could stir he sensed through his whiskers that Jennie was awake too; and for the first time using this means of communication with him so that there should not be a sound, she warned: "Rat! It is serious, Peter, and very dangerous. This is something I cannot teach you or help you with. You'll just have to watch me and try to learn as best you can. And, above all, whatever happens, don't move a muscle, don't stir, and don't make a sound, even if you want to. Now remember. I'm off."

Through the shadowing gloom Peter watched the stalk, his heart thumping in his chest, for this was different from the gay, almost lighthearted hunt of mice. Jennie's entire approach and attitude were those of complete concentration—the carriage of her body, the expression of her head, flattened forward, the glitter in her eyes, and the slow, fluid, amazingly controlled movement of her body. There was a care, caution, and deadly earnestness about her that Peter had never seen before, and his own throat felt dry and his skin and mustache twitched nervously. But he did his best to hold himself rigid and motionless as she had told him, lest some slip of his might bring her into trouble.

The wicked red eyes were glowing like two hot coals now, and Peter's acute hearing could make out the nasty sniffling noises of the rat, and the dry scrabbling of its toes on the storeroom floor. Jennie had gone quite flat now and was crawling along the boards on her belly. She stopped and held herself long and rigid for a moment, her eyes intent upon her prey, measuring, measuring. . . .

Then, inch by inch, she began to draw herself up into a little ball of fur-covered steel muscles for the spring. The rat was broadside to her. She took only two waggles, one to the left, one to the right, and then she was in the air aimed at the flank of the rat.

But lightning fast as she was, the rodent seemed to be even faster, for his head came around over his shoulder, and his white teeth were bared in a wicked slashing movement and Peter wanted to shout to his friend: "Jennie, *look out!*" but just in time he remembered her admonition under no circumstances to make a sound, and he choked it down.

And then he saw what seemed to him to be a miracle, for launched as she was and in midair, Jennie saw the swift movement of the rat and, swifter herself, avoided the sharp ripping teeth; and making a turn in the air, a kind of half-twist such as Peter had seen the high divers do in the pool at Wembley one summer, she landed on the back of the rat and immediately sank her teeth in its spine just below the head.

Then followed a dreadful moment of banging and slamming and scraping and squealing and the sharp snick of teeth as the rat snapped viciously and fought to escape, while Jennie hung on for dear life, her jaws clamping deeper and deeper until there was a sharp click and the next moment the rat hung limp and paralyzed and a few seconds later it was all over.

Jennie came away from it a little shaken and agitated, saying, "Phew! Filthy, sickening beasts! I *hate* rats—next to people. . . . They're all unclean and diseased, and if you let them bite you anywhere, then *you* get sick, for their teeth are all poisoned, and sometimes you die from it. I'm always afraid of that."

Peter said with deep sincerity: "Jennie, I think you are the bravest and most wonderful person—I mean cat—I ever saw. *Nobody* could have done that the way you did."

For once, Jennie did not preen herself or parade before Peter, for she was worried now since it was she who had coaxed him into this adventure. She said: "That's just it, Peter. We can't practice and learn on the rats the way we did on the mice, because it's too dangerous. One mistake and—well, I don't want it to happen. I *can* show you the twist, because you have to know how to do it to avoid the slash of theirs, but the spring, the distance, the timing, and, above all, just the exact place to bite them behind the neck to get at their spines—well, you must do it one hundred percent right when the time comes, and that's all there is. If you get them too high on the head, they can kick loose or even shake you off. Some of the big fellows weigh almost as much as you do, and if you seize them too far down the back they can turn their heads and cut you."

"But how will I learn, then?" Peter asked.

"Let me handle them for the time being," she replied, "and watch me closely each time I kill one. You'll be learning something. Then if and when the moment comes when you have to do it yourself, you'll either do it right the first time and never forget it thereafter or—" Jennie did not finish the sentence but instead went into the washing routine, and Peter felt a little cold chill run down his spine.

When they were finally discovered, it was some seven hours after sailing, as the *Countess of Greenock* was thumping her slow, plodding way down the broad reaches of the Thames Estuary. When the cook, an oddly triangular-shaped Jamaican Negro by the name of Mealie, came into the storeroom for some tinned corned beef, they had a bag of eight mice and three rats lined up in lieu of references and transportation. Three of the mice were Peter's, and he felt inordinately proud of them and wished there could have been some way whereby he might have had his name on them, like autographing a book perhaps: "Caught by Peter Brown, Storeroom, *Countess of Greenock,* April 15, 1949."

The Negro grinned widely, increasing the triangular effect, for his face and head were narrower at the top than at the bottom. He said: "By Jominy dat good. Hit pays to hodvertise. I tell dat to Coptain," and forthwith he went up on the bridge, taking Jennie's and Peter's samples with him. It was the kind of ship where the cook did go up on the bridge if he felt like having a word with the captain. There he told him the story of finding the two stowaways and then added: "But by Jominy they pay possage already. Look you dat!" and, unrolling his apron, showed him the fruits of their industry.

The captain, whose name was Sourlies and who was that rare specimen, a fat Scotsman, looked and felt ill and commanded Mealie in no uncertain language to throw the mess over the side and go back to his galley. It was the beginning of his time of deep unhappiness anyway, for he hated the sea and everything connected with it and was reasonably contented only when in port, or near it, or proceeding up and down an estuary or river with plenty of land on both sides.

He carried this queer notion to the point of refusing even to dress the part of a ship's captain, and conducted the affairs of the *Countess of Greenock* wearing a tweed pepper-and-salt business suit with a gold watch chain across his large expanse of stomach and a mustard-colored fedora hat, or trilby, with the brim turned up all around.

As Mealie was leaving, however, he did decree that inasmuch as the cats seemed to have got aboard and appeared inclined to work their passage, they might remain, but told him to shift one of them to the fo'c'sle as the men had been complaining of the rats there.

Mealie took his time going aft and told his story and showed the bag to everyone he met, with the result that there arrived back in the storeroom quite a committee, consisting of Mr. Strachan, the first mate, Mr. Carluke, the second, Chief Engineer McDunkeld, and the bos'n, whose name appeared to be only Angus.

They held a meeting, the gist of which Peter tried to translate rapidly for Jennie's benefit, and before they knew it, the two friends found themselves separated for the first time, Jennie being sent forward to live with the crew and Peter retained, chiefly through the insistence of Mr. Strachan, in the officers' quarters.

Jennie had only time to say to Peter: "Don't worry. We'll find ways to get together. Do your best. And if you come across a rat, don't hesitate and don't play. Kill!"

Then the bos'n picked her up by the scruff of the neck and carried her forward.

Using the smooth sides of a huge packing case as a practice ground, Peter learned the secret of the double jump-up, or second lift; or rather, after long hours of trial with Jennie coaching, it suddenly came to him. One moment he had been slipping, sliding, and falling back as he essayed to scale the perpendicular sides, and the next he had achieved it, a lightninglike thrust with the hind legs, which somehow this time stuck to the sides of the case and gave him added impetus upward, and thereafter he could always do it.

Jennie was most pleased with him, for as she explained it, this particular trick of leaping up the side of a blank wall without so much as a crack or an irregularity to give a toehold was peculiar to cats, and it was also one that could be neither wholly explained, demonstrated, or taught. The best she was able to tell him was: "You *think* you're 'way to the top, Peter. You just know you are going to be able to do it, and then you can."

Well, once the old *Countess* had taken a bit of a roll in the trough of a sea, and that helped Peter a little and gave him confidence. And the next time he felt certain he was going to be able to do it and he did.

Jennie was endlessly patient in teaching Peter control of his body in the air for she maintained that few things are of so much importance to cats. With her he studied the twist in midair from the spring so that, once he had left the ground, he could change his direction almost as in flying, and Peter loved the sense of power and freedom that came to him when he turned himself in the air like an acrobat, or a high diver, and this he practiced more than anything else. And he had to learn, too, how to drop from any normal height and twist in falling so that he would always land on his feet; and soon, with Jennie's help, he became so expert that he could roll off a case no more than a yard from the ground and still, turning like a flash, whip round so that his four paws touched the deck first, and that without a sound.

But their free time was not all devoted to hard work and practice. There were quiet hours when they rested side by side on a hatch roaming and Peter would ask Jennie questions —for instance, why she always preferred to perch on high things and look down—and she would explain about the deep instincts that survived from the days millions and millions of years ago when no doubt all cats were alike in size and shape and had to learn to protect themselves to survive. To escape the dangers that lurked on or near the ground from things that crawled, slithered, or trampled, they took to living high up in rocky caves, or perched along branches of trees where they could look down and see everything that approached them.

In the same manner, Jennie explained, cats liked to sleep in boxes, or bureau drawers, because they felt completely surrounded on all sides by high walls, as they were deep in their caves, and therefore felt relaxed and secure and able to sleep.

Or again, Peter would say: "Jennie, why when you are pleased and happy and relaxed, do your claws work in and out in that queer way? Once back home—I mean when we lived in the warehouse—I noticed that you were moving your paws up and down, almost as though you were making the bed. I never do that, though I do purr when I am happy."

Jennie was lying on her side on the canvas hatch cover when Peter asked that question, and she raised her head and gave him a most tender glance before she replied: "I know, Peter. And it is just another of those things that tell me that in spite of your shape and form, you are really human, and perhaps always will be. But maybe I can explain it to you. Peter, say something sweet to me."

The only thing Peter could think of to say was: "Oh, Jennie, I wish that I could be all cat—so that I might be more like you."

The most beatific smile stole over Jennie's face. Her throat throbbed with purring, and slowly her white paws began to work, the claws moving in and out as though she were kneading dough.

"You see?" she said to Peter. "It has to do with feeling happy. It goes all the way back to our being kittens and being nursed by our mothers. We cannot even see at first, but only feel, for when we are first born we are blind, and our eyes open only after a few weeks. But we can feel our way to our mother's breast and bury ourselves in her soft, sweet-smelling fur to find her milk, and when we are there, we work our paws gently up and down to help the food we want so much to flow more freely. Then when it does, we feel it in our throats, warm and satisfying; it stops our hunger and our thirst, it soothes our fears and desires, and oh, Peter, we are *so* blissful and contented at that moment, so secure and peaceful and—well, just happy. We never forget those moments with our mothers. They remain with us all the rest of our lives. And later on, long after we are grown, when something makes us very happy, our paws and claws go in and out the same way, in memory of those early times of our first real happiness. And that is all I can tell you about it."

Peter found that after this recital he had need to wash himself energetically for a few moments, and then he went over to where Jennie was lying and washed her face too, giving her several caresses beneath her soft chin and along the side of her muzzle that conveyed more to her than words. She made a little soft crooning sound in her throat, and her claws worked in and out, kneading the canvas hatch cover faster than ever.

But likewise during the long days of the leisurely voyage, and particularly when they were imprisoned in Dartmouth Harbor for two days by pea-soup fog, there was mock fighting to teach Peter how to take care of himself should he ever find himself in any trouble, as well as all the feline sports and games for one or two that Jennie knew or remembered and could teach him, and they spent hours rolling about, growling and spitting, locked in play combat, waiting in ambush to surprise each other, playing hide-seek-and-jump-out, or chasing each other madly up and down the gangways and passages below deck, their pads ringing oddly on the iron floors of the ancient *Countess,* like the hoofs of tiny galloping horses.

And here again Peter was to learn not only that there were method and strict rules that governed play as well as the more serious encounters between cat and cat but that he needed to study as well as practice them with Jennie in order to acquire by repetition the feeling of the rhythms that were a part of these games.

Thus Jennie would coach him: "I make a move to attack you, maybe a pass at your tail, or a feint at one of your legs; raise your left paw and be ready to strike with it. That's it. That makes me think twice before coming in. No, no, Peter, don't take your eyes off me just because I've stopped. Be ready as long as I am tense. But you've got to *feel* it when I've changed my mind and relaxed a little. You can drop your left paw, but keep watching. There! *I've* looked away for a moment—now *wash!* That stops everything. I can't do anything until you've finished except wash too, and that puts the next move up to you and it's your advantage."

Most difficult for him was the keeping of the upper hand by eye and body position and acquiring by experience the feeling of when it was safe to relax and turn away to rest, how to break up the other's plans by washing, luring and drawing the opponent on by pretending to look away, and then timing his own attack to the split second when the other was off balance and unprepared for it, and yet not violate the rules, which often made no rhyme or reason to him at all.

None of these things would Peter have done instinctively as a boy, and he had to learn them from Jennie by endless repetition. Often he marveled at her patience as she drilled him over and over: "Crouch, Peter. Now sit up quickly and look away. . . . *Wash!* Size up the situation out of the corner of your eye as you wash. I'm waiting to jump you as soon as you stop washing. Then turn and get ready. Here I come. Roll with it, onto your back. Hold me with your forepaws and kick with the hind legs. Harder—harder. . . . No, stay there, Peter. I'm coming back for a second try. Chin down so I can't get at your throat. Kick. Now roll over and sit up, paw ready, and threaten with it. If I blink my eyes and back away, *wash.* Now pretend you are interested in something imaginary. That's it. If you make it real enough you can get me to look at it, and when I do, then you spring!"

Jennie had a system of scoring these bouts, so many points for buffets, so many for knockdowns and rollovers, for breakaways and washes, for chases and ambushes, for the amount of fur that flew by tufts to be counted later, for numbers of back-kicks delivered, for bluffs and walkaways, feints and ducking, with bonuses for position and length of time in control, and game plus one hundred points called any time one maneuvered into position to grip teeth on the throat of the other.

And gradually, almost imperceptibly at first, the scores drew nearer level and soon Peter found himself winning regularly over Jennie in the training ring they had arranged among the crates and boxes in the forward hold. And when this happened and Peter won almost every time, none was prouder and happier over it than Jennie. "Soon," she said with satisfaction, "you'll be cat through and through."

And yet when the tragedy happened, it was just as well that Peter was not all cat.

In a way it began when Peter caught his first rat. The *Countess of Greenock* was plowing the Irish Sea 'twixt the Isle of Man and the Cumberland coast, close enough inshore so that one could see the peaks of the Cumbrian Mountains inland, shining in the sun. The ocean was flat calm and glassy, and the only cloud in the sky was the one made by the black smoke poured forth by the *Countess,* which, owing to a following breeze over the surface, she carried along with her over her head like an untidy old charwoman shielding herself from the sun with an old black cotton umbrella. They were on the reach between Liverpool and Port Carlisle on the Scottish border, and Captain Sourlies was in a great hurry to make it before nightfall. That was why the *Countess* was under forced draft, emitting volumes of soft-coal smoke and shuddering from the vibrations of her hurrying engines.

Peter had an appointment with Jennie on the afterdeck at six bells of the early afternoon watch, or three o'clock, for he had quickly learned to tell the ship's time from the strokes of the bell struck by the lookout on the bridge. This was always a kind of do-as-you-please time aboard the *Countess,* for then Captain Sourlies would be taking his afternoon nap in his cabin, Mr. Carluke, torn from his latest literary composition, which he was calling *The Bandit of Golden Gulch,* was on duty on the bridge, and everybody else followed his hobby or loafed by the rail or snoozed in the sun. And since Mr. Strachan, the first mate, still had a badly aching arm from the stitches taken in it, his dummy lurked in a corner in disgrace and the red-haired mate on this day was yarning with Mr. Box, the carpenter, about an episode that had happened to him in Gibraltar during the war and as proof produced an 1890 Queen Victoria copper penny that he had happened to be carrying on his person at the time of the adventure.

Jennie was already dozing in the soft spring sunshine, squatted down atop the stern rail. She liked to perch there because it was fairly high and gave her an overall view, and also to show her superiority, for everyone was always prophesying that some day she would be knocked or fall off from there into the sea. But of course there never was a cat more certain or surefooted than Jennie Baldrin.

Peter awoke promptly at ten minutes to three—he found that he could now awake at exactly any time he desired—and made a rough toilet with his tongue. He stretched and strolled casually from the lower storeroom, which was his quarters and which it was also his job to keep clear of vermin. Up to that moment there had been only mice, which Peter had kept down quite handily.

He should have smelled the rat long before he saw it, but although his smell senses were feline and quite sharp, his mind was still human, and he had been thinking that he must tell Jennie about a member of the black gang, a stoker who fed the furnace, who was such an admirer of Winston Churchill that he had a picture of the former Prime Minister tattooed on his chest, cigar and all. And so he had not been alert. When he saw the rat he was in a very bad position.

The beast was almost as large as a fox terrier and it was cornered in a small alcove made by some piled-up wooden cases of tinned baked beans, from which several boxes had been removed from the center. Also it was daylight, Peter wasn't stalking, and the rat saw Peter at the same time that Peter saw the rat. It uttered an ugly squeal of rage and bared long, yellow teeth, teeth that Peter knew were so unclean that a single scratch from them might well poison him beyond help. And for the first time he really understood what people meant by the expression "fight like a cornered rat," or rather he was about to understand. For in spite of the fact that Jennie had warned him never to go after a rat except when it was out in the open, he meant to attack this one and prove himself.

He was surprised to find that now in this moment of danger he was not thinking of lessons he had learned, or what he had seen or heard or what Jennie had said, but that his mind seemed to be extraordinarily calm and clear and that, almost as though it had always been there ready and waiting, his plan unfolded itself in his mind. It was only much later he found out that this was the result of discipline, study, patience, and practice that he had put behind him at Jennie's behest.

His spring, seemingly launched directly at the foe, appeared to be sheer folly, and the rat rose up on its hind legs to meet him head on, slashing at him viciously. But not for nothing had Peter learned and practiced the secret of continuing on up a smooth wall from a single leap from the floor. A split second faster than the rat, his fore and hind legs touched the slippery sides of one of the piles of cases for an instant and propelled him high into the air so that the flashing incisors of the rodent, like two hideously curved yataghans, whizzed between his legs, missing him by the proverbial hair's breadth.

The extra impetus upward now gave Peter the speed and energy to twist not half- but the whole way around in a complete reverse and drop onto the back of the rat to sink his own teeth deep into its spine just behind the ears.

For one dreadful moment Peter felt that he might yet be beaten, for the rat gave such a mighty heave and surge and lashed so desperately to and fro that Peter was thumped and banged up against the sides of the boxes until he felt himself growing sick and dizzy and no longer certain whether he could hold on. And if once he let go, the big fellow would turn on him and cut him to ribbons.

In desperation he set his teeth with all his might and bit, one, two, three times, hard. At the third bite he felt the rat suddenly stiffen. The swaying and banging stopped. The rodent kicked twice with its hind legs and then was still. It never moved again. Peter unclamped his aching jaws and sat down quickly and did some washing. He was badly shaken and most emphatically needed to recover his composure.

Nevertheless it was exactly at six bells that he came trotting onto the afterdeck carrying the rat in his mouth, or rather dragging it, because it was so large that when he held it in the middle, its head and tail hung down to the deck. It was so heavy that he could barely lift it. But of course he managed because he simply had to show it off to Jennie and anyone else who happened to be around.

It was Mr. Box who saw him first and let out a yell: "Blimey, looka there! The white un's caught a bloomin' helephant."

Mr. Strachan also gave a shout, for Peter passed quite close to him and the rat dragged over his foot, causing him to jump as though he had been stung. The cries brought several deckhands over on the run to see. They also woke up Jennie Baldrin.

She had not meant to fall so soundly asleep, but the peaceful sea and the warm afternoon sun had lulled her deeper than she had intended, and now the sudden cries sent alarms tingling down her spine. And when she opened her eyes they fell on Peter and his rat and in the first confusion she was not certain whether the rat was carrying Peter or vice versa, whether it was alive or dead, whether Peter was still engaged in fighting it. The sound of running feet added to her confusion, and she recoiled from the unknown and the uncertain and the thought of possible danger to Peter.

But there was no place to recoil to from her precarious perch on the ship's rail, and with an awful cry, her four paws widespread, and turning over once in the air, she fell into the sea and was swept away in the white salt froth of propeller wash.

"Cat overboard!" a deckhand cried, and then laughed.

"Good-bye, pussy," said Mr. Box. "Arskin' for it, she was, perched up there loike that."

Mr. Strachan stared with his mouth open.

The sailor who had been a hermit said to Peter: "There goes yer pal, Whitey. Ye'll no see Coptain Sourlies tairnen his ship aboot to rrrrrrescue a wee puss Baldrin."

But Peter was no longer there. There was only a white streak of fur as he dropped the rat, leaped to the rail, and from it, long and low, shot straight into the sea after Jennie.

(Ed. note: Jennie and Peter were saved, needless to say, and continued their travels.)

It was only half true that Peter wanted to go home. For boy and cat were becoming so intermingled that Peter was not at all certain any longer which he really was.

More than once during his voyage aboard the *Countess of Greenock* and the subsequent adventures Peter had thought of his mother and father and Scotch nanny and wondered how they were, if they were missing him, and whether they had any explanation for his mysterious disappearance. For certainly none of them, not even Nanny, who had been right there at the time, could be expected to guess that he had changed suddenly from a boy into a snow-white tomcat under her very eyes almost and had been pitched out into the street by her as a stray.

He thought it was probable that they would have notified the police, or perhaps, believing that he had run away, placed an advertisement in the "Personal" columns of the *Times* saying: "Peter: Come home, all is forgiven—Mummy, Daddy, and Nanny," or possibly it might have been more formally worded: "Will anyone who can give information as to the whereabouts of Master Peter Brown, vanished from No. 1A Cavendish Mews, London, W.C. 2, kindly communicate with Colonel and Mrs. Alastair Brown of that address. Reward!"

But, in the main, when he thought of those at home he did not believe that he was much missed except by Nanny, who of course had been busy with him almost from morning until night, leaving out the hours when he was at school, and now that he was gone would have nothing to do. His father was away from home so much of the time that except for their occasional evening romps he could hardly be expected to notice the difference. And as for his mother—Peter always felt sad and heavyhearted when he thought about his mother, because she had been so beautiful and he had loved her so much. But it was the kind of sadness that is connected with a memory of something long ago. Looking back to what life had been like in those now but dimly recollected days, he felt certain that his mother had been a little unhappy herself at first when he was missed, but then, after all, she never seemed to have much time, and now that he was gone, perhaps it would not have taken her long to get used to it.

Really it was Jennie who had come more and more to mean family to him and upon whom he leaned for advice, help, companionship, trust, and even affection. It was true she talked a great deal and was not the most beautiful cat in the world, but there was an endearing and ingratiating warmth and grace about her that made Peter feel comfortable and happy when they slept coiled up close to each other, or even when he only looked at her sometimes and saw her sweet attitudes, kindly eyes, gamin-wise face, and soft white throat.

The world was full of all kinds of beautiful cats, prize specimens whose pictures he had seen in the illustrated magazines during the times of the cat shows. Compared with them, Jennie was rather plain, but it was an appealing plainness he would not have exchanged for all the beauty in the world.

Nor was it his newly acquired cat-self that was seeking a return to Cavendish Mews in quest of a home, though to some extent the cat in him was now prey to curiosity about how things were there without him and what everyone was doing. But he knew quite definitely that his mother and father were people who had little or no interest in animals and appeared to have no need of them and hence would be hardly likely to offer a haven to a pair of stray cats come wandering in off the streets—namely, Jennie and himself.

Peter's suggestion that Jennie accompany him on a trip home to Cavendish Mews was perhaps more than anything born out of the memory that when he had been unhappy and upset about their treatment of Mr. Grims at the time of their first encounter with him, *she* had managed to interest and distract him by proposing the journey to Scotland. When he saw her sunk in the depths of grief and guilt over the fate of the poor old man, Peter had plucked a leaf out of her book of experience in the hope that it would take her mind off the tragedy and particularly what she considered her share in it. By instinct he seemed to have known that nothing actually would have moved her from the spot but his expression of his need for her.

Anyway, it was clear after they had set out for Cavendish Mews that she was in a more cheerful frame of mind and anxious to help him achieve his objective.

It is not easy for cats to move about in a big city, particularly on long journeys, and Jennie could be of no assistance to Peter in finding his way back to Cavendish Mews, since she had never lived or even been there and hence could not use her homing instinct, a kind of automatic direction-finder that communicated itself through her sensitive whiskers and enabled her to travel unerringly to any place where she had once spent some time.

Peter at least had the unique—from a cat's point of view —ability to know what people around him were saying, as well as being able to read signs, such as for instance appeared on the front of omnibuses and in general terms announced where they were going. One then had but to keep going in that direction and eventually one would arrive at the same destination or vicinity. In his first panic at finding himself a cat and out in the street, Peter had fled far from his home, with never any account taken of the twistings and turnings he had made. He was quite familiar with his own neighborhood, however, and knew if he could once reach Oxford and Regent streets he would find his way. But when it came to the lore of the city and knowing how to preserve one's skin whole, eat, drink, and sleep, Jennie as usual proved invaluable.

En route he learned from her all the important things there were to know about dogs and how to handle them— that, for instance, he must beware of terriers of every kind, that the average street mongrel was to be despised. Dogs on leashes could be ignored even though they put up a terrific fuss and roared, threatened, growled, and strained. They only did it because they *were* on the leash, which of course injured their dignity, and they had to put up a big show of what they would do if they were free. They behaved exactly the same when sighting another dog, and the whole thing, according to Jennie, was nothing but a lot of bluff. She, for one, never paid the slightest attention to them.

"Never run from a dog if you can control it," she admonished Peter, "because most of them are half blind anyway, and inclined to be hysterical. They will chase anything that moves. But if you stand your ground and don't run, chances are he will go right by you and pretend he neither sees you nor smells you, particularly if he has tangled with one of us before. Dogs have long memories.

"Small dogs you can keep in their places by swatting them the way we do when we play-box, only you run your claws out and hit fast and hard, because most of them are scared of having their eyes scratched and they don't like their noses clawed either, because they are tender. Here, for instance, is one looking for trouble and I'll show you what I mean."

They were walking through Settle Street near White-chapel, looking for a meal, when a fat, overfed Scotty ran barking from a doorway and made a good deal of attacking them, barking, yelping, and charging in short rushes, with an amount of snapping its teeth, bullying, and bravado.

Jennie calmly squatted down on the pavement facing the foe with a kind of humiliating disinterest, which he mistook for fear and abject cringing and which gave him sufficient courage to close in and risk a real bite at Jennie's flank. Like lightning flashes her left paw shot out three times, while she leaned away from the attack just enough to let the Scotty miss her. The next moment, cut on the end of the nose and just below the right eye, he was legging it for the cover and safety of the doorway, screaming: "Help! Murder! Watch!!"

"Come on," Jennie said to Peter. "Now *we've* got to move out. You'll see why in a minute." Peter had long since learned not to question her, particularly about anything that called for split-second timing, and he quickly ran after her out of range, just as the owner of the dog, a slatternly woman, evidently the proprietress of the dingy greengrocery, came out and threw a dishpanful of water after them, but missed, thanks to Jennie's wisdom and speedy action.

"I'm out of practice," Jennie said with just a touch of her old-time showing off for Peter. "I missed him with my third. Still, they'll run off screaming for help, and if you stay around you're likely to catch it, as you saw, though not from *them*. . . . And you don't always have to do that. Quite often they've been brought up with cats or are used to them and are just curious or want to play, and come sniffing and snuffling and smelling around with their tails wagging, which, as you know, means that *they* are pleased and friendly, and not angry or agitated or nervous over something, as it does with us. Then you can either bear up under it and pretend not to notice it, or try to walk away or get up on top of something they can't reach. I, for one, just don't care for a wet, cold, drooly nose messing about in my fur, so I usually give them just a little tap with the paw, unloaded, as a reminder that we are after all quite totally different species and their way of playing isn't ours."

"But supposing it's a bigger dog," Peter said, "like the ones in Glasgow."

Jennie gave a little shudder. "Ugh!" she said. "Don't remind me of those. As I told you then, any time you see a bull terrier, run, or, better still, start climbing. But a great many of the others you can bluff and scare by swelling up and pretending to be bigger than you actually are. Let me show you. You should have been taught this long ago, because you can never tell when you are going to need it."

They were walking near Paternoster Row in the wide-open spaces created by the bombs before St. Paul's Cathedral, and Jennie went over a low coping and into some weeds and fireflowers that were growing there. "Now," she said, "do just as I do. Take a deep breath—that's it, way in. Now blow, but hold your breath at the same time. Hard! There you go."

And, as she said, there indeed Peter went, swelling up to nearly twice his size, just as Jennie was, all puffed out into a kind of lopsided fur ball. He was sure that he was looking perfectly enormous and quite out of plumb, and he felt rather foolish. He said as much to Jennie, adding: "I think that's silly."

She answered: "Not at all. You don't realize it, but you really looked quite alarming. It's sort of preventive warfare, and it makes a good deal of sense. If you can win a battle without having to fight it, or the enemy is so scared of you that he won't even start it and goes away and there is no battle at all, that's better than anything. It doesn't do any harm, and it's always worth trying, even with other cats. For in spite of the fact that you know it's all wind and fur, it will still give you the creeps when someone does it to you."

Peter suddenly thought back to Dempsey and how truly terrifying the battle-scarred veteran of a thousand fights had looked when he had swelled up and gone all crooked and menacing on him.

"And anyway," Jennie concluded the lesson, "if it shouldn't happen to work, it's just as well to be filled up with air, because then you are ready to let out a perfect rouser of a battle cry, and very often that *does* work, provided that you can get it out of your system before the other one does. A dog will usually back away from that and remember another engagement."

In the main, on this walk across a portion of London, Peter found cats to be very like people. Some were mean and small and persnickety and insisted upon all their rights even when asked politely to share; others were broad-minded and hospitable, with a cheery, "Certainly, do come right in. There's plenty of room here," before Jennie had even so much as finished her gentle request for permission to remain. Some were snobs who refused to associate with them because they were strays; others had once been strays themselves, remembered their hardships, and were sympathetic. There were cantankerous cats always spoiling for a fight, and others who fought just for the fun of fighting and asserting their superiority; and many a good-natured cat belonging to a butcher, or a pub, or a snack bar or greengrocer would steer them toward a meal, or share what they had, or give them a tip on where to get a bite.

Also Peter learned, not only from Jennie, but from bitter experience, to be wary of children and particularly those not old enough to understand cats, or even older ones with a streak of cruelty. And since one could not tell in advance what they would be like, or whether they would fondle or tease, one had no choice, if one was a London stray, but to act in the interest of one's own safety.

This sad piece of knowledge Peter acquired in a most distressful manner as they threaded their way past Petticoat Lane in Whitechapel, where a grubby little boy was playing in the gutter outside a fish-and-chips bar. He was about Peter's age, or at least the age Peter had been before the astonishing transformation had happened to him, and about his height, and he called to them as they hurried by: "Here, puss. Come here, Whitey. . . ."

Before ever Jennie could warn him or breathe a "Peter, be careful!" he went to him trustingly, because in a way the boy reminded him of himself and he remembered how much he had loved every cat he saw in the streets, and particularly the strays and wanderers. He went over and held up his head and face to be rubbed. The next moment the most sharp and agonizing pain shot through his body from head to foot so that he thought he would die on the spot. He cried out half with hurt and half with fear, for he did not know yet what had happened to him.

Then he realized that the boy had twined his fingers firmly about his tail and was pulling. *Pulling his tail.* Nothing had ever hurt him so much or so excruciatingly.

"Nah, then," laughed the boy, nastily, "let's see yer get away."

With a cry of horror and outrage, and digging his claws into the cracks in the pavement, Peter made a supreme effort and managed to break loose, certain that he had left his tail behind him in the hand of the boy, and only after he had run half a block did he determine that it was still streaming out behind and safely attached to him.

And here Peter discovered yet another thing about cats that he had never known before. There was involved not only the pain of having his tail pulled, but the humiliation. Never had he felt so small, ashamed, outraged, and dishonored. And all in front of Jennie. He felt that he would not be able to look at her again. It was much worse than being stood in a corner when he had been a boy, or being spoken to harshly, or having his ear tweaked or knuckles cracked in front of company.

What served to make it endurable was that Jennie seemed to understand. She neither spoke to him sympathizingly, which at that moment Peter felt he would not have been able to bear, not even so much as glanced at him, but simply trotted alongside, minding her own business and pretending in a way that he was not there at all, which was a great help. Gradually the pain and the memory began to fade, and finally, after a long while, when Jennie turned to him and out of a clear sky said: "Do you know, I think it might rain tonight. What do *your* whiskers say?" he was able to thrust his mustache forward and wrinkle the skin on his back to the weather-forecasting position and reply:

"There might be a shower or two. We'd better hurry if we want to reach Cavendish Square before it starts. Oh, look there! There's the proper bus just going by now. We can't go wrong if we keep in the same direction."

It was a number 7, and the sign on the front of it read: OXFORD STREET AND MARBLE ARCH.

"For Oxford Street crosses Regent, and then comes Princes, and if we turn up Princes, we can't help coming into Cavendish Square," Peter explained, "and then it's only a short step to the Mews and home."

Jennie echoed the word "home" in so sad and wistful a voice that Peter looked at her sharply, but she said nothing more, and, proceeding quickly by little short rushes from shop door to shop door, as it were, the two soon had passed from Holborn through New Oxford into Oxford Street and across Regent to Princes, where they turned up to the right for Cavendish Square.

Manly Wade Wellman

THE WITCH'S CAT

Old Jael Bettiss, who lived in the hollow among the cypresses, was not a real witch.

It makes no difference that folk thought she was, and walked fearfully wide of her shadow. Nothing can be proved by the fact that she was as disgustingly ugly without as she was wicked within. It is quite irrelevant that evil was her study and profession and pleasure. She was no witch; she only pretended to be.

Jael Bettiss knew that all laws providing for the punishment of witches had been repealed, or at the least forgotten.

As to being feared and hated, that was meat and drink to Jael Bettiss, living secretly alone in the hollow.

The house and the hollow belonged to a kindly old villager, who had been elected marshal and was too busy to look after his property. Because he was easygoing and perhaps a little daunted, he let Jael Bettiss live there rent free. The house was no longer snug; the back of its roof was broken in, the eaves drooped slackly. At some time or other the place had been painted brown, before that with ivory black. Now both coats of color peeled away in huge flakes, making the clapboards seem scrofulous. The windows had been broken in every small, grubby pane, and mended with coarse brown paper, so that they were like cast and blurred eyes. Behind was the muddy, bramble-choked backyard, and behind that yawned the old quarry, now abandoned and full of black water. As for the inside—but few ever saw it.

Jael Bettiss did not like people to come into her house. She always met callers on the old cracked doorstep, draped in a cloak of shadowy black, with gray hair straggling, her nose as hooked and sharp as the beak of a buzzard, her eyes filmy and sore-looking, her wrinkle-bordered mouth always grinning and showing her yellow, chisel-shaped teeth.

The nearby village was an old-fashioned place, with stone flags instead of concrete for pavements, and the villagers were the simplest of men and women. From them Jael Bettiss made a fair living, by selling love philters, or herbs to cure sickness, or charms to ward off bad luck. When she wanted extra money, she would wrap her old black cloak about her and, tramping along a country road, would stop at a cowpen and ask the farmer what he would do if his cows went dry. The farmer, worried, usually came at dawn next day to her hollow and bought a good-luck charm. Occasionally the cows would go dry anyway, by accident of nature, and their owner would pay more and more, until their milk returned to them.

Now and then, when Jael Bettiss came to the door, there came with her the gaunt black cat, Gib.

Gib was not truly black, any more than Jael Bettiss was truly a witch. He had been born with white markings at muzzle, chest, and forepaws, so that he looked to be in full evening dress. Left alone, he would have grown fat and fluffy. But Jael Bettiss, who wanted a fearsome pet, kept all his white spots smeared with thick soot, and underfed him to make him look rakish and lean.

On the night of the full moon, she would drive poor Gib from her door. He would wander to the village in search of food, and would wail mournfully in the yards. Awakened householders would angrily throw boots or pans or sticks of kindling. Often Gib was hit, and his cries were sharpened by pain. When that happened, Jael Bettiss took care to be seen next morning with a bandage on head or wrist. Some of the simplest villagers thought that Gib was really the old woman, magically transformed. Her reputation grew, as did Gib's unpopularity. But Gib did not deserve mistrust—like all cats, he was a practical philosopher, who wanted to be comfortable and quiet and dignified. At bottom, he was amiable. Like all cats, too, he loved his home above all else; and the house in the hollow, be it ever so humble and often cruel, was home. It was unthinkable to him that he might live elsewhere.

In the village he had two friends—black-eyed John Frey, the storekeeper's son, who brought the mail to and from the county seat, and Ivy Hill, pretty blonde daughter of the town marshal, the same town marshal who owned the hollow and let Jael Bettiss live in the old house. John Frey and Ivy Hill were so much in love with each other that they loved everything else, even black-stained, hungry Gib. He was grateful; if he had been able, he would have loved them in return. But

his little heart had room for one devotion only, and that was
given to the house in the hollow.

One day, Jael Bettiss slouched darkly into old Mr. Frey's
store, and up to the counter that served as a post office.
Leering, she gave John Frey a letter. It was directed to a
certain little-known publisher, asking for a certain little-
known book. Several days later, she appeared again, received
a parcel, and bore it to her home.

In her gloomy, secret parlor, she unwrapped her purchase. It was a small, drab volume, with no title on cover or
back. Sitting at the rickety table, she began to read. All evening and most of the night she read, forgetting to give Gib
his supper, though he sat hungrily at her feet.

At length, an hour before dawn, she finished. Laughing
loudly and briefly, she turned her beak-nose toward the kero-
sene lamp on the table. From the book she read aloud two
words. The lamp went out, though she had not blown at it.
Jael Bettiss spoke one commanding word more, and the lamp
flamed alight again.

"At last!" she cried out in shrill exultation, and grinned
down at Gib. Her lips drew back from her yellow chisels of
teeth. "At last!" she crowed again. "Why don't you speak to
me, you little brute? . . . Why don't you, indeed?"

She asked that final question as though she had been
suddenly inspired. Quickly she glanced through the back part
of the book, howled with laughter over something she found
there, then sprang up and scuttled like a big, filthy crab into
the dark, windowless cell that was her kitchen. There she
mingled salt and malt in the palm of her skinny right hand.
After that, she rummaged out a bundle of dried herbs,
chewed them fine, and spat them into the mixture. Stirring
again with her forefinger, she returned to the parlor. Scanning
the book to refresh her memory, she muttered a nasty little
rhyme. Finally she dashed the mess suddenly upon Gib.

He retreated, shaking himself, outraged and startled. In a corner he sat down, and bent his head to lick the smeared fragments of the mixture away. But they revolted his tongue and palate, and he paused in the midst of this chore, so important to cats; and meanwhile Jael Bettiss yelled, "Speak!"

Gib crouched and blinked, feeling sick. His tongue came out and steadied his lips. Finally he said: "I want something to eat."

His voice was small and high, like a little child's, but entirely understandable. Jael Bettiss was so delighted that she laughed and clapped her bony knees with her hands, in self-applause.

"It worked!" she cried. "No more humbug about me, you understand? I'm a real witch at last, and not a fraud!"

Gib found himself able to understand all this, more clearly than he had ever understood human affairs before. "I want something to eat," he said again, more definitely than before. "I didn't have any supper, and it's nearly—"

"Oh, stow your gab!" snapped his mistress. "It's this book, crammed with knowledge and strength, that made me able to do it. I'll never be without it again, and it'll teach me all the things I've only guessed at and mumbled about. I'm a real witch now, I say. And if you don't think I'll make those ignorant sheep of villagers realize it—"

Once more she went off into gales of wild, cracked mirth, and threw a dish at Gib. He darted away into a corner just in time, and the missile crashed into blue-and-white china fragments against the wall. But Jael Bettiss read aloud from her book an impressive gibberish, and the dish re-formed itself on the floor; the bits crept together and joined and the cracks disappeared, as trickling drops of water form into a pool. And finally, when the witch's twiglike forefinger beckoned, the dish floated upward like a leaf in a breeze and set itself gently back on the table. Gib watched warily.

"That's small to what I shall do hereafter," swore Jael
Bettiss.

When next the mail was distributed at the general store, a
dazzling stranger appeared.

She wore a cloak, an old-fashioned black coat, but its
drapery did not conceal the tall perfection of her form. As for
her face, it would have stirred interest and admiration in
larger and more sophisticated gatherings than the knot of
letter-seeking villagers. Its beauty was scornful but inviting,
classic but warm, with something in it of Grecian sculpture
and Oriental allure. If the nose was cruel, it was straight; if the
lips were sullen, they were full; if the forehead was a suspicion
low, it was white and smooth. Thick, thunder-black hair swept
up from that forehead, and backward to a knot at the neck.
The eyes glowed with strange, hot lights, and wherever they
turned they pierced and captivated.

People moved away to let her have a clear, sweeping
pathway forward to the counter. Until this stranger had entered, Ivy Hill was the loveliest person present; now she
looked only modest and fresh and blonde in her starched
gingham, and worried to boot. As a matter of fact, Ivy Hill's
insides felt cold and topsy-turvy, because she saw how fascinated was the sudden attention of John Frey.

"Is there," asked the newcomer in a deep, creamy voice,
"any mail for me?"

"Wh-what name, ma'am?" asked John Frey, his brown
young cheeks turning full crimson.

"Bettiss. Jael Bettiss."

He began to fumble through the sheaf of envelopes, with
hands that shook. "Are you," he asked, "any relation to the
old lady of that name, the one who lives in the hollow?"

"Yes, of a sort." She smiled a slow, conquering smile.
"She's my—aunt. Yes. Perhaps you see the family resemblance?" Wider and wider grew the smile with which she

assaulted John Frey. "If there isn't any mail," she went on, "I would like a stamp. A one-cent stamp."

Turning to his little metal box on the shelf behind, John Frey tore a single green stamp from the sheet. His hand shook still more as he gave it to the customer and received in exchange a copper cent.

There was really nothing exceptional about the appearance of that copper cent. It looked brown and a little worn, with Lincoln's head on it, and a date—1917. But John Frey felt a sudden glow in the hand that took it, a glow that shot along his arm and into his heart. He gazed at the coin as if he had never seen its like before. And he put it slowly into his pocket, a different pocket from the one in which he usually kept change, and placed another coin in the till to pay for the stamp. Poor Ivy Hill's blue eyes grew round and downright miserable. Plainly he meant to keep that copper piece as a souvenir. But John Frey gazed only at the stranger, raptly, as though he were suddenly stunned or hypnotized.

The dark, sullen beauty drew her cloak more tightly around her and moved regally out of the store and away toward the edge of town.

As she turned up the brush-hidden trail to the hollow, a change came. Not that her step was less young and free, her figure less queenly, her eyes dimmer, or her beauty short of perfect. All these were as they had been; but her expression became set and grim, her body tense, and her head high and truculent. It was as though, beneath that young loveliness, lurked an old and evil heart, which was precisely what did lurk there, it does not boot to conceal. But none saw except Gib, the black cat with soot-covered white spots, who sat on the doorstep of the ugly cottage. Jael Bettiss thrust him aside with her foot and entered.

In the kitchen she filled a tin basin from a wooden bucket, and threw into the water a pinch of coarse green powder with an unpleasant smell. As she stirred it in with her hands, they seemed to grow skinny and harsh. Then she threw great palmfuls of the liquid into her face and over her head, and other changes came. . . .

The woman who returned to the front door, where Gib watched with a cat's apprehensive interest, was hideous old Jael Bettiss, whom all the village knew and avoided.

"He's trapped," she shrilled triumphantly. "That penny, the one I soaked for three hours in a love philter, trapped him the moment he touched it!" She stumped to the table, and patted the book as though it were a living, lovable thing.

"You taught me," she crooned to it. "You're winning me the love of John Frey!" She paused, and her voice grew harsh again. "Why not? I'm old and ugly and queer, but I can love, and John Frey is the handsomest man in the village!"

The next day she went to the store again, in her new and dazzling person as a dark, beautiful girl. Gib, left alone in the hollow, turned over in his mind the things that he had heard. The new gift of human speech had brought with it, of necessity, a human quality of reasoning; but his viewpoint and his logic were as strongly feline as ever.

Jael Bettiss's dark love that lured John Frey promised no good to Gib. There would be plenty of trouble, he was inclined to think, and trouble was something that all sensible cats avoided. He was wise now, but he was weak. What could he do against danger? And his desires, as they had been since kittenhood, were food and warmth and a cozy sleeping place, and a little respectful affection. Just now he was getting none of the four.

He thought also of Ivy Hill. She liked Gib, and often had shown it. If she won John Frey despite the witch's plan, the two would build a house all full of creature comforts—cushions, open fires, probably fish and chopped liver. Gib's tongue caressed his soot-stained lips at the savory thought. It would be good to have a home with Ivy Hill and John Frey, if once he was quit of Jael Bettiss. . . .

But he put the thought from him. The witch had never held his love and loyalty. That went to the house in the hollow, his home since the month that he was born. Even magic had not taught him how to be rid of that cat-instinctive obsession for his own proper dwelling place. The sinister, strife-sodden hovel would always call and claim him, would draw him back from the warmest fire, the softest bed, the most savory food in the world. Only John Howard Payne could have appreciated Gib's yearnings to the full, and he died long ago, in exile from the home he loved.

When Jael Bettiss returned, she was in a fine trembling rage. Her real self shone through the glamor of her disguise, like murky fire through a thin porcelain screen.

Gib was on the doorstep again and tried to dodge away as she came up, but her enchantments, or something else, had made Jael Bettiss too quick even for a cat. She darted out a hand and caught him by the scruff of the neck.

"Listen to me," she said, in a voice as deadly as the trickle of poisoned water. "You understand human words. You can talk, and you can hear what I say. You can do what I say, too." She shook him, by way of emphasis. "Can't you do what I say?"

"Yes," said Gib weakly, convulsed with fear.

"All right, I have a job for you. And mind you do it well, or else—" She broke off and shook him again, letting him imagine what would happen if he disobeyed.

"Yes," said Gib again, panting for breath in her tight grip. "What's it about?"

"It's about that little fool, Ivy Hill. She's not quite out of his heart. Go to the village tonight," ordered Jael Bettiss, "and to the house of the marshal. Steal something that belongs to Ivy Hill."

"Steal something?"

"Don't echo me, as if you were a silly parrot." She let go of him, and hurried back to the book that was her constant study. "Bring me something that Ivy Hill owns and touches —and be back here with it before dawn."

Gib carried out her orders. Shortly after sundown he crept through the deepened dusk to the home of Marshal Hill. Doubly black with the soot habitually smeared upon him by Jael Bettiss, he would have been almost invisible, even had anyone been on guard against his coming. But nobody watched; the genial old man sat on the front steps, talking to his daughter.

"Say," the father teased, "isn't young Johnny Frey coming over here tonight, as usual?"

"I don't know, daddy," said Ivy Hill wretchedly.

"What's that, daughter?" The marshal sounded surprised. "Is there anything gone wrong between you two young 'uns?"

"Perhaps not, but—oh, daddy, there's a new girl come to town—"

And Ivy Hill burst into tears, groping dolefully on the step beside her for her little wadded handkerchief. But she could not find it.

For Gib, stealing near, had caught it up in his mouth and was scampering away toward the edge of town, and beyond to the house in the hollow.

Meanwhile, Jael Bettiss worked hard at a certain project of wax modeling. Any witch, or student of witchcraft, would have known at once why she did this.

After several tries, she achieved something quite interesting and even clever—a little female figure, that actually resembled Ivy Hill.

Jael Bettiss used the wax of three candles to give it enough substance and proportion. To make it more realistic, she got some fresh, pale-gold hemp, and of this made hair, like the wig of a blonde doll, for the wax head. Drops of blue ink served for eyes, and a blob of berry juice for the red mouth. All the while she worked, Jael Bettiss was muttering and mumbling words and phrases she had gleaned from the rearward pages of her book.

When Gib brought in the handkerchief, Jael Bettiss snatched it from his mouth, with a grunt by way of thanks. With rusty scissors and coarse white thread, she fashioned for the wax figure a little dress. It happened that the handkerchief was of gingham, and so the garment made all the more striking the puppet's resemblance to Ivy Hill.

"You're a fine one!" tittered the witch, propping her finished figure against the lamp. "You'd better be scared!"

For it happened that she had worked into the waxen face an expression of terror. The blue ink of the eyes made wide round blotches, a stare of agonized fear; and the berry-juice mouth seemed to tremble, to plead shakily for mercy.

Again Jael Bettiss refreshed her memory of goetic spells by poring over the back of the book, and after that she dug from the bottom of an old pasteboard box a handful of rusty pins. She chuckled over them, so that one would think triumph already hers. Laying the puppet on its back, so that the lamplight fell full upon it, she began to recite a spell.

"I have made my wish before," she said in measured tones. "I will make it now. And there was never a day that I did not see my wish fulfilled." Simple, vague—but how many have died because those words were spoken in a certain way over images of them?

The witch thrust a pin into the breast of the little wax figure and drove it all the way in, with a murderous pressure of her thumb. Another pin she pushed into the head, another into an arm, another into a leg; and so on, until the gingham-clad puppet was fairly studded with transfixing pins.

"Now," she said, "we shall see what we shall see."

Morning dawned, as clear and golden as though wickedness had never been born into the world. The mysterious new paragon of beauty—not a young man of the village but mooned over her, even though she was the reputed niece and namesake of that unsavory old vagabond, Jael Bettiss—walked into the general store to make purchases. One delicate pink ear turned to the gossip of the housewives.

Wasn't it awful, they were agreeing, how poor little Ivy Hill was suddenly sick almost to death; she didn't seem to know her father or her friends. Not even Doctor Melcher could find out what was the matter with her. Strange that John Frey was not interested in her troubles; but John Frey sat behind the counter, slumped on his stool like a mud idol, and his eyes lighted up only when they spied lovely young Jael Bettiss with her market basket.

When she had heard enough, the witch left the store and went straight to the town marshal's house. There she spoke gravely and sorrowfully about how she feared for the sick girl, and was allowed to visit Ivy Hill in her bedroom. To the father and the doctor, it seemed that the patient grew stronger and felt less pain while Jael Bettiss remained to wish her a quick recovery; but, not long after this new acquaintance departed, Ivy Hill grew worse. She fainted, and recovered only to vomit.

And she vomited—pins, rusty pins. Something like that happened in old Salem Village, and earlier still in Scotland, before the grisly cult of North Berwick was literally burned out. But Doctor Melcher, a more modern scholar, had never seen or heard of anything remotely resembling Ivy Hill's disorder.

So it went, for three full days. Gib, too, heard the doleful gossip as he slunk around the village to hunt for food and to avoid Jael Bettiss, who did not like him near when she did magic. Ivy Hill was dying, and he mourned her, as for the boons of fish and fire and cushions and petting that might have been his. He knew, too, that he was responsible for her doom and his loss—that handkerchief that he had stolen had helped Jael Bettiss to direct her spells.

But philosophy came again to his aid. If Ivy Hill died, she died. Anyway, he had never been given the chance to live as her pensioner and pet. He was not even sure that he would have taken the chance—thinking of it, he felt strong, accustomed clamps upon his heart. The house in the hollow was his home forever. Elsewhere he'd be an exile.

Nothing would ever root it out of his feline soul.

On the evening of the third day, witch and cat faced each other across the tabletop in the old house in the hollow.

"They've talked loud enough to make his dull ears hear," grumbled the fearful old woman—with none but Gib to see her, she had washed away the disguising enchantment that, though so full of lure, seemed to be a burden upon her. "John Frey has agreed to take Ivy Hill out in his automobile. The doctor thinks that the fresh air, and John Frey's company, will make her feel better—but it won't. It's too late. She'll never return from that drive."

She took up the pin-pierced wax image of her rival, rose, and started toward the kitchen.

"What are you going to do?" Gib forced himself to ask.

"Do?" repeated Jael Bettiss, smiling murderously. "I'm going to put an end to that baby-faced chit, but why are you so curious? Get out, with your prying!"

And, snarling curses and striking with her clawlike hands, she made him spring down from his chair and run out of the house. The door slammed, and he crouched in some brambles and watched. No sound, and at the half-blinded windows no movement; but, after a time, smoke began to coil upward from the chimney. Its first puffs were dark and greasy-looking. Then it turned dull gray, then white, then blue as indigo. Finally it vanished altogether.

When Jael Bettiss opened the door and came out, she was

once more in the semblance of a beautiful dark girl. Yet Gib recognized a greater terror about her than ever before.

"You be gone from here when I get back," she said to him.

"Gone?" stammered Gib, his little heart turning cold. "What do you mean?"

She stooped above him, like a threatening bird of prey.

"You be gone," she repeated. "If I ever see you again, I'll kill you—or I'll make my new husband kill you."

He still could not believe her. He shrank back, and his eyes turned mournfully to the old house that was the only thing he loved.

"You're the only witness to the things I've done," Jael Bettiss continued. "Nobody would believe their ears if a cat started telling tales, but anyway, I don't want any trace of you around. If you leave, they'll forget that I used to be a witch. So run!"

She turned away. Her mutterings were now only her thoughts aloud:

If my magic works—and it always works—that car will find itself idling around through the hill road to the other side of the quarry. John Frey will stop there. And so will Ivy Hill —forever.

Drawing her cloak around her, she stalked purposefully toward the old quarry behind the house.

Left by himself, Gib lowered his lids and let his yellow eyes grow dim and deep with thought. His shrewd beast's mind pawed and probed at this final wonder and danger that faced him and John Frey and Ivy Hill.

He must run away if he would live. The witch's house in the hollow, which had never welcomed him, now threatened him. No more basking on the doorstep, no more ambushing woodmice among the brambles, no more dozing by the kitchen fire. Nothing for Gib henceforth but strange, forbidding wilderness, and scavenger's food, and no shelter, not on the coldest night. The village? But his only two friends, John Frey and Ivy Hill, were being taken from him by the magic of Jael Bettiss and her book. . . .

That book had done this. That book must undo it. There was no time to lose.

The door was not quite latched, and he nosed it open, despite the groans of its hinges. Hurrying in, he sprang up on the table.

It was gloomy in that tree-invested house, even for Gib's sharp eyes. Therefore, in a trembling fear almost too big for his little body, he spoke a word that Jael Bettiss had spoken, on her first night of power. As had happened then, so it happened now; the dark lamp glowed alight.

Gib pawed at the closed book, and contrived to lift its cover. Pressing it open with one front foot, with the other he painstakingly turned leaves, more leaves, and more yet. Finally he came to the page he wanted.

Not that he could read; and, in any case, the characters were strange in their shapes and combinations. Yet, if one looked long enough and levelly enough—even though one were a cat, and afraid—they made sense, conveyed intelligence.

And so into the mind of Gib, beating down his fears, there stole a phrase:

Beware of mirrors . . .

So that was why Jael Bettiss never kept a mirror—not even now, when she could assume such dazzling beauty.

Beware of mirrors, the book said to Gib, *for they declare the truth, and truth is fatal to sorcery. Beware also, of crosses, which defeat all spells.*

That was definite inspiration. He moved back from the book, and let it snap shut. Then, pushing with head and paws, he coaxed it to the edge of the table and let it fall. Jumping down after it, he caught a corner of the book in his teeth and dragged it to the door, more like a retriever than a cat. When he got it into the yard, into a place where the earth was soft, he dug furiously until he had made a hole big enough to contain the volume. Then, thrusting it in, he covered it up.

Nor was that all his effort, so far as the book was concerned. He trotted a little way off to where lay some dry, tough twigs under the cypress trees. To the little grave he bore first one, then another of these, and laid them across each other, in the form of an **X**. He pressed them well into the earth, so that they would be hard to disturb. Perhaps he would keep an eye on that spot henceforth, after he had done the rest of the things in his mind, to see that the cross remained. And, though he acted thus only by chance reasoning, all the demonologists, even the Reverend Montague Summers, would have nodded approval. Is this not the way to foil the black wisdom of the *Grand Albert?* Did not Prospero thus inter his grimoires, in the fifth act of *The Tempest?*

Now back to the house once more and into the kitchen. It was even darker than the parlor, but Gib could make out a basin on a stool by the moldy wall, and smelled an ugly pungency: Jael Bettiss had left her mixture of powdered water after last washing away her burden of false beauty.

Gib's feline nature rebelled at a wetting; his experience of witchcraft bade him be wary, but he rose on his hind legs and with his forepaws dragged at the basin's edge. It tipped and toppled. The noisome fluid drenched him. Wheeling, he ran back into the parlor, but paused on the doorstep. He spoke two more words that he remembered from Jael Bettiss. The lamp went out again.

And now he dashed around the house and through the brambles and to the quarry beyond.

It lay amid uninhabited wooded hills, a wide excavation from which had once been quarried all the stones for the village houses and pavements. Now it was full of water, from many thaws and torrents. Almost at its lip was parked John

Frey's touring car, with the top down, and beside it he lolled, slack-faced and dreamy. At his side, cloak-draped and enigmatically queenly, was Jael Bettiss, her back to the quarry, never more terrible or handsome. John Frey's eyes were fixed dreamily upon her, and her eyes were fixed commandingly on the figure in the front seat of the car—a slumped, defeated figure, hard to recognize as poor sick Ivy Hill.

"Can you think of no way to end all this pain, Miss Ivy?" the witch was asking. Though she did not stir, or glance behind her, it was as though she had gestured toward the great quarry pit, full to unknown depths with black, still water. The sun, at the very point of setting, made angry red lights on the surface of that stagnant pond.

"Go away," sobbed Ivy Hill, afraid without knowing why. "Please, please!"

"I'm only trying to help," said Jael Bettiss. "Isn't that so, John?"

"That's so, Ivy," agreed John, like a little boy who is prompted to an unfamiliar recitation. "She's only trying to help."

Gib, moving silently as fate, crept to the back of the car. None of the three human beings, so intent upon each other, saw him.

"Get out of the car," persisted Jael Bettiss. "Get out, and look into the water. You will forget your pain."

"Yes, yes," chimed in John Frey mechanically. "You will forget your pain."

Gib scrambled stealthily to the running board, then over the side of the car and into the rear seat. He found what he had hoped to find. Ivy Hill's purse—and open.

He pushed his nose into it. Tucked into a little side pocket was a hard, flat rectangle, about the size and shape of a visiting card. All normal girls carry mirrors in their purses; all mirrors show the truth. Gib clamped the edge with his mouth, and struggled to drag the thing free.

"Miss Ivy," Jael Bettiss was commanding, "get out of this car, and come and look into the water of the quarry."

No doubt what would happen if once Ivy Hill should gaze into that shiny black abyss; but she bowed her head, in agreement or defeat, and began slowly to push aside the catch of the door.

Now or never, thought Gib. He made a little noise in his throat, and sprang up on the side of the car next to Jael Bettiss. His black-stained face and yellow eyes were not a foot from her.

She alone saw him; Ivy Hill was too sick, John Frey too dull. "What are you doing here?" she snarled, like a bigger and fiercer cat than he; but he moved closer still, holding up the oblong in his teeth. Its back was uppermost, covered with imitation leather, and hid the real nature of it. Jael Bettiss was mystified, for once in her relationship with Gib. She took the thing from him, turned it over, and saw a reflection.

She screamed.

The other two looked up, horrified through their stupor. The scream that Jael Bettiss uttered was not deep and rich and young; it was the wild, cracked cry of a terrified old woman.

"I don't look like that," she choked out, and drew back from the car. "Not old—ugly—"

Gib sprang at her face. With all four claw-bristling feet he seized and clung to her. Again Jael Bettiss screamed, flung up her hands, and tore him away from his hold; but his soggy fur had smeared the powdered water upon her face and head.

Though he fell to earth, Gib twisted in midair and landed upright. He had one glimpse of his enemy. Jael Bettiss, no mistake—but a Jael Bettiss with hooked beak, rheumy eyes, hideous wry mouth and yellow chisel teeth—Jael Bettiss exposed for what she was, stripped of her lying mask of beauty!

And she drew back a whole staggering step. Rocks were just behind her. Gib saw, and flung himself. Like a flash he clawed his way up her cloak, and with both forepaws ripped at the ugliness he had betrayed. He struck for his home that was forbidden him—Marco Bozzaris never strove harder for Greece, or Stonewall Jackson for Virginia.

Jael Bettiss screamed yet again, a scream loud and full of horror. Her feet had slipped on the edge of the abyss. She flung out her arms, the cloak flapped from them like frantic wings. She fell, and Gib fell with her, still tearing and fighting.

The waters of the quarry closed over them both.

Gib thought that it was a long way back to the surface and a longer way to shore. But he got there, and scrambled out with the help of projecting rocks. He shook his drenched body, climbed back into the car and sat upon the rear seat. At least Jael Bettiss would no longer drive him from the home he loved. He'd find food some way, and take it back there each day to eat. . . .

With tongue and paws he began to rearrange his sodden fur.

John Frey, clear-eyed and wide awake, was leaning in and talking to Ivy Hill. As for her, she sat up straight, as though she had never known a moment of sickness.

"But just what did happen?" she was asking.

John Frey shook his head, though all the stupidity was gone from his face and manner. "I don't quite remember. I seem to have wakened from a dream. But are you all right, darling?"

"Yes, I'm all right." She gazed toward the quarry, and the black water that had already subsided above what it had swallowed. Her eyes were puzzled, but not frightened. "I was dreaming, too," she said. "Let's not bother about it."

She lifted her gaze, and cried out with joy. "There's that old house that daddy owns. Isn't it interesting?"

John Frey looked, too. "Yes. The old witch has gone away—I seem to have heard she did."

Ivy Hill was smiling with excitement. "Then I have an

inspiration. Let's get daddy to give it to us. And we'll paint it over and fix it up, and then—" she broke off, with a cry of delight. "I declare, there's a cat in the car with me!"

It was the first she had known of Gib's presence.

John Frey stared at Gib. He seemed to have wakened only the moment before. "Yes, and isn't he a thin one? But he'll be pretty when he gets through cleaning himself. I think I see a white shirt front."

Ivy Hill put out a hand and scratched Gib behind the ear. "He's bringing us good luck, I think. John, let's take him to live with us when we have the house fixed up and move in."

"Why not?" asked her lover. He was gazing at Gib. "He looks as if he was getting ready to speak."

But Gib was not getting ready to speak. The power of speech was gone from him, along with Jael Bettiss and her enchantments. But he understood, in a measure, what was being said about him and the house in the hollow. There would be new life there, joyful and friendly this time. And he would be a part of it, forever, and of his loved home.

He could only purr to show his relief and gratitude.

Lael J. Littke

A FELINE FELONY

Jerome Kotter looked like a cat. However, this did not bring him any undue attention from his schoolmates since almost all of them had an unusual quality or two. Beverly Baumgartner had a laugh like a horse. Bart Hansen was as rotund as an elephant. Carla Seaver's long neck resembled that of a giraffe. And Randy Ramsbottom always smelled remarkably like a dog on a rainy day.

The only person who worried about Jerome's unusual appearance was his father, who quietly set about arming his son to face a world in which he was a bit different. He taught Jerome gentle manners, assuring him that no matter how different he looked he would always get along fine if he acted right. He taught him to recite all the verses of "The Star-Spangled Banner" by heart. He encouraged him to read the Bible. And he taught him to sing the songs from the best-known Gilbert and Sullivan operettas. He felt Jerome was well equipped to face the world.

When Jerome got to high school he became the greatest track star that Quigley High had ever produced, although he had to be careful because the coaches from rival schools cried foul when Jerome resorted to running on all fours.

Altogether, Jerome's school years would have been quite happy—if it hadn't been for Benny Rhoades.

Whereas Jerome was tall, polite, studious, and well groomed with silken fur and sparkling whiskers, Benny was wizened, unkempt, rude, and sly. His face was pinched and pointed and his hair stuck up in uneven wisps. He hated anyone who excelled him in anything. Almost everybody excelled him in everything, and since Jerome surpassed him in the one thing he did do fairly well—running—he hated Jerome most of all. When Jerome took away his title of champion runner of Quigley High, Benny vowed he would get even if it took him the rest of his life.

One of Benny's favorite harassments was to tread on Jerome's tail in study hall, causing him to yowl and thereby incurring the wrath of the monitor. Benny tweaked Jerome's whiskers and poured honey in his fur. He did everything he could think of to make Jerome's life miserable.

When it came to Benny Rhoades, Jerome found it hard to follow the admonitions of his father—that he should love his enemies and do good even to those who used him spitefully. He looked forward to the day when he would finish school and get away, for he had to admit in his heart that he loathed the odious Benny. It rankled him to think that Benny was the only person who could make him lose his composure and caterwaul in public, thus making people notice that despite his suave manner and intellectual conversation he was a bit different. To keep his temper he took to declaiming "The Star-Spangled Banner" or passages from the Bible. Once he got all the way through the "begats" in Genesis before he took hold of himself and regained his composure.

Just before Jerome was graduated from college, Benny stole all the fish from Old Man Walker's little fish cart and deposited them in Jerome's car, after which he made an anonymous phone call to the police. The police, who had always regarded Jerome as the embodiment of what they would like all young men to be, preferred to believe his claim of innocence; but then again, looking as he did, it was natural for them to believe that he might have swiped a mess of fish.

People began to whisper about Jerome when he passed on the street. They pointed out that although his manners were perfect, he did have those long swordlike claws, and they certainly wouldn't want to be caught alone with him in any alley on a dark night. And wasn't there a rather feline craftiness in his slanted eyes?

Jerome left town after graduation enveloped in an aura of suspicion and an aroma of rotting fish which he never could dispel completely from his car.

Jerome decided to pursue a career as a writer of advertising copy in New York, reasoning that what with all the strange creatures roaming about in that city no one was apt to notice anything a bit different about him. He was hired at the first place he applied, Bobble, Babble, and Armbruster, Inc., on Madison Avenue. Mr. Armbruster had been out celebrating his fourteenth wedding anniversary the night before and had imbibed himself into near oblivion trying to forget what devastation those fourteen years had wrought. When Jerome walked into his office he naturally figured him to be related to the ten-foot polka-dot cobra that had pursued him the night before, and thought he would fade with the hangover. After ducking behind his desk for a little hair-of-the-dog, he hired Jerome. By the time Mr. Armbruster had fully recovered from his celebration, Jerome had proved himself capable at his job and affable with the other employees, so he was allowed to stay. Mr. Armbruster naturally put him on the cat-food account.

Before long Jerome fell in love with his secretary, Marie, a shapely blonde, who thought Jerome's sleek fur and golden eyes sexy. He wanted to ask her for a date, but first, in all fairness, he thought he should find out how she felt about him.

"Marie," he said one day as he finished the day's dictation, "do you like me as a boss?"

"Oh, yes," breathed Marie. "Gee, Mr. Kotter, you're the swellest boss I ever had. You're so different."

Jerome's heart sank. "Different? In what way, Marie?"

"Well," said Marie, "Mr. Leach, my old boss, used to pinch me sometimes. And he used to sneak up behind me and kiss me." She peered coyly at Jerome from under her lashes. "You're a perfect gentleman, Mr. Kotter. You're real different."

Jerome was enchanted and wasted no further time asking her out to dinner.

For several weeks everything was wonderful. Then, unexpectedly, Benny Rhoades turned up. Jerome looked up from his desk one day to see his nemesis standing in the doorway.

"Man," said Benny, "if it ain't Jerome Kotter." He grinned.

"Benny Rhoades," exclaimed Jerome. "What are you doing here?"

"Man, you're the most," said Benny softly. "I work in the mail room, man. You're gonna see a lot of me, Jerome."

Jerome's tail twitched.

"Why did you come here?" he asked. "Why don't you leave me alone?"

Offended innocence replaced the calculating look on Benny's pasty face.

"Why, man, I ain't done a thing. A man's got to work. And I work here." He lounged against the doorjamb. "I hear you're a real swingin' cat around here. I wonder how long that's gonna last."

"Get out," said Jerome.

"Sure, Mr. Kotter, sir. Sure. Think I'll drop by your secretary's desk. Quite a dish, that Marie."

"You stay away from her." Jerome could feel the fur around his neck rising. His whiskers bristled.

Benny smiled and glided away like an insidious snake.

From that time on Benny did what he could to torment Jerome. He held up his mail until important clients called the bosses to complain about lack of action on their accounts. He slammed Jerome's tail in doors, usually when some VIP was visiting the office. Worst of all, he vexed Marie by hanging around her desk asking for dates and sometimes sneaking up to nibble at her neck. Marie hated him almost as much as Jerome did.

Jerome didn't know quite what he could do about it without jeopardizing his job, of which he had become very fond. The other people at the agency liked him, although they regarded him as a trifle eccentric since he always insisted on sampling the cat food he wrote about. But then, everyone to his own tastes, they said.

Things came to a head one evening when Jerome invited Marie to his apartment for a fish dinner before going out to a show. They were just sitting down to eat when the doorbell rang.

It was Benny.

"Cozy," he murmured, surveying the scene. He slammed the door shut behind him.

"A real swingin' cat," he said, sidling into the room. He produced a small pistol from his pocket.

"Are you out of your mind, Benny?" said Jerome. "What do you think you're doing?"

"I lost my job," smiled Benny.

"What's that got to do with me?"

"Marie complained that I bothered her. They fired me." Benny's small eyes glittered. "I'll repay her for the favor, then I'll take care of you, Jerome. I'll fix it so they'll think you shot her for resisting your charms, and then shot yourself. Everybody knows a big cat like you could go beserk anytime."

"You're a rat," said Marie. "You're a miserable, black-hearted little rat."

Jerome stepped protectively in front of her.

"Sticks and stones may break my bones but names will never hurt me," chanted Benny gleefully.

Jerome was looking at Benny thoughtfully. "A rat," he said. "That's what he is. A rat. Funny it never occurred to me before." His tail twitched nervously.

Benny didn't like the look on Jerome's face. "Stay away from me, man. I'll shoot."

Before Benny could aim, Jerome leaped across the room with the swift, fluid motion of a tiger. He knocked Benny to the floor and easily took the gun from him.

"A rat," repeated Jerome softly.

Benny looked at Jerome's face so close to his own. "What are you going to do?" he squeaked, his own face pinched and white and his beady eyes terror-stricken. "What are you going to do?"

Jerome ate him.

It took a long time to get the police sergeant to take the matter seriously. Marie had urged Jerome to forget the whole thing, but Jerome felt he must confess.

"You say you ate this guy Benny?" the sergeant asked for the twentieth time.

"I ate him," said Jerome.

"He was a rat," said Marie.

The sergeant shook his head. "We get all kinds," he muttered. "Go home. Sleep it off." He sighed. "Self-defense, you say?"

"Benny was going to shoot both of us," said Marie.

"Where's the body?" asked the sergeant.

Jerome shook his head. "There is no body. I ate him."

"He was a rat," said Marie.

"There's no body," said the sergeant. "We sent a coupla men up to your apartment and there's no body and no sign of anybody getting killed. We even called this Benny's family long distance to find out if they knew where he is, but his old man said as far as they are concerned he died at birth. So go home."

"I ate him," insisted Jerome.

"So you performed a public service. I got six kids to support, buddy. I don't want to spend the next two years on a headshrinker's couch for trying to make the Chief believe I got a six-foot cat here who ate a guy. Now go home, you two, before I get mad."

Jerome remained standing in front of the desk.

"Look," said the sergeant. "You ate a guy."

"A rat," corrected Marie.

"A rat," said the sergeant. "So how do you feel?"

"Terrible," said Jerome. "I have a most remarkable case of indigestion."

"You ate a rat," said the sergeant. "Now you've got a bellyache. That's your punishment. Remember when you ate green apples as a kid?" He sighed. "Now go home."

As they turned to leave, Jerome heard the sergeant muttering to himself about not having had a vacation in four years.

Despite his indigestion, Jerome felt marvelous. "Let the punishment fit the crime," he said with satisfaction. He took Marie's arm in a courtly fashion and sang softly as they walked along. "My object all sublime, I shall achieve in time, to let the punishment fit the crime, the punishment fit the crime. . . ."

"Gee, Mr. Kotter," said Marie, gazing up at him in admiration. "You're so different from anyone else I ever went with."

"Different?" asked Jerome. "How, Marie?"

"Gee," said Marie, "I never went out before with anybody who quoted poetry."

Dorothy L. Sayers

THE CYPRIAN CAT

It's extraordinarily decent of you to come along and see me like this, Harringay. Believe me, I do appreciate it. It isn't every busy K.C. who'd do as much for such a hopeless sort of client. I only wish I could spin you a more workable kind of story, but honestly I can only tell you exactly what I told Peabody. Of course, I can see he doesn't believe a word of it, and I don't blame him. He thinks I ought to be able to make up a more plausible tale than that, and I suppose I could, but where's the use? One's almost bound to fall down somewhere if one tries to swear to a lie. What I'm going to tell you is the absolute truth. I fired one shot and one shot only, and that was at the cat. It's funny that one should be hanged for shooting at a cat.

Merridew and I were always the best of friends, school and college and all that sort of thing. We didn't see very much of each other after the war, because we were living at opposite ends of the country; but we met in town from time to time and wrote occasionally, and each of us knew that the other was there in the background, so to speak. Two years ago he wrote and told me he was getting married. He was just turned forty and the girl was fifteen years younger, and he was tremendously in love. It gave me a bit of a jolt. You know how it is when your friends marry. You feel they will never be quite the same again, and I'd got used to the idea that Merridew and I were cut out to be old bachelors. But of course I congratulated him and sent him a wedding present, and I did sincerely hope he'd be happy. He was obviously over head and ears, almost dangerously so, I thought, considering all things. Though except for the difference of age, it seemed suitable enough. He told me he had met her at—of all places —a rectory garden party down in Norfolk, and that she had actually never been out of her native village. I mean literally —not so much as a trip to the nearest town. I'm not trying to convey that she wasn't pukka, or anything like that. Her father was some queer sort of recluse—a medievalist or something —desperately poor. He died shortly after their marriage.

I didn't see anything of them for the first year or so. Merridew is a civil engineer, you know, and he took his wife away after the honeymoon to Liverpool, where he was doing something in connection with the harbor. It must have been a big change for her from the wilds of Norfolk. I was in Birmingham, with my nose kept pretty close to the grindstone, so we only exchanged occasional letters. His were what I can only call deliriously happy, especially at first. Later on, he seemed a little worried about his wife's health. She was restless; town life didn't suit her; he'd be glad when he could finish up his Liverpool job and get her away into the country. There wasn't any doubt about their happiness, you understand. She'd got him body and soul as they say, and as far as I could make out it was mutual. I want to make that perfectly clear.

Well, to cut a long story short, Merridew wrote to me at the beginning of last month and said he was just off to a new job, a waterworks extension scheme down in Somerset, and he asked if I could possibly cut loose and join them there for a few weeks. He wanted to have a yarn with me, and Felice was longing to make my acquaintance. They had got rooms at the village inn. It was rather a remote spot, but there was fishing and scenery and so forth, and I should be able to keep Felice company while he was working up at the dam. I was about fed up with Birmingham, what with the heat and one thing and another, and it looked pretty good to me, and I was due for a holiday anyhow, so I fixed up to go. I had a bit of business to do in town, which I calculated would take me about a week, so I said I'd go down to Little Hexham on June 20.

As it happened, my business in London finished itself off unexpectedly soon, and on the sixteenth I found myself absolutely free and stuck in a hotel with road drills working just under the windows and a tar-spraying machine to make things livelier. You remember what a hot month it was—flaming June and no mistake about it. I didn't see any point in waiting, so I sent off a wire to Merridew, packed my bag, and took the train for Somerset the same evening. I couldn't get a compartment to myself, but I found a first-class smoker with only three seats occupied and stowed myself thankfully into the fourth corner. There was a military-looking old boy, an elderly female with a lot of bags and baskets, and a girl. I thought I should have a nice peaceful journey.

So I should have, if it hadn't been for the unfortunate way I'm built. It was quite all right at first. As a matter of fact,

I think I was half asleep, and I only woke up properly at seven o'clock, when the waiter came to say that dinner was on. The other people weren't taking it, and when I came back from the restaurant car I found that the old boy had gone, and there were only the two women left. I settled down in my corner again, and gradually, as we went along, I found a horrible feeling creeping over me that there was a cat in the compartment somewhere. I'm one of those wretched people who can't stand cats. I don't mean just that I prefer dogs. I mean that the presence of a cat in the same room with me makes me feel like nothing on earth. I can't describe it, but I believe quite a lot of people are affected that way. Something to do with electricity, or so they tell me. I've read that very often the dislike is mutual, but it isn't so with me. The brutes seem to find me abominably fascinating, make a beeline for my legs every time. It's a funny sort of complaint, and it doesn't make me at all popular with dear old ladies.

Anyway, I began to feel more and more awful, and I realized that the old girl at the other end of the seat must have a cat in one of her innumerable baskets. I thought of asking her to put it out in the corridor or calling the guard and having it removed, but I knew how silly it would sound and made up my mind to try and stick it. I couldn't say the animal was misbehaving itself or anything, and she looked a pleasant old lady; it wasn't her fault that I was a freak. I tried to distract my mind by looking at the girl.

She was worth looking at, too—very slim and dark with one of those dead-white skins that make you think of magnolia blossom. She had the most astonishing eyes, too—I've never seen eyes quite like them—a very pale brown, almost amber, set wide apart and a little slanting, and they seemed to have a kind of luminosity of their own, if you get what I mean. I don't know if this sounds—I don't want you to think I was bowled over or anything. As a matter of fact, she held no sort of attraction for me, though I could imagine a different type of man going potty about her. She was just unusual, that was all. But however much I tried to think of other things I couldn't get rid of the uncomfortable feeling, and eventually I gave it up and went out into the corridor. I just mention this because it will help you to understand the rest of the story. If you can only realize how perfectly awful I feel when there's a cat about—even when it's shut up in a basket—you'll understand better how I came to buy the revolver.

Well, we got to Hexham Junction, which was the nearest station to Little Hexham, and there was old Merridew waiting on the platform. The girl was getting out too—but not the old lady with the cat, thank goodness—and I was just handing her traps out after her when he came galloping up and hailed us.

"Hullo," he said, "why that's splendid! Have you introduced yourselves?" So I tumbled to it then that the girl was Mrs. Merridew, who'd been up to Town on a shopping expedition, and I explained to her about my change of plans, and she said how jolly it was that I could come—the usual things. I noticed what an attractive low voice she had and how graceful her movements were, and I understood—though, mind you, I didn't share—Merridew's infatuation.

We got into his car; Mrs. Merridew sat in the back, and I got up beside Merridew and was very glad to feel the air and to get rid of the oppressive electric feeling I'd had in the train. He told me the place suited them wonderfully and had given Felice an absolutely new lease on life, so to speak. He said he was very fit, too, but I thought myself that he looked rather fagged and nervy.

You'd have liked that inn, Harringay. The real, old-fashioned stuff, as quaint as you make 'em, and everything genuine—none of your Tottenham Court Road antiques. We'd all had our grub, and Mrs. Merridew said she was tired; so she went up to bed early, and Merridew and I had a drink and went for a stroll around the village. It's a tiny hamlet quite at the other end of nowhere; lights out at ten, little thatched houses with pinched-up attic windows like furry ears. The place purred in its sleep. Merridew's working gang didn't sleep there, of course; they'd put up huts for them at the dams, a mile beyond the village.

The landlord was just locking up the bar when we came in, a block of a man with an absolutely expressionless face. His wife was a thin, sandy-haired woman who looked as though she was too downtrodden to open her mouth. But I found out afterward that was a mistake, for one evening when he'd taken one or two over the eight and showed signs of wanting to make a night of it, his wife sent him off upstairs with a gesture and a look that took the heart out of him. That first night she was sitting on the porch and hardly glanced at us as we passed her. I always thought her an uncomfortable kind of woman, but she certainly kept her house most exquisitely neat and clean.

They'd given me a noble bedroom, close under the eaves with a long, low casement window overlooking the garden. The sheets smelled of lavender, and I was between them and asleep almost before you could count ten. I was tired, you see. But later in the night I woke up. I was too hot, so took off some of the blankets and then strolled across to the window to get a breath of air. The garden was bathed in moonshine, and on the lawn I could see something twisting and turning oddly. I stared a bit before I made it out to be two cats. They didn't worry me at that distance, and I watched them for a bit before I turned in again. They were rolling over one another and jumping away again and chasing their own shadows on the grass, intent on their own mysterious business, taking themselves seriously, the way cats always do. It looked like a kind of ritual dance. Then something seemed to startle them, and they scampered away.

I went back to bed, but I couldn't get to sleep again. My nerves seemed to be all on edge. I lay watching the window and listening to a kind of soft rustling noise that seemed to be going on in the big wisteria that ran along my side of the house. And then something landed with a soft thud on the sill —a great Cyprian cat.

What did you say? Well, one of those striped gray-and-black cats. Tabby, that's right. In my part of the country they call them Cyprus cats, or Cyprian cats. I'd never seen such a monster. It stood with its head cocked sideways, staring into the room and rubbing its ears very softly against the upright bar of the casement.

Of course, I couldn't do with that. I shooed the brute away, and it made off without a sound. Heat or no heat, I shut and fastened the window. Far out in the shrubbery I thought I heard a faint meowing, then silence. After that, I went straight off to sleep again and lay like a log till the girl came in to call me.

The next day Merridew ran us up in his car to see the place where they were making the dam, and that was the first time I realized that Felice's nerviness had not been altogether cured. He showed us where they had diverted part of the river into a swift little stream that was to be used for working the dynamo of an electrical plant. There were a couple of planks laid across the stream, and he wanted to take us over to show us the engine. It wasn't extraordinarily wide or dangerous, but Mrs. Merridew peremptorily refused to cross it and got quite hysterical when he tried to insist. Eventually he and I went over and inspected the machinery by ourselves. When we got back, she had recovered her temper and apologized for being so silly. Merridew abased himself, of course, and I began to feel a little *de trop.* She told me afterward that she had once fallen into the river as a child and been nearly drowned, and it had left her with a what d'ye call it—a complex about running water. And but for this one trifling episode, I never heard a single sharp word pass between them all the time I was there; nor, for a whole week, did I notice anything else to suggest a flaw in Mrs. Merridew's radiant health. Indeed, as the days wore on to midsummer and the heat grew more intense, her whole body seemed to glow with vitality. It was as though she was lit up from within.

Merridew was out all day and working very hard. I thought he was overdoing it and asked him if he was sleeping badly. He told me that, on the contrary, he fell asleep every night the moment his head touched the pillow and—what was most unusual with him—had no dreams of any kind. I myself felt well enough, but the hot weather made me languid and disinclined for exertion. Mrs. Merridew took me out for long drives in the car. I would sit for hours, lulled into a half slumber by the rush of warm air and the purring of the engine and gazing at my driver, upright at the wheel, her eyes fixed unwaveringly upon the spinning road. We explored the whole of the country to the south and east of Little Hexham, and once or twice went as far north as Bath. Once I suggested that we should turn eastward over the bridge and run down into what looked like rather beautiful wooded country, but Mrs. Merridew didn't care for the idea; she said it was a bad road and that the scenery on that side was disappointing.

Altogether I spent a pleasant week at Little Hexham, and if it had not been for the cats I should have been perfectly comfortable. Every night the garden seemed to be haunted by them—the Cyprian cat that I had seen the first night of my stay, a little ginger one, and a horrible stinking black tom were especially tiresome. And one night there was a terrified white kitten that mewed for an hour on end under my window. I flung boots and books at my visitors till I was heartily weary, but they seemed determined to make the inn garden their rendezvous. The nuisance grew worse from night to night; on one occasion I counted fifteen of them, sitting on their hinder ends in a circle, while the Cyprian cat danced her shadow dance among them, working in and out like a weaver's shuttle. I had to keep my window shut, for the Cyprian cat evidently made a habit of climbing up by the wisteria. The door, too, for once when I had gone down to fetch something from the sitting room, I found her on my bed, kneading the coverlet with her paws—*pr'rp, pr'rp, pr'rp* —with her eyes closed in a sensuous ecstasy. I beat her off, and she spat at me as she fled into the dark passage.

I asked the landlady about her, but she replied rather curtly that they kept no cat at the inn, and it is true that I never saw any of the beasts in the daytime. One evening, however, about dusk I caught the landlord in one of the outhouses. He had the ginger cat on his shoulder and was feeding her with something that looked like strips of liver. I remonstrated with him for encouraging the cats about the place and asked whether I could have a different room, explaining that the nightly caterwauling disturbed me. He half opened his slits of eyes and murmured that he would ask his wife about it, but nothing was done, and in fact I believe there was no other bedroom in the house.

And all this time the weather got hotter and heavier, working up for thunder, with the sky like brass and the earth like iron, and the air quivering over it so that it hurt your eyes to look at it.

All right, Harringay, I am trying to keep to the point. And I'm not concealing anything from you. I say that my relations with Mrs. Merridew were perfectly ordinary. Of course, I saw a good deal of her, because as I explained Merridew was out all day. We went up to the dam with him in the morning and brought the car back, and naturally we had to amuse one another as best we could till the evening. She seemed quite pleased to be in my company, and I couldn't dislike her. I can't tell you what we talked about—nothing in particular. She was not a talkative woman. She would sit or lie for hours in the sunshine, hardly speaking, only stretching out her body to the light and heat. Sometimes she would spend a whole afternoon playing with a twig or a pebble, while I sat and smoked. Restful! No. No, I shouldn't call her a restful personality exactly. Not to me, at any rate. In the evening she would liven up and talk a little more, but she generally went up to bed early and left Merridew and me to yarn together in the garden.

Oh, about the revolver! Yes. I bought that in Bath, when I had been at Little Hexham exactly a week. We drove over in the morning, and while Mrs. Merridew got some things for her husband, I prowled around the secondhand shops. I had intended to get an air gun or a peashooter or something of that kind, when I saw this. You've seen it, of course. It's very tiny—what people in books describe as "little more than a toy"—but deadly enough. The old boy who sold it to me didn't seem to know much about firearms. He'd taken it in pawn sometime back, he told me, and there were ten rounds of ammunition with it. He made no bones about a license or anything, glad enough to make a sale, no doubt, without putting difficulties in a customer's way. I told him I knew how to handle it and mentioned by way of a joke that I meant to take a potshot or two at the cats. That seemed to wake him up a bit. He was a dried-up little fellow, with a scrawny gray beard and a stringy neck. He asked me where I was staying. I told him at Little Hexham.

"You better be careful, sir," he said. "They think a heap of their cats down there, and it's reckoned unlucky to kill them." And then he added something I couldn't quite catch, about a silver bullet. He was a doddering old fellow, and he seemed to have some sort of scruple about letting me take the parcel away, but I assured him that I was perfectly capable of looking after it and myself. I left him standing in the door of his shop, pulling at his beard and staring after me.

That night the thunder came. The sky had turned to lead before evening, but the dull heat was more oppressive than the sunshine. Both the Merridews seemed to be in a state of nerves—he sulking and swearing at the weather and the flies, and she wrought up to a queer kind of vivid excitement.

Thunder affects some people that way. I wasn't much better, and to make things worse I got the feeling that the house was full of cats. I couldn't see them, but I knew they were there, lurking behind the cupboards and flitting noiselessly about the corridors. I could scarcely sit in the parlor and was thankful to escape to my room.

Cats or no cats I had to open the window, and I sat there with my pajama jacket unbuttoned, trying to get a breath of air. But the place was like the inside of a copper furnace. And pitch-dark. I could scarcely see from my window where the bushes ended and the lawn began. But I could hear and feel the cats. There were little scrapings in the wisteria and scufflings among the leaves, and about eleven o'clock one of them started the concert with a loud and hideous wail. Then another and another joined in—I'll swear there were fifty of them. And presently I got that foul sensation of nausea, and the flesh crawled on my bones, and I knew that one of them was slinking close to me in the darkness.

I looked around quickly, and there she stood, the great Cyprian, right against my shoulder, her eyes glowing like green lamps. I yelled and struck out at her, and she snarled as she leaped out and down. I heard her thump the gravel, and the yowling burst out all over the garden with renewed vehemence. And then all in a moment there was utter silence, and in the far distance there came a flickering blue flash and then another. In the first of them I saw the far garden wall, topped along all its length with cats, like a nursery frieze. When the second flash came the wall was empty.

At two o'clock the rain came. For three hours before that I had sat there, watching the lightning as it spat across the sky and exulting in the crash of the thunder. The storm seemed to carry off all the electrical disturbance in my body; I could have shouted with excitement and relief. Then the first heavy drops fell, then a steady downpour, then a deluge. It struck the iron-baked garden with a noise like steel rods falling. The smell of the ground came up intoxicatingly, and the wind rose and flung the rain in against my face. At the other end of the passage I heard a window thrown to and fastened, but I leaned out into the tumult and let the water drench my head and shoulders. The thunder still rumbled intermittently, but with less noise and farther off, and in an occasional flash I saw the white grille of falling water drawn between me and the garden.

It was after one of these thunderpeals that I became aware of a knocking at my door. I opened it, and there was Merridew. He had a candle in his hand, and his face was terrified.

"Felice!" he said abruptly. "She's ill. I can't wake her. For God's sake, come and give me a hand."

I hurried down the passage after him. There were two beds in his room—a great four-poster, hung with crimson damask, and a small camp bedstead drawn up near to the window. The small bed was empty, the bedclothes tossed aside; evidently he had just risen from it. In the four-poster lay Mrs. Merridew, naked, with only a sheet upon her. She was stretched flat upon her back, her long black hair in two plaits over her shoulders. Her face was waxen and shrunk, like the face of a corpse, and her pulse, when I felt it, was so faint that at first I could scarcely feel it. Her breathing was very slow and shallow and her flesh cold. I shook her, but there was no response at all. I lifted her eyelids and noticed how the eyeballs were turned up under the upper lid, so that only the whites were visible. The touch of my fingertip upon the sensitive ball evoked no reaction. I immediately wondered whether she took drugs.

Merridew seemed to think it necessary to make some explanation. He was babbling about the heat—she couldn't bear so much as a silk nightgown—she had suggested that he should occupy the other bed—he had slept heavily—right through the thunder. The rain blowing in on his face had aroused him. He had got up and shut the window. Then he had called to Felice to know if she was all right; he thought the storm might have frightened her. There was no answer. He had struck a light. Her condition had alarmed him, and so on.

I told him to pull himself together and to try whether, by chafing his wife's hands and feet, we could restore the circulation. I had it firmly in my mind that she was under the influence of some opiate. We set to work, rubbing and pinching and slapping her with wet towels and shouting her name in her ear. It was like handling a dead woman, except for the very slight but perfectly regular rise and fall of her bosom, on which—with a kind of surprise that there should be any flaw on its magnolia whiteness—I noticed a large brown mole, just over the heart. To my perturbed fancy it suggested a wound and a menace. We had been at it for some time, with the sweat pouring off us, when we became aware of something going on outside the window—a stealthy bumping and scraping against the panes. I snatched up the candle and looked out.

On the sill, the Cyprian cat sat and clawed at the casement. Her drenched fur clung limply to her body; her eyes glared into mine; her mouth was opened in protest. She scrabbled furiously at the latch, her hind claws slipping and scratching on the woodwork. I hammered on the pane and bawled at her, and she struck back at the glass as though possessed. As I cursed her and turned away she set up a long, despairing wail.

Merridew called to me to bring back the candle and leave the brute alone. I returned to the bed, but the dismal crying went on and on incessantly. I suggested to Merridew that he should wake the landlord and get hot-water bottles and some brandy from the bar and see if a messenger could not be sent for a doctor. He departed on this errand, while I went on with my massage. It seemed to me that the pulse was growing still fainter. Then I suddenly recollected that I had a small brandy flask in my bag. I ran out to fetch it, and as I did so the cat suddenly stopped its howling.

As I entered my own room the air blowing through the open window struck gratefully upon me. I found my bag in the dark and was rummaging for the flask among my shirts and socks when I heard a loud, triumphant mew and turned around in time to see the Cyprian cat crouched for a moment on the sill, before it sprang in past me and out at the door. I found the flask and hastened back with it, just as Merridew and the landlord came running up the stairs.

We all went into the room together. As we did so, Mrs. Merridew stirred, sat up, and asked us what in the world was the matter.

I have seldom felt quite such a fool.

Next day the weather was cooler; the storm had cleared the air. What Merridew had said to his wife I do not know. None of us made any public allusion to the night's disturbance, and to all appearance Mrs. Merridew was in the best of health and spirits. Merridew took a day off from the waterworks, and we all went for a long drive and picnic together. We were on the best of terms with one another. Ask Merridew. He will tell you the same thing. He would not—he could not, surely—say otherwise. I can't believe, Harringay, I simply cannot believe that he could imagine or suspect me. I say, there was nothing to suspect. Nothing.

Yes—this is the important date—the twenty-fourth of June. I can't tell you any more details; there is nothing to tell. We came back and had dinner just as usual. All three of us were together all day, till bedtime. On my honor I had no private interview of any kind that day, either with him or with her. I was the first to go to bed, and I heard the others come upstairs about half an hour later. They were talking cheerfully.

It was a moonlight night. For once, no caterwauling came

to trouble me. I didn't even bother to shut the window or the door. I put the revolver on the chair beside me before I lay down. Yes, it was loaded. I had no special object in putting it there, except that I meant to have a go at the cats if they started their games again.

I was desperately tired and thought I should drop off to sleep at once, but I didn't. I must have been overtired, I suppose. I lay and looked at the moonlight. And then, about midnight, I heard what I had been half expecting: a stealthy scrabbling in the wisteria and a faint meowing sound.

I sat up in bed and reached for the revolver. I heard the *plop* as the big cat sprang up onto the window ledge; I saw her black-and-silver flanks and the outline of her round head, pricked ears, and upright tail. I aimed and fired, and the beast let out one frightful cry and sprang down into the room.

I jumped out of bed. The crack of the shot had sounded terrific in the silent house, and somewhere I heard a distant voice call out. I pursued the cat into the passage, revolver in hand, with some idea of finishing it off, I suppose. And then, at the door of the Merridews' room, I saw Mrs. Merridew. She stood with one hand on each doorpost, swaying to and fro. Then she fell down at my feet. Her bare breast was all stained with blood. And as I stood staring at her, clutching the revolver, Merridew came out and found us—like that.

Well, Harringay, that's my story, exactly as I told it to Peabody. I'm afraid it won't sound very well in court, but what can I say? The trail of blood led from my room to hers; the cat must have run that way; I *know* it was the cat I shot. I can't offer any explanation. I don't know who shot Mrs. Merridew, or why. I can't help it if the people at the inn say they never saw the Cyprian cat; Merridew saw it that other night, and I know he wouldn't lie about it. Search the house, Harringay. That's the only thing to do. Pull the place to pieces, till you find the body of the Cyprian cat. It will have my bullet in it.

James H. Schmitz

NOVICE

There was, Telzey Amberdon thought, someone besides TT and herself in the garden. Not, of course, Aunt Halet, who was in the house waiting for an early visitor to arrive, and not one of the servants. Someone or something else must be concealed among the thickets of magnificently flowering native Jontarou shrubs about Telzey.

She could think of no other way to account for Tick-Tock's spooked behavior—nor, to be honest about it, for the manner her own nerves were acting up without visible cause this morning.

Telzey plucked a blade of grass, slipped the end between

her lips, and chewed it gently, her face puzzled and concerned. She wasn't ordinarily afflicted with nervousness. Fifteen years old, genius level, brown as a berry, and not at all bad-looking in her sunbriefs, she was the youngest member of one of Orado's most prominent families and a second-year law student at one of the most exclusive schools in the Federation of the Hub. Her physical, mental, and emotional health, she'd always been informed, was excellent. Aunt Halet's frequent cracks about the inherent instability of the genius level could be ignored; Halet's own stability seemed questionable at best.

But none of that made the present odd situation any less disagreeable. . . .

The trouble might have begun, Telzey decided, during the night, within an hour after they arrived from the spaceport at the guesthouse Halet had rented in Port Nichay for their vacation on Jontarou. Telzey had retired at once to her second-story bedroom with Tick-Tock; but she barely got to sleep before something awakened her again. Turning over, she discovered TT reared up before the window, her forepaws on the sill, big cat-head outlined against the star-hazed night sky, staring fixedly down into the garden.

Telzey, only curious at that point, climbed out of bed and joined TT at the window. There was nothing in particular to be seen, and if the scents and minor night sounds which came from the garden weren't exactly what they were used to, Jontarou was after all an unfamiliar planet. What else would one expect here?

But Tick-Tock's muscular back felt tense and rigid when Telzey laid her arm across it, and, except for an absentminded dig with her forehead against Telzey's shoulder, TT refused to let her attention be distracted from whatever had absorbed it. Now and then, a low, ominous rumble came from her furry throat, a half-angry, half-questioning sound. Telzey began to feel a little uncomfortable. She managed finally to coax Tick-

Tock away from the window, but neither of them slept well the rest of the night. At breakfast, Aunt Halet made one of her typical nasty-sweet remarks.

"You look so fatigued, dear—as if you were under some severe mental strain—which, of course, you might be," Halet added musingly. With her gold-blond hair piled high on her head and her peaches-and-cream complexion, Halet looked fresh as a daisy herself—a malicious daisy. "Now wasn't I right in insisting to Jessamine that you needed a vacation away from that terribly intellectual school?" She smiled gently.

"Absolutely," Telzey agreed, restraining the impulse to fling a spoonful of egg yolk at her father's younger sister. Aunt Halet often inspired such impulses, but Telzey had promised her mother to avoid actual battles on the Jontarou trip, if possible. After breakfast, she went out into the back garden with Tick-Tock, who immediately walked into a thicket, camouflaged herself, and vanished from sight. It seemed to add up to something. But what?

Telzey strolled about the garden awhile, maintaining a pretense of nonchalant interest in Jontarou's flowers and colorful bug life. She experienced the most curious little chills of alarm from time to time, but discovered no signs of a lurking intruder, or of TT either. Then, for half an hour or more, she'd just sat cross-legged in the grass, waiting quietly for Tick-Tock to show up of her own accord. And the big lunkhead hadn't obliged.

Telzey scratched a tanned kneecap, scowling at Port Nichay's park trees beyond the garden wall. It seemed idiotic to feel scared when she couldn't even tell whether there was anything to be scared about! And, aside from that, another unreasonable feeling kept growing stronger by the minute now. This was to the effect that she should be doing some unstated but specific thing. . . .

In fact, that Tick-Tock *wanted* her to do some specific thing!

Completely idiotic!

Abruptly, Telzey closed her eyes, thought sharply, "Tick-Tock?" and waited—suddenly very angry at herself for having given in to her fancies to this extent—for whatever might happen.

She had never really established that she was able to tell, by a kind of symbolic mind-picture method, like a short waking dream, approximately what TT was thinking and feeling. Five years before, when she'd discovered Tick-Tock—an odd-looking and odder-behaved stray kitten then—in the woods near the Amberdons' summer home on Orado, Telzey had thought so. But it might never have been more than a colorful play of her imagination; and after she got into law school and grew increasingly absorbed in her studies, she almost forgot the matter again.

Today, perhaps because she was disturbed about Tick-Tock's behavior, the customary response was extraordinarily prompt. The warm glow of sunlight shining through her closed eyelids faded out quickly and was replaced by some inner darkness. In the darkness there appeared then an image of Tick-Tock sitting a little way off beside an open door in an old stone wall, green eyes fixed on Telzey. Telzey got the impression that TT was inviting her to go through the door, and, for some reason, the thought frightened her.

Again, there was an immediate reaction. The scene with Tick-Tock and the door vanished; and Telzey felt she was standing in a pitch-black room, knowing that if she moved even one step forward, something that was waiting there silently would reach out and grab her.

Naturally, she recoiled . . . and at once found herself sitting, eyes still closed and the sunlight bathing her lids, in the grass of the guesthouse garden.

She opened her eyes, looked around. Her heart was

thumping rapidly. The experience couldn't have lasted more than four or five seconds, but it had been extremely vivid, a whole compact little nightmare. None of her earlier experiments at getting into mental communication with TT had been like that.

It served her right, Telzey thought, for trying such a childish stunt at the moment! What she should have done at once was to make a methodical search for the foolish beast— TT was bound to be *somewhere* nearby—locate her behind her camouflage, and hang on to her then until this nonsense in the garden was explained! Talented as Tick-Tock was at blotting herself out, it usually was possible to spot her if one directed one's attention to shadow patterns. Telzey began a surreptitious study of the flowering bushes about her.

Three minutes later, off to her right, where the ground was banked beneath a six-foot step in the garden's terraces, Tick-Tock's outline suddenly caught her eye. Flat on her belly, head lifted above her paws, quite motionless, TT seemed like a transparent wraith stretched out along the terrace, barely discernible even when stared at directly. It was a convincing illusion; but what seemed to be rocks, plant leaves, and sun-splotched earth seen through the wraith outline was simply the camouflage pattern TT had printed for the moment on her hide. She could have changed it completely in an instant to conform to a different background.

Telzey pointed an accusing finger.

"See you!" she announced, feeling a surge of relief which seemed as unaccountable as the rest of it.

The wraith twitched one ear in acknowledgment, the head outlines shifting as the camouflaged face turned toward Telzey. Then the inwardly uncamouflaged, very substantial-looking mouth opened slowly, showing Tick-Tock's red tongue and curved white tusks. The mouth stretched in a wide yawn, snapped shut with a click of meshing teeth, became indistinguishable again. Next, a pair of camouflaged lids drew back from TT's round, brilliant-green eyes. The eyes stared across the lawn at Telzey.

Telzey said irritably, "Quit clowning around, TT!"

The eyes blinked, and Tick-Tock's natural bronze-brown color suddenly flowed over her head, down her neck, and across her body into legs and tail. Against the side of the terrace, as if materializing into solidity at that moment, appeared two hundred pounds of supple, rangy, long-tailed cat . . . or catlike creature. TT's actual origin had never been established. The best guesses were that what Telzey had found playing around in the woods five years ago was either a biostructural experiment which had got away from a private laboratory on Orado, or some spaceman's lost pet, brought to the capital planet from one of the remote colonies beyond the Hub. On top of TT's head was a large, fluffy pom-pom of white fur, which might have looked ridiculous on another animal, but didn't on her. Even as a fat kitten, hanging head down from the side of a wall by the broad sucker pads in her paws, TT had possessed enormous dignity.

Telzey studied her, the feeling of relief fading again. Tick-Tock, ordinarily the most restful and composed of companions, definitely was still tensed up about something. That big, lazy yawn a moment ago, the attitude of stretched-out relaxation . . . all pure sham!

"What *is* eating you?" she asked in exasperation.

The green eyes stared at her, solemn, watchful, seeming for that fleeting instant quite alien. And why, Telzey thought, should the old question of what Tick-Tock really was pass through her mind just now? After her rather alarming rate of growth began to taper off last year, nobody had cared anymore.

For a moment, Telzey had the uncanny certainty of having had the answer to this situation almost in her grasp. An answer which appeared to involve the world of Jontarou, Tick-Tock, and—of all unlikely factors—Aunt Halet.

She shook her head. TT's impassive green eyes blinked.

Jontarou? The planet lay outside Telzey's sphere of personal interests, but she'd read up on it on the way here from Orado. Among all the worlds of the Hub, Jontarou was *the* paradise for zoologists and sportsmen, a gigantic animal preserve, its continents and seas swarming with magnificent game. Under Federation law, it was being retained deliberately in the primitive state in which it had been discovered. Port Nichay, the only city, actually the only inhabited point on Jontarou, was beautiful and quiet, a pattern of vast but elegantly slender towers, each separated from the others by four or five miles of rolling parkland and interconnected only by the threads of transparent skyways. Near the horizon, just visible from the garden, rose the tallest towers of all, the green and gold spires of the Shikaris' Club, a center of Federation affairs and of social activity. From the aircar which brought them across Port Nichay the evening before, Telzey had seen occasional strings of guesthouses, similar to the one Halet had rented, nestling along the park slopes.

Nothing very sinister about Port Nichay or green Jontarou, surely!

Halet? That blond, slinky, would-be Machiavelli? What could—?

Telzey's eyes narrowed reflectively. There'd been a minor occurrence—at least, it seemed minor—just before the spaceliner docked last night. A young woman from one of the newscasting services had asked for an interview with the daughter of Federation Councilwoman Jessamine Amberdon. This happened occasionally; and Telzey had no objections until the news hen's gossipy persistence in inquiring about the "unusual pet" she was bringing to Port Nichay with her began to be annoying. TT might be somewhat unusual, but that was not a matter of general interest; and Telzey said so. Then Halet moved smoothly into the act and held forth on Tick-Tock's appearance, habits, and mysterious antecedents, in considerable detail.

Telzey had assumed that Halet was simply going out of her way to be irritating, as usual. Looking back on the incident, however, it occurred to her that the chatter between her aunt and the newscast woman had sounded oddly stilted— almost like something the two might have rehearsed.

Rehearsed for what purpose? Tick-Tock . . . Jontarou.

Telzey chewed gently on her lower lip. A vacation on Jontarou for the two of them and TT had been Halet's idea, and Halet had enthused about it so much that Telzey's mother at last talked her into accepting. Halet, Jessamine explained privately to Telzey, had felt they were intruders in the Amberdon family, had bitterly resented Jessamine's political honors and, more recently, Telzey's own emerging promise of brilliance. This invitation was Halet's way of indicating a change of heart. Wouldn't Telzey oblige?

So Telzey had obliged, though she took very little stock in Halet's change of heart. She wasn't, in fact, putting it past her aunt to have some involved dirty trick up her sleeve with this trip to Jontarou. Halet's mind worked like that.

So far there had been no actual indications of purposeful mischief. But logic did seem to require a connection between the various puzzling events here. . . . A newscaster's rather forced-looking interest in Tick-Tock—Halet could easily have paid for that interview. Then TT's disturbed behavior during their first night in Port Nichay, and Telzey's own formless anxieties and fancies in connection with the guesthouse garden.

The last remained hard to explain. But Tick-Tock—and Halet—might know something about Jontarou that she didn't know.

Her mind returned to the results of the half-serious attempt she'd made to find out whether there was something Tick-Tock "wanted her to do." An open door? A darkness where somebody waited to grab her if she took even one step forward? It couldn't have had any significance. Or could it?

So you'd like to try magic, Telzey scoffed at herself. Baby games. . . . How far would you have got at law school if you'd asked TT to help with your problems?

Then why had she been thinking about it again?

She shivered, because an eerie stillness seemed to settle on the garden. From the side of the terrace, TT's green eyes watched her.

Telzey had a feeling of sinking down slowly into a sunlit dream, into something very remote from law-school problems.

"Should I go through the door?" she whispered.

The bronze cat-shape raised its head slowly. TT began to purr.

Tick-Tock's name had been derived in kittenhood from the manner in which she purred—a measured, oscillating sound, shifting from high to low, as comfortable and often as continuous as the unobtrusive pulse of an old clock. It was the first time, Telzey realized now, that she'd heard the sound since their arrival on Jontarou. It went on for a dozen seconds or so, then stopped. Tick-Tock continued to look at her.

It appeared to have been an expression of definite assent. . . .

The dreamlike sensation increased, hazing over Telzey's thoughts. If there was nothing to this mind-communication thing, what harm could symbols do? This time, she wouldn't let them alarm her. And if they did mean something . . .

She closed her eyes.

The sunglow outside faded instantly. Telzey caught a fleeting picture of the door in the wall, and knew in the same moment that she'd already passed through it.

She was not in the dark room then, but poised at the edge of a brightness which seemed featureless and without limit, spread out around her with a feeling-tone like "sea" or "sky." But it was an unquiet place. There was a sense of unseen things on all sides watching her and waiting.

Was this another form of the dark room—a trap set up in her mind? Telzey's attention did a quick shift. She was seated in the grass again; the sunlight beyond her closed eyelids seemed to shine in quietly through rose-tinted curtains. Cautiously, she let her awareness return to the bright area; and *it* was still there. She had a moment of excited elation. She was controlling this! And why not, she asked herself. These things were happening in *her* mind, after all!

She would find out what they seemed to mean, but she would be in no rush to—

An impression as if, behind her, Tick-Tock had thought, Now I can help again!

Then a feeling of being swept swiftly, irresistibly forward, thrust out and down. The brightness exploded in thundering colors around her. In fright, she made the effort to snap her eyes open, to be back in the garden; but now she couldn't make it work. The colors continued to roar about her, like a confusion of excited, laughing, triumphant voices. Telzey felt caught in the middle of it all, suspended in invisible spiderwebs. Tick-Tock seemed to be somewhere nearby, looking on. Faithless, treacherous TT!

Telzey's mind made another wrenching effort, and there was a change. She hadn't got back into the garden, but the noisy, swirling colors were gone and she had the feeling of reading a rapidly moving microtape now, though she didn't actually see the tape.

The tape, she realized, was another symbol for what was happening, a symbol easier for her to understand. There were voices, or what might be voices, around her; on the invisible tape she seemed to be reading what they said.

A number of speakers, apparently involved in a fast, hot argument about what to do with her. Impressions flashed past. . . .

Why waste time with her? It was clear that kitten talk was all she was capable of! . . . Not necessarily; that was a normal first step. Give her a little time! . . . But what—exasperatedly—could *such* a small-bite *possibly* know that would be of significant value?

There was a slow, blurred, awkward-seeming interruption. Its content was not comprehensible to Telzey at all, but in some unmistakable manner it was defined as Tick-Tock's thought.

A pause as the circle of speakers stopped to consider whatever TT had thrown into the debate.

Then another impression—one that sent a shock of fear through Telzey as it rose heavily into her awareness. Its sheer intensity momentarily displaced the tape-reading symbolism. A savage voice seemed to rumble:

"Toss the tender small-bite to *me*"—malevolent crimson eyes fixed on Telzey from somewhere not far away—"and let's be done here!"

Startled, stammering protest from Tick-Tock, accompanied by gusts of laughter from the circle. Great sense of humor these characters had, Telzey thought bitterly. That crimson-eyed thing wasn't joking at all!

More laughter as the circle caught her thought. Then a kind of majority opinion found sudden expression:

"Small-bite *is* learning! No harm to wait—We'll find out quickly—Let's . . ."

The tape ended; the voices faded; the colors went blank. In whatever jumbled-up form she'd been getting the impressions at that point—Telzey couldn't have begun to describe it—the whole thing suddenly stopped.

She found herself sitting in the grass, shaky, scared, eyes open. Tick-Tock stood beside the terrace, looking at her. An air of hazy unreality still hung about the garden.

She might have flipped! She didn't think so; but it certainly seemed possible! Otherwise . . . Telzey made an attempt to sort over what had happened.

Something *had* been in the garden! Something had been inside her mind. Something that was at home on Jontarou.

There'd been a feeling of perhaps fifty or sixty of these . . . well, beings. Alarming beings! Reckless, wild, hard—and that red-eyed nightmare! Telzey shuddered.

They'd contacted Tick-Tock first, during the night. TT understood them better than she could. Why? Telzey found no immediate answer.

Then Tick-Tock had tricked her into letting her mind be invaded by these beings. There must have been a very definite reason for that.

She looked over at Tick-Tock. TT looked back. Nothing stirred in Telzey's thoughts. Between *them* there was still no direct communication.

Then how had the beings been able to get through to her?

Telzey wrinkled her nose. Assuming this was real, it seemed clear that the game of symbols she'd made up between herself and TT had provided the opening. Her whole experience just now had been in the form of symbols, translating whatever occurred into something she could consciously grasp.

"Kitten talk" was how the beings referred to the use of symbols; they seemed contemptuous of it. Never mind, Telzey told herself; they'd agreed she was learning.

The air over the grass appeared to flicker. Again she had

the impression of reading words off a quickly moving, not-quite-visible tape.

"You're being taught and you're learning," was what she seemed to read. "The question was whether you were capable of partial understanding as your friend insisted. Since you were, everything else that can be done will be accomplished very quickly." A pause, then with a touch of approval, "You're a well-formed mind, a small-bite! Odd and with incomprehensibilities, but well formed—"

One of the beings, and a fairly friendly one—at least not unfriendly. Telzey framed a tentative mental question. "Who are you?"

"You'll know very soon." The flickering ended; she realized she and the question had been dismissed for the moment. She looked over at Tick-Tock again.

"Can't *you* talk to me now, TT?" she asked silently.

A feeling of hesitation.

"Kitten talk!" was the impression that formed itself with difficulty then. It was awkward, searching; but it came unquestionably from TT. "Still learning, too, Telzey!" TT seemed half anxious, half angry. "We—"

A sharp buzz-note reached Telzey's ears, wiping out the groping thought-impression. She jumped a little, glanced down. Her wrist-talker was signaling. For a moment, she seemed poised uncertainly between a world where unseen, dangerous-sounding beings referred to one as small-bite and where TT was learning to talk, and the familiar other world where wrist communicators buzzed periodically in a matter-of-fact manner. Settling back into the more familiar world, she switched on the talker.

"Yes?" she said. Her voice sounded husky.

"Telzey, dear," Halet murmured honey-sweet from the talker, "would you come back into the house, please? The living room—We have a visitor who very much wants to meet you."

Telzey hesitated, eyes narrowing. Halet's visitor wanted to meet *her?*

"Why?" she asked.

"He has something *very* interesting to tell you, dear." The edge of triumphant malice showed for an instant, vanished in murmuring sweetness again. "So please hurry!"

"All right." Telzey stood up. "I'm coming."

"Fine, dear!" The talker went dead.

Telzey switched off the instrument, noticed that Tick-Tock had chosen to disappear meanwhile.

Flipped? She wondered, starting up toward the house. It was clear Aunt Halet had prepared some unpleasant surprise to spring on her, which was hardly more than normal behavior for Halet. The other business? She couldn't be certain of anything there. Leaving out TT's strange actions—which might have a number of causes, after all—that entire string of events could have been created inside her head. There was no contradictory evidence so far.

But it could do no harm to take what *seemed* to have happened at face value. Some pretty grim event might be shaping up, in a very real way, around here. . . .

"You reason logically!" The impression now was of a voice speaking to her, a voice that made no audible sound. It was the same being who'd addressed her a minute or two ago.

The two worlds between which Telzey had felt suspended seemed to glide slowly together and become one.

"I go to law school," she explained to the being, almost absently.

Amused agreement. "So we heard."

"What do you want of me?" Telzey inquired.

"You'll know soon enough."

"Why not tell me now?" Telzey urged. It seemed about to dismiss her again.

Quick impatience flared at her. "Kitten pictures! Kitten

thoughts! Kitten talk! Too slow, too slow! *Your* pictures—too much *you!* Wait till the . . ."

Circuits close . . . channels open. . . . Obstructions clear? What *had* it said? There'd been only the blurred image of a finicky, delicate, but perfectly normal technical operation of some kind.

". . . minutes now!" the voice concluded. A pause, then another thought tossed carelessly at her. "This is more important to you, small-bite, than to *us!*" The voice impression ended as sharply as if a communicator had snapped off.

Not *too* friendly! Telzey walked on toward the house, a new fear growing inside her, a fear like the awareness of a storm gathered nearby, still quiet—deadly quiet, but ready to break.

"Kitten pictures!" a voice seemed to jeer distantly, a whispering in the park trees beyond the garden wall.

Halet's cheeks were lightly pinked; her blue eyes sparkled. She looked downright stunning, which meant to anyone who knew her that the worst side of Halet's nature was champing at the bit again. On uninformed males it had a dazzling effect, however; and Telzey wasn't surprised to find their visitor wearing a tranced expression when she came into the living room. He was a tall, outdoorsy man with a tanned, bony face, a neatly trained black mustache, and a scar down one cheek, which would have seemed dashing if it hadn't been for the stupefied look. Beside his chair stood a large, clumsy instrument which might have been some kind of telecamera.

Halet performed introductions. Their visitor was Dr. Droon, a zoologist. He had been tuned in on Telzey's newscast interview on the liner the night before, and wondered whether Telzey would care to discuss Tick-Tock with him.

"Frankly, no," Telzey said.

Dr. Droon came awake and gave Telzey a surprised look. Halet smiled easily.

"My niece doesn't intend to be discourteous, Doctor," she explained.

"Of course not," the zoologist agreed doubtfully.

"It's just," Halet went on, "that Telzey is a little, oh, sensitive where Tick-Tock is concerned. In her own way, she's attached to the animal. Aren't you, dear?"

"Yes," Telzey said blandly.

"Well, we hope this isn't going to disturb you too much, dear." Halet glanced significantly at Dr. Droon. "Dr. Droon, you must understand, is simply doing . . . well, there is something very important he must tell you now."

Telzey transferred her gaze back to the zoologist. Dr. Droon cleared his throat. "I, ah, understand, Miss Amberdon, that you're unaware of what kind of creature your, ah, Tick-Tock is?"

Telzey started to speak, then checked herself, frowning. She had been about to state that she knew exactly what kind of creature TT was . . . but she didn't, of course!

Or did she? She . . .

She scowled absentmindedly at Dr. Droon, biting her lip.

"Telzey!" Halet prompted gently.

"Huh?" Telzey said. "Oh . . . please go on, Doctor!"

Dr. Droon steepled his fingers. "Well," he said, "she . . . your pet . . . is, ah, a young crest cat. Nearly full grown now, apparently, and—"

"Why, yes!" Telzey cried.

The zoologist looked at her. "You knew that—"

"Well, not really," Telzey admitted. "Or sort of." She laughed, her cheeks flushed. "This is the most . . . go ahead please! Sorry I interrupted." She stared at the wall beyond Dr. Droon with a rapt expression.

The zoologist and Halet exchanged glances. Then Dr. Droon resumed cautiously. The crest cats, he said, were a species native to Jontarou. Their existence had been known for only eight years. The species appeared to have had a somewhat limited range—the Baluit Mountains on the opposite side of the huge continent on which Port Nichay had been built. . . .

Telzey barely heard him. A very curious thing was happening. For every sentence Dr. Droon uttered, a dozen other sentences appeared in her awareness. More accurately, it was as if an instantaneous smooth flow of information relevant to whatever he said arose continuously from what might have been almost her own memory, but wasn't. Within a minute or two, she knew more about the crest cats of Jontarou than Dr. Droon could have told her in hours—much more than he'd ever known.

She realized suddenly that he'd stopped talking, that he had asked her a question. "Miss Amberdon?" he repeated now, with a note of uncertainty.

"Yar-rrr-REE!" Telzey told him softly. "I'll drink your blood!"

"Eh?"

Telzey blinked, focused on Dr. Droon, wrenching her mind away from a splendid view of the misty-blue peaks of the Baluit range.

"Sorry," she said briskly. "Just a joke!" She smiled. "Now what were you saying?"

The zoologist looked at her in a rather odd manner for a moment. "I was inquiring," he said then, "whether you were familiar with the sporting rules established by the various hunting associations of the Hub in connection with the taking of game trophies?"

Telzey shook her head. "No, I never heard of them."

The rules, Dr. Droon explained, laid down the type of equipment—weapons, spotting and tracking instruments, number of assistants, and so forth—a sportsman could legitimately use in the pursuit of any specific type of game. "Before the end of the first year after their discovery," he went on, "the Baluit crest cats had been placed in the ultraequipment class."

"What's ultraequipment?" Telzey asked.

"Well," Dr. Droon said thoughtfully, "it doesn't quite involve the use of full battle armor—not quite! And, of course, even with that classification the sporting principle of mutual accessibility must be observed."

"Mutual . . . oh, I see!" Telzey paused as another wave of silent information rose into her awareness; went on, "So the game has to be able to get at the sportsman too, eh?"

"That's correct. Except in the pursuit of various classes of flying animals, a shikari would not, for example, be permitted the use of an aircar other than as a means of simple transportation. Under these conditions, it was soon established that crest cats were being obtained by sportsmen who went after them at a rather consistent one-to-one ratio."

Telzey's eyes widened. She'd gathered something similar from her other information source but hadn't quite believed it. "One hunter killed for each cat bagged?" she said. "That's pretty rough sport, isn't it?"

"Extremely rough sport!" Dr. Droon agreed dryly. "In fact, when the statistics were published, the sporting interest in winning a Baluit cat trophy appears to have suffered a sudden and sharp decline. On the other hand, a more scientific interest in these remarkable animals was coincidingly created, and many permits for their acquisition by the agents of museums, universities, public and private collections were issued. Sporting rules, of course, do not apply to that activity."

Telzey nodded absently. "I see! *They* used aircars, didn't they? A sort of heavy knockout gun—"

"Aircars, long-range detectors and stun guns are standard equipment in such work," Dr. Droon acknowledged. "Gas and poison are employed, of course, as circumstances dictate. The collectors were relatively successful for a while.

"And then a curious thing happened. Less than two years after their existence became known, the crest cats of the Baluit range were extinct! The inroads made on their numbers by man cannot begin to account for this, so it must be assumed that a sudden plague wiped them out. At any rate, not another living member of the species has been seen on Jontarou until you landed here with your pet last night."

Telzey sat silent for some seconds. Not because of what he had said, but because the other knowledge was still flowing into her mind. On one very important point that was at variance with what the zoologist had stated; and from there a coldly logical pattern was building up. Telzey didn't grasp the pattern in complete detail yet, but what she saw of it stirred her with a half-incredulous dread.

She asked, shaping the words carefully but with only a small part of her attention on what she was really saying, "Just what does all that have to do with Tick-Tock, Dr. Droon?"

Dr. Droon glanced at Halet, and returned his gaze to Telzey. Looking very uncomfortable but quite determined, he told her, "Miss Amberdon, there is a Federation law which states that when a species is threatened with extinction, any available survivors must be transferred to the Life Banks of the University League, to ensure their indefinite preservation. Under the circumstances, this law applies to, ah, Tick-Tock!"

So that had been Halet's trick. She'd found out about the crest cats, might have put in as much as a few months arranging to make the discovery of TT's origin on Jontarou seem a regrettable mischance—something no one could have foreseen or prevented. In the Life Banks, from what Telzey had heard of them, TT would cease to exist as an individual awareness while scientists tinkered around with the possibilities of reconstructing her species.

Telzey studied her aunt's carefully sympathizing face for an instant, asked Dr. Droon, "What about the other crest cats you said were collected before they became extinct here? Wouldn't they be enough for what the Life Banks need?"

He shook his head. "Two immature male specimens are known to exist, and they are at present in the Life Banks. The others that were taken alive at the time have been destroyed —often under nearly disastrous circumstances. They are enormously cunning, enormously savage creatures, Miss Amberdon! The additional fact that they can conceal themselves to the point of being virtually undetectable except by the use of instruments makes them one of the most dangerous animals known. Since the young female which you raised as a pet has remained docile—so far—you may not really be able to appreciate that."

"Perhaps I can," Telzey said. She nodded at the heavy-looking instrument standing beside his chair. "And that's—?"

"It's a life detector combined with a stun gun, Miss Amberdon. I have no intention of harming your pet, but we can't take chances with any animal of that type. The gun's charge will knock it unconscious for several minutes, just long enough to let me secure it with paralysis belts."

"You're a collector for the Life Banks, Dr. Droon?"

"That's correct."

"Dr. Droon," Halet remarked, "has obtained a permit from the Planetary Moderator, authorizing him to claim Tick-Tock for the University League and remove her from the planet, dear. So you see there is simply nothing we can do about the matter! Your mother wouldn't like us to attempt to obstruct the law, would she?" Halet paused. "The permit should have your signature, Telzey, but I can sign in your stead if necessary."

That was Halet's way of saying it would do no good to appeal to Jontarou's Planetary Moderator. She'd taken the precaution of getting his assent to the matter first.

"So now if you'll just call Tick-Tock, dear. . . ," Halet went on.

Telzey barely heard the last words. She felt herself stiffening slowly, while the living room almost faded from her sight. Perhaps, in that instant, some additional new circuit had closed in her mind, or some additional new channel had opened, for TT's purpose in tricking her into contact with the reckless, mocking beings outside was suddenly and numbingly clear.

And what it meant immediately was that she'd have to get out of the house without being spotted at it, and go someplace where she could be undisturbed for half an hour.

She realized that Halet and the zoologist were both staring at her.

"Are you ill, dear?"

"No." Telzey stood up. It would be worse than useless to try to tell these two anything! Her face must be pretty white at the moment—she could feel it—but they assumed, of course, that the shock of losing TT had just now sunk in on her.

"I'll have to check on that law you mentioned before I sign anything," she told Dr. Droon.

"Why, yes . . ." He started to get out of his chair. "I'm sure that can be arranged, Miss Amberdon!"

"Don't bother to call the Moderator's office," Telzey said. "I brought my law library along. I'll look it up myself." She turned to leave the room.

"My niece," Halet explained to Dr. Droon who was beginning to look puzzled, "attends law school. She's always so absorbed in her studies. . . . Telzey?"

"Yes, Halet?" Telzey paused at the door.

"I'm very glad you've decided to be sensible about this, dear. But don't take too long, will you? We don't want to waste Dr. Droon's time."

"It shouldn't take more than five or ten minutes," Telzey told her agreeably. She closed the door behind her, and went directly to her bedroom on the second floor. One of her two valises was still unpacked. She locked the door behind her, opened the unpacked valise, took out a pocket-edition law library, and sat down at the table with it.

She clicked on the library's viewscreen, tapped the clearing and index buttons. Behind the screen, one of the multiple rows of pinhead tapes shifted slightly as the index was flicked into reading position. Half a minute later, she was glancing over the legal section on which Dr. Droon had based his claim. The library confirmed what he had said.

Very neat of Halet, Telzey thought, very nasty—and pretty idiotic! Even a second-year law student could think immediately of two or three ways in which a case like that could have been dragged out in the Federation's courts for a couple of decades before the question of handing Tick-Tock over to the Life Banks became too acute.

Well, Halet simply wasn't really intelligent. And the plot to shanghai TT was hardly even a side issue now.

Telzey snapped the tiny library shut, fastened it to the belt of her sunsuit, and went over to the open window. A two-foot ledge passed beneath the window, leading to the roof of a patio on the right. Fifty yards beyond the patio, the garden ended in a natural-stone wall. Behind it lay one of the big wooded park areas which formed most of the ground level of Port Nichay.

Tick-Tock wasn't in sight. A sound of voices came from ground-floor windows on the left. Halet had brought her maid and chauffeur along; and a chef had showed up in time to make breakfast this morning, as part of the city's guesthouse service. Telzey took the empty valise to the window, set it on end against the left side of the frame, and let the window slide down until its lower edge rested on the valise. She went back to the house guard-screen panel beside the door, put her finger against the lock button, and pushed.

The sound of voices from the lower floor was cut off as outer doors and windows slid silently shut all about the house.

Telzey glanced back at the window. The valise had creaked a little as the guard field drove the frame down on it, but it was supporting the thrust. She returned to the window, wriggled feet foremost through the opening, twisted around, and got a footing on the ledge.

A minute later, she was scrambling quietly down a vine-covered patio trellis to the ground. Even after they discovered she was gone, the guard screen would keep everybody in the house for some little while. They'd either have to disengage the screen's main mechanisms and start poking around in them, or force open the door to her bedroom and get the lock unset. Either approach would involve confusion, upset tempers, and generally delay any organized pursuit.

Telzey edged around the patio and started toward the wall, keeping close to the side of the house so she couldn't be seen from the windows. The shrubbery made minor rustling noises as she threaded her way through it—and then there was a different stirring, which might have been no more than a slow, steady current of air moving among the bushes behind her. She shivered involuntarily but didn't look back.

She came to the wall, stood still, measuring its height, jumped and got an arm across it, swung up a knee, and squirmed up and over. She came down on her feet with a small thump in the grass on the other side, glanced back once at the guesthouse, crossed a path, and went on among the park trees.

Within a few hundred yards, it became apparent that she had an escort. She didn't look around for them; but, spread out to right and left like a skirmish line, keeping abreast with her, occasional shadows slid silently through patches of open, sunlit ground, disappeared again under the trees. Otherwise, there was hardly anyone in sight. Port Nichay's human residents appeared to make almost no personal use of the vast parkland spread out beneath their tower apartments; and its traffic moved over the airways, visible from the ground only as rainbow-hued ribbons which bisected the sky between the upper tower levels. An occasional private aircar went by overhead.

Wisps of thought which were not her own thoughts flicked through Telzey's mind from moment to moment as the silent line of shadows moved deeper into the park with her. She realized she was being sized up, judged, evaluated again. No more information was coming through; they had given her as much information as she needed. In the main, perhaps, they were simply curious now. This was the first human mind they'd been able to make heads or tails of, and that hadn't seemed deaf and silent to their form of communication. They were taking time out to study it. They'd been assured she would have something of genuine importance to tell them; and there was some derision about that. But they were willing to wait a little, and find out. They were curious and they liked games. At the moment, Telzey and what she might try to do to change their plans was the game on which their attention was fixed.

Twelve minutes passed before the talker on Telzey's wrist began to buzz. It continued to signal off and on for another few minutes, then stopped. Back in the guesthouse they couldn't be sure yet whether she wasn't simply locked inside her room and refusing to answer them. But Telzey quickened her pace.

The park's trees gradually became more massive, reached higher above her, stood spaced more widely apart. She passed through the morning shadow of the residential tower nearest the guesthouse, and emerged from it presently on the shore of a small lake. On the other side of the lake, a number of dappled grazing animals like long-necked, tall horses lifted their heads to watch her. For some seconds they seemed only mildly interested, but then a breeze moved across the lake, crinkling the surface of the water; and as it touched the opposite shore, abrupt panic exploded among the grazers. They wheeled, went flashing away in effortless twenty-foot strides, and were gone among the trees.

Telzey felt a crawling along her spine. It was the first objective indication she'd had of the nature of the company she had brought to the lake, and while it hardly came as a surprise, for a moment her urge was to follow the example of the grazers.

"Tick-Tock?" she whispered, suddenly a little short of breath.

A single up-and-down purring note replied from the bushes on her right. TT was still around, for whatever good that might do. Not too much, Telzey thought, if it came to serious trouble. But the knowledge was somewhat reassuring . . . and this, meanwhile, appeared to be as far as she needed to get from the guesthouse. They'd be looking for her by aircar presently, but there was nothing to tell them in which direction to turn first.

She climbed the bank of the lake to a point where she was screened both by thick, green shrubbery and the top of a single immense tree from the sky, sat down on some dry, mossy growth, took the law library from her belt, opened it, and placed it in her lap. Vague stirrings indicated that her escort was also settling down in an irregular circle about her; and apprehension shivered on Telzey's skin again. It wasn't that their attitude was hostile; they were simply overawing. And no one could predict what they might do next. Without looking up, she asked a question in her mind.

"Ready?"

Sense of multiple acknowledgment, variously tinged: sardonic; interestedly amused; attentive; doubtful. Impatience quivered through it too, only tentatively held in restraint, and

Telzey's forehead was suddenly wet. Some of them seemed on the verge of expressing disapproval with what was being done here—

Her fingers quickly flicked in the index tape, and the stir of feeling about her subsided, their attention captured again for the moment. Her thoughts became to some degree detached, ready to dissect another problem in the familiar ways and present the answers to it. Not a very involved problem essentially, but this time it wasn't a school exercise. Her company waited, withdrawn, silent, aloof once more, while the index blurred, checked, blurred and checked. Within a minute and a half, she had noted a dozen reference symbols. She tapped in another of the pinhead tapes, glanced over a few paragraphs, licked salty sweat from her lip, and said in her thoughts, emphasizing the meaning of each detail of the sentence so that there would be no misunderstanding, "This is the Federation law that applies to the situation which existed originally on this planet. . . ."

There were no interruptions, no commenting thoughts, no intrusions of any kind, as she went step by step through the section, turned to another one, and another. In perhaps twelve minutes she came to the end of the last one, and stopped. Instantly, argument exploded about her.

Telzey was not involved in the argument; in fact, she could grasp only scraps of it. Either they were excluding her deliberately, or the exchange was too swift, practiced, and varied to allow her to keep up. But their vehemence was not encouraging. And was it reasonable to assume that the Federation's laws would have any meaning for minds like these? Telzey snapped the library shut with fingers that had begun to tremble, and placed it on the ground. Then she stiffened. In the sensations washing about her, a special excitement rose suddenly, a surge of almost gleeful wildness that choked away her breath. Awareness followed of a pair of malignant crimson eyes fastened on her, moving steadily closer. A kind of nightmare paralysis seized Telzey—they'd turned her over to that red-eyed horror! She sat still, feeling mouse-sized.

Something came out with a crash from a thicket behind her. Her muscles went tight. But it was TT who rubbed a hard head against her shoulder, took another three stiff-legged steps forward, and stopped between Telzey and the bushes on their right, back rigid, neck fur erect, tail twisting.

Expectant silence closed in about them. The circle was waiting. In the greenery on the right something made a slow, heavy stir.

TT's lips peeled back from her teeth. Her head swung toward the motion, ears flattening, transformed to a split, snarling demon-mask. A long shriek ripped from her lungs, raw with fury, blood lust and challenge.

The sound died away. For some seconds the tension about them held; then came a sense of gradual relaxation mingled with a partly amused approval. Telzey was shaking violently. It had been, she was telling herself, a deliberate test . . . not of herself, of course, but of TT. And Tick-Tock had passed with honors. That her nerves had been half ruined in the process would seem a matter of no consequence to this rugged crew. . . .

She realized next that someone here was addressing her personally.

It took a few moments to steady her jittering thoughts enough to gain a more definite impression than that. This speaker, she discovered then, was a member of the circle of whom she hadn't been aware before. The thought-impressions came hard and cold as iron—a personage who was very evidently in the habit of making major decisions and seeing them carried out. The circle, its moment of sport over, was listening with more than a suggestion of deference. Tick-Tock, far from conciliated, green eyes still blazing, nevertheless was settling down to listen, too.

Telzey began to understand.

Her suggestions, Iron Thoughts informed her, might appear without value to a number of foolish minds here, but *he* intended to see they were given a fair trial. Did he perhaps hear, he inquired next of the circle, throwing in a casual but horridly vivid impression of snapping spines and slashed shaggy throats spouting blood, any objection to that?

Dead stillness all around. There was, definitely, no objection! Tick-Tock began to grin like a pleased kitten.

That point having been settled in an orderly manner now, Iron Thoughts went on coldly to Telzey, what specifically did she propose they should do?

Halet's long, pearl-gray sports car showed up above the park trees twenty minutes later. Telzey, face turned down toward the open law library in her lap, watched the car from the corner of her eyes. She was in plain view, sitting beside the lake, apparently absorbed in legal research. Tick-Tock, camouflaged among the bushes thirty feet higher up the bank, had spotted the car an instant before she did and announced the fact with a three-second break in her purring. Neither of them made any other move.

The car was approaching the lake but still a good distance off. Its canopy was down, and Telzey could just make out the heads of three people inside. Delquos, Halet's chauffeur, would be flying the vehicle, while Halet and Dr. Droon looked around for her from the sides. Three hundred yards away, the aircar began a turn to the right. Delquos didn't like his employer much; at a guess, he had just spotted Telzey and was trying to warn her off.

Telzey closed the library and put it down, picked up a handful of pebbles, and began flicking them idly, one at a time, into the water. The aircar vanished to her left.

Three minutes later, she watched its shadow glide across the surface of the lake toward her. Her heart began to thump almost audibly, but she didn't look up. Tick-Tock's purring continued, on its regular, unhurried note. The car came to a stop almost directly overhead. After a couple of seconds, there was a clicking noise. The purring ended abruptly.

Telzey climbed to her feet as Delquos brought the car down to the bank of the lake. The chauffeur grinned ruefully at her. A side door had been opened, and Halet and Dr. Droon stood behind it. Halet watched Telzey with a small smile while the naturalist put the heavy life-detector-and-stun-gun device carefully down on the floorboards.

"If you're looking for Tick-Tock," Telzey said, "she isn't here."

Halet just shook her head sorrowfully.

"There's no use lying to us, dear! Dr. Droon just stunned her."

They found TT collapsed on her side among the shrubs, wearing her natural color. Her eyes were shut; her chest rose and fell in a slow breathing motion. Dr. Droon, looking rather apologetic, pointed out to Telzey that her pet was in no pain, that the stun gun had simply put her comfortably to sleep. He also explained the use of the two sets of webbed paralysis belts which he fastened about TT's legs. The effect of the stun charge would wear off in a few minutes, and contact with the inner surfaces of the energized belts would then keep TT anesthetized and unable to move until the belts were removed. She would, he repeated, be suffering no pain throughout the process.

Telzey didn't comment. She watched Delquos raise TT's limp body above the level of the bushes with a gravity hoist belonging to Dr. Droon, and maneuver her back to the car, the others following. Delquos climbed into the car first, opened the big trunk compartment in the rear. TT was slid inside and the trunk compartment locked.

"Where are you taking her?" Telzey asked sullenly as Delquos lifted the car into the air.

"To the spaceport, dear," Halet said. "Dr. Droon and I both felt it would be better to spare your feelings by not prolonging the matter unnecessarily."

Telzey wrinkled her nose disdainfully, and walked up the aircar to stand behind Delquos' seat. She leaned against the back of the seat for an instant. Her legs felt shaky.

The chauffeur gave her a sober wink from the side.

"That's a dirty trick she's played on you, Miss Telzey!" he murmured. "I tried to warn you."

"I know." Telzey took a deep breath. "Look, Delquos, in just a minute something's going to happen! It'll look dangerous, but it won't be. Don't let it get you nervous . . . right?"

"Huh?" Delquos appeared startled, but kept his voice low. "Just *what's* going to happen?"

"No time to tell you. Remember what I said."

Telzey moved back a few steps from the driver's seat, turned around, said unsteadily, "Halet . . . Dr. Droon—"

Halet had been speaking quietly to Dr. Droon; they both looked up.

"If you don't move, and don't do anything stupid," Telzey said rapidly, "you won't get hurt. If you do . . . well, I don't know! You see, there's another crest cat in the car. . . ." In her mind she added, "Now!"

It was impossible to tell in just what section of the car Iron Thoughts had been lurking. The carpeting near the rear passenger seats seemed to blur for an instant. Then he was there, camouflage dropped, sitting on the floorboards five feet from the naturalist and Halet.

Halet's mouth opened wide; she tried to scream but fainted instead. Dr. Droon's right hand started out quickly toward the big stun-gun device beside his seat. Then he checked himself and sat still, ashen-faced.

Telzey didn't blame him for changing his mind. She felt he must be a remarkably brave man to have moved at all. Iron

Thoughts, twice as broad across the back as Tick-Tock, twice as massively muscled, looked like a devil-beast even to her. His dark-green marbled hide was crisscrossed with old scar patterns; half his tossing crimson crest appeared to have been ripped away. He reached out now in a fluid, silent motion, hooked a paw under the stun gun, and flicked upward. The big instrument rose in an incredibly swift, steep arc eighty feet into the air, various parts flying away from it, before it started curving down toward the treetops below the car. Iron Thoughts lazily swung his head around and looked at Telzey with yellow fire-eyes.

"Miss Telzey! Miss Telzey!" Delquos was muttering behind her. "You're sure it won't . . ."

Telzey swallowed. At the moment, she felt barely mouse-sized again. "Just relax!" she told Delquos in a shaky voice. "He's really quite t-t-t-tame."

Iron Thoughts produced a harsh but not unamiable chuckle in her mind.

The pearl-gray sports car, covered now by its streamlining canopy, drifted down presently to a parking platform outside the suite of offices of Jontarou's Planetary Moderator, on the fourteenth floor of the Shikaris' Club Tower. An attendant waved it on into a vacant slot.

Inside the car, Delquos set the brakes, switched off the engine, asked, "Now what?"

"I think," Telzey said reflectively, "we'd better lock you in the trunk compartment with my aunt and Dr. Droon while I talk to the Moderator."

The chauffeur shrugged. He'd regained most of his aplomb during the unhurried trip across the parklands. Iron Thoughts had done nothing but sit in the center of the car, eyes half shut, looking like instant death enjoying a dignified nap, and occasionally emitting a ripsawing noise which might have been either his style of purring or a snore. And Tick-

Tock, when Delquos peeled the paralysis belts off her legs at Telzey's direction, had greeted him with her usual reserved affability. What the chauffeur was suffering from at the moment was intense curiosity, which Telzey had done nothing to relieve.

"Just as you say, Miss Telzey," he agreed. "I hate to miss whatever you're going to be doing here, but if you *don't* lock me up now, Miss Halet will figure I was helping you and fire me as soon as you let her out."

Telzey nodded, then cocked her head in the direction of the rear compartment. Faint sounds coming through the door indicated that Halet had regained consciousness and was having hysterics.

"You might tell her," Telzey suggested, "that there'll be a grown-up crest cat sitting outside the compartment door." This wasn't true, but neither Delquos nor Halet could know it. "If there's too much racket before I get back, it's likely to irritate him. . . ."

A minute later, she set both car doors on lock and went outside, wishing she were less informally clothed. Sunbriefs and sandals tended to make her look juvenile.

The parking attendant appeared startled when she approached him with Tick-Tock striding alongside.

"They'll never let you into the offices with that thing, miss," he informed her. "Why, it doesn't even have a collar!"

"Don't worry about it," Telzey told him aloofly.

She dropped a two-credit piece she'd taken from Halet's purse into his hand, and continued on toward the building entrance. The attendant squinted after her, trying unsuccessfully to dispel an odd impression that the big catlike animal with the girl was throwing a double shadow.

The Moderator's chief receptionist also had some doubts about TT, and possibly about the sunbriefs, though she seemed impressed when Telzey's identification tag informed her she was speaking to the daughter of Federation Council-woman Jessamine Amberdon.

"You feel you can discuss this . . . emergency . . . only with the Moderator himself, Miss Amberdon?" she repeated.

"Exactly," Telzey said firmly. A buzzer sounded as she spoke. The receptionist excused herself and picked up an earphone. She listened a moment, said blandly, "Yes . . . Of course . . . Yes, I understand," replaced the earphone, and stood up, smiling at Telzey.

"Would you come with me, Miss Amberdon?" she said. "I think the Moderator will see you immediately."

Telzey followed her, chewing thoughtfully at her lip. This was easier than she'd expected—in fact, too easy! Halet's work? Probably. A few comments to the effect of "A highly imaginative child . . . overexcitable," while Halet was arranging to have the Moderator's office authorize Tick-Tock's transfer to the Life Banks, along with the implication that Jessamine Amberdon would appreciate a discreet handling of any disturbance Telzey might create as a result.

It was the sort of notion that would appeal to Halet.

They passed through a series of elegantly equipped offices and hallways, Telzey grasping TT's neck fur in lieu of a leash, their appearance creating a tactfully restrained wave of surprise among secretaries and clerks. And if somebody here and there was troubled by a fleeting, uncanny impression that not one large beast but two seemed to be trailing the Moderator's visitor down the aisles, no mention was made of what could have been only a momentary visual distortion. Finally, a pair of sliding doors opened ahead, and the receptionist ushered Telzey into a large, cool balcony garden on the shaded side of the great building. A tall, gray-haired man stood up from the desk at which he was working, and bowed to Telzey. The receptionist withdrew again.

"My pleasure, Miss Amberdon," Jontarou's Planetary Moderator said, "be seated, please." He studied Tick-Tock with more than casual interest while Telzey was settling herself into a chair, added, "And what may I and my office do for you?"

Telzey hesitated. She'd observed his type on Orado in her mother's circle of acquaintances—a senior diplomat, a man not easy to impress. It was a safe bet that he'd had her brought out to his balcony office only to keep her occupied while Halet was quietly informed where the Amberdon problem child was and requested to come over and take charge.

What she had to tell him now would have sounded rather wild even if presented by a presumably responsible adult. She could provide proof, but until the Moderator was already nearly sold on her story, that would be a very unsafe thing to do. Old Iron Thoughts was backing her up, but if it didn't look as if her plans were likely to succeed, he would be willing to ride herd on his devil's pack just so long. . . .

Better start the ball rolling without any preliminaries, Telzey decided. The Moderator's picture of her must be that of a spoiled, neurotic brat in a stew about the threatened loss of a pet animal. He expected her to start arguing with him immediately about Tick-Tock.

She said, "Do you have a personal interest in keeping the Baluit crest cats from becoming extinct?"

Surprise flickered in his eyes for an instant. Then he smiled.

"I admit I do, Miss Amberdon," he said pleasantly. "I should like to see the species reestablished. I count myself almost uniquely fortunate in having had the opportunity to bag two of the magnificent brutes before disease wiped them out on the planet."

The last seemed a less than fortunate statement just now. Telzey felt a sharp tingle of alarm, then sensed that in the minds which were drawing the meaning of the Moderator's speech from her mind there had been only a brief stir of interest.

She cleared her throat, said, "The point is that they weren't wiped out by disease."

He considered her quizzically, seemed to wonder what she was trying to lead up to. Telzey gathered her courage, plunged on. "Would you like to hear what did happen?"

"I should be much interested, Miss Amberdon," the Moderator said, without change of expression. "But first, if you'll excuse me a moment . . ."

There had been some signal from his desk which Telzey hadn't noticed, because he picked up a small communicator now, said, "Yes?" After a few seconds, he resumed, "That's rather curious, isn't it? . . . Yes, I'd try that. . . . No, that shouldn't be necessary. . . . Yes, please do. Thank you." He replaced the communicator, his face very sober; then, his eyes flicking for an instant to TT, he drew one of the upper desk drawers open a few inches, and turned back to Telzey.

"Now, Miss Amberdon," he said affably, "you were about to say? About these crest cats . . ."

Telzey swallowed. She hadn't heard the other side of the conversation, but she could guess what it had been about. His office had called the guesthouse, had been told by Halet's maid that Halet, the chauffeur, and Dr. Droon were out looking for Miss Telzey and her pet. The Moderator's office had then checked on the sports car's communication number and attempted to call it. And, of course, there had been no response.

To the Moderator, considering what Halet would have told him, it must add up to the grim possibility that the young lunatic he was talking to had let her three-quarters-grown crest cat slaughter her aunt and the two men when they caught up with her! The office would be notifying the police now to conduct an immediate search for the missing aircar.

When it would occur to them to look for it on the Moderator's parking terrace was something Telzey couldn't know. But if Halet and Dr. Droon were released before the Moderator accepted her own version of what had occurred, and the two reported the presence of wild crest cats in Port Nichay, there would be almost no possibility of keeping the situation under control. Somebody was bound to make some idiotic move, and the fat would be in the fire.

Two things might be in her favor. The Moderator seemed to have the sort of steady nerve one would expect in a man who had bagged two Baluit crest cats. The partly opened desk drawer beside him must have a gun in it; apparently he considered that a sufficient precaution against an attack by TT. He wasn't likely to react in a panicky manner. And the mere fact that he suspected Telzey of homicidal tendencies would make him give the closest attention to what she said. Whether he believed her then was another matter, of course.

Slightly encouraged, Telzey began to talk. It did sound like a thoroughly wild story, but the Moderator listened with an appearance of intent interest. When she had told him as much as she felt he could be expected to swallow for a start, he said musingly, "So they weren't wiped out—they went into hiding! Do I understand you to say they did it to avoid being hunted?"

Telzey chewed her lip frowningly before replying. "There's something about that part I don't quite get," she admitted. "Of course I don't quite get either why you'd want to go hunting . . . twice . . . for something that's just as likely to bag you instead!"

"Well, those are, ah, merely the statistical odds," the Moderator explained. "If one has enough confidence, you see—"

"I don't really. But the crest cats seem to have felt the same way—at first. They were getting around one hunter for every cat that got shot. Humans were the most exciting game they'd ever run into.

"But then that ended, and the humans started knocking

them out with stun guns from aircars where they couldn't be got at, and hauling them off while they were helpless. After it had gone on for a while, they decided to keep out of sight.

"But they're still around, thousands and thousands of them! Another thing nobody's known about them is that they weren't only in the Baluit Mountains. There were crest cats scattered all through the big forests along the other side of the continent."

"Very interesting," the Moderator commented. "Very interesting, indeed!" He glanced toward the communicator, then returned his gaze to Telzey, drumming his fingers lightly on the desktop.

She could tell nothing at all from his expression now, but she guessed he was thinking hard. There was supposed to be no native intelligent life in the legal sense on Jontarou, and she had been careful to say nothing so far to make the Baluit cats look like more than rather exceptionally intelligent animals. The next—rather large—question should be how she'd come by such information.

If the Moderator asked her that, Telzey thought, she could feel she'd made a beginning at getting him to buy the whole story.

"Well," he said abruptly, "if the crest cats are not extinct or threatened with extinction, the Life Banks obviously have no claim on your pet." He smiled confidingly at her. "And that's the reason you're here, isn't it?"

"Well, no," Telzey began, dismayed. "I—"

"Oh, it's quite all right, Miss Amberdon! I'll simply rescind the permit which was issued for the purpose. You need feel no further concern about that." He paused. "Now, just one question: Do you happen to know where your aunt is at present?"

Telzey had a dead, sinking feeling. So he hadn't believed a word she said. He'd been stalling her along until the aircar could be found.

She took a deep breath. "You'd better listen to the rest of it."

"Why, is there more?" the Moderator asked politely.

"Yes. The important part! The kind of creatures they are, they wouldn't go into hiding indefinitely just because someone was after them."

Was there a flicker of something beyond watchfulness in his expression? "What would they do, Miss Amberdon?" he asked quietly.

"If they couldn't get at the men in the aircars and couldn't communicate with them"—the flicker again!— "they'd start looking for the place the men came from, wouldn't they? It might take them some years to work their way across the continent and locate us here in Port Nichay. But supposing they did it finally and a few thousand of them are sitting around in the parks down there right now? They could come up the side of these towers as easily as they go up the side of a mountain. And supposing they'd decided that the only way to handle the problem was to clean out the human beings in Port Nichay?"

The Moderator stared at her in silence a few seconds. "You're saying," he observed then, "that they're rational beings—above the Critical I.Q. level."

"Well," Telzey said, "legally they're rational. I checked on that. About as rational as we are, I suppose."

"Would you mind telling me now how you happen to know this?"

"They told me," Telzey said.

He was silent again, studying her face. "You mentioned, Miss Amberdon, that they have been unable to communicate with other human beings. This suggests then that you are a xenotelepath. . . ."

"I am?" Telzey hadn't heard the term before. "If it means that I can tell what the cats are thinking, and they can tell what I'm thinking, I guess that's the word for it." She considered him, decided she had him almost on the ropes, went on quickly.

"I looked up the laws, and told them they could conclude a treaty with the Federation which would establish them as an Affiliated Species . . . and that would settle everything the way they would want it settled, without trouble. Some of them believed me. They decided to wait until I could talk to you. If it works out, fine! If it doesn't"—she felt her voice falter for an instant—"they're going to cut loose fast!"

The Moderator seemed undisturbed. "What am I supposed to do?"

"I told them you'd contact the Council of the Federation on Orado."

"Contact the Council?" he repeated coolly. "With no more proof for this story than your word, Miss Amberdon?"

Telzey felt a quick, angry stirring begin about her, felt her face whiten.

"All right," she said. "I'll give you proof! I'll have to now. But that'll be it. Once they've tipped their hand all the way, you'll have about thirty seconds left to make the right move. I hope you remember that!"

He cleared his throat. "I—"

"NOW!" Telzey said.

Along the walls of the balcony garden, beside the ornamental flower stands, against the edges of the rock pool, the crest cats appeared. Perhaps thirty of them. None quite as physically impressive as Iron Thoughts, who stood closest to the Moderator; but none very far from it. Motionless as rocks, frightening as gargoyles, they waited, eyes glowing with hellish excitement.

"This is *their* council, you see," Telzey heard herself saying.

The Moderator's face had also paled. But he was, after all, an old shikari and a senior diplomat. He took an unhurried look around the circle, said quietly, "Accept my pro-

found apologies for doubting you, Miss Amberdon!'' and
reached for the desk communicator.

Iron Thoughts swung his demon head in Telzey's direction. For an instant, she picked up the mental impression of
a fierce yellow eye closing in an approving wink.

''An open transmitter line to Orado,'' the Moderator was
saying into the communicator. ''The Council. And snap it up!
Some very important visitors are waiting.''

The offices of Jontarou's Planetary Moderator became an
extremely busy and interesting area then. Quite two hours
passed before it occurred to anyone to ask Telzey again
whether she knew where her aunt was at present.

Telzey smote her forehead.

''Forgot all about that!'' she admitted, fishing the sports
car's keys out of the pocket of her sunbriefs. ''They're out on
the parking platform.''

The preliminary treaty arrangements between the Federation
of the Hub and the new Affiliated Species of the Planet of
Jontarou were formally ratified two weeks later, the ceremony
taking place on Jontarou, in the Champagne Hall of the Shikaris' Club.

Telzey was able to follow the event only by news viewer
in her ship cabin, she and Halet being on the return trip to
Orado by then. She wasn't too interested in the treaty's details
—they conformed almost exactly to what she had read out to
Iron Thoughts and his co-chiefs and companions in the park.
It was the smooth bridging of the wide language gap between
the contracting parties by a row of interpreting machines and
a handful of human xenotelepaths which held her attention.

As she switched off the viewer, Halet came wandering in
from the adjoining cabin.

''I was watching it, too!'' Halet observed. She smiled. ''I
was hoping to see dear Tick-Tock.''

Telzey looked over at her. ''Well, TT would hardly be

likely to show up in Port Nichay," she said. "She's having too good a time now finding out what life in the Baluit range is like."

"I suppose so," Halet agreed doubtfully, sitting down on a hassock. "But I'm glad she promised to get in touch with us again in a few years. I'll miss her."

Telzey regarded her aunt with a reflective frown. Halet meant it quite sincerely, of course; she had undergone a profound change of heart during the past two weeks. But Telzey wasn't without some doubts about the actual value of a change of heart brought on by telepathic means. The learning process the crest cats had started in her mind appeared to have continued automatically several days longer than her rugged teachers had really intended; and Telzey had reason to believe that by the end of that time she'd developed associated latent abilities of which the crest cats had never heard. She'd barely begun to get it all sorted out yet, but, as an example, she'd found it remarkably easy to turn Halet's more obnoxious attitudes virtually upside down. It had taken her a couple of days to get the hang of her aunt's personal symbolism, but after that there had been no problem.

She was reasonably certain she'd broken no laws so far, though the sections in the law library covering the use and abuse of psionic abilities were veiled in such intricate and downright obscure phrasing—deliberately, Telzey suspected —that it was really difficult to say what they did mean. But even aside from that, there were a number of arguments in favor of exercising great caution.

Jessamine, for one thing, was bound to start worrying about her sister-in-law's health if Halet turned up on Orado in her present state of mind, even though it would make for a far more agreeable atmosphere in the Amberdon household.

"Halet," Telzey inquired mentally, "do you remember what an all-out stinker you used to be?"

"Of course, dear," Halet said aloud. "I can hardly wait to tell dear Jessamine how much I regret the many times I—"

"Well," Telzey went on, still verbalizing it silently, "I think you'd really enjoy life more if you were, let's say, about halfway between your old nasty self and the sort of sickening-good kind you are now."

"Why, Telzey!" Halet cried out with dopey amiability. "What a delightful idea!"

"Let's try it," Telzey said.

There was silence in the cabin for some twenty minutes then, while she went painstakingly about remolding a number of Halet's character traits for the second time. She still felt some misgiving about it; but if it became necessary, she probably could always restore the old Halet *in toto.*

These, she told herself, definitely were powers one should treat with respect. Better rattle through law school first; then, with that out of the way, she could start hunting around to see who in the Federation was qualified to instruct a genius-level novice in the proper handling of psionics.

Q. Patrick

THE FAT CAT

The marines found her when they finally captured the old mission house at Fufa. After two days of relentless pounding, they hadn't expected to find anything alive there—least of all a fat cat.

And she was a very fat cat, sandy as a Scotsman, with enormous agate eyes and a fat amiable face. She sat there on the mat—or rather what was left of the mat—in front of what had been the mission porch, licking her paws as placidly as if the shell-blasted jungle were a summer lawn in New Jersey.

One of the men, remembering his childhood primer, quoted: "The fat cat sat on the mat."

The other men laughed; not that the remark was really funny, but laughter broke the tension and expressed their relief at having at last reached their objective, after two days of bitter fighting.

The fat cat, still sitting on the mat, smiled at them, as if to show she didn't mind the joke being on her. Then she saw Corporal Randy Jones, and for some reason known only to herself ran toward him as though he were her long-lost master. With a refrigerator purr, she weaved in and out of his muddy legs.

Everyone laughed again as Randy picked her up and pushed his ugly face against the sleek fur. It was funny to see any living thing show a preference for the dour, solitary Randy.

A sergeant flicked his fingers. "Kitty. Come here. We'll make you B Company mascot."

But the cat, perched on Randy's shoulder like a queen on her throne, merely smiled down majestically as much as to say: "You can be my subjects if you like. But this is my man —my royal consort."

And never for a second did she swerve from her devotion. She lived with Randy, slept with him, ate only food provided by him. Almost every man in Company B tried to seduce her with caresses and morsels of canned ration, but all advances were met with a yawn of contempt.

For Randy this new love was ecstasy. He guarded her with the possessive tenderness of a mother. He combed her fur sleek; he almost starved himself to maintain her fatness. And all the time there was a strange wonder in him. The homeliest and ungainliest of ten in a West Virginia mining family, he had never before aroused affection in man or woman. No one had counted for him until the fat cat.

Randy's felicity, however, was short-lived. In a few days B Company was selected to carry out a flanking movement to surprise and possibly capture the enemy's headquarters, known to be twenty miles away through dense, sniper-infested jungle. The going would be rugged. Each man would carry his own supply of food and water, and sleep in foxholes with no support from the base.

The C.O. was definite about the fat cat: the stricken Randy was informed that the presence of a cat would seriously endanger the safety of the whole company. If it were seen following him, it would be shot on sight. Just before their scheduled departure, Randy carried the fat cat over to the mess of Company H, where she was enthusiastically received by an equally fat cook. Randy could not bring himself to look back at the reproachful stare which he knew would be in the cat's agate eyes.

But all through that first day of perilous jungle travel, the thought of the cat's stare haunted him, and he was prey to all the heartache of parting; in leaving the cat, he had left behind wife, mother, and child.

Darkness, like an immense black parachute, had descended hours ago on the jungle, when Randy was awakened from exhausted sleep. Something soft and warm was brushing his cheek; and his foxhole resounded to a symphony of purring. He stretched out an incredulous hand, but this was no dream. Real and solid, the cat was curled in a contented ball at his shoulder.

His first rush of pleasure was chilled as he remembered his C.O.'s words. The cat, spurning the blandishments of H Company's cuisine, had followed him through miles of treacherous jungle, only to face death the moment daylight revealed her presence. Randy was in an agony of uncertainty. To carry her back to the base would be desertion. To beat and drive her away was beyond the power of his simple nature.

The cat nuzzled his face again and breathed a mournful meow. She was hungry, of course, after her desperate trek. Suddenly Randy saw what he must do. If he could bring himself not to feed her, hunger would surely drive her back to the sanctuary of the cook.

She meowed again. He shushed her and gave her a half-hearted slap. "Ain't got nothing for you, honey. Scram. Go home. Scat."

To his mingled pleasure and disappointment, she leaped silently out of the foxhole. When morning came there was no sign of her.

As B Company inched its furtive advance through the dense undergrowth, Randy felt the visit from the cat must have been a dream. But on the third night it came again. It brushed against his cheek and daintily took his ear in its teeth. When it meowed, the sound was still soft and cautious, but held a pitiful quaver of beseechment which cut through Randy like a Japanese bayonet.

On its first visit, Randy had not seen the cat, but tonight some impulse made him reach for his flashlight. Holding it carefully downward, he turned it on. What he saw was the ultimate ordeal. The fat cat was fat no longer. Her body sagged; her sleek fur was matted and mud-stained, her paws torn and bloody. But it was the eyes, blinking up at him, that were the worst. There was no hint of reproach in them, only an expression of infinite trust and pleading.

Forgetting everything but those eyes, Randy tugged out one of his few remaining cans of ration. At the sight of it, the cat weakly licked its lips. Randy moved to open the can. Then the realization that he would be signing the cat's death warrant surged over him. And, because the pent-up emotion in him had to have some outlet, it turned into unreasoning anger against this animal whose suffering had become more than he could bear. "Scat," he hissed. But the cat did not move.

He lashed out at her with the heavy flashlight. For a second she lay motionless under the blow. Then with a little moan she fled.

The next night she did not come back and Randy did not sleep.

On the fifth day they reached really dangerous territory. Randy and another marine, Joe, were sent forward to scout for the Japanese command headquarters. Suddenly, weaving through the jungle, they came upon it.

A profound silence hung over the glade, with its two hastily erected shacks. Peering through the dense foliage, they saw traces of recent evacuation—waste paper scattered on the grass, a pile of fresh garbage, a Japanese army shirt flapping on a tree. Outside one of the shacks, under an awning, stretched a rough table strewn with the remains of a meal. "They must have got wind of us and scrammed," breathed Joe.

Randy edged forward—then froze as something stirred in the long grasses near the door of the first shack. As he watched, the once fat cat hobbled out into the sunlight.

A sense of heightened danger warred with Randy's pride that she had not abandoned him. Stiff with suspense, he watched it disappear into the shack. Soon it padded out.

"No Japs," said Joe. "That cat'd have raised 'em sure as shooting."

He started boldly into the glade. "Hey, Randy, there's a whole chicken on that table. Chicken's going to taste good after K rations."

He broke off, for the cat had seen the chicken too, and with pitiful clumsiness had leaped onto the table. With an angry yell Joe stooped for a rock and threw it.

Indignation blazed in Randy. He'd starved and spurned the cat, and yet she'd followed him with blind devotion. The chicken, surely, should be her reward. In his slow, simple mind it seemed the most important thing in the world for his beloved to have her fair share of the booty.

The cat, seeing the rock coming, lumbered off the table, just in time, for the rock struck the chicken squarely, knocking it off its plate.

Randy leaped into the clearing. As he did so, a deafening explosion made him drop to the ground. A few seconds later, when he raised himself, there was no table, no shack, nothing but a blazing wreckage of wood.

Dazedly he heard Joe's voice: "Booby trap under that chicken. Gee, if that cat hadn't jumped for it, I wouldn't have hurled the rock; we'd have grabbed it ourselves—and we'd be in heaven now." His voice dropped to an awed whisper. "That cat, I guess it's blown to hell. . . . But it saved our lives." Randy couldn't speak. There was a constriction in his throat. He lay there, feeling more desolate than he'd ever felt in his life before.

Then from behind came a contented purr.

He spun round. Freakishly, the explosion had hurled a crude rush mat out of the shack. It had come to rest on the grass behind him.

And, seated serenely on the mat, the cat was smiling at him.

Henry Slesar

MY FATHER, THE CAT

My mother was a lovely, delicate woman from the coast of Brittany, who was miserable sleeping on less than three mattresses, and who, it is said, was once injured by a falling leaf in her garden. My grandfather, a descendant of the French nobility whose family had ridden the tumbrils of the Revolution, tended her fragile body and spirit with the same loving care given rare, brief-blooming flowers. You may imagine from this his attitude concerning marriage. He lived in terror of the vulgar, heavy-handed man who would one day win my mother's heart, and at last, this persistent dread killed him. His concern was unnecessary, however, for my mother chose a suitor who was as free of mundane brutality as a husband could be. Her choice was Dauphin, a remarkable white cat which strayed onto the estate shortly after his death.

Dauphin was an unusually large Angora, and his ability to speak in cultured French, English, and Italian was sufficient to cause my mother to adopt him as a household pet. It did not take long for her to realize that Dauphin deserved a higher status, and he became her friend, protector, and confidant. He never spoke of his origin, nor where he had acquired the classical education which made him such an entertaining companion. After two years, it was easy for my mother, an unworldly woman at best, to forget the dissimilarity in their species. In fact, she was convinced that Dauphin was an enchanted prince, and Dauphin, in consideration of her illusions, never dissuaded her. At last, they were married by an understanding clergyman of the locale, who solemnly filled in the marriage application with the name of M. Edouard Dauphin.

I, Etienne Dauphin, am their son.

To be candid, I am a handsome youth, not unlike my mother in the delicacy of my features. My father's heritage is evident in my large, feline eyes, and in my slight body and quick movements. My mother's death, when I was four, left me in the charge of my father and his coterie of loyal servants, and I could not have wished for a finer upbringing. It is to my father's patient tutoring that I owe whatever graces I now possess. It was my father, the cat, whose gentle paws guided me to the treasure houses of literature, art, and music, whose whiskers bristled with pleasure at a goose well cooked, at a meal well served, at a wine well chosen. How many happy hours we shared! He knew more of life and the humanities, my father, the cat, than any human I have met in all my twenty-three years.

Until the age of eighteen, my education was his personal

challenge. Then, it was his desire to send me into the world outside the gates. He chose for me a university in America, for he was deeply fond of what he called "that great raw country," where he believed my feline qualities might be tempered by the aggressiveness of the rough-coated barking dogs I would be sure to meet.

I must confess to a certain amount of unhappiness in my early American years, torn as I was from the comforts of the estate and the wisdom of my father, the cat. But I became adapted, and even upon my graduation from the university, sought and held employment in a metropolitan art museum. It was there I met Joanna, the young woman I intended to make my bride.

Joanna was a product of the great American Southwest, the daughter of a cattle raiser. There was a blooming vitality in her face and her body, a lustiness born of open skies and desert. Her hair was not the gold of antiquity; it was new gold, freshly mined from the black rock. Her eyes were not like old-world diamonds; their sparkle was that of sunlight on a cascading river. Her figure was bold, an open declaration of her sex.

She was, perhaps, an unusual choice for the son of a fairylike mother and an Angora cat. But from the first meeting of our eyes, I knew that I would someday bring Joanna to my father's estate to present her as my fiancée.

I approached that occasion with understandable trepidation. My father had been explicit in his advice before I departed for America, but on no point had he been more emphatic than secrecy concerning himself. He assured me that revelation of my paternity would bring ridicule and unhappiness upon me. The advice was sound, of course, and not even Joanna knew that our journey's end would bring us to the estate of a large, cultured, and conversing cat. I had deliberately fostered the impression that I was orphaned, believing that the proper place for revealing the truth was the atmosphere of my father's home in France. I was certain that Joanna would accept her father-in-law without distress. Indeed, hadn't nearly a score of human servants remained devoted to their feline master for almost a generation?

We had agreed to be wed on the first of June, and on May the fourth, enplaned in New York for Paris. We were met at Orly Field by François, my father's solemn manservant, who had been delegated not so much as escort as he was chaperone, my father having retained much of the Old World proprieties. It was a long trip by automobile to our estate in Brittany, and I must admit to a brooding silence throughout the drive which frankly puzzled Joanna.

However, when the great stone fortress that was our home came within view, my fears and doubts were quickly dispelled. Joanna, like so many Americans, was thrilled at the aura of venerability and royal custom surrounding the estate. François placed her in charge of Madame Jolinet, who clapped her plump old hands with delight at the sight of her fresh blond beauty, and chattered and clucked like a mother hen as she led Joanna to her room on the second floor. As for myself, I had one immediate wish: to see my father, the cat.

He greeted me in the library, where he had been anxiously awaiting our arrival, curled up in his favorite chair by the fireside, a wide-mouthed goblet of Cognac by his side. As I entered the room, he lifted a paw formally, but then his reserve was dissolved by the emotion of our reunion, and he licked my face in unashamed joy.

François refreshed his glass, and poured another for me, and we toasted each other's well-being.

"To you, *mon purr*," I said, using the affectionate name of my childhood memory.

"To Joanna," my father said. He smacked his lips over the Cognac, and wiped his whiskers gravely. "And where is this paragon?"

"With Madame Jolinet. She will be down shortly."

"And you have told her everything?"

I blushed. "No, *mon purr,* I have not. I thought it best to wait until we were home. She is a wonderful woman," I added impulsively. "She will not be—"

"Horrified?" my father said. "What makes you so certain, my son?"

"Because she is a woman of great heart," I said stoutly. "She was educated at a fine college for women in Eastern America. Her ancestors were rugged people, given to legend and folklore. She is a warm, human person—"

"Human," my father sighed, and his tail swished. "You are expecting too much of your beloved, Etienne. Even a woman of the finest character may be dismayed in this situation."

"But my mother—"

"Your mother was an exception, a changeling of the Fairies. You must not look for your mother's soul in Joanna's eyes." He jumped from his chair, and came toward me, resting his paw upon my knee. "I am glad you have not spoken of me, Etienne. Now you must keep your silence forever."

I was shocked. I reached down and touched my father's silky fur, saddened by the look of his age in his gray, gold-flecked eyes, and by the tinge of yellow in his white coat.

"No, *mon purr,*" I said. "Joanna must know the truth. Joanna must know how proud I am to be the son of Edouard Dauphin."

"Then you will lose her."

"Never! That cannot happen!"

My father walked stiffly to the fireplace, staring into the gray ashes. "Ring for François," he said. "Let him build the fire. I am cold, Etienne."

I walked to the cord and pulled it. My father turned to me and said: "You must wait, my son. At dinner this evening, perhaps. Do not speak of me until then."

"Very well, Father."

When I left the library, I encountered Joanna at the head of the stairway, and she spoke to me excitedly.

"Oh, Etienne! What a *beautiful* old house. I know I will love it! May we see the rest?"

"Of course," I said.

"You look troubled. Is something wrong?"

"No, no. I was thinking how lovely you are."

We embraced, and her warm full body against mine confirmed my conviction that we should never be parted. She put her arm in mine, and we strolled through the great rooms of the house. She was ecstatic at their size and elegance, exclaiming over the carpeting, the gnarled furniture, the ancient silver and pewter, the gallery of family paintings. When she came upon an early portrait of my mother, her eyes misted.

"She was lovely," Joanna said. "Like a princess! And what of your father? Is there no portrait of him?"

"No," I said hurriedly. "No portrait." I had spoken my first lie to Joanna, for there was a painting, half-completed, which my mother had begun in the last year of her life. It was a whispering little watercolor, and Joanna discovered it, to my consternation.

"What a magnificent cat!" she said. "Was it a pet?"

"It is Dauphin," I said nervously.

She laughed. "He has your eyes, Etienne."

"Joanna, I must tell you something—"

"And this ferocious gentleman with the mustaches? Who is he?"

"My grandfather. Joanna, you must listen—"

François, who had been following our inspection tour at shadow's-length, interrupted. I suspected that his timing was no mere coincidence.

"We will be serving dinner at seven-thirty," he said. "If the lady would care to dress . . ."

"Of course," Joanna said. "Will you excuse me, Etienne?"

I bowed to her, and she was gone.

At fifteen minutes to the appointed dining time, I was ready, and hastened below to talk once more with my father. He was in the dining room, instructing the servants as to the placement of the silver and accessories. My father was proud of the excellence of his table, and took all his meals in the splendid manner. His appreciation of food and wine was unsurpassed in my experience, and it had always been the greatest of pleasures for me to watch him at table, stalking across the damask and dipping delicately into the silver dishes prepared for him. He pretended to be too busy with his dinner preparations to engage me in conversation, but I insisted.

"I must talk to you," I said. "We must decide together how to do this."

"It will not be easy," he answered with a twinkle. "Consider Joanna's view. A cat as large and as old as myself is cause enough for comment. A cat that speaks is alarming. A cat that dines at table with the household is shocking. And a cat whom you must introduce as your—"

"Stop it!" I cried. "Joanna must know the truth. You must help me reveal it to her."

"Then you will not heed my advice?"

"In all things but this. Our marriage can never be happy unless she accepts you for what you are."

"And if there is no marriage?"

I would not admit to this possibility. Joanna was mine; nothing could alter that. The look of pain and bewilderment in my eyes must have been evident to my father, for he touched my arm gently with his paw and said:

"I will help you, Etienne. You must give me your trust."

"Always!"

"Then come to dinner with Joanna and explain nothing. Wait for me to appear."

I grasped his paw and raised it to my lips. "Thank you, Father!"

He turned to François, and snapped: "You have my in-structions?"

"Yes, sir," the servant replied.

"Then all is ready. I shall return to my room now, Etienne. You may bring your fiancée to dine."

I hastened up the stairway, and found Joanna ready, strik-ingly beautiful in shimmering white satin. Together, we de-scended the grand staircase and entered the room.

Her eyes shone at the magnificence of the service set upon the table, at the soldierly array of fine wines, some of them already poured into their proper glasses for my father's enjoyment: Haut Médoc, from St. Estèphe, authentic Chablis, Epernay Champagne, and an American import from the Napa Valley of which he was fond. I waited expectantly for his appearance as we sipped our aperitif, while Joanna chatted about innocuous matters, with no idea of the tormented state I was in.

At eight o'clock, my father had not yet made his appear-ance, and I grew ever more distraught as François signaled for the serving of the *bouillon au madère.* Had he changed his mind? Would I be left to explain my status without his help? I hadn't realized until this moment how difficult a task I had allotted for myself, and the fear of losing Joanna was terrible within me. The soup was flat and tasteless on my tongue, and the misery in my manner was too apparent for Joanna to miss.

"What is it, Etienne?" she said. "You've been so morose all day. Can't you tell me what's wrong?"

"No, it's nothing. It's just—" I let the impulse take pos-session of my speech. "Joanna, there's something I should tell you. About my mother, and my father—"

"Ahem," François said.

He turned to the doorway, and our glances followed his.

"Oh, Etienne!" Joanna cried, in a voice ringing with delight.

It was my father, the cat, watching us with his gray,

gold-flecked eyes. He approached the dining table, regarding Joanna with timidity and caution.

"It's the cat in the painting!" Joanna said. "You didn't tell me he was here, Etienne. He's beautiful!"

"Joanna, this is—"

"Dauphin! I would have known him anywhere. Here, Dauphin! Here, kitty, kitty, kitty!"

Slowly, my father approached her outstretched hand, and allowed her to scratch the thick fur on the back of his neck.

"Aren't you the pretty little pussy! Aren't you the sweetest little thing!"

"Joanna!"

She lifted my father by the haunches, and held him in her lap, stroking his fur and cooing the silly little words that women address to their pets. The sight pained and confused me, and I sought to find an opening word that would allow me to explain, yet hoping all the time that my father would himself provide the answer.

Then my father spoke.

"Meow," he said.

"Are you hungry?" Joanna asked solicitously. "Is the little pussy hungry?"

"Meow," my father said, and I believe my heart broke then and there. He leaped from her lap and padded across the room. I watched him through blurred eyes as he followed François to the corner, where the servant had placed a shallow bowl of milk. He lapped at it eagerly, until the last white drop was gone. Then he yawned and stretched, and trotted back to the doorway, with one fleeting glance in my direction that spoke articulately of what I must do next.

"What a wonderful animal," Joanna said.

"Yes," I answered. "He was my mother's favorite."

Lilian Jackson Braun

THE SIN OF
MADAME PHLOI

From the very beginning Madame Phloi felt an instinctive distaste for the man who moved into the apartment next door. He was fat, and his trouser cuffs had the unsavory odor of fire hydrant.

They met for the first time in the decrepit elevator as it lurched up to the tenth floor of the old building, once fashionable but now coming apart at the seams. Madame Phloi had been out for a stroll in the city park, chewing city grass and chasing faded butterflies, and as she and her companion stepped on the elevator for the slow ride upward, the car was already half filled with the new neighbor.

The fat man and the Madame presented a contrast that was not unusual in this apartment house, which had a brilliant past and no future. He was bulky, uncouth, sloppily attired. Madame Phloi was a long-legged, blue-eyed aristocrat whose creamy fawn coat shaded into brown at the extremities.

The Madame deplored fat men. They had no laps, and of what use is a lapless human? Nevertheless, she gave him the common courtesy of a sniff at his trouser cuffs and immediately backed away, twitching her nose and breathing through the mouth.

"*Get* that cat away from me," the fat man roared, stamping his feet thunderously at Madame Phloi. Her companion pulled on the leash, although there was no need—the Madame with one backward leap had retreated to a safe corner of the elevator, which shuddered and continued its groaning ascent.

"Don't you like animals?" asked the gentle voice at the other end of the leash.

"Filthy, sneaky beasts," the fat man said with a snarl. "Last place I lived, some lousy cat got in my room and et my parakeet."

"I'm sorry to hear that. Very sorry. But you don't need to worry about Madame Phloi and Thapthim. They never leave the apartment except on a leash."

"You got *two?* That's just fine, that is! Keep 'em away from me, or I'll break their rotten necks. I ain't wrung a cat's neck since I was fourteen, but I remember how."

And with the long black box he was carrying, the fat man lunged at the impeccable Madame Phloi, who sat in her corner, flat-eared and tense. Her fur bristled, and she tried to dart away. Even when her companion picked her up in protective arms, Madame Phloi's body was taut and trembling.

Not until she was safely home in her modest but well-cushioned apartment did she relax. She walked stiff-legged to the sunny spot on the carpet where Thapthim was sleeping and licked the top of his head. Then she had a complete bath herself—to rid her coat of the fat man's odor. Thapthim did not wake.

This drowsy, unambitious, amiable creature—her son—was a puzzle to Madame Phloi, who was sensitive and spirited herself. She didn't try to understand him; she merely loved him. She spent hours washing his paws and breast and other parts he could easily have reached with his own tongue. At dinnertime she chewed slowly so there would be something left on her plate for his dessert, and he always gobbled the extra portion hungrily. And when he slept, which was most of the time, she kept watch by his side, sitting with a tall, regal posture until she swayed with weariness. Then she made herself into a small bundle and dozed with one eye open.

Thapthim was lovable, to be sure. He appealed to other cats, large and small dogs, people, and even ailurophobes in a limited way. He had a face like a beautiful flower and large blue eyes, tender and trusting. Ever since he was a kitten, he had been willing to purr at the touch of a hand—any hand. Eventually he became so agreeable that he purred if anyone looked at him across the room. What's more, he came when called; he gratefully devoured whatever was served on his dinner plate; and when he was told to get down, he got down.

His wise parent disapproved this uncatly conduct; it indicated a certain lack of character, and no good would come of it. By her own example she tried to guide him. When dinner was served, she gave the plate a haughty sniff and walked away, no matter how tempting the dish. That was the way it was done by any self-respecting feline. In a minute or two she returned and condescended to dine, but never with open enthusiasm.

Furthermore, when human hands reached out, the catly thing was to bound away, lead them a chase, flirt a little before allowing oneself to be caught and cuddled. Thapthim, sorry to say, greeted any friendly overture by rolling over, purring, and looking soulful.

From an early age he had known the rules of the apartment:

> *No sleeping in a cupboard with the pots and pans.*
> *Sitting on the table with the inkwell is permissible.*
> *Sitting on the table with the coffeepot is never allowed.*

The sad truth was that Thapthim obeyed these rules. Madame Phloi, on the other hand, knew that a rule was a challenge, and it was a matter of integrity to violate it. To obey was to sacrifice one's dignity. . . . It seemed that her son would never learn the true values in life.

To be sure, Thapthim was adored for his good nature in the human world of inkwells and coffeepots. But Madame Phloi was equally adored—and for the correct reasons. She was respected for her independence, admired for her clever methods of getting her own way, and loved for the cowlick on her white breast, the kink in her tail, and the squint in her delphinium-blue eyes. She was more truly Siamese than her son. Her face was small and perky. By cocking her head and staring with heart-melting eyes, slightly crossed, she could charm a porterhouse steak out from under a knife and fork.

Until the fat man and his black box moved in next door, Madame Phloi had never known an unfriendly soul. She had two companions in her tenth-floor apartment—genial creatures without names who came and went a good deal. One was an easy mark for between-meal snacks; a tap on his ankle always produced a spoonful of cottage cheese. The other served as a hot-water bottle on cold nights and punctually obliged whenever the Madame wished to have her underside stroked or her cheekbones massaged. This second one also murmured compliments in a gentle voice that made one squeeze one's eyes in pleasure.

Life was not all love and cottage cheese, however. Madame Phloi had her regular work. She was official watcher and listener for the household.

There were six windows that needed watching, for a wide ledge ran around the building flush with the tenth-floor windowsills, and this was a promenade for pigeons. They strutted, searched their feathers, and ignored the Madame, who sat on the sill and watched them dispassionately but thoroughly through the window screen.

While watching was a daytime job, listening was done after dark and required greater concentration. Madame Phloi listened for noises in the walls. She heard termites chewing, pipes sweating, and sometimes the ancient plaster cracking; but mostly she listened to the ghosts of generations of deceased mice.

One evening, shortly after the incident in the elevator, Madame Phloi was listening, Thapthim was asleep, and the other two were quietly turning pages of books, when a strange and horrendous sound came from the wall. The Madame's ears flicked to attention, then flattened against her head.

An interminable screech was coming out of that wall, like nothing the Madame had ever heard before. It chilled the blood and tortured the eardrums. So painful was the shrillness that Madame Phloi threw back her head and complained with a piercing howl of her own. The strident din even waked Thapthim. He looked about in alarm, shook his head wildly, and clawed at his ears to get rid of the offending noise.

The others heard it, too.

"Listen to that!" said the one with the gentle voice.

"It must be that new man next door," said the other. "It's incredible."

"I can't imagine anyone so crude producing anything so exquisite. Is it Prokofiev he's playing?"

"No, I think it's Bartók."

"He was carrying his violin in the elevator today. He tried to hit Phloi with it."

"He's a nut. . . . Look at the cats—apparently they don't care for violin."

Madame Phloi and Thapthim, bounding from the room, collided with each other as they rushed to hide under the bed.

That was not the only kind of noise which emanated from the adjoining apartment in those upsetting days after the fat man moved in. The following evening, when Madame Phloi walked into the living room to commence her listening, she heard a fluttering sound dimly through the wall, accompanied by highly conversational chirping. This was agreeable music, and she settled down on the sofa to enjoy it, tucking her brown paws neatly under her creamy body.

Her contentment was soon disturbed, however, when the fat man's voice burst through the wall like thunder.

"Look what you done, you dirty skunk!" he bellowed. "Right in my fiddle! Get back in your cage before I brain you."

There was a frantic beating of wings.

"*Get* down off that window, or I'll bash your head in."

This threat brought only a torrent of chirping.

"Shut up, you stupid cluck! Shut up and get back in that cage, or I'll . . ."

There was a splintering crash, and after that all was quiet except for an occasional pitiful "Peep!"

Madame Phloi was fascinated. In fact, when she resumed her watching the next day, pigeons seemed rather insipid entertainment. She had waked the family that morning in her usual way—by staring intently at their foreheads as they slept. Then she and Thapthim had a game of hockey in the bathtub with a Ping-Pong ball, followed by a dish of mackerel, and after breakfast the Madame took up her post at the living-room window. Everyone had left for the day but not before opening the window and placing a small cushion on the chilly marble sill.

There she sat—Madame Phloi—a small but alert package of fur, sniffing the welcome summer air, seeing all, and knowing all. She knew, for example, that the person who was at that moment walking down the tenth-floor hallway, wearing old tennis shoes and limping slightly, would halt at the door of her apartment, set down his pail, and let himself in with a passkey.

Indeed, she hardly bothered to turn her head when the window washer entered. He was one of her regular court of admirers. His odor was friendly, although it suggested damp basements and floor mops, and he talked sensibly—indulging in none of that falsetto foolishness with which some people insulted the Madame's intelligence.

"Hop down, kitty," he said in a musical voice. "Charlie's gotta take out that screen. See, I brought you some cheese."

He held out a modest offering of rat cheese, and Madame Phloi investigated it. Unfortunately, it was the wrong variety, and she shook one fastidious paw at it.

"Mighty fussy cat," Charlie laughed. "Well, now, you set there and watch Charlie clean this here window. Don't you go jumpin' out on the ledge, because Charlie ain't runnin' after you. No sir! That old ledge, she's startin' to crumble. Some day them pigeons'll stamp their feet hard, and down she goes! . . . Hey, lookit the broken glass out here. Somebody busted a window."

Charlie sat on the marble sill and pulled the upper sash down in his lap, and while Madame Phloi followed his movements carefully, Thapthim sauntered into the room, yawning and stretching, and swallowed the cheese.

"Now Charlie puts the screen back in, and you two guys can watch them crazy pigeons some more. This screen, she's comin' apart, too. Whole buildin' seems to be crackin' up."

Remembering to replace the cushion on the cool, hard sill, he then went on to clean the next window, and the Madame resumed her post, sitting on the very edge of the cushion so that Thapthim could have most of it.

The pigeons were late that morning, probably frightened away by the window washer. It was while Madame Phloi patiently waited for the first visitor to skim in on a blue-gray wing that she noticed the tiny opening in the screen. Every aperture, no matter how small, was a temptation; she had to prove she could wriggle through any tight space, whether there was a good reason or not.

She waited until Charlie had limped out of the apartment before she began pushing at the screen with her nose, first gingerly and then stubbornly. Inch by inch the rusted mesh ripped away from the frame until the whole corner formed a loose flap, and Madame Phloi slithered through—nose and ears, slender shoulders, dainty Queen Anne forefeet, svelte torso, lean flanks, hind legs like steel springs, and finally proud brown tail. For the first time in her life she found herself on the pigeon promenade. She gave a delicious shudder.

Inside the screen the lethargic Thapthim, jolted by this strange turn of affairs, watched his daring parent with a quarter inch of his pink tongue hanging out. They touched noses briefly through the screen, and the Madame proceeded to explore. She advanced cautiously and with mincing step, for the pigeons had not been tidy in their habits.

The ledge was about two feet wide. To its edge Madame Phloi moved warily, nose down and tail high. Ten stories below there were moving objects but nothing of interest, she decided. Walking daintily along the extreme edge to avoid the broken glass, she ventured in the direction of the fat man's apartment, impelled by some half-forgotten curiosity.

His window stood open and unscreened, and Madame Phloi peered in politely. There, sprawled on the floor, lay the fat man himself, snorting and heaving his immense paunch in a kind of rhythm. It always alarmed her to see a human on the floor, which she considered feline domain. She licked her nose apprehensively and stared at him with enormous eyes, one iris hypnotically off-center. In a dark corner of the room something fluttered and squawked, and the fat man waked.

"SHcrrff! *Get* out of here!" he shouted, struggling to his feet.

In three leaps Madame Phloi crossed the ledge back to her own window and pushed through the screen to safety. Looking back to see if the fat man might be chasing her and being reassured that he wasn't, she washed Thapthim's ears and her own paws and sat down to wait for pigeons.

Like any normal cat, Madame Phloi lived by the Rule of Three. She resisted every innovation three times before accepting it, tackled an obstacle three times before giving up, and tried each new activity three times before tiring of it. Consequently she made two more sallies to the pigeon promenade and eventually convinced Thapthim to join her.

Together they peered over the edge at the world below. The sense of freedom was intoxicating. Recklessly Thapthim made a leap at a low-flying pigeon and landed on his mother's back. She cuffed his ear in retaliation. He poked her nose. They grappled and rolled over and over on the ledge, oblivious of the long drop below them, taking playful nips of each other's hide and snarling guttural expressions of glee.

Suddenly and instinctively Madame Phloi scrambled to her feet and crouched in a defensive position. The fat man was leaning from his window.

"Here, kitty, kitty," he was saying in one of those despised falsetto voices, offering some tidbit in a saucer. The Madame froze, but Thapthim turned his beautiful trusting eyes on the stranger and advanced along the ledge. Purring and waving his tail cordially, he walked into the trap. It all happened in a matter of seconds: the saucer was withdrawn, and a long black box was swung at Thapthim like a ball bat, sweeping him off the ledge and into space. He was silent as he fell.

When the family came home, laughing and chattering, with their arms full of packages, they knew at once something was amiss. No one greeted them at the door. Madame Phloi hunched moodily on the windowsill staring at a hole in the screen, and Thapthim was not to be found.

"Look at the screen!" cried the gentle voice.

"I'll bet he got out on the ledge."

"Can you lean out and look? Be careful."

"You hold Phloi."

"Do you see him?"

"Not a sign of him! There's a lot of glass scattered around, and the window's broken next door."

"Do you suppose that man . . . ? I feel sick."

"Don't worry, dear. We'll find him. . . . There's the doorbell! Maybe someone's bringing him home."

It was Charlie standing at the door. He fidgeted uncomfortably. " 'Scuse me, folks," he said. "You missin' one of your kitties?"

"Yes! Have you found him?"

"Poor little guy," said Charlie. "Found him lyin' right under your windows—where the bushes is thick."

"He's dead!" the gentle one moaned.

"Yes, ma'am. That's a long way down."

"Where is he now?"

"I got him down in the basement, ma'am. I'll take care of him real nice. I don't think you'd want to see the poor guy."

Still Madame Phloi stared at the hole in the screen and waited for Thapthim. From time to time she checked the other windows, just to be sure. As time passed and he did not return, she looked behind the radiators and under the bed. She pried open the cupboard door where the pots and pans were stored. She tried to burrow her way into the closet. She sniffed all around the front door. Finally she stood in the middle of the living room and called loudly in a high-pitched, wailing voice.

Later that evening Charlie paid another visit to the apartment.

"Only wanted to tell you, ma'am, how nice I took care of him," he said. "I got a box that was just the right size. A white box, it was. And I wrapped him up in a piece of old blue curtain. The color looked real pretty with his fur. And I buried the little guy right under your window behind the bushes."

And still the Madame searched, returning again and again to watch the ledge from which Thapthim had disappeared. She scorned food. She rebuffed any attempts at consolation. And all night she sat wide-eyed and waiting in the dark.

The living-room window was now tightly closed, but the following day the Madame—after she was left by herself in the lonely apartment—went to work on the bedroom screens. One was new and hopeless, but the second screen was slightly corroded, and she was soon nosing through a slit that lengthened as she struggled out onto the ledge.

Picking her way through the broken glass, she approached the spot where Thapthim had vanished. And then it all happened again. There he was—the fat man—reaching forth with a saucer.

"Here, kitty, kitty."

Madame Phloi hunched down and backed away.

"Kitty want some milk?" It was that ugly falsetto, but she didn't run home this time. She crouched there on the ledge, a few inches out of reach.

"Nice kitty. Nice kitty."

Madame Phloi crept with caution toward the saucer in the outstretched fist, and stealthily the fat man extended another hand, snapping his fingers as one would call a dog.

The Madame retreated diagonally—half toward home and half toward the dangerous brink.

"Here, kitty. Here, kitty," he cooed, leaning farther out. But muttering, he said, "You dirty sneak! I'll get you if it's the last thing I ever do. Comin' after my bird, weren't you?"

Madame Phloi recognized danger with all her senses. Her ears went back, her whiskers curled, and her white underside hugged the ledge.

A little closer she moved, and the fat man made a grab for her. She jerked back a step, with unblinking eyes fixed on his sweating face. He was furtively laying the saucer aside, she noticed, and edging his fat paunch farther out the window.

Once more she advanced almost into his grasp, and again he lunged at her with both powerful arms.

The Madame leaped lightly aside.

"This time I'll get you, you stinkin' cat," he cried, and raising one knee to the windowsill, he threw himself at Madame Phloi. As she slipped through his fingers, he landed on the ledge with all his weight.

A section of it crumbled beneath him. He bellowed, clutching at the air, and at the same time a streak of creamy brown flashed out of sight. The fat man was not silent as he fell.

As for Madame Phloi, she was found doubled in half in a patch of sunshine on her living-room carpet, innocently washing her fine brown tail.

Stephen Vincent Benét

THE KING
OF THE CATS

"But, my *dear,*" said Mrs. Culverin, with a tiny gasp, "you can't actually mean—a *tail!*"

Mrs. Dingle nodded impressively. "Exactly. I've actually seen him. Twice. Paris, of course, and then, a command appearance at Rome—we were in the Royal box. He conducted —my dear, you've never heard such effects from an orchestra —and, my dear," she hesitated slightly, "he conducted *with it.*"

"How perfectly, fascinatingly too horrid for words!" said Mrs. Culverin in a dazed but greedy voice. "We *must* have him to dinner as soon as he comes over—he is coming over, isn't he?"

"The twelfth," said Mrs. Dingle with a gleam in her eyes. "The New Symphony people have asked him to be guest conductor for three special concerts—I do hope you can dine with *us* some night while he's here—he'll be very busy, of course—but he's promised to give us what time he can spare."

"Oh, thank you, dear," said Mrs. Culverin abstractedly, her last raid upon Mrs. Dingle's pet British novelist still fresh in her mind. "You're always so delightfully hospitable—but you mustn't wear yourself out—the rest of us must do *our* part —I know Harry and myself would be only too glad to—"

"That's very sweet of you, darling." Mrs. Dingle also remembered the larceny of the British novelist. "But we're just going to give Monsieur Tibault—sweet name, isn't it! They say he's descended from the Tybalt in *Romeo and Juliet* and that's why he doesn't like Shakespeare—we're just going to give Monsieur Tibault the simplest sort of time—a little reception after his first concert, perhaps. He hates," she looked around the table, "large, mixed parties. And then, of course, his—er—little idiosyncrasy." She coughed delicately. "It makes him feel a trifle shy with strangers."

"But I don't understand yet, Aunt Emily," said Tommy Brooks, Mrs. Dingle's nephew. "Do you really mean this Tibault bozo has a tail? Like a monkey and everything?"

"Tommy dear," said Mrs. Culverin crushingly, "in the first place Monsieur Tibault is not a bozo—he is a very distinguished musician—the finest conductor in Europe. And in the second place—"

"He has." Mrs. Dingle was firm. "He has a tail. He conducts with it."

"Oh, but honestly!" said Tommy, his ears pinkening. "I mean—of course, if you say so, Aunt Emily, I'm sure he has

—but still, it sounds pretty steep, if you know what I mean! How about it, Professor Tatto?"

Professor Tatto cleared his throat. "Tck," he said, putting his fingertips together cautiously. "I shall be very anxious to see this Monsieur Tibault. For myself, I have never observed a genuine specimen of *homo caudatus,* so I should be inclined to doubt, and yet . . . In the Middle Ages, for instance, the belief in men—er—tailed or with caudal appendages of some sort, was both widespread and, as far as we can gather, well founded. As late as the eighteenth century, a Dutch sea captain with some character for veracity recounts the discovery of a pair of such creatures in the island of Formosa. They were in a low state of civilization, I believe, but the appendages in question were quite distinct. And in 1860 Dr. Grimbrook, the English surgeon, claims to have treated no less than three African natives with short but evident tails—though his testimony rests upon his unsupported word. After all, the thing is not impossible, though doubtless unusual. Web feet—rudimentary gills—these occur with some frequency. The appendix we have with us always. The chain of our descent from the apelike form is by no means complete. For that matter," he beamed around the table, "what can we call the last few vertebrae of the normal spine but the beginnings of a rudimentary tail? Oh, yes—yes—it's possible—quite—that in an extraordinary case—a reversion to type—a survival—"

"I told you so," said Mrs. Dingle triumphantly. *"Isn't* it fascinating? Isn't it, Princess?"

The Princess Vivrakanarda's eyes, blue as a field of larkspur, fathomless as the center of heaven, rested lightly for a moment on Mrs. Dingle's excited countenance.

"Ve-ry fascinating," she said, in a voice like stroked, golden velvet. "I should like ve-ry much to meet this Monsieur Tibault."

"Well, *I* hope he breaks his neck!" said Tommy Brooks

under his breath—but nobody ever paid much attention to Tommy.

Nevertheless, as the time for Monsieur Tibault's arrival in these States drew nearer and nearer, people in general began to wonder whether the Princess had spoken quite truthfully—for there was no doubt of the fact that, up till then, she had been the unique sensation of the season—and you know what social lions and lionesses are.

It was a Siamese season, and genuine Siamese were at quite as much of a premium as Russian accents had been in the quaint old days when the Chauve-Souris was a novelty. The Siamese Art Theater, imported at terrific expense, was playing to packed houses at the Century Theater. *Gushuptzgu,* an epic novel of Siamese farm life, in nineteen closely printed volumes, had just been awarded the Nobel Prize. Prominent pet-and-newt dealers reported no cessation in the appalling demand for Siamese cats. And upon the crest of this wave of interest in things Siamese the Princess Vivrakanarda poised with the elegant nonchalance of a Hawaiian water baby upon his surfboard. She was indispensable. She was incomparable. She was everywhere.

Youthful, enormously wealthy, allied on one hand to the royal family of Siam and on the other to the Cabots (and yet with the first eighteen of her twenty-one years shrouded from speculation in a golden zone of mystery), the mingling of races in her had produced an exotic beauty as distinguished as it was strange. She moved with a feline, effortless grace, and her skin was as if it had been gently powdered with tiny grains of the purest gold—yet the blueness of her eyes, set just a trifle slantingly, was as pure and startling as the sea on the rocks of Maine. Her brown hair fell to her knees—she had been offered extraordinary sums by the Master Barbers' Protective Association to have it shingled. Straight as a waterfall tumbling over brown rocks, it had a vague perfume of sandalwood and suave spices and held tints of rust and the sun. She did not talk very much—but then she did not have to; her voice had an odd, small, melodious huskiness that haunted the mind. She lived alone and was reputed to be very lazy—at least it was known that she slept during most of the day—but at night she bloomed like a moonflower, and a depth came into her eyes.

It was no wonder that Tommy Brooks fell in love with her. The wonder was that she let him. There was nothing exotic or distinguished about Tommy—he was just one of those pleasant, normal young men who seem created to carry on the bond business by reading the newspapers in the University Club during most of the day, and can always be relied upon at night to fill an unexpected hole in a dinner party. It is true that the Princess could hardly be said to do more than tolerate any of her suitors—no one had ever seen those aloof and arrogant eyes enliven at the entrance of any male. But she seemed to be able to tolerate Tommy a little more than the rest—and that young man's infatuated daydreams were beginning to be beset by smart solitaires and imaginary apartments on Park Avenue when the famous Monsieur Tibault conducted his first concert at Carnegie Hall.

Tommy Brooks sat beside the Princess. The eyes he turned upon her were eyes of longing and love, but her face was as impassive as a Benda mask, and the only remark she made during the preliminary bustlings was that there seemed to be a number of people in the audience. But Tommy was relieved, if anything, to find her even a little more aloof than usual, for, ever since Mrs. Culverin's dinner party, a vague disquiet as to the possible impression which this Tibault creature might make upon her had been growing in his mind. It shows his devotion that he was present at all. To a man whose simple Princetonian nature found in "Just a Little Love, a Little Kiss," the quintessence of musical art, the average symphony was a positive torture, and he looked forward to the evening's program itself with a grim, brave smile.

"Ssh!" said Mrs. Dingle breathlessly. "He's coming!" It seemed to the startled Tommy as if he were suddenly back in the trenches under a heavy barrage, as Monsieur Tibault made his entrance to a perfect bombardment of applause.

Then the enthusiastic noise was sliced off in the middle, and a gasp took its place—a vast, windy sigh, as if every person in that multitude had suddenly said "Ah!" For the papers had not lied about him. The tail was there.

They called him theatric—but how well he understood the uses of theatricalism! Dressed in unrelieved black from head to foot (the black dress shirt had been a special token of Mussolini's esteem), he did not walk on, he strolled, leisurely, easily, aloofly, the famous tail curled nonchalantly about one wrist—a suave, black panther lounging through a summer garden with that little mysterious weave of the head that panthers have when they pad behind bars—the glittering darkness of his eyes unmoved by any surprise or elation. He nodded, twice in regal acknowledgment, as the clapping reached an apogee of frenzy. To Tommy there was something dreadfully reminiscent of the Princess in the way he nodded. Then he turned to his orchestra.

A second and louder gasp went up from the audience at this point, for, as he turned, the tip of that incredible tail twined with dainty carelessness into some hidden pocket and produced a black baton. But Tommy did not even notice. He was looking at the Princess instead.

She had not even bothered to clap, at first, but now. . . . Poor Tommy had never seen her moved like this, never. She was not applauding, her hands were clenched in her lap, but her whole body was rigid, rigid as a steel bar, and the blue flowers of her eyes were bent upon the figure of Monsieur Tibault in a terrible concentration. The pose of her entire figure was so still and intense that for an instant Tommy had the lunatic idea that any moment she might leap from her seat beside him as lightly as a moth, and land, with no sound, at Monsieur Tibault's side to—yes—to rub her proud head against his coat in worship. Even Mrs. Dingle would notice in a moment.

"Princess—" he said, in a horrified whisper, "Princess—"

Slowly the tenseness of her body relaxed, her eyes veiled again, she grew calm.

"Yes, Tommy?" she said, in her usual voice, but there was still something about her. . . .

"Nothing, only—oh, hang—he's starting!" said Tommy, as Monsieur Tibault, his hands loosely clasped before him, turned and *faced* the audience. His eyes dropped; his tail switched once impressively, then gave three little preliminary taps with his baton on the floor.

Seldom has Gluck's overture to *Iphigenia in Aulis* received such an ovation. But it was not until the Eighth Symphony that the hysteria of the audience reached its climax. Never before had the New Symphony been played so superbly—and certainly never before had it been led with such genius. Three prominent conductors in the audience were sobbing with the despairing admiration of envious children toward the close, and one at least was heard to offer wildly ten thousand dollars to a well-known facial surgeon there present for a shred of evidence that tails of some variety could by any stretch of science be grafted upon a normally decaudate form. There was no doubt about it—no mortal hand and arm, be they ever so dexterous, could combine the delicate élan and powerful grace displayed in every gesture of Monsieur Tibault's tail.

A sable staff, it dominated the brasses like a flicker of black lightning; an ebon, elusive whip, it drew the last exquisite breath of melody from the woodwinds and ruled the stormy strings like a magician's rod. Monsieur Tibault bowed and bowed again—roar after roar of frenzied admiration

shook the hall to its foundations—and when he finally staggered, exhausted, from the platform, the president of the
Wednesday Sonata Club was only restrained by force from
flinging her ninety-thousand-dollar string of pearls after him
in an excess of aesthetic appreciation. New York had come
and seen—and New York was conquered. Mrs. Dingle was
immediately besieged by reporters, and Tommy Brooks
looked forward to the "little party" at which he was to meet
the new hero of the hour with feelings only a little less lugubrious than those that would have come to him just before
taking his seat in the electric chair.

The meeting between his princess and Monsieur Tibault
was worse and better than he expected. Better because, after
all, they did not say much to each other—and worse because
it seemed to him, somehow, that some curious kinship of
mind between them made words unnecessary. They were
certainly the most distinguished-looking couple in the room,
as he bent over her hand. "So darlingly foreign, both of them,
and yet so different," babbled Mrs. Dingle—but Tommy
couldn't agree.

They were very different, yes—the dark, lithe stranger
with that bizarre appendage tucked carelessly in his pocket,
and the blue-eyed, brown-haired girl. But that difference only
accentuated what they had in common—something in the way
they moved, in the suavity of their gestures, in the set of their
eyes. Something deeper, even, than race. He tried to puzzle
it out—then, looking around at the others, he had a flash of
revelation. It was as if that couple were foreign, indeed—not
only to New York but to all common humanity. As if they
were polite guests from a different star.

Tommy did not have a happy evening, on the whole. But his
mind worked slowly, and it was not until much later that the
mad suspicion came upon him in full force.

Perhaps he is not to be blamed for his lack of immediate

comprehension. The next few weeks were weeks of bewildered misery for him. It was not that the Princess's attitude toward him had changed—she was just as tolerant of him as before; but Monsieur Tibault was always there. He had a faculty of appearing as out of thin air—he walked, for all his height, as lightly as a butterfly—and Tommy grew to hate that faintest shuffle on the carpet that announced his presence as he had never hated the pound of the guns.

And then, hang it all, the man was so smooth, so infernally, unrufflably smooth! He was never out of temper, never embarrassed. He treated Tommy with the extreme of urbanity, and yet his eyes mocked, deep down, and Tommy could do nothing. And gradually, the Princess became more and more drawn to this stranger, in a soundless communion that found little need for speech—and that, too, Tommy saw and hated, and that, too, he could not mend.

He began to be haunted not only by Monsieur Tibault in the flesh but by Monsieur Tibault in the spirit. He slept badly, and when he slept he dreamed—of Monsieur Tibault, a man no longer, but a shadow, a specter, the limber ghost of an animal whose words came purringly between sharp little pointed teeth. There was certainly something odd about the whole shape of the fellow—his fluid ease, the mold of his head, even the cut of his fingernails—but just what it was escaped Tommy's intensest cogitation. And when he did put his finger on it at length, at first he refused to believe.

A pair of petty incidents decided him, finally, against all reason. He had gone to Mrs. Dingle's, one winter afternoon, hoping to find the Princess. She was out with his aunt, but was expected back for tea, and he wandered idly into the library to wait. He was just about to switch on the lights, for the library was always dark even in summer, when he heard a sound of light breathing that seemed to come from the leather couch in the corner. He approached it cautiously and dimly made out the form of Monsieur Tibault, curled up on the couch, peacefully asleep.

The sight annoyed Tommy so that he swore under his breath and was back near the door on his way out, when the feeling we all know and hate, the feeling that eyes we cannot see are watching us, arrested him. He turned back—Monsieur Tibault had not moved a muscle of his body, to all appearance —but his eyes were open now. And those eyes were black and human no longer. They were green—Tommy could have sworn it—and he could have sworn that they had no bottom and gleamed like little emeralds in the dark. It lasted only a moment, for Tommy pressed the light button automatically— and there was Monsieur Tibault, his normal self, yawning a little but urbanely apologetic, but it gave Tommy time to think. Nor did what happened a trifle later increase his peace of mind.

They had lit a fire and were talking in front of it—by now, Tommy hated Monsieur Tibault so thoroughly that he felt that odd yearning for his company that often occurs in such cases. Monsieur Tibault was telling some anecdote, and Tommy was hating him worse than ever for basking with such obvious enjoyment in the heat of the flames and the ripple of his own voice.

Then they heard the street door open, and Monsieur Tibault jumped up—and, jumping, caught one sock on a sharp corner of the brass fire rail and tore it open in a jagged flap. Tommy looked down mechanically at the tear—a second's glance, but enough—for Monsieur Tibault, for the first time in Tommy's experience, lost his temper completely. He swore violently in some spitting, foreign tongue—his face distorted suddenly—he clapped his hand over his sock. Then, glaring furiously at Tommy, he fairly sprang from the room, and Tommy could hear him scaling the stairs in long, agile bounds. Tommy sank into a chair, careless for once of the fact that he heard the Princess's light laugh in the hall. He didn't want to see the Princess. He didn't want to see anybody. There had been something revealed when Monsieur Tibault had torn that hole in his sock—and it was not the skin of a man. Tommy had caught a glimpse of—black plush. Black velvet. And then had come Monsieur Tibault's sudden explosion of fury. Good *Lord*—did the man wear black velvet stockings under his ordinary socks? Or could he—could he—but here Tommy held his fevered head in his hands.

He went to Professor Tatto that evening with hypothetical questions, but as he did not dare confide his real suspicions to the professor, the hypothetical answers he received served only to confuse him the more. Then he thought of Billy Strang. Billy was a good sort, and his mind had a turn for the bizarre. Billy might be able to help.

He couldn't get hold of Billy for three days, and lived through the interval in a fever of impatience. But finally they had dinner together at Billy's apartment, where his queer books were, and Tommy was able to blurt out the whole disordered jumble of his suspicions.

Billy listened without interrupting until Tommy was quite through. Then he pulled at his pipe. "But, my dear man—" he said protestingly.

"Oh, I know—I know," said Tommy, and waved his hands, "I know I'm crazy—you needn't tell me that—but I tell you, the man's a cat all the same—no, I don't see how he could be, but he is—why, hang it, in the first place, everybody knows he's got a *tail!*"

"Even so," said Billy Strang, puffing. "Oh, my dear Tommy, I don't doubt you saw, or think you saw, everything you say. But, even so . . ." He shook his head.

"But what about those other birds, werewolves and things?" said Tommy.

306

Billy looked dubious. "We-ll," he admitted, "you've got me there, of course. At least—a tailed man *is* possible. And the yarns about werewolves go back far enough so that—well, *I* wouldn't say there aren't or haven't been werewolves—but then I'm willing to believe more things than most people. But a werecat—or a man that's a cat and a cat that's a man— honestly, Tommy—"

"If I don't get some real advice I'll go clean off my hinge. For heaven's sake, tell me something to *do!*"

"Lemme think," said Billy. "First, you're pizen-sure this man is—"

"A cat. Yeah," and Tommy nodded violently.

"Check. And second—if it doesn't hurt your feelings, Tommy—you're afraid this girl you're in love with has—er— at least a streak of—felinity—in her—and so she's drawn to him?"

"Oh, Lord, Billy, if I only knew!"

"Well—er—suppose she really is, too, you know— would you still be keen on her?"

"I'd marry her if she turned into a dragon every Wednesday!" said Tommy fervently.

Billy smiled. "Hmm," he said, "then the obvious thing to do is to get rid of this Monsieur Tibault. Lemme think."

He thought about two pipes full, while Tommy sat on pins and needles. Then, finally, he burst out laughing.

"What's so darn funny?" said Tommy aggrievedly.

"Nothing, Tommy, only I've just thought of a stunt— something so blooming crazy—but if he is—hmm—what you think he is—it *might* work." And, going to the bookcase, he took down a book.

"If you think you're going to quiet my nerves by reading me a bedtime story—"

"Shut up, Tommy, and listen to this—if you really want to get rid of your feline friend."

"What is it?" asked Tommy gloomily.

"Book of Agnes Repplier's. About cats. Listen.

" 'There is also a Scandinavian version of the ever famous story which Sir Walter Scott told to Washington Irving, which Monk Lewis told to Shelley, and which, in one form or another, we find embodied in the folklore of every land'—now, Tommy, pay attention—'the story of the traveler who saw within a ruined abbey, a procession of cats, lowering into a grave a little coffin with a crown upon it. Filled with horror, he hastened from the spot; but when he had reached his destination he could not forbear relating to a friend the wonder he had seen. Scarcely had the tale been told when his friend's cat, who lay curled up tranquilly by the fire, sprang to its feet, cried out, "Then I am the King of the Cats!" and disappeared in a flash up the chimney.'

"Well?" said Billy, shutting the book.

"By gum!" said Tommy, staring. "By gum! Do you really think there's a chance?"

"*I* think we're both in the booby hatch. But if you want to try it—"

"Try it! I'll spring it on him the next time I see him. But —listen—I can't make it a ruined abbey."

"Oh, use your imagination! Make it Central Park. Tell it as if it happened to you—seeing the funeral procession and all that. You can lead into it somehow—let's see, some general line—oh, yes—'Strange, isn't it, how fact so often copies fiction? Why, only yesterday . . .' See?"

"Strange, isn't it, how fact so often copies fiction," repeated Tommy dutifully. "Why, only yesterday . . ."

"I happened to be strolling through Central Park when I saw something very odd."

"I happened to be strolling through—here, gimme that book!" said Tommy. "I want to learn the rest of it by heart!"

Mrs. Dingle's farewell dinner to the famous Monsieur Tibault, on the occasion of his departure for his Western tour, was looked forward to with the greatest expectations. Not only could everybody be there, including the Princess Vivrakanarda, but Mrs. Dingle, a hinter if there ever was one, had let it be known that at this dinner an announcement of very unusual interest to Society might be made. So everyone, for once, was almost on time, except for Tommy. He was at least fifteen minutes early, for he wanted to have speech with his aunt alone. Unfortunately, however, he had hardly taken off his overcoat when she was whispering some news in his ear so rapidly that he found it difficult to understand a word of it.

"And you mustn't breathe it to a soul!" she ended, beaming. "That is, not before the announcement—I think we'll have *that* with the salad—people never pay very much attention to salad—"

"Breathe what, Aunt Emily?" said Tommy, confused.

"The Princess, darling—the dear Princess and Monsieur Tibault—they just got engaged this afternoon, dear things! Isn't it *fascinating?*"

"Yeah," said Tommy, and started to walk blindly through the nearest door. His aunt restrained him.

"Not there, dear, not in the library. You can congratulate them later. They're just having a sweet little moment alone there now." And she turned away to harry the butler, leaving Tommy stunned.

But his chin came up after a moment. He wasn't beaten yet.

"Strange, isn't it, how often fact copies fiction?" he repeated to himself in dull mnemonics, and, as he did so, he shook his fist at the closed library door.

Mrs. Dingle was wrong, as usual. The Princess and Monsieur Tibault were not in the library—they were in the conservatory, as Tommy discovered when he wandered aimlessly past the glass doors.

He didn't mean to look, and after a second he turned away. But that second was enough.

Tibault sat in a chair and she was crouched on a stool at his side, while his hand, softly, smoothly, stroked her brown hair. Black cat and Siamese kitten. Her face was hidden from Tommy, but he could see Tibault's face. And he could hear.

They were not talking, but there was a sound between them. A warm and contented sound like the murmur of giant bees in a hollow tree—a golden, musical rumble, deep-throated, that came from Tibault's lips and was answered by hers—a golden purr.

Somehow Tommy found himself back in the drawing room, shaking hands with Mrs. Culverin, who said frankly that she had seldom seen him look so pale.

The first two courses of the dinner passed Tommy like dreams, but Mrs. Dingle's cellar was notable, and by the middle of the meat course he began to come to himself. He had only one resolve now.

For the next few moments he tried desperately to break into the conversation, but Mrs. Dingle was talking, and even Gabriel will have a time interrupting Mrs. Dingle. At last, though, she paused for breath, and Tommy saw his chance.

"Speaking of that," said Tommy piercingly, without knowing in the least what he was referring to, "speaking of that—"

"As I was saying," said Professor Tatto. But Tommy would not yield. The plates were being taken away. It was time for salad.

"Speaking of that," he said again, so loudly and strangely that Mrs. Culverin jumped, and an awkward hush fell over the table. "Strange, isn't it, how often fact copies fiction?" There, he was started. His voice rose even higher. "Why, only today I was strolling through . . ." and, word for word, he repeated his lesson. He could see Tibault's eyes glowing at him as he described the funeral. He could see the Princess, tense.

He could not have said what he had expected might happen when he came to the end. But it was not bored silence everywhere, to be followed by Mrs. Dingle's acrid, "Well, Tommy, is that *quite* all?"

He slumped back in his chair, sick at heart. He was a fool, and his last resource had failed. Dimly he heard his aunt's voice saying, "Well, then—" and realized that she was about to make the fatal announcement.

But just then Monsieur Tibault spoke.

"One moment, Mrs. Dingle," he said, with extreme politeness, and she was silent. He turned to Tommy.

"You are . . . positive, I suppose, of what you saw this afternoon, Brooks?" he said in tones of light mockery.

"Absolutely," said Tommy sullenly. "Do you think I'd—"

"Oh, no, no, no," Monsieur Tibault waved the implication aside, "but—such an interesting story—one likes to be sure of the details—and, of course, you *are* sure—*quite* sure —that the kind of crown you describe was on the coffin?"

"Of course," said Tommy, wondering, "but—"

"Then I'm the King of the Cats!" cried Monsieur Tibault in a voice of thunder, and, even, as he cried it, the house lights blinked—there was the soft thud of an explosion that seemed muffled in cotton wool from the minstrel galley—and the scene was lit for a second by an obliterating and painful burst of light that vanished in an instant and was succeeded by heavy, blinding clouds of white, pungent smoke.

"Oh, those *horrid* photographers," came Mrs. Dingle's voice in a melodious wail. "I *told* them not to take the flash-light picture till dinner was over, and now they've taken it *just* as I was nibbling lettuce!"

Someone tittered a little nervously. Someone coughed.

Then, gradually, the veils of smoke dislimned and the green and black spots in front of Tommy's eyes died away.

They were blinking at each other like people who have just come out of a cave into brilliant sun. Even yet their eyes stung with the fierceness of that abrupt illumination, and Tommy found it hard to make out the faces across the table from him.

Mrs. Dingle took command of the half-blinded company with her accustomed poise. She rose, glass in hand. "And now, dear friends," she said in a clear voice, "I'm sure all of us are very happy to—" Then she stopped, open-mouthed, an expression of incredulous horror on her features. The lifted glass began to spill its contents on the tablecloth in a little stream of amber. As she spoke she had turned directly to Monsieur Tibault's place at the table—and Monsieur Tibault was no longer there.

Some say there was a bursting flash of fire that disappeared up the chimney—some say it was a giant cat that leaped through the window at a bound, without breaking the glass. Professor Tatto puts it down to a mysterious chemical disturbance operating only over Monsieur Tibault's chair. Be that as it may, one thing is certain: in the instant of fictive darkness which followed the glare of the flashlight, Monsieur Tibault, the great conductor, disappeared forever from mortal sight, tail and all.

Mrs. Culverin swears he was an international burglar and that she was just about to unmask him, but no one who sat at that historic table believes her. No, there are no sound explanations, but Tommy thinks he knows, and he will never be able to pass a cat again without wondering.

Mrs. Tommy is quite of her husband's mind regarding cats—she was Gretchen Woolwine, of Chicago (*you* know the Woolwines!)—for Tommy told her his whole story.

Doubtless it would have been more romantic to relate

how Tommy's daring won him his princess—but, unfortunately, it would not be veracious. For the Princess Vivrakanarda, also, is with us no longer. Her nerves, shattered by the spectacular denouement of Mrs. Dingle's dinner, required a sea voyage, and from that voyage she has never returned to America.

Of course, there are the usual stories—one hears of her, a nun in a Siamese convent, or a masked dancer at *Le Jardin de ma Soeur*—one hears that she has been murdered in Patagonia or married in Trebizond—but, as far as can be ascertained, not one of these gaudy fables has the slightest basis in fact. I believe that Tommy, in his heart of hearts, is quite convinced that the sea voyage was only a pretext, and that by some unheard-of means she has managed to rejoin the formidable Monsieur Tibault, in fact, that in some ruined city or subterranean palace they reign together now, King and Queen of all the mysterious Kingdom of Cats. But that, of course, is quite impossible.

Cordwainer Smith

THE GAME OF RAT AND DRAGON

1. The Table

Pinlighting is a hell of a way to earn a living. Underhill was furious as he closed the door behind himself. It didn't make much sense to wear a uniform and look like a soldier if people didn't appreciate what you did.

He sat down in his chair, laid his head back in the head-rest, and pulled the helmet down over his forehead.

As he waited for the pin-set to warm up, he remembered the girl in the outer corridor. She had looked at it, then looked at him scornfully.

"Meow." That was all she had said. Yet it had cut him like a knife.

What did she think he was—a fool, a loafer, a uniformed nonentity? Didn't she know that for every half-hour of pin-lighting, he got a minimum of two months' recuperation in the hospital?

By now the set was warm. He felt the squares of space around him, sensed himself at the middle of an immense grid, a cubic grid, full of nothing. Out in that nothingness, he could sense the hollow aching horror of space itself and could feel the terrible anxiety which his mind encountered whenever it met the faintest trace of inert dust.

As he relaxed, the comforting solidity of the Sun, the clockwork of the familiar planets and the Moon rang in on him. Our own solar system was as charming and as simple as an ancient cuckoo clock filled with familiar ticking and with reassuring noises. The odd little moons of Mars swung around their planet like frantic mice, yet their regularity was itself an assurance that all was well. Far above the plane of the ecliptic, he could feel half a ton of dust more or less drifting outside the lanes of human travel.

Here there was nothing to fight, nothing to challenge the mind, to tear the living soul out of a body with its roots dripping in effluvium as tangible as blood.

Nothing ever moved in on the solar system. He could wear the pin-set forever and be nothing more than a sort of telepathic astronomer, a man who could feel the hot, warm protection of the Sun throbbing and burning against his living mind.

Woodley came in.

"Same old ticking world," said Underhill. "Nothing to report. No wonder they didn't develop the pin-set until they began to planoform. Down here with the hot sun around us, it feels so good and so quiet. You can feel everything spinning and turning. It's nice and sharp and compact. It's sort of like sitting around home."

Woodley grunted. He was not much given to flights of fantasy.

Undeterred, Underhill went on, "It must have been pretty good to have been an ancient man. I wonder why they burned up their world with war. They didn't have to planoform. They didn't have to go out to earn their livings among the stars. They didn't have to dodge the rats or play the game. They couldn't have invented pinlighting because they didn't have any need of it, did they, Woodley?"

Woodley grunted, "Uh-huh." Woodley was twenty-six years old and due to retire in one more year. He already had a farm picked out. He had gotten through ten years of hard work pinlighting with the best of them. He had kept his sanity by not thinking very much about his job, meeting the strains of the task whenever he had to meet them, and thinking nothing more about his duties until the next emergency arose.

Woodley never made a point of getting popular among the partners. None of the partners liked him very much. Some of them even resented him. He was suspected of thinking ugly thoughts of the partners on occasion, but since none of the partners ever thought a complaint in articulate form, the other pinlighters and the chiefs of the Instrumentality left him alone.

Underhill was still full of the wonder of their job. Happily he babbled on, "What does happen to us when we planoform? Do you think it's sort of like dying? Did you ever see anybody who had his soul pulled out?"

"Pulling souls is just a way of talking about it," said Woodley. "After all these years, nobody knows whether we have souls or not."

"But I saw one once. I saw what Dogwood looked like when he came apart. There was something funny. It looked wet and sort of sticky as if it were bleeding and it went out of him—and you know what they did to Dogwood? They took him away, up in that part of the hospital where you and

I never go—way up at the top part where the others are, where the others always have to go if they are alive after the rats of the up-and-out have gotten them."

Woodley sat down and lit an ancient pipe. He was burning something called tobacco in it. It was a dirty sort of habit, but it made him look very dashing and adventurous.

"Look here, youngster. You don't have to worry about that stuff. Pinlighting is getting better all the time. The partners are getting better. I've seen them pinlight two rats forty-six million miles apart in one and a half milliseconds. As long as people had to try to work the pin-sets themselves, there was always the chance that with a minimum of four hundred milliseconds for the human mind to set a pinlight, we wouldn't light the rats up fast enough to protect our planoforming ships. The partners have changed all that. Once they get going, they're faster than rats. And they always will be. I know it's not easy, letting a partner share your mind—"

"It's not easy for them, either," said Underhill.

"Don't worry about them. They're not human. Let them take care of themselves. I've seen more pinlighters go crazy from monkeying around with partners than I have ever seen caught by the rats. How many of them do you actually know of that got grabbed by rats?"

Underhill looked down at his fingers, which shone green and purple in the vivid light thrown by the tuned-in pin-set, and counted ships. The thumb for the *Andromeda,* lost with crew and passengers, the index finger and the middle finger for *Release Ships* 43 and 56, found with their pin-sets burned out and every man, woman, and child on board dead or insane. The ring finger, the little finger, and the thumb of the other hand were the first three battleships to be lost to the rats —lost as people realized that there was something out there *underneath space itself* which was alive, capricious, and malevolent.

Planoforming was sort of funny. It felt like—

Like nothing much.

Like the twinge of a mild electric shock.

Like the ache of a sore tooth bitten on for the first time.

Like a slightly painful flash of light against the eyes.

Yet in that time, a forty-thousand-ton ship lifting free above Earth disappeared somehow or other into two dimensions and appeared half a light-year or fifty light-years off.

At one moment, he would be sitting in the Fighting Room, the pin-set ready and the familiar solar system ticking around inside his head. For a second or a year (he could never tell how long it really was, subjectively), the funny little flash went through him and then he was loose in the up-and-out, the terrible open spaces between the stars, where the stars themselves felt like pimples on his telepathic mind and the planets were too far away to be sensed or read.

Somewhere in this outer space, a gruesome death awaited, death and horror of a kind which man had never encountered until he reached out for interstellar space itself. Apparently the light of the suns kept the dragons away.

Dragons. That was what people called them. To ordinary people, there was nothing, nothing except the shiver of planoforming and the hammerblow of sudden death or the dark spastic note of lunacy descending into their minds.

But to the telepaths, they were dragons.

In the fraction of a second between the telepaths' awareness of a hostile something out in the black, hollow nothingness of space and the impact of a ferocious, ruinous psychic blow against all living things within the ship, the telepaths had sensed entities something like the dragons of ancient human lore, beasts more clever than beasts, demons more tangible than demons, hungry vortices of aliveness and hate compounded by unknown means out of the thin, tenuous matter between the stars.

It took a surviving ship to bring back the news—a ship in which, by sheer chance, a telepath had a light-beam ready, turning it out at the innocent dust so that, within the panorama of his mind, the dragon dissolved into nothing at all and the other passengers, themselves nontelepathic, went about their way not realizing that their own immediate deaths had been averted.

From then on, it was easy—almost.

Planoforming ships always carried telepaths. Telepaths had their sensitiveness enlarged to an immense range by the pin-sets, which were telepathic amplifiers adapted to the mammal mind. The pin-sets in turn were electronically geared into small dirigible light-bombs. Light did it.

Light broke up the dragons, allowed the ships to reform three-dimensionally, skip, skip, skip, as they moved from star to star.

The odds suddenly moved down from a hundred to one against mankind to sixty to forty in mankind's favor.

This was not enough. The telepaths were trained to become ultrasensitive, trained to become aware of the dragons in less than a millisecond.

But it was found that the dragons could move a million miles in just under two milliseconds and that this was not enough for the human mind to activate the light beams.

Attempts had been made to sheath the ships in light at all times.

This defense wore out.

As mankind learned about the dragons, so too, apparently, the dragons learned about mankind. Somehow they flattened their own bulk and came in on extremely flat trajectories very quickly.

Intense light was needed, light of sunlike intensity. This could be provided only by the light-bombs. Pinlighting came into existence.

Pinlighting consisted of the detonation of ultravivid miniature photonuclear bombs, which converted a few ounces of a magnesium isotope into pure visible radiance.

The odds kept coming down in mankind's favor, yet ships were being lost.

It became so bad that people didn't even want to find the ships because the rescuers knew what they would see. It was sad to bring back to Earth three hundred bodies ready for burial and two hundred or three hundred lunatics, damaged beyond repair, to be wakened, and fed, and cleaned, and put to sleep, wakened, and fed again until their lives were ended.

Telepaths tried to reach into the minds of the psychotics who had been damaged by the dragons, but they found nothing there beyond vivid spouting columns of fiery terror bursting from the primordial id itself, the volcanic source of life.

Then came the partners.

Man and partner could do together what man could not do alone. Men had the intellect. Partners had the speed.

The partners rode their tiny craft, no larger than footballs, outside the spaceships. They planoformed with the ships. They rode beside them in their six-pound craft ready to attack.

The tiny ships of the partners were swift. Each carried a dozen pinlights, bombs no bigger than thimbles.

The pinlighters threw the partners—quite literally threw —by means of mind-to-firing relays directly at the dragons.

What seemed to the human mind to be dragons appeared in the form of gigantic rats in the minds of the partners.

Out in the pitiless nothingness of space, the partners' minds responded to an instinct as old as life. The partners attacked, striking with a speed faster than man's, going from attack to attack until the rats or themselves were destroyed. Almost all the time it was the partners who won.

With the safety of the interstellar skip, skip, skip of the ships, commerce increased immensely, the population of all the colonies went up, and the demand for trained partners increased.

Underhill and Woodley were a part of the third generation of pinlighters and yet, to them, it seemed as though their craft had endured forever.

Gearing space into minds by means of the pin-set, adding the partners to those minds, keying up the minds for the tension of a fight on which all depended—this was more than human synapses could stand for long. Underhill needed his two months' rest after half an hour of fighting. Woodley needed his retirement after ten years of service. They were young. They were good. But they had limitations.

So much depended on the choice of partners, so much on the sheer luck of who drew whom.

2. *The Shuffle*

Father Moontree and the little girl named West entered the room. They were the other two pinlighters. The human complement of the Fighting Room was now complete.

Father Moontree was a red-faced man of forty-five who had lived the peaceful life of a farmer until he reached his fortieth year. Only then, belatedly, did the authorities find he was telepathic and agree to let him late in life enter upon the career of pinlighter. He did well at it, but he was fantastically old for this kind of business.

Father Moontree looked at the glum Woodley and the musing Underhill. "How're the youngsters today? Ready for a good fight?"

"Father always wants a fight," giggled the little girl named West. She was such a little little girl. Her giggle was high and childish. She looked like the last person in the world one would expect to find in the rough, sharp dueling of pinlighting.

Underhill had been amused one time when he found one of the most sluggish of the partners coming away happy from contact with the mind of the girl named West.

Usually the partners didn't care much about the human minds with which they were paired for the journey. The partners seemed to take the attitude that human minds were complex and fouled up beyond belief, anyhow. No partner ever questioned the superiority of the human mind, though very few of the partners were much impressed by that superiority.

The partners liked people. They were willing to fight with them. They were even willing to die for them. But when a partner liked an individual the way, for example, that Captain Wow or the Lady May liked Underhill, the liking had nothing to do with intellect. It was a matter of temperament, of feel.

Underhill knew perfectly well that Captain Wow regarded his, Underhill's, brains as silly. What Captain Wow liked was Underhill's friendly emotional structure, the cheerfulness and glint of wicked amusement that shot through Underhill's unconscious thought patterns, and the gaiety with which Underhill faced danger. The words, the history books, the ideas, the science—Underhill could sense all that in his own mind—reflected back from Captain Wow's mind as so much rubbish.

Miss West looked at Underhill. "I bet you've put stickum on the stones."

"I did not!"

Underhill felt his ears grow red with embarrassment. During his novitiate, he had tried to cheat in the lottery because he got particularly fond of a special partner, a lovely young mother named Murr. It was so much easier to operate with Murr and she was so affectionate toward him that he forgot pinlighting was hard work and that he was not instructed to have a good time with his partner. They were both designed and prepared to go into deadly battle together.

One cheating had been enough. They had found him out and he had been laughed at for years.

Father Moontree picked up the imitation-leather cup and shook the stone dice which assigned them their partners for the trip. By senior rights he took first draw.

He grimaced. He had drawn a greedy old character, a tough old male whose mind was full of slobbering thoughts of food, veritable oceans full of half-spoiled fish. Father Moontree had once said that he burped cod liver oil for weeks after drawing that particular glutton, so strongly had the telepathic image of fish impressed itself upon his mind. Yet the glutton was a glutton for danger as well as for fish. He had killed sixty-three dragons, more than any other partner in the service, and was quite literally worth his weight in gold.

The little girl West came next. She drew Captain Wow. When she saw who it was, she smiled.

"I *like* him," she said. "He's such fun to fight with. He feels so nice and cuddly in my mind."

"Cuddly, hell," said Woodley. "I've been in his mind, too. It's the most leering mind in this ship, bar none."

"Nasty man," said the little girl. She said it declaratively, without reproach.

Underhill, looking at her, shivered.

He didn't see how she could take Captain Wow so calmly. Captain Wow's mind *did* leer. When Captain Wow got excited in the middle of a battle, confused images of dragons, deadly rats, luscious beds, the smell of fish, and the shock of space all scrambled together in his mind as he and Captain Wow, their consciousnesses linked together through the pin-set, became a fantastic composite of human being and Persian cat.

That's the trouble with working with cats, thought Underhill. It's a pity that nothing else anywhere will serve as partner. Cats were all right once you got in touch with them telepathically. They were smart enough to meet the needs of the flight, but their motives and desires were certainly different from those of humans.

They were companionable enough as long as you thought tangible images at them, but their minds just closed up and went to sleep when you recited Shakespeare or Colegrove, or if you tried to tell them what space was.

It was sort of funny realizing that the partners who were so grim and mature out here in space were the same cute little animals that people had used as pets for thousands of years back on Earth. He had embarrassed himself more than once while on the ground saluting perfectly ordinary nontelepathic cats because he had forgotten for the moment that they were not partners.

He picked up the cup and shook out his stone dice.

He was lucky—he drew the Lady May.

The Lady May was the most thoughtful partner he had ever met. In her, the finely bred pedigree mind of a Persian cat had reached one of its highest peaks of development. She was more complex than any human woman, but the complexity was all one of emotions, memory, hope, and discriminated experience—experience sorted through without benefit of words.

When he had first come into contact with her mind, he was astonished at its clarity. With her he remembered her kittenhood. He remembered every mating experience she had ever had. He saw in a half-recognizable gallery all the other pinlighters with whom she had been paired for the fight. And he saw himself radiant, cheerful, and desirable.

He even thought he caught the edge of a longing—

A very flattering and yearning thought: *What a pity he is not a cat.*

Woodley picked up the last stone. He drew what he deserved—a sullen, scarred old tomcat with none of the verve of Captain Wow. Woodley's partner was the most animal of all the cats on the ship, a low, brutish type with a dull mind.

Even telepathy had not refined his character. His ears were half chewed off from the first fights in which he had engaged. He was a serviceable fighter, nothing more.

Woodley grunted.

Underhill glanced at him oddly. Didn't Woodley ever do anything but grunt?

Father Moontree looked at the other three. "You might as well get your partners now. I'll let the Go-captain know we're ready to go into the up-and-out."

3. The Deal

Underhill spun the combination lock on the Lady May's cage. He woke her gently and took her into his arms. She humped her back luxuriously, stretched her claws, started to purr, thought better of it, and licked him on the wrist instead. He did not have the pin-set on, so their minds were closed to each other, but in the angle of her mustache and in the movement of her ears, he caught some sense of the gratification she experienced in finding him as her partner.

He talked to her in human speech, even though speech meant nothing to a cat when the pin-set was not on.

"It's a damn shame, sending a sweet little thing like you whirling around in the coldness of nothing to hunt for rats that are bigger and deadlier than all of us put together. You didn't ask for this kind of fight, did you?"

For answer, she licked his hand, purred, tickled his cheek with her long fluffy tail, turned around, and faced him, golden eyes shining.

For a moment they stared at each other, man squatting, cat standing erect on her hind legs, front claws digging into his knee. Human eyes and cat eyes looked across an immensity which no words could meet, but which affection spanned in a single glance.

"Time to get in," he said.

She walked docilely to her spheroid carrier. She climbed in. He saw to it that her miniature pin-set rested firmly and comfortably against the base of her brain. He made sure that her claws were padded so that she could not tear herself in the excitement of battle.

Softly he said to her, "Ready?"

For answer, she preened her back as much as her harness would permit and purred softly within the confines of the frame that held her.

He slapped down the lid and watched the sealant ooze around the seam. For a few hours, she was welded into her projectile; later, a workman with a short cutting arc would remove her after she had done her duty.

He picked up the entire projectile and slipped it into the ejection tube. He closed the door of the tube, spun the lock, seated himself in his chair, and put his own pin-set on.

Once again he flung the switch.

He sat in a small room, *small, small, warm, warm,* the bodies of the other three people moving close around him, the tangible light in the ceiling bright and heavy against his closed eyelids.

As the pin-set warmed, the room fell away. The other people ceased to be people and became small glowing heaps of fire, embers, dark red fire, with the consciousness of life burning like old red coals in a country fireplace.

As the pin-set warmed a little more, he felt Earth just below him, felt the ship slipping away, felt the turning Moon as it swung on the far side of the world, felt the planets and the hot, clear goodness of the Sun which kept the dragons so far from mankind's native ground.

Finally, he reached complete awareness.

He was telepathically alive to a range of millions of miles. He felt the dust which he had noticed earlier high above the ecliptic. With a thrill of warmth and tenderness, he felt the consciousness of the Lady May pouring over into his own. Her consciousness was as gentle and clear and yet sharp to the taste of his mind as if it were scented oil. It felt relaxing and reassuring. He could sense her welcome of him. It was scarcely a thought, just a raw emotion of greeting.

At last they were one again.

In a tiny remote corner of his mind, as tiny as the smallest toy he had ever seen in his childhood, he was still aware of the room and the ship, and of Father Moontree picking up a telephone and speaking to a Go-captain in charge of the ship.

His telepathic mind caught the idea long before his ears could frame the words. The actual sound followed the idea the way that thunder on an ocean beach follows the lightning inward from far out over the seas.

"The Fighting Room is ready. Clear to planoform, sir."

4. *The Play*

Underhill was always a little exasperated at the way that Lady May experienced things before he did.

He was braced for the quick vinegar thrill of planoforming, but he caught her report of it before his own nerves could register what happened.

Earth had fallen so far away that he groped for several milliseconds before he found the Sun in the upper rear right-hand corner of his telepathic mind.

That was a good jump, he thought. *This way we'll get there in four or five skips.*

A few hundred miles outside the ship, the Lady May thought back at him. *O warm, O generous, O gigantic man! O brave, O friendly, O tender and huge partner! O wonderful with you, with you so good, good, good, warm, warm, now to fight, now to go, good with you . . .*

He knew that she was not thinking words, that his mind

took the clear amiable babble of her cat intellect and translated it into images which his own thinking could record and understand.

Neither one of them was absorbed in the game of mutual greeting. He reached out far beyond her range of perception to see if there was anything near the ship. It was funny how it was possible to do two things at once. He could scan space with his pin-set mind and yet at the same time catch a vagrant thought of hers, a lovely, affectionate thought about a son who had had a golden face and a chest covered with soft, incredibly downy white fur.

While he was still searching, he caught the warning from her.

We jump again!

And so they had. The ship had moved to a second planoform. The stars were different. The Sun was immeasurably far behind. Even the nearest stars were barely in contact. This was good dragon country, this open, nasty, hollow kind of space. He reached farther, faster, sensing and looking for danger, ready to fling the Lady May at danger wherever he found it.

Terror blazed up in his mind, so sharp, so clear, that it came through as a physical wrench.

The little girl named West had found something—something immense, long, black, sharp, greedy, horrific. She flung Captain Wow at it.

Underhill tried to keep his own mind clear. "Watch out!" he shouted telepathically at the others, trying to move the Lady May around.

At one corner of the battle, he felt the lustful rage of Captain Wow as the big Persian tomcat detonated light while he approached the streak of dust which threatened the ship and the people within.

The light scored near misses.

The dust flattened itself, changing from the shape of a stingray into the shape of a spear.

Not three milliseconds had elapsed.

Father Moontree was talking human words and was saying in a voice that moved like cold molasses out of a heavy jar. "C-a-p-t-a-i-n." Underhill knew that the sentence was going to be "Captain, move fast!"

The battle would be fought and finished before Father Moontree got through talking.

Now, fractions of a millisecond later, the Lady May was directly in line.

Here was where the skill and speed of the partners came in. She could react faster than he. She could see the threat as an immense rat coming directly at her.

She could fire the light-bombs with a discrimination which he might miss.

He was connected with her mind, but he could not follow it.

His consciousness absorbed the tearing wound inflicted by the alien enemy. It was like no wound on Earth—raw, crazy pain which started like a burn at his navel. He began to writhe in his chair.

Actually he had not yet had time to move a muscle when the Lady May struck back at their enemy.

Five evenly spaced photonuclear bombs blazed out across a hundred thousand miles.

The pain in his mind and body vanished.

He felt a moment of fierce, terrible, feral elation running through the mind of the Lady May as she finished her kill. It was always disappointing to the cats to find out that their enemies disappeared at the moment of destruction.

Then he felt her hurt, the pain and the fear that swept over both of them as the battle, quicker than the movement of an eyelid, had come and gone. In the same instant there came the sharp and acid twinge of planoform.

Once more the ship went skip.

He could hear Woodley thinking at him. *You don't have*

to bother much. This old son of a gun and I will take over for a while.

Twice again the twinge, the skip.

He had no idea where he was until the lights of the Caledonia spaceport shone below.

With a weariness that lay almost beyond the limits of thought, he threw his mind back into rapport with the pin-set, fixing the Lady May's projectile gently and neatly in its launching tube.

She was half dead with fatigue, but he could feel the beat of her heart, could listen to her panting, and he grasped the grateful edge of a *Thanks* reaching from her mind to his.

5. *The Score*

They put him in the hospital at Caledonia.

The doctor was friendly but firm. "You actually got touched by that dragon. That's as close a shave as I've ever seen. It's all so quick that it'll be a long time before we know what happened scientifically, but I suppose you'd be ready for the insane asylum now if the contact had lasted several tenths of a millisecond longer. What kind of cat did you have out in front of you?"

Underhill felt the words coming out of him slowly. Words were such a lot of trouble compared with the speed and the joy of thinking, fast and sharp and clear, mind to mind! But words were all that could reach ordinary people like this doctor.

His mouth moved heavily as he articulated words. "Don't call our partners cats. The right thing to call them is partners. They fight for us in a team. You ought to know we call them partners, not cats. How is mine?"

"I don't know," said the doctor contritely. "We'll find out for you. Meanwhile, old man, you take it easy. There's nothing but rest that can help you. Can you make yourself sleep, or would you like us to give you some kind of sedative?"

"I can sleep," said Underhill. "I just want to know about the Lady May."

The nurse joined in. She was a little antagonistic. "Don't you want to know about the other people?"

"They're okay," said Underhill. "I knew that before I came in here."

He stretched his arms and sighed and grinned at them. He could see they were relaxing and were beginning to treat him as a person instead of a patient.

"I'm all right," he said. "Just let me know when I can go see my partner."

A new thought struck him. He looked wildly at the doctor. "They didn't send her off with the ship, did they?"

"I'll find out right away," said the doctor. He gave Underhill a reassuring squeeze of the shoulder and left the room.

The nurse took a napkin off a goblet of chilled fruit juice.

Underhill tried to smile at her. There seemed to be something wrong with the girl. He wished she would go away. First she had started to be friendly and now she was distant again. *It's a nuisance being telepathic,* he thought. *You keep trying to reach even when you are not making contact.*

Suddenly she swung around on him.

"You pinlighters! You and your damn cats!"

Just as she stamped out, he burst into her mind. He saw himself a radiant hero, clad in his smooth suede uniform, the pin-set crown shining like ancient royal jewels around his head. He saw his own face, handsome and masculine, shining out of her mind. He saw himself very far away and he saw himself as she hated him.

She hated him in the secrecy of her own mind. She hated him because he was—she thought—proud and strange and rich, better and more beautiful than people like her.

He cut off the sight of her mind and, as he buried his face in the pillow, he caught an image of the Lady May.

She is *a cat,* he thought. *That's all she is—a cat!*

But that was not how his mind saw her—quick beyond all dreams of speed, sharp, clever, unbelievably graceful, beautiful, wordless and undemanding.

Where would he ever find a woman who could compare with her?

L. P. Hartley

PODOLO

The evening before we made the expedition to Podolo we talked it over, and I agreed there was nothing against it really.

"But why did you say you'd feel safer if Walter were going too?" Angela asked me. And he said, "What good should I be? I can't help to row the gondola, you know."

Then I felt rather silly, for everything I had said about Podolo was merely conversational exaggeration, meant to whet their curiosity, like a newspaper headline: and I knew that when Angela actually saw the dull little island, its stony and inhospitable shore littered with broken bottles and empty tins, she would think what a fool I was, with my romancing. So I took back everything I said, called my own bluff, as it were, and explained that I only avoided Podolo because of its exposed position: it was four miles from Venice, and if a boisterous bora got up (as it sometimes did, without warning), we should find getting back hard work, and might be home late. "And what will Walter say," I wound up, "if he comes back from Trieste" (he was going there for the day on business) "and finds no wife to welcome him?" Walter said, on the contrary, he had often wished such a thing might happen. And so, after some playful recriminations between this lately married, charming, devoted couple, we agreed that Podolo should be the goal for tomorrow's picnic. "You must curb my wife's generous impulses," Walter warned me; "she always wants to do something for somebody. It's an expensive habit." I assured him at Podolo she would find no calls on her heart or her purse. Except perhaps for a rat or two it was quite uninhabited. Next morning in brilliant sunshine Walter gulped down his breakfast and started for the station. It seemed hard that he should have to spend six hours of this divine day in a stuffy train. I stood on the balcony watching his departure.

The sunlight sparkled on the water; the gondola, in its best array, glowed and glittered. "Say good-bye to Angela for me," cried Walter as the gondolier braced himself for the first stroke. "And what is your postal address at Podolo?"

"Full fathom five," I called out, but I don't think my reply reached him.

Until you get right up to Podolo you can form no estimate of its size. There is nothing nearby to compare it with. On the horizon it looks like a ruler. Even now, though I have been there many times, I cannot say whether it is a hundred yards long or two hundred. But I have no wish to go back and make certain.

We cast anchor a few feet from the stony shore. Podolo, I must say, was looking its best, green, flowery, almost welcoming. One side is rounded to form the shallow arc of a circle: the other is straight. Seen from above, it must look like the moon in its first quarter. Seen as we saw it from the water line with the grassy rampart behind, it forms a kind of natural amphitheater. The slim withy-like acacia trees give a certain charm to the foreground, and to the background where they grow in clumps, and cast darker shadows, an air of mystery. As we sat in the gondola we were like theatergoers in the stalls, staring at an empty stage.

It was nearly two o'clock when we began lunch. I was very hungry, and, charmed by my companion and occupied by my food, I did not let my eyes stray out of the boat. To Angela belonged the honor of discovering the first denizen of Podolo.

"Why," she exclaimed, "there's a cat." Sure enough there was: a little cat, hardly more than a kitten, very thin and scraggy, and mewing with automatic regularity every two or three seconds. Standing on the weedy stones at the water's edge it was a pitiful sight. "It's smelled the food," said Angela. "It's hungry. Probably it's starving."

Mario, the gondolier, had also made the discovery but he received it in a diffident spirit. *"Povera bestia,"* he cried in sympathetic accents, but his eyes brightened. "Its owners did not want it. It has been put here on purpose, one sees." The idea that the cat had been left to starve caused him no great concern, but it shocked Angela profoundly.

"How abominable!" she exclaimed. "We must take it something to eat at once."

The suggestion did not recommend itself to Mario, who had to haul up the anchor and see the prospect of his own lunch growing more remote: I, too, thought we might wait till the meal was over. The cat would not die before our eyes. But Angela could brook no delay. So to the accompaniment of a good deal of stamping and heavy breathing, the prow of the gondola was turned to land.

Meanwhile the cat continued to meow, though it had retreated a little and was almost invisible, a thin wisp of tabby fur, against the parched stems of the outermost grasses.

Angela filled her hands with chicken bones.

"I'll try to win its confidence with these," she said, "and then if I can I shall catch it and put it in the boat and we'll take it to Venice. If it's left here it'll certainly starve."

She climbed along the knifelike gunwale of the gondola and stepped delicately onto the slippery boulders.

Continuing to eat my chicken in comfort, I watched her approach the cat. It ran away, but only a few yards; its hunger was obviously keeping its fear at bay. She threw a bit of food and it came nearer; another, and it came nearer still. Its demeanor grew less suspicious; its tail rose into the air; it came right up to Angela's feet. She pounced. But the cat was too quick for her; it slipped through her hands like water. Again hunger overpowered mistrust. Back it came. Once more Angela made a grab at it; once more it eluded her. But the third time she was successful. She got hold of its leg.

I shall never forget seeing it dangle from Angela's (fortunately) gloved hand. It wiggled and squirmed and fought, and in spite of its tiny size, the violence of its struggles made Angela quiver like a twig in a gale. And all the while it made the most extraordinary noise, the angriest, wickedest sound I ever heard. Instead of growing louder as its fury mounted, the sounds actually decreased in volume, as though the creature were being choked by its own rage. The spitting died away into the thin ghost of a snarl, infinitely malevolent, but hardly more audible from where I was than the hiss of air from a punctured tire.

Mario was distressed by what he felt to be Angela's brutality. "Poor beast!" he exclaimed with pitying looks. "She ought not to treat it like that." And his face gleamed with satisfaction when, intimidated by the whirling claws, she let the cat drop. It streaked away into the grass, its belly to the ground.

Angela climbed back into the boat. "I nearly had it," she said, her voice still unsteady from the encounter. "I think I shall get it next time. I shall throw a coat over it." She ate her asparagus in silence, throwing the stalks over the side. I saw that she was preoccupied and couldn't get the cat out of her mind. Any form of suffering in others affected her almost like an illness. I began to wish we hadn't come to Podolo; it was not the first time a picnic there had gone badly.

"I tell you what," Angela said suddenly, "if I can't catch it I'll kill it. It's only a question of dropping one of these boulders on it. I could do it quite easily." She disclosed her plan to Mario, who was horror-struck. His code was different from hers. He did not mind the animal dying of slow starvation; that was in the course of nature. But deliberately to kill it! *"Poveretto!* it has done no one any harm," he exclaimed with indignation. But there was another reason, I suspected, for his attitude. Venice is overrun with cats, chiefly because it is considered unlucky to kill them. If they fall into the water and are drowned, so much the better, but woe betide anyone who pushed them in.

I expounded the gondolier's point of view to Angela, but she was not impressed. "Of course I don't expect him to do it," she said, "nor you either, if you'd rather not. It may be a messy business but it will soon be over. Poor little brute, it's in a horrible state. Its life can't be any pleasure to it."

"But we don't know that," I urged, still cravenly averse to the deed of blood. "If it could speak, it might say it preferred to live at all costs." But I couldn't move Angela from her purpose.

"Let's go and explore the island," she said, "until it's time to bathe. The cat will have got over its fright and be hungry again by then, and I'm sure I shall be able to catch it. I promise I won't murder it except as a last resource."

The word *murder* lingered unpleasantly in my mind as we made our survey of the island. You couldn't imagine a better place for one. During the war a battery had been mounted there. The concrete emplacement, about as long as a tennis court, remained; but nature and the weather had conspired to break it up, leaving black holes large enough to admit a man. These holes were like crevasses in a glacier, but masked by vegetation instead of snow. Even in the brilliant afternoon sunlight one had to tread cautiously. "Perhaps the cat has its lair down there," I said, indicating a gloomy cavern with a jagged edge. "I suppose its eyes would shine in the dark." Angela lay down on the pavement and peered in. "I thought I heard something move," she said, "but it might be any-where in this rabbit warren."

Our bath was a great success. The water was so warm one hardly felt the shock of going in. The only drawback was the mud, which clung to Angela's white bathing shoes, nasty sticky stuff. A little wind had got up. But the grassy rampart sheltered us; we leaned against it and smoked. Suddenly I noticed it was past five.

"We ought to go soon," I said. "We promised, do you remember, to send the gondola to meet Walter's train."

"All right," said Angela, "just let me have a go at the cat first. Let's put the food" (we had brought some remnants of lunch with us) "here where we last saw it, and watch."

There was no need to watch, for the cat appeared at once and made for the food. Angela and I stole up behind it, but I inadvertently kicked a stone and the cat was off like a flash. Angela looked at me reproachfully. "Perhaps you could man-age better alone," I said. Angela seemed to think she could. I retreated a few yards, but the cat, no doubt scenting a trap, refused to come out.

Angela threw herself on the pavement. "I can see it," she

muttered. "I must win its confidence again. Give me three minutes and I'll catch it."

Three minutes passed. I felt concern for Angela, her lovely hair floating over the dark hole, her face, as much as one could see of it, a little red. The air was getting chilly.

"Look here," I said. "I'll wait for you in the gondola. When you've caught it, give a shout and I'll have the boat brought to land." Angela nodded; she dare not speak for fear of scaring her prey.

So I returned to the gondola. I could just see the line of Angela's shoulders; her face of course was hidden. Mario stood up, eagerly watching the chase. "She loves it so much," he said, "that she wants to kill it." I remembered Oscar Wilde's epigram, rather uncomfortably; still, nothing could be more disinterested than Angela's attitude to the cat. "We ought to start," the gondolier warned me. "The signore will be waiting at the station and wonder what has happened."

"What about Walter?" I called across the water. "He won't know what to do."

Her mind was clearly on something else as she said: "Oh, he'll find his own way home."

More minutes passed. The gondolier smiled. "One must have patience with ladies," he said. "Always patience."

I tried a last appeal. "If we started at once we could just do it."

She didn't answer. Presently I called out again. "What luck, Angela? Any hope of catching him?"

There was a pause; then I heard her say, in a curiously tense voice: "I'm not trying to *catch* him now."

The need for immediate hurry had passed, since we were irrevocably late for Walter. A sense of relaxation stole over me; I wrapped the rug round me to keep off the treacherous cold sirocco and I fell asleep. Almost at once, it seemed, I began to dream. In my dream it was night; we were hurrying across the lagoon trying to be in time for Walter's train. It was so dark I could see nothing but the dim blur of Venice ahead, and the little splash of whitish water where the oar dipped. Suddenly I stopped rowing and looked around. The seat behind me seemed to be empty. "Angela!" I cried; but there was no answer. I grew frightened. "Mario!" I shouted. "Where's the signora? We have left her behind! We must go back at once!" The gondolier, too, stopped rowing and came toward me. I could just distinguish his face; it had a wild look. "She's there, signore," he said. "But where? She's not on the seat." "She wouldn't stay on it," said the gondolier. And then, as is the way in dreams, I knew what his next words would be. "We loved her so we had to kill her."

An uprush of panic woke me. The feeling of relief at getting back to actuality was piercingly sweet. I was restored to the sunshine. At least I thought so, in the ecstasy of returning consciousness. The next moment I began to doubt, and an uneasiness, not unlike the beginning of nightmare, stirred in me again. I opened my eyes to the daylight but they didn't receive it. I looked out onto darkness. At first I couldn't believe my eyes; I wondered if I was fainting. But a glance at my watch explained everything. It was past seven o'clock. I had slept the brief twilight through and now it was night, though a few gleams lingered in the sky over Fusina.

Mario was not to be seen. I stood up and looked around. There he was on the poop, his knees drawn up, asleep. Before I had time to speak he opened his eyes, like a dog.

"Signore," he said, "you went to sleep, so I did too." To sleep out of hours is considered a joke all the world over; we both laughed. "But the signora," he said, "is *she* asleep? Or is she still trying to catch the cat?"

We strained our eyes toward the island, which was much darker than the surrounding sky.

"That's where she was," said Mario, pointing, "but I can't see her now."

"Angela!" I called.

There was no answer, indeed no sound at all but the noise of the waves slapping against the gondola.

We stared at each other.

"Let us hope she has taken no harm," said Mario, a note of anxiety in his voice. "The cat was very fierce, but it wasn't big enough to hurt her, was it?"

"No, no," I said. "It might have scratched her when she was putting her face—you know—into one of those holes."

"She was trying to kill it, wasn't she?" asked Mario.

I nodded.

"*Ha fatto male,*" said Mario. "In this country we are not accustomed to kill cats."

"*You* call, Mario," I said impatiently. "Your voice is stronger than mine."

Mario obeyed with a shout that might have raised the dead. But no answer came.

"Well," I said briskly, trying to conceal my agitation, "we must go and look for her or else we shall be late for dinner and the signore will be getting worried. She must be a *dormiotta*—a heavy sleeper."

Mario didn't answer.

"*Avanti!*" I said. "*Andiamo! Coraggio!*" I could not understand why Mario, usually so quick to execute an order, did not move. He was staring straight in front of him.

"There *is* someone on the island," he said at last, "but it's not the signora."

I must say, to do us justice, that within a couple of minutes we had beached the boat and landed. To my surprise Mario kept the oar in his hand. "I have a pocketknife," he remarked, "but the blade is only so long," indicating the third joint of a stalwart little finger.

"It was a man, then?" said I.

"It looked like a man's head."

"But you're not sure?"

"No, because it didn't walk like a man."

"How then?"

Mario bent forward and touched the ground with his free hand. I couldn't imagine why a man should go on all fours, unless he didn't want to be seen.

"He must have come while we were asleep," I said. "There'll be a boat round the other side. But let's look here first."

We were standing by the place where we had last seen Angela. The grass was broken and bent; she had left a handkerchief as though to mark the spot. Otherwise there was no trace of her.

"Now let's find the boat," I said.

We climbed the grassy rampart and began to walk round the shallow curve, stumbling over concealed brambles.

"Not here, not here," muttered Mario.

From our little eminence we could see clusters of lights twinkling across the lagoon; Fusina three or four miles away on the left, Malamocco the same distance on the right. And straight ahead Venice, floating on the water like a swarm of fireflies. But no boat. We stared at each other, bewildered.

"So he didn't come by water," said Mario at last. "He must have been here all the time."

"But are you quite certain it wasn't the signora you saw?" I asked. "How could you tell in the darkness?"

"Because the signora was wearing a white dress," said Mario. "And this one is all in black—unless he is a Negro."

"That's why it's so difficult to see him."

"Yes, we can't see him, but he can see us all right."

I felt a curious sensation up my spine.

"Mario," I said, "he must have seen her, you know. Do you think he's got anything to do with her not being here?"

Mario didn't answer.

"I don't understand why he doesn't speak to us."

"Perhaps he can't speak."

"But you thought he was a man. . . . Anyhow, we are two

against one. Come on. You take the right. I'll go to the left."

We soon lost sight of each other in the darkness, but once or twice I heard Mario swearing as he scratched himself on the acacia bushes. My search was more successful than I expected. Right at the corner of the island, close to the water's edge, I found one of Angela's bathing shoes; she must have taken it off in a hurry, for the button was torn away. A little later I made a grisly discovery. It was the cat, dead, its head crushed. The pathetic little heap of fur would never suffer the pangs of hunger again. Angela had been as good as her word.

I was going to call Mario when the bushes parted and something hurled itself upon me. I was swept off my feet. Alternately dragging and carrying me, my captor continued his headlong course. The next thing I knew I was pitched pell-mell into the gondola and felt the boat move under me.

"Mario!" I gasped. And then—absurd question—"What have you done with the oar?"

The gondolier's white face stared down at me.

"The oar? I left it—it wasn't any use, signore. I tried. . . . What it wants is a machine gun."

He was rowing frantically with my oar; the island began to recede.

"But we can't go away," I cried.

The gondolier said nothing, but rowed with all his strength. Then he began to talk under his breath. "It was a good oar, too," I heard him mutter. Suddenly he left the poop, climbed over the cushions, and sat down beside me.

"When I found her," he whispered, "she wasn't quite dead."

I began to speak but he held up his hand.

"She asked me to kill her."

"But, Mario!"

" 'Before it comes back,' she said. And then she said, 'It's starving too and it won't wait . . .' " Mario bent his head nearer but his voice was inaudible.

343

"Speak up," I cried. The next moment I implored him to stop.

Mario clambered onto the poop.

"You don't want to go to the island now, signore?"

"No, no. Straight home."

I looked back. Transparent darkness covered the lagoon save for one shadow that stained the horizon black. Podolo . . .

Fritz Leiber

SPACE–TIME FOR SPRINGERS

Gummitch was a superkitten, as he knew very well, with an I.Q. of about 160. Of course, he didn't talk. But everybody knows that I.Q. tests based on language ability are very one-sided. Besides, he would talk as soon as they started setting a place for him at table and pouring him coffee. Ashurbanipal and Cleopatra ate horsemeat from pans on the floor and they didn't talk. Baby dined in his crib on milk from a bottle and he didn't talk. Sissy sat at table but they didn't pour her coffee and she didn't talk—not one word. Father and Mother (whom Gum-

mitch had nicknamed Old Horsemeat and Kitty-Come-
Here) sat at table and poured each other coffee and they *did*
talk. Q.E.D.

Meanwhile, he would get by very well on thought projection and intuitive understanding of all human speech—
not even to mention cat patois, which almost any civilized
animal could play by ear. The dramatic monologues and So-
cratic dialogues, the quiz- and panel-show appearances, the
felidological expedition to darkest Africa (where he would
uncover the real truth behind lions and tigers), the exploration of the outer planets—all these could wait. The same
went for the books for which he was ceaselessly accumulat-
ing material: *The Encyclopedia of Odors, Anthropofeline Psychol-
ogy, Invisible Signs and Secret Wonders, Space-Time for Springers,
Slit Eyes Look at Life,* et cetera. For the present it was enough
to live existence to the hilt and soak up knowledge, missing
no experience proper to his age level—to rush about with
tail aflame.

So to all outward appearances Gummitch was just a vividly normal kitten, as shown by the succession of nicknames
he bore along the magic path that led from blue-eyed infancy
toward puberty: Little One, Squawker, Portly, Bumble (for
purring not clumsiness), Old Starved-to-Death, Fierso, Lover
Boy (affection not sex), Spook, and Catnik. Of these only the
last perhaps requires further explanation: the Russians had
just sent Muttnik up after Sputnik, so that when one evening
Gummitch streaked three times across the firmament of the
living-room floor in the same direction, past the fixed stars of
the humans and the comparatively slow-moving heavenly
bodies of the two older cats, and Kitty-Come-Here quoted the
line from Keats:

> *Then felt I like some watcher of the skies*
> *When a new planet swims into his ken;*

it was inevitable that Old Horsemeat would say, "Ah—Cat-nik!"

The new name lasted all of three days, to be replaced by Gummitch, which showed signs of becoming permanent.

The little cat was on the verge of truly growing up, at least so Gummitch overheard Old Horsemeat comment to Kitty-Come-Here. A few short weeks, Old Horsemeat said, and Gummitch's fiery flesh would harden, his slim neck thicken, the electricity vanish from everything but his fur, and all his delightful kittenish qualities rapidly give way to the earthbound single-mindedness of a tom. They'd be lucky, Old Horsemeat concluded, if he didn't turn completely surly like Ashurbanipal.

Gummitch listened to these predictions with gay uncon-cern and with secret amusement from his vantage point of superior knowledge, in the same spirit that he accepted so many phases of his outwardly conventional existence: the murderous sidelong looks he got from Ashurbanipal and Cleopatra as he devoured his own horsemeat from his own little tin pan, because they sometimes were given canned catfood but he never; the stark idiocy of Baby, who didn't know the difference between a live cat and a stuffed teddy bear and who tried to cover up his ignorance by making goo-goo noises and poking indiscriminately at all eyes; the far more serious—because cleverly hidden—maliciousness of Sissy, who had to be watched out for warily—especially when you were alone—and whose retarded—even warped—devel-opment, Gummitch knew, was Old Horsemeat and Kitty-Come-Here's deepest, most secret, worry (more of Sissy and her evil ways soon); the limited intellect of Kitty-Come-Here, who despite the amounts of coffee she drank was quite as featherbrained as kittens are supposed to be and who firmly believed, for example, that kittens operated in the same space-time as other beings—that to get from *here* to *there* they had to cross the space *between*—and similar fallacies; the mental stodginess of even Old Horsemeat, who although he understood quite a bit of the secret doctrine and talked intelligently to Gummitch when they were alone, nevertheless suffered from the limitations of his status—a rather nice old god but a maddeningly slow-witted one.

But Gummitch could easily forgive all this massed inadequacy and downright brutishness in his felinohuman household, because he was aware that he alone knew the real truth about himself and about other kittens and babies as well, the truth which was hidden from weaker minds, the truth that was as intrinsically incredible as the germ theory of disease or the origin of the whole great universe in the explosion of a single atom.

As a baby kitten Gummitch had believed that Old Horsemeat's two hands were hairless kittens permanently attached to the ends of Old Horsemeat's arms but having an independent life of their own. How he had hated and loved those two five-legged sallow monsters, his first playmates, comforters and battle opponents!

Well, even that fantastic discarded notion was but a trifling fancy compared to the real truth about himself!

The forehead of Zeus split open to give birth to Athena. Gummitch had been born from the waist-fold of a dirty old terry-cloth bathrobe, Old Horsemeat's basic garment. The kitten was intuitively certain of it and had proved it to himself as well as any Descartes or Aristotle. In a kitten-size tuck of that ancient bathrobe the atoms of his body had gathered and quickened into life. His earliest memories were of snoozing wrapped in terry-cloth, warmed by Old Horsemeat's heat. Old Horsemeat and Kitty-Come-Here were his true parents. The other theory of his origin, the one he heard Old Horsemeat and Kitty-Come-Here recount from time to time—that he had been the only surviving kitten of a litter abandoned next door, that he had had the shakes from vitamin deficiency and lost the tip of his tail and the hair on his paws and had to be nursed back to life and health with warm yellowish milk-and-vitamins fed from an eyedropper—that other theory was just one of those rationalizations with which mysterious nature cloaks the birth of heroes, perhaps wisely veiling the truth from minds unable to bear it, a rationalization as false as Kitty-Come-Here and Old Horsemeat's touching belief that Sissy and Baby were their children rather than the cubs of Ashurbanipal and Cleopatra.

The day that Gummitch had discovered by pure intuition the secret of his birth he had been filled with a wild instant excitement. He had only kept it from tearing him to pieces by rushing out to the kitchen and striking and devouring a fried scallop, torturing it fiendishly first for twenty minutes.

And the secret of his birth was only the beginning. His intellectual faculties aroused, Gummitch had two days later intuited a further and greater secret: since he was the child of humans he would, upon reaching this maturation date of which Old Horsemeat had spoken, turn not into a sullen tom but into a godlike human youth with reddish golden hair the color of his present fur. He would be poured coffee; and he would instantly be able to talk, probably in all languages. While Sissy (how clear it was now!) would at approximately the same time shrink and fur out into a sharp-clawed and vicious she-cat dark as her hair, sex and self-love her only concerns, fit harem-mate for Cleopatra, concubine to Ashurbanipal.

Exactly the same was true, Gummitch realized at once, for all kittens and babies, all humans and cats, wherever they might dwell. Metamorphosis was as much a part of the fabric of their lives as it was of the insects'. It was also the basic fact

349

underlying all legends of werewolves, vampires, and witches' familiars.

If you just rid your mind of preconceived notions, Gummitch told himself, it was all very logical. Babies were stupid, fumbling, vindictive creatures without reason or speech. What could be more natural than that they should grow up into mute sullen selfish beasts bent only on rapine and reproduction? While kittens were quick, sensitive, subtle, supremely alive. What other destiny were they possibly fitted for except to become the deft, word-speaking, book-writing, music-making, meat-getting-and-dispensing masters of the world? To dwell on the physical differences, to point out that kittens and men, babies and cats, are rather unlike in appearance and size, would be to miss the forest for the trees—very much as if an entomologist should proclaim metamorphosis a myth because his microscope failed to discover the wings of a butterfly in a caterpillar's slime or a golden beetle in a grub.

Nevertheless it was such a mind-staggering truth, Gummitch realized at the same time, that it was easy to understand why humans, cats, babies, and perhaps most kittens were quite unaware of it. How to safely explain to a butterfly that he was once a hairy crawler, or to a dull larva that he will one day be a walking jewel? No, in such situations the delicate minds of man- and feline-kind are guarded by a merciful mass amnesia, such as Velikovsky has explained prevents us from recalling that in historical times the Earth was catastrophically bumped by the planet Venus operating in the manner of a comet before settling down (with a cosmic sigh of relief, surely!) into its present orbit.

This conclusion was confirmed when Gummitch in the first fever of illumination tried to communicate his great insight to others. He told it in cat patois, as well as that limited jargon permitted, to Ashurbanipal and Cleopatra and even, on the off chance, to Sissy and Baby. They showed no interest whatever, except that Sissy took advantage of his unguarded preoccupation to stab him with a fork.

Later, alone with Old Horsemeat, he projected the great new thoughts, staring with solemn yellow eyes at the old god, but the latter grew markedly nervous and even showed signs of real fear, so Gummitch desisted. ("You'd have sworn he was trying to put across something as deep as the Einstein theory or the doctrine of original sin," Old Horsemeat later told Kitty-Come-Here.)

But Gummitch was a man now in all but form, the kitten reminded himself after these failures, and it was part of his destiny to shoulder secrets alone when necessary. He wondered if the general amnesia would affect him when he metamorphosed. There was no sure answer to this question, but he hoped not—and sometimes felt that there was reason for his hopes. Perhaps he would be the first true kitten-man, speaking from a wisdom that had no locked doors in it.

Once he was tempted to speed up the process by the use of drugs. Left alone in the kitchen, he sprang onto the table and started to lap up the black puddle in the bottom of Old Horsemeat's coffee cup. It tasted foul and poisonous and he withdrew with a little snarl, frightened as well as revolted. The dark beverage would not work its tongue-loosening magic, he realized, except at the proper time and with the proper ceremonies. Incantations might be necessary as well. Certainly unlawful tasting was highly dangerous.

The futility of expecting coffee to work any wonders by itself was further demonstrated to Gummitch when Kitty-Come-Here, wordlessly badgered by Sissy, gave a few spoonfuls to the little girl, liberally lacing it first with milk and sugar. Of course Gummitch knew by now that Sissy was destined shortly to turn into a cat and that no amount of coffee would ever make her talk, but it was nevertheless instructive to see how she spat out the first mouthful, drooling a lot of saliva after it, and dashed the cup and its contents at the chest of Kitty-Come-Here.

Gummitch continued to feel a great deal of sympathy for his parents in their worries about Sissy and he longed for the day when he would metamorphose and be able as an acknowledged man-child truly to console them. It was heartbreaking to see how they each tried to coax the little girl to talk, always attempting it while the other was absent, how they seized on each accidentally wordlike note in the few sounds she uttered and repeated it back to her hopefully, how they were more and more possessed by fears not so much of her retarded (they thought) development as of her increasingly obvious maliciousness, which was directed chiefly at Baby . . . though the two cats and Gummitch bore their share. Once she had caught Baby alone in his crib and used the sharp corner of a block to dot Baby's large-domed lightly downed head with triangular red marks. Kitty-Come-Here had discovered her doing it, but the woman's first action had been to rub Baby's head to obliterate the marks so that Old Horsemeat wouldn't see them. That was the night Kitty-Come-Here hid the abnormal-psychology books.

Gummitch understood very well that Kitty-Come-Here and Old Horsemeat, honestly believing themselves to be Sissy's parents, felt just as deeply about her as if they actually were and he did what little he could under the present circumstances to help them. He had recently come to feel a quite independent affection for Baby—the miserable little proto-cat was so completely stupid and defenseless—and so he unofficially constituted himself the creature's guardian, taking his naps behind the door of the nursery and dashing about noisily whenever Sissy showed up. In any case he realized that as a potentially adult member of a felinohuman household he had his natural responsibilities.

Accepting responsibilities was as much a part of a kitten's life, Gummitch told himself, as shouldering unsharable intuitions and secrets, the number of which continued to grow from day to day.

There was, for instance, the Affair of the Squirrel Mirror.

Gummitch had early solved the mystery of ordinary mirrors and of the creatures that appeared in them. A little observation and sniffing and one attempt to get behind the heavy wall-job in the living room had convinced him that mirror beings were insubstantial or at least hermetically sealed into their other world, probably creatures of pure spirit, harmless imitative ghosts—including the silent Gummitch Double who touched paws with him so softly yet so coldly.

Just the same, Gummitch had let his imagination play with what would happen if one day, while looking into the mirror world, he should let loose his grip on his spirit and let it slip into the Gummitch Double while the other's spirit slipped into his body—if, in short, he should change places with the scentless ghost kitten. Being doomed to a life consisting wholly of imitation and completely lacking in opportunities to show initiative—except for behind-the-scenes judgment and speed needed in rushing from one mirror to another to keep up with the real Gummitch—would be sickeningly dull, Gummitch decided, and he resolved to keep a tight hold on his spirit at all times in the vicinity of mirrors.

But that isn't telling about the Squirrel Mirror. One morning Gummitch was peering out the front bedroom window that overlooked the roof of the porch. Gummitch had already classified windows as semi-mirrors having two kinds of space on the other side: the mirror world and that harsh region filled with mysterious and dangerously organized-sounding noises called the outer world, into which grown-up humans reluctantly ventured at intervals, donning special garments for the purpose and shouting loud farewells that were meant to be reassuring but achieved just the opposite effect. The coexistence of two kinds of space presented no paradox to the kitten who carried in his mind the twenty-seven-chapter outline of *Space-Time for Springers*—indeed, it constituted one of the minor themes of the book.

This morning the bedroom was dark and the outer world was dull and sunless, so the mirror world was unusually difficult to see. Gummitch was just lifting his face toward it, nose twitching, his front paws on the sill, when what should rear up on the other side, exactly in the space that the Gummitch Double normally occupied, but a dirty brown, narrow-visaged image with savagely low forehead, dark evil walleyes, and a huge jaw filled with shovellike teeth.

Gummitch was enormously startled and hideously frightened. He felt his grip on his spirit go limp, and without volition he teleported himself three yards to the rear, making use of that faculty for cutting corners in space-time, traveling by space-warp in fact, which was one of his powers that Kitty-Come-Here refused to believe in and that even Old Horsemeat accepted only on faith.

Then, not losing a moment, he picked himself up by his furry seat, swung himself around, dashed downstairs at top speed, sprang to the top of the sofa, and stared for several seconds at the Gummitch Double in the wall mirror—not relaxing a muscle strand until he was completely convinced that he was still himself and had not been transformed into the nasty brown apparition that had confronted him in the bedroom window.

"Now what do you suppose brought that on?" Old Horsemeat asked Kitty-Come-Here.

Later Gummitch learned that what he had seen had been a squirrel, a savage, nut-hunting being belonging wholly to the outer world (except for forays into attics) and not at all to the mirror one. Nevertheless he kept a vivid memory of his profound momentary conviction that the squirrel had taken the Gummitch Double's place and been about to take his own. He shuddered to think what would have happened if the squirrel had been actively interested in trading spirits with him. Apparently mirrors and mirror-situations, just as he had always feared, were highly conducive to spirit transfers. He filed the information away in the memory cabinet reserved for dangerous, exciting, and possibly useful information, such as plans for climbing straight up glass (diamond-tipped claws!) and flying higher than the trees.

These days his thought cabinets were beginning to feel filled to bursting and he could hardly wait for the moment when the true rich taste of coffee, lawfully drunk, would permit him to speak.

He pictured the scene in detail: the family gathered in conclave at the kitchen table, Ashurbanipal and Cleopatra respectfully watching from floor level, himself sitting erect on chair with paws (or would they be hands?) lightly touching his cup of thin china, while Old Horsemeat poured the thin black steaming stream. He knew the Great Transformation must be close at hand.

At the same time he knew that the other critical situation in the household was worsening swiftly. Sissy, he realized now, was far older than Baby and should long ago have undergone her own somewhat less glamorous though equally necessary transformation (the first tin of raw horsemeat could hardly be as exciting as the first cup of coffee). Her time was long overdue. Gummitch found increasing horror in this mute vampirish being inhabiting the body of a rapidly growing girl, though inwardly equipped to be nothing but a most bloodthirsty she-cat. How dreadful to think of Old Horsemeat and Kitty-Come-Here having to care all their lives for such a monster! Gummitch told himself that if any opportunity for alleviating his parents' misery should ever present itself to him, he would not hesitate for an instant.

Then one night, when the sense of Change was so burstingly strong in him that he knew tomorrow must be the Day, but when the house was also exceptionally unquiet with boards creaking and snapping, taps adrip, and curtains mysteriously rustling at closed windows (so that it was clear that the many spirit worlds including the mirror one must be pressing very close), the opportunity came to Gummitch.

Kitty-Come-Here and Old Horsemeat had fallen into especially sound, drugged sleeps, the former with a bad cold, the latter with one unhappy highball too many (Gummitch knew he had been brooding about Sissy). Baby slept too, though with uneasy whimperings and joggings—moonlight shone full on his crib past a window shade which had whirringly rolled itself up without human or feline agency. Gummitch kept vigil under the crib, with eyes closed but with wildly excited mind pressing outward to every boundary of the house and even stretching here and there into the outer world. On this night of all nights sleep was unthinkable.

Then suddenly he became aware of footsteps, footsteps so soft they must, he thought, be Cleopatra's.

No, softer than that, so soft they might be those of the Gummitch Double escaped from the mirror world at last and padding up toward him through the darkened halls. A ribbon of fur rose along his spine.

Then into the nursery Sissy came prowling. She looked slim as an Egyptian princess in her long thin yellow nightgown and as sure of herself, but the cat was very strong in her tonight, from the flat intent eyes to the dainty canine teeth slightly bared—one look at her now would have sent Kitty-Come-Here running for the telephone number she kept hidden, the telephone number of the special doctor—and Gummitch realized he was witnessing a monstrous suspension of natural law in that this being should be able to exist for a moment without growing fur and changing round pupils for slit eyes.

He retreated to the darkest corner of the room, suppressing a snarl.

Sissy approached the crib and leaned over Baby in the moonlight, keeping her shadow off him. For a while she gloated. Then she began softly to scratch his cheek with a long hatpin she carried, keeping away from his eye, but just barely. Baby awoke and saw her and Baby didn't cry. Sissy continued to scratch, always a little more deeply. The moonlight glittered on the jeweled end of the pin.

Gummitch knew he faced a horror that could not be countered by running about or even spitting and screeching. Only magic could fight so obviously supernatural a manifestation. And this was also no time to think of consequences, no matter how clearly and bitterly etched they might appear to a mind intensely awake.

He sprang up onto the other side of the crib, not uttering a sound, and fixed his golden eyes on Sissy's in the moonlight. Then he moved forward straight at her evil face, stepping slowly, not swiftly, using his extraordinary knowledge of the properties of space *to walk straight through her hand and arm as they flailed the hatpin at him.* When his nose-tip finally paused a fraction of an inch from hers his eyes had not blinked once, and she could not look away. Then he unhesitatingly flung his spirit into her like a fistful of flaming arrows and he worked the Mirror Magic.

Sissy's moonlit face, feline and terrified, was in a sense the last thing that Gummitch, the real Gummitch-kitten, ever saw in this world. For the next instant he felt himself enfolded by the foul black blinding cloud of Sissy's spirit, which his own had displaced. At the same time he heard the little girl scream, very loudly but even more distinctly, *"Mommy!"*

That cry might have brought Kitty-Come-Here out of her grave, let alone from sleep merely deep or drugged. Within seconds she was in the nursery, closely followed by Old

Horsemeat, and she had caught up Sissy in her arms and the little girl was articulating the wonderful word again and again, and miraculously following it with the command—there could be no doubt, Old Horsemeat heard it too—"Hold me tight!"

Then Baby finally dared to cry. The scratches on his cheek came to attention and Gummitch, as he had known must happen, was banished to the basement amid cries of horror and loathing chiefly from Kitty-Come-Here.

The little cat did not mind. No basement would be one-tenth as dark as Sissy's spirit that now enshrouded him for always, hiding all the file drawers and the labels on all the folders, blotting out forever even the imagining of the scene of first coffee-drinking and first speech.

In a last intuition, before the animal blackness closed in utterly, Gummitch realized that the spirit, alas, is not the same thing as the consciousness and that one may lose—sacrifice—the first and still be burdened with the second.

Old Horsemeat had seen the hatpin (and hid it quickly from Kitty-Come-Here) and so he knew that the situation was not what it seemed and that Gummitch was at the very least being made into a sort of scapegoat. He was quite apologetic when he brought the tin pans of food to the basement during the period of the little cat's exile. It was a comfort to Gummitch, albeit a small one. Gummitch told himself, in his new black halting manner of thinking, that after all a cat's best friend is his man.

From that night Sissy never turned back in her development. Within two months she had made three years' progress in speaking. She became an outstandingly bright, light-footed, high-spirited little girl. Although she never told anyone this, the moonlit nursery and Gummitch's magnified face were her first memories. Everything before that was inky blackness. She was always very nice to Gummitch in a careful sort of way. She could never stand to play the game Owl Eyes.

After a few weeks Kitty-Come-Here forgot her fears and Gummitch once again had the run of the house. But by then the transformation Old Horsemeat had always warned about had fully taken place. Gummitch was a kitten no longer but an almost burly tom. In him it took the psychological form not of sullenness or surliness but an extreme dignity. He seemed at times rather like an old pirate brooding on treasures he would never live to dig up, shores of adventure he would never reach. And sometimes when you looked into his yellow eyes you felt that he had in him all the materials for the book *Slit Eyes Look at Life*— three or four volumes at least—although he would never write it. And that was natural when you come to think of it, for as Gummitch knew very well, bitterly well indeed, his fate was to be the only kitten in the world that did not grow up to be a man.

Eleanor Farjeon

SPOONER

$\mathbf{M}$y cousin, William Saunders, died suddenly and tragically in a road accident in London. He had a 1915 bullet in his leg, and hobbled. As children, and as boy and girl in our teens, we had been like brother and sister to each other. We were both only children, lived in adjacent roads in South Hampstead, and spent much of our free time together. It was from Bill I caught fire about cricket. I did not shape well in our back-garden games, but Bill drilled the science into me theoretically, taught me how to score, and companioned me to Lords as often as he could scrape up the time and the pocket money. I learned to love the game as a saga, even the dull patches which were an essential part of it. Tennis is lyrical; but cricket is epic. No epic remains at inspiration point from start to finish. You live through a cricket match, as you live through much of life, on expectation. To the critic who criticized his longer poems for their dull patches, Byron replied: "The night cannot be all stars." The stars show up all the brighter for the night.

Of course we chose our teams, or rather were chosen by them. I couldn't say by what inevitable process I became Lancashire and Bill Yorkshire. Every summer the rivalry waxed fierce between us two young Londoners who had never been to Lancaster or York. The rivalry of sport is an indisseverable bond. We honored each other's hierarchies, but swore by our own. When I, in our schoolroom strife, shouted, "Maclaren!", Bill hurled back "Jackson!" like a thunderbolt. Just before the First World War we began to see less of each other, and after it we never met at all. He settled down with his war wound in a little house he bought in St. John's Wood; I had drifted by circumstance up north, and was earning my living in a large industrial town. Even kinship did not save us from one of those almost complete separations which happen to childhood friends, the mere thought of which, in the first decade of the century, would have seemed laughable to us. There was no estrangement of any sort. We were not letter writers. We exchanged notes at Christmas, and once a year, on our birthdays, something else. The two days fell in the same week in June, and I never let Bill's pass without posting him a red rose. A few days later he responded with a white one. It was the postscript to our cricket rivalry.

I did not even know that Bill had died when I heard from a solicitor that he had left me the little house in Selina Place, just as it stood, lock, stock, and barrel. I was on the eve of retiring on a pension which was not much more than a pleasant competence, so Bill's legacy came as a godsend. The house, which stood detached in a quarter of an acre of garden, was furnished, I was told, from top to toe, and all it contained was mine, free of legacy duty. I instantly abandoned the tentative plans I had been considering for my retirement, blessed my old Bill from a grateful heart, packed my modest possessions, strapped Spooner into his basket, and traveled to London with as little delay as possible.

Spooner was my red tabby. When I say he had the most exquisite stance, and, running, carried his tail with enchanting style, anyone whose cricket memories extend back to the turn of the century will know why I gave him that name. I had never ceased to worship the gods of my youth; and if Maclaren was the Zeus, Spooner was the Apollo at whose shrine I had poured my most ardent libations. Many a time he had been a feather in my red-rosed cap, when Yorkshire lost a match, and Bill could hardly wish me a civil good night.

We arrived in time for late tea, on Midsummer Eve. Midsummer Day was Bill's birthday; he would have been sixty-one. On June 27 I was to become sixty-three. But the Bill who had just hobbled to his death with his years upon him was still to me the lithe young man I had seen racing balls to the boundary from long-on (Bill insisted on keen fielding). And Mary Shearn, the elderly woman to whom he had bequeathed his house behind Lords Cricket Ground, to him no doubt was still little pigtailed Molly, biting the end of her pencil as she worked out a bowling average. In winter we played elaborate paper cricket, assisted by a pack of cards and a dice box. So as the front door was opened to me by a nice Mrs. Meadows, who had looked after Bill and was prepared to look after me, I had the strange feeling of four or five decades slipping away behind me, and almost expected that in another minute I should encounter Bill himself, toweling his shoulders after a sweating innings, and teasing me because my unaccustomed hairpins were falling out. The very look of the house made it easy to think so; the oddly shaped rooms, furnished simply and shabbily with the kindly furniture of his boyhood, the maple frames of the pictures, the old-fashioned French windows opening onto a low balcony with three ironwork steps down to the sunny-shady garden: all had retained the air of our adolescence. I stood still, feeling and smelling rather than seeing it.

"I've laid your tea under the weeping ash, Miss Shearn. Poor Mr. Saunders liked it best there; he could hear the appeals, he said."

"The appeals, Mrs. Meadows?"

"From the cricket ground. I can't say I ever hear them myself, but then my ears aren't so quick, I expect."

No, I expect not, I thought. Sitting in his garden, within range of the lordly pitch, Bill's ears were sharpened on the hone of half a century.

"Did he go often to the matches, Mrs. Meadows?"

"Oh, yes, very often, when he was at his best. What a dear little puss. Shall you let her out in the garden?"

"Him, Mrs. Meadows. I won't unstrap him till there's something for him to eat. What is there in the house?"

"I was doing you some fried fillets for supper."

"That will do beautifully. Bring me one with the tea, please, and some margarine."

"To butter his feet, yes, miss. What do you call him?"

"Spooner."

"Spooner—Spooner—Spooner!" Mrs. Meadows let out the high call peculiar to women who call in their cats at night. Spooner opened a wary eye, but made no sign. Mrs. Meadows departed. I would have much to ask her later on, I knew; but not today. I did not want the present imposed on this delicious sense of the past in which I was swimming as on a summer sea: the sort of sea children dream of before and after their holidays. Mrs. Meadows returned with the teapot (a table was ready-laid under the tree), a tin plate of fish, an extra saucer, and a pat of margarine.

"Thank you, Mrs. Meadows. Perhaps you'd better leave us before I undo him."

"Very well, miss. He'll soon get used to me. They know who's fond of them, don't you, pretty? Meadows is more one for dogs. It near broke his heart when Mr. Saunders—" Mrs. Meadows gulped and wiped her eyes on her apron. I respected her grief, but her unfinished sentence left me faintly puzzled. "Meadows has taken your boxes up to your room. Mr. Bill's room it is. One of the cupboards isn't quite cleared out. Shall I unpack for you?"

"No, thank you. I'd better settle everything myself, and get my bearings. I haven't brought very much, but I'll clear the cupboard if I need more room."

"I'll leave the key in it then, miss."

"Did Bill—did Mr. Saunders keep it locked?"

"He didn't like me ever to touch what was in it. I often thought perhaps he kept some savings there, but when the valuers came they found nothing of any account."

Mrs. Meadows left me, and I unstrapped the basket with endearing sounds and caresses. I caught Spooner on the stretch, buttered his protesting paws, and put the plate of fish under his nose. He turned his head away and roamed leisurely round my deck chair, stopping here and there to lick his white pads. Then he came round to the fish, discovered it for himself, fell to, devoured half of it heartily, eyed the remainder with loathing, stood before me with milk-demanding eyes, refused it out of his own saucer, drank it lavishly from mine, and began to prowl the garden with great caution. He nosed lions and jackals in every rosebush.

Roses! Suddenly I was overwhelmed with the scent of them. I turned my head and found myself looking at a small rosebed of great beauty. Eleven exquisite white standard trees dominated it, below them sprawled a mat of red rosebushes: eleven more. I burst out laughing.

"Bill! You *rotter!*"

I recognized the white roses at once. From these standards my rival had plucked his annual trophy, never hinting that the white rose had dominated the red. In a single moment I heard some thirty-five years of chuckles, as Bill snipped from the upper-team the most perfect specimen he could find to rout me with. I even imagined him apostrophizing it by name. . . .

Of course! I jumped to my feet. I knew in a flash he had done what I would have done. Yes, each bush and each standard had its tag. The upright Frau Karl Druschkis were labeled: "Hobbs"—"Hirst"—"Sutcliffe." The crawling Hugh Dicksons: "A. C. Maclaren"—"Tyldesley"—"R. H. Spooner."

"I'll Spooner you!" I cried. "Here! Spooner, Spooner!"

A low growl answered me, the jungle growl that the gentlest cat can emit when you touch his kill. Spooner was crouched in the grass, hairs bristling, eyes glittering. It always gives me a shiver when I see a cat seeing what I can't see. Spooner was seeing—what?

He made ready to spring; then suddenly dashed in frantic haste up the ash, and stood with steeply arched spine, glaring down. At such moments his electric eyes change from honey to tomato red.

I did my best to coax him to come down. He would not. Only when Mr. Meadows arrived with a ladder was Spooner restored to my arms, trembling, I thought, with equal fear and fury. I carried him at once into the house, where he ate the rest of his fish avidly, drank copious water, and followed me to my bedroom. Here he fell asleep very suddenly on my bed, coiled round on himself like a golden ammonite.

It did not take me long to settle my things. There was no wardrobe, but the fireplace was flanked, in the Victorian fashion, by painted cupboards fixed against the wallpaper, not reaching quite to the ceiling. One would have shelves, the other hanging space. There were two chests of drawers, an old one of mahogany with drop-handles, and a light yellow one with china knobs. I remembered this cheap chest as being part of Bill's boyish outfit; the varnish was worn off, and I had some difficulty in opening a drawer from which a knob had gone. An insufficient doily stood on the top; the surface it left exposed was scored with Bill's penknife: "B. S." cut several times, and in one place, with particular care, "F. S." I tried to recall to what Saunders the *F* belonged, and remembered that his father, with whom he did not get on very well, was called Francis. My heart warmed to Bill cherishing the furniture of his youth; it was this heterogeneousness, this loving tastelessness, that gave the rooms in his house their wistful quality. I found I did not want to alter anything, and hoped I need not shift what Bill kept in his cupboard. Luckily for me, the empty cupboard was the hanging one. A modern rail had been fitted, which took my dress hangers. When my wardrobe was arranged I examined the ones with shelves in it. The first thing I took out was a cricket bat.

Then I knew. I knew what it was the valuers did not value. Everything on the shelves had to do with Bill's passion. It delved deep back to his seventh or eighth year. Small bats, growing bigger and bigger, pads the same, balls broken at the seams, a split bail marked in red ink "T. Richardson," photographs, picture postcards and newspaper prints, of batsmen, bowlers, umpires; newspaper cuttings, too, of hundreds of games, Wisdens galore, Snaith's *Willow the King* read to saturation point; cardboard shoe boxes crammed with letters and autographs: Townsend's among them. I recalled how at one match when the small boys broke loose, Bill had chased Townsend almost to the Pavilion, pestering him for his signature; and how Townsend had muttered, "Oh, I *can't!*" and fled. Bill had returned to me red-faced with shame, and eyes suspiciously moist. So you did get him after all, Bill. I'm so glad!—And among the shoe boxes a larger one, containing old copybooks with marbled covers in which Bill had kept the scores of our paper games. An incomplete, very dirty pack of cards. And a scribbled sheet that seemed strangely familiar—yes! a bowling score, the dots very black from Molly's well-sucked pencil, and the maiden M's marked scrupulously from corner to corner. Oh Bill, dear Bill! I won't disturb your boyhood's treasure house. All my old junk shall be scrapped ere one scrap of yours.

I shut the door gently, everything replaced, and as gently pushed Spooner away with my foot, for I felt him trying to shove his way into the cupboard.

"This is not the place for pusscats," I admonished him, stooping to soften the admonition with a caress—and found that there was nothing to caress; for Spooner was still coiled up, sound asleep, on my quilt.

I kicked off my slippers, had a bath in the old-fashioned bath with a mahogany surround, dressed in something fresh, and went down to dinner. It was simple and nicely cooked, and I began to feel that I and Spooner were batting on a good wicket. Mrs. Meadows brought the dishes in and out, and I had an impression that Meadows was helping her, for I caught a glimpse of him in the passage when the door was ajar, saw rather than heard him whisper something, and Mrs. Meadows shake her head at him. "I wouldn't, not tonight," I heard her say; and then she came in and put the summer pudding before me.

I decided to ask no questions; for the moment I was the visiting team on the Meadows's home ground. I did not yet belong, things must come about in their own way. So I merely said, "I shall go to bed early tonight. We'll have plenty to talk about in the next few days."

"Yes, miss. Where did you want Spooner to sleep?"

"He sleeps with me. He usually tucks down, but he may

be restless tonight, especially as there's a moon. I shall only open my window at the top."

"We'll have to keep an eye on him," agreed Mrs. Meadows. "Goodness knows, we don't want no more accidents."

I couldn't think of an adequate answer to this. I helped myself again to the pudding, saying, "This is delicious, Mrs. Meadows. By the way—or really, not at all by the way, of course—I'm sure you know that tomorrow is Mr. Bill's birthday."

"Oh, yes, indeed, miss! But he won't be here to play his cricket match."

"His cricket match, Mrs. Meadows?"

"It was just a bit of playacting, of course, but on his birthday he always made Meadows buckle on his pads for him, and he'd put on his gloves, and take his bat (he always kept it oiled), and Meadows had to bowl to him in the garden. He couldn't run, of course; but he scored by where his hits went, so many for the ash, so many for the conservatory end, a boundary for the fig tree on the far wall, and so on. He was no end bucked one year when he broke a pane in the top of the conservatory. 'What price Jessop?' he said. It was you, miss, wasn't it, always sent him that red rose?"

"Yes, Mrs. Meadows. We'll put one in the vase in front of his picture tomorrow."

"I don't think he was ever merrier than when he went out to cut you your white one. 'The return match, Mrs. Meadows,' he used to say, 'ba goom, this'll dish her, so much for Spooner!' he'd say—Spooner!" ejaculated Mrs. Meadows. "Well, I never! Did he know about your little cat, miss?"

"No, I'm sure he didn't. We didn't really write to each other, you know. But I did call my cat Spooner because of an old joke between us when we were little. And he was thinking of it when he cut the rose."

"It's what you might call a coincidence, mightn't you, miss."

"Perhaps, Mrs. Meadows." And perhaps not, Mrs. Meadows.

When I went up to bed the room was not as I had left it. I had been careful not quite to close the knobless drawer in the yellow chest, till I got it mended. It had been dragged still farther out, and the contents were messed up, and some of them were on the floor. Among these my best pair of gloves, the left one badly chewed; and my second-best pair in a corner, torn to shreds; and in the fireplace the string gloves a friend had knitted, restored to their original string. Whose doing? Spooner's? He had long given up his masticating kittenhood, and his elegant limbs and delicate little head could not have pushed and jammed the drawer as I now found it. But where *was* Spooner? He seemed to have disappeared.

I spied him on the top of the hanging cupboard. He was in a strange state, and for the second time that day refused to come down. When I stood on a chair and reached for him, he snarled. But not, I thought, at me. I could not blame him for being perturbed; I was rather perturbed myself, the difference being that I did not know what was perturbing me; and I was quite sure Spooner did know.

"Is it a poltergeist?" I asked him. "What is it, Spooner?"

He tried to struggle out of my arms to the cupboard again; I soothed him, and presently he quieted down, and paraded the carpet gingerly, sniffing at my damaged finery, until I had tidied it up and put it away. I decided to shut the knobless drawer for the night; I didn't want anything rummaging while I slept.

But though I was puzzled, I wasn't really afraid. I felt no malice in the air, no antagonism, only the agitation of something itself perturbed, but in no sense dangerous. Should I consult Mrs. Meadows? Better not. I would investigate the mystery in the daylight. I got into bed, and Spooner, after his fashion, lay on my pillow with one pad on my cheek.

I woke in moonlight to the baying of a dog. Spooner was sitting upright by my ear. I sat up too. The baying sounded like a call, a challenge. Spooner made a mad rush at the window, clawed at the frame, at the sashes, at the glass. I had carried out my plan of shutting the lower half, leaving only a little opening at the top. To my horror, Spooner scrambled up the curtain like a monkey, and pressed his way through the crack. Cats are more fluid than solid, they can pour themselves through any sluice like water. I saw my red cat tremble half-in, half-out, and disappear like a meteor into the garden. I flung up the sash, called him sternly by name, and without waiting for the answer I did not expect, ran down as I was, hoping to be in time to stop him from leaping a wall. The moonlight was warm, the garden seemed scarcely to breathe, the rose scent was intolerably strong. I did not know roses smelled so strong at night. Drawn to the bed, with its teams of red and white, I saw Spooner standing almost erect against one of the standards. He was beautifully poised and perfectly calm. Once more he was looking at what I could not see, and seemed to be listening too. After few moments he dropped on all fours, stood sniffing as he might a fellow cat, turned tail, and walked with composure into the house. I followed meekly. Whatever was toward, Spooner now had it in charge. As he led me up the stairs his tail was erect; so I knew that there was nothing to worry about.

Back in the bedroom Spooner proceeded to the cupboard with the shelves. There he planted himself, looking at me expectantly. I hesitated, like the crass human I am; but I have never yet known a cat who could not make its commands imperative, even if not explicable. Spooner stood on his hind legs, stretched himself like elastic as high as the keyhole, and laid a paw on either side of the key. I turned it, and opened the cupboard.

What would Spooner do next? He did nothing at all, but merely waited with his eyes on the door of the room. Again,

I saw nothing; then the door silently opened a little further, and Nothing entered. Nor could I hear anything; but Anything was there. A disturbance now began inside the cupboard; on one of the shelves the objects became dislodged, a ball rolled out, a box of papers scattered itself at my feet, bit by bit the shelf was cleared of its litter—until, among other things, the ancient batting glove dropped on the floor. It did not remain there. It appeared to drag itself across the carpet, and into the passage. I heard it flopping down from stair to stair.

I looked at Spooner. He was cleaning his white pads with particular care. In the moonlight they gleamed as though they were freshly pipe-clayed. As soon as they were done to his satisfaction, he strolled back to my pillow and went to sleep.

"Did you hear a dog bay in the night, Mrs. Meadows?" I asked.

She hesitated in the act of clearing my breakfast away. "Yes, miss, I fancied I did. It sounded for all the world like poor old Jack."

"Jack?"

"Mr. Bill's Yorkshire terrier, miss."

"I never knew my cousin had a dog." (But why should I, Bill? You never knew I had dog's rival, cat.)

"Oh, yes, he was all the world to Mr. Bill. Of course, that's how it happened."

"How what happened?"

"The dreadful accident. Surely you knew about it?"

"I knew nothing, Mrs. Meadows. I didn't even know my cousin had died till I heard from his lawyer. Do you mind telling me?"

Mrs. Meadows began to sob uncontrollably. As though he had been waiting for his cue, Mr. Meadows appeared in the doorway.

"Now Mother, doan't take on. You go to t' kitchen an'

recover yersel.' *Ah'll* tell Miss Shearn." The burly red-faced little man stood before me, twisting his cap in his hands. "Middlesex were playin' Yarksheer, ye see. Mr. Bill never missed a Yarksheer match if he could help it. Ah were goin' to arm him there, as Ah allus did, but he thought he'd be late, an' got ahead o' me. The tyke dashed after him, out into t' road. Mr. Bill cried summat like *'Save it!'* because one o' them big house-movin' vans were coming. It got the tyke an' knocked the maister flat. We brought 'em home together, tyke in t' maister's arms, dead as a doornail. Maister he died before t' ambulance come."

"And that was the end," I whispered. (Bill—giving his life to save Yorkshire.)

"No, miss, not quite. It's summat Ah've got to speak to you about, if you doan't mind."

"Go on, Meadows."

"When he wur lyin' there, gaspin' to fetch his breath, he sez to me, 'Bury Jack in t' garden under t' fig, an' put a wood cross wi' his name on it same as it is on his collar. "In Lovin' Memory," doan't forget,' he sez. In a little while he fetched his breath agen. 'When you lay Jack to rest, lay wi' him my bat, and see it's oiled, an' my pads an' my gloves, an' the new ball. Jack an' me'll want 'em on Midsummer Day.' "

"That's today, Meadows."

"It's t' day he allus played his match, d'ye see. The tyke played too. He allus fielded t' ball. He fielded under t' fig tree at long-on. Jack were a gradely fielder."

"Did you do what he asked, Meadows?"

"Ah did, miss. But t' missus thought the sight of the cross might upset you, if you saw it sudden, not knowin' nawthen about it; so Ah hid it yesterday afore you come, an' thought to tell you about it today. Which now Ah've done."

Little Mr. Meadows wiped his arm across his brow.

"Come along," I said. "We'll put Jack's cross up together." We went into the garden, where the wooden cross was concealed in the fig-tree corner.

"On'y one thing troubles me," he said as we went. "Ah found t' maister's bat, an' t' new ball he allus bought in March, an' t' right-'and battin' glove. But *could* Ah find that left-'and glove? Ah could not. Ah'm afraid if t' ball rises," said Mr. Meadows with a watery smile, "t' maister'll get grazed bad upon t' knuckles."

"I don't think you need worry, Meadows," I said. "I think Jack will see to it that he's all right."

"Ba goom, Ah 'ope so. Now then, Tommy, 'oo do you think you are?" Spooner was sitting on the dog's little grave, still cleaning his white forelegs meticulously. Meadows gave him a not-too-gentle shove with his thick boot. "Get off t' pitch, son." But Spooner had taken center and seemed set for a century. He moved only just enough aside to allow Meadows to set up the wooden cross, on which was inscribed:

IN LOVING MEMORY OF F. S. JACKSON

P. G. Wodehouse

THE STORY OF
WEBSTER

C ats are not dogs!"

There is only one place where you can hear good things like that thrown off quite casually in the general run of conversation, and that is the bar parlor of the Anglers' Rest. It was there, as we sat grouped about the fire, that a thoughtful Pint of Bitter had made the statement just recorded.

Although the talk up to this point had been dealing with Einstein's Theory of Relativity, we readily adjusted our minds to cope with the new topic. Regular attendance at the nightly sessions over which Mr. Mulliner presides with such unfailing dignity and geniality tends to produce mental nimbleness. In our little circle I have known an argument on the final destination of the soul to change inside forty seconds into one concerning the best method of preserving the juiciness of bacon fat.

"Cats," proceeded the Pint of Bitter, "are selfish. A man waits on a cat hand and foot for weeks, humoring its lightest whim, and then it goes and leaves him flat because it has found a place down the road where the fish is more frequent."

"What I've got against cats," said a Lemon Sour, speaking feelingly, as one brooding on a private grievance, "is their unreliability. They lack candor and are not square shooters. You get your cat and you call him Thomas or George, as the case may be. So far, so good. Then one morning you wake up and find six kittens in the hatbox and you have to reopen the whole matter, approaching it from an entirely different angle."

"If you want to know what's the trouble with cats," said a red-faced man with glassy eyes, who had been rapping on the table for his fourth whiskey, "they've got no tact. That's what's the trouble with them. I remember a friend of mine had a cat. Made quite a pet of that cat, he did. And what occurred? What was the outcome? One night he came home rather late and was feeling for the keyhole with his corkscrew; and, believe me or not, his cat selected that precise moment to jump on the back of his neck out of a tree. No tact."

Mr. Mulliner shook his head.

"I grant you all this," he said, "but still, in my opinion, you have not got to the root of the matter. The real objection to the great majority of cats is their insufferable air of superiority. Cats, as a class, have never completely got over the snootiness caused by the fact that in ancient Egypt they were worshiped as gods. This makes them too prone to set themselves up as critics and censors of the frail and erring human beings whose lot they share. They stare rebukingly. They view with concern. And on a sensitive man this often has the worst effects, inducing an inferiority complex of the gravest kind. It is odd that the conversation should have taken this turn," said Mr. Mulliner, sipping his hot Scotch and lemon, "for I was thinking only this afternoon of the rather strange case of my cousin Edward's son, Lancelot."

"I knew a cat—" began a Small Bass.

My cousin Edward's son, Lancelot (said Mr. Mulliner) was, at the time of which I speak, a comely youth of some twenty-five summers. Orphaned at an early age, he had been brought up in the home of his uncle Theodore, the saintly Dean of Bolsover; and it was a great shock to that good man when Lancelot, on attaining his majority, wrote from London to inform him that he had taken a studio in Bott Street, Chelsea, and proposed to remain in the metropolis and become an artist.

The dean's opinion of artists was low. As a prominent member of the Bolsover Watch Committee, it had recently been his distasteful duty to be present at a private showing of the super-superfilm *Palettes of Passion;* and he replied to his nephew's communication with a vibrant letter in which he emphasized the grievous pain it gave him to think that one of his flesh and blood should deliberately be embarking on a career which must inevitably lead sooner or later to the painting of Russian princesses lying on divans in the seminude with their arms round tame jaguars. He urged Lancelot to return and become a curate while there was yet time.

But Lancelot was firm. He deplored the rift between himself and a relative whom he had always respected, but he was dashed if he meant to go back to an environment where his individuality had been stifled and his soul confined in chains. And for four years there was silence between uncle and nephew.

During these years Lancelot had made progress in his chosen profession. At the time at which this story opens, his prospects seemed bright. He was painting the portrait of Brenda, only daughter of Mr. and Mrs. B. B. Carberry-Pirbright, of 11 Maxton Square, South Kensington, which meant thirty pounds in his sock on delivery. He had learned to cook eggs and bacon. He had practically mastered the ukulele. And, in addition, he was engaged to be married to a fearless young *vers libre* poetess of the name of Gladys Bingley, better known as The Sweet Singer of Garbidge Mews, Fulham—a charming girl who looked like a penwiper.

It seemed to Lancelot that life was very full and beautiful. He lived joyously in the present, giving no thought to the past.

But how true it is that the past is inextricably mixed up with the present and that we can never tell when it may spring some delayed bomb beneath our feet. One afternoon, as he sat making a few small alterations in the portrait of Brenda Carberry-Pirbright, his fiancée entered.

He had been expecting her to call, for today she was going off for a three weeks' holiday to the south of France, and she had promised to look in on her way to the station. He laid down his brush and gazed at her with a yearning affection, thinking for the thousandth time how he worshiped every spot of ink on her nose. Standing there in the doorway with her bobbed hair sticking out in every direction like a golliwog's, she made a picture that seemed to speak to his very depths.

"Hullo, Reptile!" he said lovingly.

"What ho, Worm!" said Gladys, maidenly devotion shining through the monocle which she wore in her left eye. "I can stay just half an hour."

"Oh, well, half an hour soon passes," said Lancelot. "What's that you've got there?"

"A letter, ass. What did you think it was?"

"Where did you get it?"

"I found the postman outside."

Lancelot took the envelope from her and examined it.

"Gosh!" he said.

"What's the matter?"

"It's from my uncle Theodore."

"I didn't know you had an uncle Theodore."

"Of course I have. I've had him for years."

"What's he writing to you about?"

"If you'll kindly keep quiet for two seconds, if you know how," said Lancelot, "I'll tell you."

And in a clear voice which, like that of all the Mulliners, however distant from the main branch, was beautifully modulated, he read as follows:

> *The Deanery,*
> *Bolsover, Wilts.*

My Dear Lancelot,

As you have, no doubt, already learned from your *Church Times,* I have been offered and have accepted the vacant bishopric of Bongo-Bongo, in West Africa. I sail immediately to take up my new duties, which I trust will be blessed.

In these circumstances it becomes necessary for me to find a good home for my cat, Webster. It is, alas, out of the question that he should accompany me, as the rigors of the climate and the lack of essential comforts might well sap a constitution which has never been robust.

I am dispatching him, therefore, to your address, my dear boy, in a straw-lined hamper, in the full confidence that you will prove a kindly and conscientious host.

With cordial good wishes,

> Your affectionate uncle,
> Theodore Bongo-Bongo

For some moments after he had finished reading this communication, a thoughtful silence prevailed in the studio. Finally Gladys spoke.

"Of all the nerve!" she said. "I wouldn't do it."

"Why not?"

"What do you want with a cat?"

Lancelot reflected.

"It is true," he said, "that, given a free hand, I should prefer not to have my studio turned into a cattery or cat bin. But consider the special circumstances. Relations between Uncle Theodore and self have for the last few years been a bit strained. In fact, you might say we had definitely parted brass-rags. It looks to me as if he were coming round. I should describe this letter as more or less what you might call an olive branch. If I lush this cat up satisfactorily, shall I not be in a position later on to make a swift touch?"

"He is rich, this bean?" said Gladys, interested.

"Extremely."

"Then," said Gladys, "consider my objections withdrawn. A good stout check from a grateful cat-fancier would undoubtedly come in very handy. We might be able to get married this year."

"Exactly," said Lancelot. "A pretty loathsome prospect, of course; but still, as we've arranged to do it, the sooner we get it over, the better, what?"

"Absolutely."

"Then that's settled. I accept custody of cat."

"It's the only thing to do," said Gladys. "Meanwhile, can you lend me a comb? Have you such a thing in your bedroom?"

"What do you want with a comb?"

"I got some soup in my hair at lunch. I won't be a minute."

She hurried out, and Lancelot, taking up the letter again,

found that he had omitted to read a continuation of it on the back page.

It was to the following effect:

> P.S. In establishing Webster in your home, I am actuated by another motive than the simple desire to see to it that my faithful friend and companion is adequately provided for.
>
> From both a moral and an educative standpoint, I am convinced that Webster's society will prove of inestimable value to you. His advent, indeed, I venture to hope, will be a turning point in your life. Thrown, as you must be, incessantly among loose and immoral bohemians, you will find in this cat an example of upright conduct which cannot but act as an antidote to the poison cup of temptation which is, no doubt, hourly pressed to your lips.
>
> P.P.S. Cream only at midday, and fish not more than three times a week.

He was reading these words for the second time, when the front doorbell rang and he found a man on the steps with a hamper. A discreet mew from within revealed its contents, and Lancelot, carrying it into the studio, cut the strings.

"Hi!" he bellowed, going to the door.

"What's up?" shrieked his betrothed from above.

"The cat's come."

"All right. I'll be down in a jiffy."

Lancelot returned to the studio.

"What ho, Webster!" he said cheerily. "How's the boy?"

The cat did not reply. It was sitting with bent head, performing that wash and brushup which a journey by rail renders so necessary.

In order to facilitate these toilet operations, it had raised its left leg and was holding it rigidly in the air. And there flashed into Lancelot's mind an old superstition handed on to him, for what it was worth, by one of the nurses of his infancy. If, this woman had said, you creep up to a cat when its leg is in the air and give it a pull, then you make a wish and your wish comes true in thirty days.

It was a pretty fancy, and it seemed to Lancelot that the theory might as well be put to the test. He advanced warily, therefore, and was in the act of extending his fingers for the pull, when Webster, lowering the leg, turned and raised his eyes.

He looked at Lancelot. And suddenly with sickening force there came to Lancelot the realization of the unpardonable liberty he had been about to take.

Until this moment, though the postscript to his uncle's letter should have warned him, Lancelot Mulliner had had no suspicion of what manner of cat this was that he had taken into his home. Now, for the first time, he saw him steadily and saw him whole.

Webster was very large and very black and very composed. He conveyed the impression of being a cat of deep reserves. Descendant of a long line of ecclesiastical ancestors who had conducted their decorous courtships beneath the shadow of cathedrals and on the back walls of bishops' palaces, he had that exquisite poise which one sees in high dignitaries of the Church. His eyes were clear and steady, and seemed to pierce to the very roots of the young man's soul, filling him with a sense of guilt.

Once, long ago, in his hot childhood, Lancelot, spending his summer holidays at the deanery, had been so far carried away by ginger beer and original sin as to plug a senior canon in the leg with his air gun—only to discover, on turning, that a visiting archdeacon had been a spectator of the entire incident from his immediate rear. As he had felt then, when meeting the archdeacon's eye, so did he feel now as Webster's gaze played silently upon him.

Webster, it is true, had not actually raised his eyebrows. But this, Lancelot felt, was simply because he hadn't any.

He backed, blushing.

"Sorry!" he muttered.

There was a pause. Webster continued his steady scrutiny. Lancelot edged toward the door.

"Er—excuse me—just a moment . . . ," he mumbled. And, sidling from the room, he ran distractedly upstairs.

"I say," said Lancelot.

"Now what?" asked Gladys.

"Have you finished with the mirror?"

"Why?"

"Well, I—er—I thought," said Lancelot, "that I might as well have a shave."

The girl looked at him, astonished.

"Shave? Why, you shaved only the day before yesterday."

"I know. But, all the same . . . I mean to say, it seems only respectful. That cat, I mean."

"What about him?"

"Well, he seems to expect it, somehow. Nothing actually said, don't you know, but you could tell by his manner. I thought a quick shave and perhaps change into my blue serge suit—"

"He's probably thirsty. Why don't you give him some milk?"

"Could one, do you think?" said Lancelot doubtfully. "I mean, I hardly seem to know him well enough." He paused. "I say, old girl," he went on, with a touch of hesitation.

"Hullo?"

"I know you won't mind my mentioning it, but you've got a few spots of ink on your nose."

"Of course I have. I always have spots of ink on my nose."

"Well . . . you don't think . . . a quick scrub with a bit of pumice stone. . . . I mean to say, you know how important first impressions are. . . ."

The girl stared.

"Lancelot Mulliner," she said, "if you think I'm going to skin my nose to the bone just to please a mangy cat—"

"Sh!" cried Lancelot, in agony.

"Here, let me go down and look at him," said Gladys petulantly.

As they reentered the studio, Webster was gazing with an air of quiet distaste at an illustration from *La Vie Parisienne* which adorned one of the walls. Lancelot tore it down hastily.

Gladys looked at Webster in an unfriendly way.

"So that's the blighter!"

"Sh!"

"If you want to know what I think," said Gladys, 'that cat's been living too high. Doing himself a dashed sight too well. You'd better cut his rations down a bit."

In substance, her criticism was not unjustified. Certainly, there was about Webster more than a suspicion of *embonpoint.* He had that air of portly well-being which we associate with those who dwell in cathedral closes. But Lancelot winced uncomfortably. He had so hoped that Gladys would make a good impression, and here she was, starting right off by saying the tactless thing.

He longed to explain to Webster that it was only her way; that in the bohemian circles of which she was such an ornament genial chaff of a personal order was accepted and, indeed, relished. But it was too late. The mischief had been done. Webster turned in a pointed manner and withdrew silently behind the chesterfield.

Gladys, all unconscious, was making preparations for departure.

"Well, bung-oh," she said lightly. "See you in three weeks. I suppose you and that cat'll both be out on the tiles the moment my back's turned."

"Please! Please!" moaned Lancelot. "Please!"

He had caught sight of the tip of a black tail protruding from behind the chesterfield. It was twitching slightly, and Lancelot could read it like a book. With a sickening sense of dismay, he knew that Webster had formed a snap judgment of his fiancée and condemned her as frivolous and unworthy.

It was some ten days later that Bernard Worple, the Neo-Vorticist sculptor, lunching at the Puce Ptarmigan, ran into Rodney Scollop, the powerful young Surrealist. And after talking for a while of their art:

"What's all this I hear about Lancelot Mulliner?" asked Worple. "There's a wild story going about that he was seen shaved in the middle of the week. Nothing in it, I suppose?"

Scollop looked grave. He had been on the point of mentioning Lancelot himself, for he loved the lad and was deeply exercised about him.

"It is perfectly true," he said.

"It sounds incredible."

Scollop leaned forward. His fine face was troubled.

"Shall I tell you something, Worple?"

"What?"

"I know for an absolute fact," said Scollop, "that Lancelot Mulliner now shaves every morning."

Worple pushed aside the spaghetti which he was wreathing about him and through the gap stared at his companion.

"Every morning?"

"Every single morning. I looked in on him myself the other day, and there he was, neatly dressed in blue serge and shaved to the core. And, what is more, I got the distinct impression that he had used talcum powder afterward."

"You don't mean that!"

"I do. And shall I tell you something else? There was a book lying open on the table. He tried to hide it, but he wasn't quick enough. It was one of those etiquette books!"

"An etiquette book!"

"Polite Behavior, by Constance, Lady Bodbank."

Worple unwound a stray tendril of spaghetti from about his left ear. He was deeply agitated. Like Scollop, he loved Lancelot.

"He'll be dressing for dinner next!" he exclaimed.

"I have every reason to believe," said Scollop gravely, "that he does dress for dinner. At any rate, a man closely resembling him was seen furtively buying three stiff collars and a black tie at Hope Brothers in the King's Road last Tuesday."

Worple pushed his chair back, and rose. His manner was determined.

"Scollop," he said, "we are friends of Mulliner's, you and I. It is evident from what you tell me that subversive influences are at work and that never has he needed our friendship more. Shall we not go round and see him immediately?"

"It is what I was about to suggest myself," said Rodney Scollop.

Twenty minutes later they were in Lancelot's studio, and with a significant glance Scollop drew his companion's notice to their host's appearance. Lancelot Mulliner was neatly, even foppishly, dressed in blue serge with creases down the trouser legs, and his chin, Worple saw with a pang, gleamed smoothly in the afternoon light.

At the sight of his friends' cigars, Lancelot exhibited unmistakable concern.

"You don't mind throwing those away, I'm sure," he said pleadingly.

Rodney Scollop drew himself up a little haughtily.

"And since when," he asked, "have the best fourpenny cigars in Chelsea not been good enough for you?"

Lancelot hastened to soothe him.

"It isn't me," he exclaimed. "It's Webster. My cat. I happen to know he objects to tobacco smoke. I had to give up my pipe in deference to his views."

Bernard Worple snorted.

"Are you trying to tell us," he sneered, "that Lancelot Mulliner allows himself to be dictated to by a blasted cat?"

"Hush!" cried Lancelot, trembling. "If you knew how he disapproves of strong language!"

"Where is this cat?" asked Rodney Scollop. "Is that the animal?" he said, pointing out of the window to where, in the yard, a tough-looking tom with tattered ears stood mewing in a hard-boiled way out of the corner of its mouth.

"Good heavens, no!" said Lancelot. "That is an alley cat which comes round here from time to time to lunch at the ash can. Webster is quite different. Webster has a natural dignity and repose of manner. Webster is a cat who prides himself on always being well turned out and whose high principles and lofty ideals shine from his eyes like beacon fires. . . ." And then suddenly, with an abrupt change of manner, Lancelot broke down and in a low voice added, "Curse him! Curse him! Curse him! Curse him!"

Worple looked at Scollop. Scollop looked at Worple.

"Come, old man," said Scollop, laying a gentle hand on Lancelot's bowed shoulder. "We are your friends. Confide in us."

"Tell us all," said Worple. "What's the matter?"

Lancelot uttered a bitter, mirthless laugh.

"You want to know what's the matter? Listen, then. I'm catpecked!"

"Catpecked?"

"You've heard of men being henpecked, haven't you?" said Lancelot with a touch of irritation. "Well, I'm cat-pecked."

And in broken accents he told his story. He sketched the history of his association with Webster from the latter's first entry into the studio. Confident now that the animal was not within earshot, he unbosomed himself without reserve.

"It's something in the beast's eye," he said in a shaking voice. "Something hypnotic. He casts a spell upon me. He gazes at me and disapproves. Little by little, bit by bit, I am degenerating under his influence from a wholesome, self-respecting artist into . . . well, I don't know what you call it. Suffice it to say that I have given up smoking, that I have ceased to wear carpet slippers and go about without a collar, that I never dream of sitting down to my frugal evening meal without dressing, and"—he choked—"I have sold my uku-lele."

"Not that!" said Worple, paling.

"Yes," said Lancelot. "I felt he considered it frivolous."

There was a long silence.

"Mulliner," said Scollop, "this is more serious than I had supposed. We must brood upon your case."

"It may be possible," said Worple, "to find a way out."

Lancelot shook his head hopelessly.

"There is no way out. I have explored every avenue. The only thing that could possibly free me from this intolerable bondage would be if once—just once—I could catch that cat unbending. If once—merely once—it would lapse in my presence from its austere dignity for but a single instant, I feel that the spell would be broken. But what hope is there of that?" cried Lancelot passionately. "You were pointing just now to that alley cat in the yard. There stands one who has strained every nerve and spared no effort to break down Webster's inhuman self-control. I have heard that animal say things to him which you would think no cat with red blood in its veins would suffer for an instant. And Webster merely looks at him like a suffragan bishop eyeing an erring choirboy and turns his head and falls into a refreshing sleep."

He broke off with a dry sob. Worple, always an optimist, attempted in his kindly way to minimize the tragedy.

"Ah, well," he said. "It's bad, of course, but still, I suppose there is no actual harm in shaving and dressing for dinner and so on. Many great artists . . . Whistler, for example—"

"Wait!" cried Lancelot. "You have not heard the worst."

He rose feverishly, and, going to the easel, disclosed the portrait of Brenda Carberry-Pirbright.

"Take a look at that," he said, "and tell me what you think of her."

His two friends surveyed the face before them in silence. Miss Carberry-Pirbright was a young woman of prim and glacial aspect. One sought in vain for her reasons for wanting to have her portrait painted. It would be a most unpleasant thing to have about any house.

Scollop broke the silence.

"Friend of yours?"

"I can't stand the sight of her," said Lancelot vehemently.

"Then," said Scollop, "I may speak frankly. I think she's a pill."

"A blister," said Worple.

"A boil and a disease," said Scollop, summing up.

Lancelot laughed hackingly.

"You have described her to a nicety. She stands for everything most alien to my artist soul. She gives me a pain in the neck. I'm going to marry her."

"What!" cried Scollop.

"But you're going to marry Gladys Bingley," said Worple.

"Webster thinks not," said Lancelot bitterly. "At their first meeting he weighed Gladys in the balance and found her wanting. And the moment he saw Brenda Carberry-Pirbright he stuck his tail up at right angles, uttered a cordial gargle, and rubbed his head against her leg. Then, turning, he looked at me. I could read that glance. I knew what was in his mind. From that moment he has been doing everything in his power to arrange the match."

"But, Mulliner," said Worple, always eager to point out the bright side, "why should this girl want to marry a wretched, scrubby, hard-up footler like you? Have courage, Mulliner. It is simply a question of time before you repel and sicken her."

Lancelot shook his head.

"No," he said. "You speak like a true friend, Worple, but you do not understand. Old Ma Carberry-Pirbright, this exhibit's mother, who chaperons her at the sittings, discovered at an early date my relationship to my uncle Theodore, who, as you know, has got it in gobs. She knows well enough that some day I shall be a rich man. She used to know my uncle Theodore when he was Vicar of St. Botolph's in Knightsbridge, and from the very first she assumed toward me the repellent chumminess of an old family friend. She was always trying to lure me to her at-homes, her Sunday luncheons, her little dinners. Once she actually suggested that I should escort her and her beastly daughter to the Royal Academy."

He laughed bitterly. The mordant witticisms of Lancelot Mulliner at the expense of the Royal Academy were quoted from Tite Street in the south to Holland Park in the north and eastward as far as Bloomsbury.

"To all these overtures," resumed Lancelot, "I remained firmly unresponsive. My attitude was from the start one of frigid aloofness. I did not actually say in so many words that I would rather be dead in a ditch than at one of her at-homes, but my manner indicated it. And I was just beginning to think

I had choked her off when in crashed Webster and upset everything. Do you know how many times I have been to that infernal house in the last week? Five. Webster seemed to wish it. I tell you, I am a lost man."

He buried his face in his hands. Scollop touched Worple on the arm, and together the two men stole silently out.

"Bad!" said Worple.

"Very bad," said Scollop.

"It seems incredible."

"Oh, no. Cases of this kind are, alas, by no means uncommon among those who, like Mulliner, possess to a marked degree the highly strung, ultrasensitive artistic temperament. A friend of mine, a rhythmical interior decorator, once rashly consented to put his aunt's parrot up at his studio while she was away visiting friends in the north of England. She was a woman of strong evangelical views, which the bird had imbibed from her. It had a way of putting its head on one side, making a noise like someone drawing a cork from a bottle, and asking my friend if he was saved. To cut a long story short, I happened to call on him a month later and he had installed a harmonium in his studio and was singing hymns, ancient and modern, in a rich tenor, while the parrot, standing on one leg on its perch, took the bass. A very sad affair. We were all much upset about it."

Worple shuddered.

"You appall me, Scollop! Is there nothing we can do?"

Rodney Scollop considered for a moment.

'We might wire Gladys Bingley to come home at once. She might possibly reason with the unhappy man. A woman's gentle influence . . . Yes, we could do that. Look in at the post office on your way home and send Gladys a telegram. I'll owe you for my half of it."

In the studio they had left, Lancelot Mulliner was staring dumbly at a black shape which had just entered the room. He had the appearance of a man with his back to the wall.

"No!" he was crying. "No! I'm dashed if I do!"

Webster continued to look at him.

"Why should I?" demanded Lancelot weakly.

Webster's gaze did not flicker.

"Oh, all right," said Lancelot sullenly.

He passed from the room with leaden feet, and, proceeding upstairs, changed into morning clothes and a top hat. Then, with a gardenia in his buttonhole, he made his way to 11 Maxton Square, where Mrs. Carberry-Pirbright was giving one of her intimate little teas ("just a few friends") to meet Clara Throckmorton Stooge, authoress of *A Strong Man's Kiss.*

Gladys Bingley was lunching at her hotel in Antibes when Worple's telegram arrived. It occasioned her the gravest concern.

Exactly what it was all about she was unable to gather, for emotion had made Bernard Worple rather incoherent. There were moments, reading it, when she fancied that Lancelot had met with a serious accident; others when the solution seemed to be that he had sprained his brain to such an extent that rival lunatic asylums were competing eagerly for his custom; others, again, when Worple appeared to be suggesting that he had gone into partnership with his cat to start a harem. But one fact emerged clearly. Her loved one was in serious trouble of some kind, and his best friends were agreed that only her immediate return could save him.

Gladys did not hesitate. Within half an hour of the receipt of the telegram she had packed her trunk, removed a piece of asparagus from her right eyebrow, and was negotiating for accommodation on the first train going north.

Arriving in London, her first impulse was to go straight to Lancelot. But a natural feminine curiosity urged her, before doing so, to call upon Bernard Worple and have light thrown on some of the more abstruse passages in the telegram.

Worple, in his capacity of author, may have tended toward obscurity, but, when confining himself to the spoken word, he told a plain story well and clearly. Five minutes of his society enabled Gladys to obtain a firm grasp on the salient facts, and there appeared on her face that grim, tight-lipped expression which is seen only on the faces of fiancées who have come back from a short holiday to discover that their dear one has been straying in their absence from the straight and narrow path.

"Brenda Carberry-Pirbright, eh?" said Gladys, with ominous calm. "I'll give him Brenda Carberry-Pirbright! My gosh, if one can't go off to Antibes for the merest breather without having one's betrothed getting it up his nose and starting to act like a Mormon Elder, it begins to look a pretty tough world for a girl."

Kindhearted Bernard Worple did his best.

"I blame the cat," he said. "Lancelot, to my mind, is more sinned against than sinning. I consider him to be acting under undue influence or duress."

"How like a man!" said Gladys. "Shoving it all off onto an innocent cat!"

"Lancelot says it has a sort of something in its eye."

"Well, when I meet Lancelot," said Gladys, "he'll find that I have a sort of something in my eye."

She went out, breathing flame quietly through her nostrils. Worple, saddened, heaved a sigh and resumed his Neo-Vorticist sculpting.

It was some five minutes later that Gladys, passing through Maxton Square on her way to Bott Street, stopped suddenly in her tracks. The sight she had seen was enough to make any fiancée do so.

Along the pavement leading to number 11 two figures were advancing. Or three, if you counted a morose-looking dog of a semidachshund nature which preceded them, attached to a leash. One of the figures was that of Lancelot Mulliner, natty in gray herringbone tweed and a new homburg hat. It was he who held the leash. The other Gladys recognized from the portrait which she had seen on Lancelot's easel as that modern Du Barry, that notorious wrecker of homes and breaker-up of love nests, Brenda Carberry-Pirbright.

The next moment they had mounted the steps of number 11, and had gone in to tea, possibly with a little music.

It was perhaps an hour and a half later that Lancelot, having wrenched himself with difficulty from the lair of the Philistines, sped homeward in a swift taxi. As always after an extended tête-à-tête with Miss Carberry-Pirbright, he felt dazed and bewildered, as if he had been swimming in a sea of glue and had swallowed a good deal of it. All he could think of clearly was that he wanted a drink and that the materials for that drink were in the cupboard behind the chesterfield in his studio.

He paid the cab and charged in with his tongue rattling dryly against his front teeth. And there before him was Gladys Bingley, whom he had supposed far, far away.

"You!" exclaimed Lancelot.

"Yes, me!" said Gladys.

Her long vigil had not helped to restore the girl's equanimity. Since arriving at the studio she had had leisure to tap her foot 3,142 times on the carpet, and the number of bitter smiles which had flitted across her face was 911. She was about ready for the battle of the century.

She rose and faced him, all the woman in her flashing from her eyes.

"Well, you Casanova!" she said.

"You who?" said Lancelot.

"Don't say 'Yoo-hoo!' to me!" cried Gladys. "Keep that for your Brenda Carberry-Pirbright. Yes, I know all about it, Lancelot Don Juan Henry the Eighth Mulliner! I saw you with her just now. I hear that you and she are inseparable. Bernard Worple says you said you were going to marry her."

"You mustn't believe everything a Neo-Vorticist sculptor tells you," quavered Lancelot.

"I'll bet you're going back to dinner there tonight," said Gladys.

She had spoken at a venture, basing the charge purely on a possessive cock of the head which she had noticed in Brenda Carberry-Pirbright at their recent encounter. There, she had said to herself at the time, had gone a girl who was about to invite—or had just invited—Lancelot Mulliner to dine quietly and take her to the pictures afterward. But the shot went home. Lancelot hung his head.

"There was some talk of it," he admitted.

"Ah!" exclaimed Gladys.

Lancelot's eyes were haggard.

"I don't want to go," he pleaded. "Honestly, I don't. But Webster insists."

"Webster!"

"Yes, Webster. If I attempt to evade the appointment, he will sit in front of me and look at me."

"Tchah!"

"Well, he will. Ask him for yourself."

Gladys tapped her foot six times in rapid succession on the carpet, bringing the total to 3,148. Her manner had changed and was now dangerously calm.

"Lancelot Mulliner," she said, "you have your choice. Me on the one hand, Brenda Carberry-Pirbright on the other. I offer you a home where you will be able to smoke in bed, spill the ashes on the floor, wear pajamas and carpet slippers all day and shave only on Sunday mornings. From her, what have you to hope? A house in South Kensington—possibly the Brompton Road—probably with her mother living with you. A life that will be one long round of stiff collars and tight shoes, of morning coats and top hats."

Lancelot quivered, but she went on remorselessly.

"You will be at home on alternate Thursdays, and will be expected to hand the cucumber sandwiches. Every day you will air the dog, till you become a confirmed dog-airer. You will dine out in Bayswater and go for the summer to Bournemouth or Dinard. Choose well, Lancelot Mulliner! I will leave you to think it over. But one last word. If by seven-thirty on the dot you have not presented yourself at Six-A Garbidge Mews ready to take me out to dinner at the Ham and Beef, I shall know what to think and shall act accordingly."

And brushing the cigarette ashes from her chin, the girl strode haughtily from the room.

"Gladys!" cried Lancelot.

But she had gone.

For some minutes Lancelot Mulliner remained where he was, stunned. Then, insistently, there came to him the recollection that he had not had that drink. He rushed to the cupboard and produced the bottle. He uncorked it, and was pouring out a lavish stream, when a movement on the floor below him attracted his attention.

Webster was standing there, looking up at him. And in his eyes was that familiar expression of quiet rebuke.

"Scarcely what I have been accustomed to at the Deanery," he seemed to be saying.

Lancelot stood paralyzed. The feeling of being bound hand and foot, of being caught in a snare from which there was no escape, had become more poignant than ever. The bottle fell from his nerveless fingers and rolled across the floor, spilling its contents in an amber river, but he was too heavy in spirit to notice it. With a gesture such as Job might have made on discovering a new boil, he crossed to the window and stood looking moodily out.

Then, turning with a sigh, he looked at Webster again—and, looking, stood spellbound.

The spectacle which he beheld was of a kind to stun a stronger man than Lancelot Mulliner. At first, he shrank from believing his eyes. Then, slowly, came the realization that what he saw was no mere figment of a disordered imagination. This unbelievable thing was actually happening.

Webster sat crouched upon the floor beside the widening pool of whiskey. But it was not horror and disgust that had caused him to crouch. He was crouched because, crouching, he could get nearer to the stuff and obtain crisper action. His tongue was moving in and out like a piston.

And then abruptly, for one fleeting instant, he stopped lapping and glanced up at Lancelot, and across his face there flitted a quick smile—so genial, so intimate, so full of jovial camaraderie, that the young man found himself automatically smiling back, and not only smiling but winking. And in answer to that wink Webster winked too—a wholehearted, roguish wink that said as plainly as if he had spoken the words:

"How long has this been going on?"

Then with a slight hiccup he turned back to the task of getting his drink before it soaked into the floor.

Into the murky soul of Lancelot Mulliner there poured a sudden flood of sunshine. It was as if a great burden had been lifted from his shoulders. The intolerable obsession of the last two weeks had ceased to oppress him, and he felt a free man. At the eleventh hour the reprieve had come. Webster, that seeming pillar of austere virtue, was one of the boys, after all. Never again would Lancelot quail beneath his eye. He had the goods on him.

Webster, like the stag at eve, had now drunk his fill. He had left the pool of alcohol and was walking round in slow, meditative circles. From time to time he mewed tentatively, as if he were trying to say, "British Constitution." His failure to articulate the syllables appeared to tickle him, for at the end of each attempt he would utter a slow, amused chuckle. It was about this moment that he suddenly broke into a rhythmic dance not unlike the old saraband.

It was an interesting spectacle, and at any other time Lancelot would have watched it raptly. But now he was busy at his desk, writing a brief note to Mrs. Carberry-Pirbright, the burden of which was that if she thought he was coming within a mile of her foul house that night or any other night she had vastly underrated the dodging powers of Lancelot Mulliner.

And what of Webster? The Demon Rum now had him in an iron grip. A lifetime of abstinence had rendered him a ready victim to the fatal fluid. He had now reached the stage when geniality gives way to belligerence. The rather foolish smile had gone from his face, and in its stead there lowered a fighting frown. For a few moments he stood on his hind legs, looking about him for a suitable adversary; then, losing all vestiges of self-control, he ran five times round the room at a high rate of speed and, falling foul of a small footstool, attacked it with the utmost ferocity, sparing neither tooth nor claw.

But Lancelot did not see him. Lancelot was not there. Lancelot was out in Bott Street, hailing a cab.

"Six-A Garbidge Mews, Fulham," said Lancelot to the driver.

Pamela Sargent

OUT OF PLACE

"For something is amiss or out of place
When mice with wings can wear a human face."
—THEODORE ROETHKE,
"The Bat"

Marcia was washing the breakfast dishes when she first heard her cat thinking. I'm thirsty, why doesn't she give me more water, there's dried food on the sides of my bowl. There was a pause. I wonder how she catches the food. She can't stalk anything, she always scares the birds away. She never catches any when I'm nearby. Why does she put it into those squares and round things when she just has to take it out again? What is food, anyway? What is water?

Very slowly, Marcia put down the cup she was washing, turned off the water, and faced the cat. Pearl, a slim Siamese, was sitting by her plastic bowls. She swatted the newspaper under them with one paw, then stretched out on her side. I want to be combed, I want my stomach scratched. Why isn't he here? He always goes away. They should both be here, they're supposed to serve me. Pearl's mouth did not move, but Marcia knew the words were hers. For one thing, there was no one else in the house. For another, the disembodied voice had a feline whine to it, as if the words were almost, but not quite, meows.

Oh, God, Marcia thought, I'm going crazy. Still eyeing the cat, she crept to the back door and opened it. She inhaled some fresh air and felt better. A robin was pecking at the grass. Earth, yield your treasures to me. I hunger, my young cry out for food. This voice had a musical lilt. Marcia leaned against the door frame.

I create space. The next voice was deep and sluggish. The universe parts before me. It is solid and dark and damp, it covers all, but I create space. I approach the infinite. Who has created it? A giant of massive dimensions must have moved through the world, leaving the infinite. It is before me now. The warmth—ah!

The voice broke off. The robin had caught the worm.

Marcia slammed the door shut. Help, she thought, and then: I wonder what Dr. Leroy would say. A year of transactional analysis and weekly group-therapy sessions had assured her that she was only a mildly depressed neurotic; though she had never been able to scream and pound her pillow in front of others in her group and could not bring herself to call Dr. Leroy Bill, as his other clients did, the therapy had at least diminished the frequency of her migraines, and the psychiatrist had been pleased with her progress. Now she was sure that she was becoming psychotic; only psychotics heard voices. There was some satisfaction in knowing Dr. Leroy had been wrong.

Pearl had wandered away. Marcia struggled to stay calm.

If I can hear her thoughts, she reasoned, can she hear mine? She shivered. "Pearl," she called out in a wavering voice. "Here, kitty. Nice Pearl." She walked into the hall and toward the stairs.

The cat was on the top step, crouching. Her tail twitched. Marcia concentrated, trying to transmit a message to Pearl. If you come to the kitchen right now, she thought, I'll give you a whole can of Super Supper.

The cat did not move.

If you don't come down immediately, Marcia went on, I won't feed you at all.

Pearl was still.

She doesn't hear me, Marcia thought, relieved. She was now beginning to feel a bit silly. She had imagined it all; she would have to ask Dr. Leroy what it meant.

I could leap from here, Pearl thought, and land on my feet. I could leap and sink my claws in flesh, but then I'd be punished. Marcia backed away.

The telephone rang. Marcia hurried to the kitchen to answer it, huddling against the wall as she clung to the receiver. "Hello."

"Marcia?"

"Hi, Paula."

"Marcia, I don't know what to do, you're going to think I'm crazy."

"Are you at work?"

"I called in sick. I think I'm having a nervous breakdown. I heard the Baron this morning, I mean I heard what he was thinking: They're stealing everything again, they're stealing it. And then he said: But the other man will catch them and bring some of it back, and I'll bark at him and he'll be afraid even though I'm only being friendly. I finally figured it out. He thinks the garbage men are thieves and the mailman catches them later."

"Does he think in German?"

"What?"

"German shepherds should know German, shouldn't they?" Marcia laughed nervously. "I'm sorry, Paula. I heard Pearl, too. I also overheard a bird and a worm."

"I was afraid the Baron could hear my thoughts, too. But he doesn't seem to." Paula paused. "Jesus. The Baron just came in. He thinks my perfume ruins my smell. His idea of a good time is sniffing around to see which dogs pissed on his favorite telephone poles. What are we going to do?"

"I don't know." Marcia looked down. Pearl was rubbing against her legs. Why doesn't she comb me, the cat thought. Why doesn't she pay attention to me? She's always talking to that thing. I'm much prettier.

Marcia said, "I'll call you back later."

Doug was sitting at the kitchen table when Marcia came up from the laundry room.

"You're home early."

Doug looked up, frowning under his beard. "Jimmy Barzini brought his hamster to Show and Tell, and the damn thing started to talk. We all heard it. That was the end of any order in the classroom. The kids started crowding around and asking it questions, but it just kept babbling, as if it couldn't understand them. Its mouth wasn't moving, though. I thought at first that Jimmy was throwing his voice, but he wasn't. Then I figured out that we must be hearing the hamster's thoughts somehow, and then Mrs. Price came in and told me the white rats in her class's science project were talking, too, and after that Tallman got on the P.A. system and said school would close early."

"Then I'm not crazy," Marcia said. "Or else we all are. I heard Pearl. Then Paula called up and said Baron von Ribbentrop was doing it."

They were both silent for a few moments. Then Marcia asked, "What did it say? The hamster, I mean."

"It said, I want to get out of this cage."

Did cats owned by Russians speak Russian? Marcia had wondered. Did dogs in France transmit in French? Either animals were multilingual or one heard their thoughts in one's native tongue; she had gathered this much from the news.

Press coverage and television news programs were now given over almost entirely to this phenomenon. Did it mean that animals had in fact become intelligent, or were people simply hearing, for the first time, the thoughts that had always been there? Or was the world in the midst of a mass psychosis?

It was now almost impossible to take a walk without hearing birds and other people's pets expressing themselves at length. Marcia had discovered that the cocker spaniel down the street thought she had a nice body odor, while Mr. Sampson's poodle next door longed to take a nip out of her leg. Cries of Invader approaching! had kept her from stepping on an anthill. She was afraid to spend time in her yard since listening to a small snake: I slither. The sun is warm. I coil. I strike. Strike or be struck. That is the way of it. My fangs are ready.

Marcia found herself hiding from this cacophony by staying indoors, listening instead to the babble on the radio and television as animal behaviorists, zoo officials, dog breeders, farmers, psychiatrists, and a few cranks offered their views. A presidential commission was to study the matter, an adviser to the President had spoken of training migratory birds as observers to ensure arms control. Marcia had heard many theories. People were picking up the thoughts of animals and somehow translating them into terms they could understand. They were picking up their own thoughts and projecting them onto the nearest creatures. The animals' thoughts were a manifestation of humankind's guilt over having treated other living, sentient beings as slaves and objects. They were all racists—or "speciesists," as one philosopher had put it on "Good Morning, America"; the word had gained wide currency.

Marcia had begun to follow Pearl around the house, hoping for some insight into the cat's character; it had occurred to her that understanding a cat's point of view might yield some wisdom. Pearl, however, had disappointed her. The cat's mind was almost purely associative; she thought of food, of being scratched behind the ears, of sex, of sharpening her claws on the furniture. I want to stalk those birds in the yard, she would think. I like to feel the grass on my paws but it tickles my nose, when I scratched that dog next door on the nose, he yipped, I hate him, why did my people scream at me when I caught a mouse and put it on their pillow for them, I'm thirsty, why don't they ever give me any tuna fish instead of keeping it all to themselves? Pearl reminded Marcia, more than anything, of her mother-in-law, whose conversations were a weakly linked chain.

Yet she supposed she still loved the cat, in spite of it. In the evening, Pearl would hop on her lap as she watched television with Doug, and Marcia would stroke her fur, and Pearl would say, That feels good, and begin to purr. At night, before going to bed, Marcia had always closed the bedroom door, feeling that sex should be private, even from cats. Now she was glad she had done so. She was not sure she wanted to know what Pearl would have had to say about that subject.

The President had gone on television to urge the nation to return to its daily tasks, and Doug's school had reopened. Marcia, alone again for the day, vacuumed the living room while thinking guiltily that she had to start looking for another job. The months at home had made her lazy; she had too easily settled into a homemaker's routine and wondered if this meant she was unintelligent. Persisting in her dull-wittedness, she decided to do some grocery shopping instead of making a trip to the employment agency.

Doug had taken the bus to work, leaving her the car. She felt foolish as she drove down the street. Anton's Market was only a block away and she could have taken her shopping cart, but she could not face the neighborhood's animals. It was all too evident that Mr. Sampson's poodle and a mixed-breed down the road bore her ill will because she was Pearl's owner. She had heard a report from India on the morning news. Few people there were disturbed by recent events, since audible animal contemplation had only confirmed what many had already believed: that animals had souls. Several people there had in fact identified certain creatures as dead relatives or ancestors.

As she parked behind Anton's Market and got out of the car, she noticed a collie pawing at Mr. Anton's garbage cans. Bones, the dog was thinking. I know there are bones in there. I want to gnaw on one. What a wonderful day! I smell a bitch close by. The collie barked. Why do they make it so hard for me to get the bones? The dog's mood was growing darker. It turned toward Marcia's car. I hate them, I hate those shiny rolling carapaces, I saw it, one rolled and growled as it went down the street and it didn't even see her, she barked and whined and then she died, and the thing's side opened and a man got out, and the thing just sat there on its wheels and purred. I hate them. The dog barked again.

When Marcia entered the store, she saw Mr. Anton behind the cash register. "Where's Jeannie?" she asked.

Mr. Anton usually seemed cheerful, as if three decades of waiting on his customers had set his round face in a perpetual smile. But today his brown eyes stared at her morosely. "I had to let her go, Mrs. Bochner," he replied. "I had to let the other butchers go, too. Thirty years, and I don't know how long I can keep going. My supplier won't be able to get me any more meat. There's a run on it now in the big cities, but after that—" He shrugged. "May I help you?" he went on, and smiled, as if old habits were reasserting themselves.

Marcia, peering down the aisle of canned goods, noticed that the meat counter was almost empty. Another customer, a big-shouldered, gray-haired man, wandered over with a six-pack of beer. "I don't know what things are coming to," the man said as he fumbled for his wallet. "I was out in the country with my buddy last weekend. You can't hardly sleep with all the noise. I heard one of them coyotes out there. You know what it said? It said, I must beware the two-legged stalker. And you know who it meant. Then it howled."

"You should have seen '60 Minutes,' " Mr. Anton said. "They did a story about the tuna fishermen, and how they're going out of business. They showed one of the last runs. They shouldn't have stuff like that on when kids are watching. My grandson was crying all night." He draped an arm over the register. "A guy has a farm," he said. "How does he know it's actually a concentration camp? All the cows are bitching, that's what they say. You can't go into a barn now without hearing their complaints." He sighed. "At least we can still get milk—the cows can't wander around with swollen udders. But what the hell happens later? They want bigger stalls, they want better feed, they want more pasture. What if they want to keep all the milk for their calves?"

"I don't know," Marcia said, at a loss.

"The government should do something," the gray-haired man uttered.

"The chickens. They're all crazy from being crowded. It's like a nuthouse, a chicken farm. The pigs—they're the worst, because they're the smartest. You know what I feel like? I feel like a murderer—I've got blood on my hands. I feel like a cannibal."

Marcia had left the house with thoughts of hamburgers and slices of baked Virginia ham. Now she had lost her appetite. "What are you going to do?"

"I don't know," Mr. Anton replied. "I'm trying to get into legumes, vegetables, fresh produce, but that puts me in competition with John Ramey's fruit and vegetable market. I'm going to have to get a vegetarian adviser, so I'll know what to stock. There's this vegetarian college kid down the street from me. She's thinking of setting up a consulting firm."

"Well," Marcia said, looking down at the floor.

"I can give you some potato salad, my wife made it up fresh. At least potatoes don't talk. Not yet."

Doug nibbled at his dinner of bean curd and vegetables. "Have you noticed? People are getting thinner."

"Not everybody. Some people are eating more starch."

"I guess so," Doug said. "Still, it's probably better for us in the long run. We'll live longer. I know I feel better."

"I suppose. I don't know what we're going to do when Pearl's cat food runs out." Marcia lowered her voice when she spoke of Pearl.

After supper, they watched the evening news. Normality, of a sort, had returned to the network broadcast; the first part of the program consisted of the usual assortment of international crises, congressional hearings, and press conferences. Halfway through the broadcast, it was announced that the President's Labrador retriever had died; the *Washington Post* was claiming that the Secret Service had disposed of the dog as a security risk.

"My God," Marcia said.

There was more animal news toward the end of the program. Family therapists in California were asking their clients to bring their pets to sessions. Animal shelters all over the country were crowded with dogs and cats that workers refused to put to sleep. Medical researchers were abandoning animal studies and turning to computer models. Racetracks were closing because too many horseplayers were getting inside information from the horses. There were rumors in Moscow that the Kremlin had been secretly and extensively fumigated, and that there were thousands of dead mice in the city's sewers. There was a story about a man named Mac-Donald, whose column, "MacDonald's Farm," was made up of sayings and aphorisms he picked up from his barnyard animals. His column had been syndicated and was being published in several major newspapers, putting him in direct competition with Farmer Bob, a "Today" show commentator who also had a column. Marcia suspected editorial tampering on the part of both men, since MacDonald's animals sounded like Will Rogers, while Farmer Bob's reminded her of Oscar Wilde.

Pearl entered the room as the news was ending and began to claw at the rug. "I saw an interesting cat on Phil Donahue this morning," Marcia said. "A Persian. Kind of a philosopher. His owner said that he has a theory of life after death and thinks cats live on in a parallel world. The cat thinks that all those strange sounds you sometimes hear in the night are actually the spirits of cats. What's interesting is that he doesn't think birds or mice have souls."

"Why don't you look for a job instead of watching the tube all day?"

"I don't watch it all day. I have to spend a lot of time on meals, you know. Vegetarian cooking is very time-consuming when you're not used to it."

"That's no excuse. You know I'll do my share when you're working."

"I'm afraid to leave Pearl alone all day."

"That never bothered you before."

"I never heard what she was thinking before."

Pearl was stretching, front legs straight out, back arched. I want to sleep on the bed tonight, the cat was thinking. Why can't I sleep on it at night, I sleep there during the day. They keep it all to themselves. They let that woman with the red fur on her head sleep there at night, but not me.

Doug sucked in his breath. Marcia sat up. He pushed her on it, the cat went on, and they shed their outer skins, and he rolled around and rubbed her, but when I jumped up on the bed, he shooed me away.

Marcia said, "You bastard." Doug was pulling at his beard. "When did this happen?" He did not answer. "It must have been when I was visiting my sister, wasn't it? You son of a bitch." She got to her feet, feeling as though someone had punched her in the stomach. "Red fur on her head. It must have been Emma. I always thought she was after you. Jesus Christ, you couldn't even go to a motel."

"I went out with some friends for a few beers," Doug said in a low voice. "She drove me home. I didn't expect anything to happen. It didn't mean anything. I would have told you if I thought it was important, but it wasn't, so why bother you with it? I don't even like Emma that much." He was silent for a moment. "You haven't exactly been showing a lot of interest in sex, you know. And ever since you stopped working, you don't seem to care about anything. At least Emma talks about something besides housework and gossip and Phil Donahue."

"You didn't even close the door," Marcia said, making fists of her hands. "You didn't even think of Pearl."

"For God's sake, Marcia, do you think normal people care if a cat sees them?"

"They do now."

I'm thirsty, Pearl said. I want some food. Why doesn't anybody clean my box? It stinks all the time. I wish I could piss where I like.

Doug said, "I'm going to kill that cat." He started to lunge across the room.

"No, you're not." Marcia stepped in front of him, blocking his way. Pearl scurried off.

"Let me by."

"No."

She struggled with him. He knocked her aside and she screamed, swung at him, and began to cry. They both sat down on the floor. Marcia cursed at him between sobs while he kept saying he was sorry. The television set blared at them until Doug turned it off and got out some wine. They drank for a while and Marcia thought of throwing him out, then remembered that she didn't have a job and would be alone with Pearl.

Doug went to bed early, exhausted by his apologizing. Marcia glared at the sofa resentfully; it was Doug who should sleep there, not she.

Before she went to sleep, she called Pearl. The cat crept up from the cellar while Marcia took out some cat food. "Your favorite," she whispered to the cat. "Chicken livers. Your reward. Good kitty."

Marcia had heard a sharp crack early that morning. The poodle next door was dead, lying in the road. When Mr. Sampson found out, he strode across the street and started shouting at Mr. Hornig's door.

"Come out, you murderer," he hollered. "You come out here and tell me why you shot my dog. You bastard, get out here!"

Marcia stood in her front yard, watching; Doug was staring out the bay window at the scene. The Novaks' cocker spaniel sat on the edge of Marcia's lawn. I smell death, the spaniel thought. I smell rage. What is the matter? We are the friends of man, but must we die to prove our loyalty? We are not friends, we are slaves. We die licking our masters' hands.

Mr. Hornig opened his door; he was holding a rifle. "Get the hell off my lawn, Sampson."

"You shot my dog." Mr. Sampson was still wearing his

pajamas; his bald pate gleamed in the sun. "I want to know why. I want an answer right now before I call the cops."

Mr. Hornig walked out on his porch and down the steps; Mrs. Hornig came to the door, gasped, and went after her husband, wresting the weapon from him. He pulled away from her and moved toward Mr. Sampson.

"Why?" Mr. Sampson cried. "Why did you do it?"

"I'll tell you why. I can live with your damn dog yapping all the time, even though I hate yappy dogs. I don't even care about him leaving turds all over my yard and running around loose. But I won't put up with his spying and his goddamn insults. That dog of yours has a dirty mind."

"Had," Mr. Sampson shouted. "He's dead now. You killed him and left him in the street."

"He insulted my wife. He was laughing at her tits. He was right outside our bedroom window, and he was making fun of her tits." Mrs. Hornig retreated with the rifle. "He says we stink. That's what he said. He said we smell like something that's been lying outside too long. I take a shower every day, and he says I stink. And he said some other things I won't repeat."

Mr. Sampson leaned forward. "You fool. He didn't understand. How the hell could he help what he thought? You didn't have to listen."

"I'll bet I know where he got his ideas. He wouldn't have thought them up all by himself. I shot him and I'm glad. What do you think of that, Sampson?"

Mr. Sampson answered with his fist. Soon the two pudgy men were rolling in the grass, trading punches. A few neighborhood children gathered to watch the display. A police car appeared; Marcia looked on as the officers pulled the two men away from each other.

"My God," Marcia said as she went inside. "The police came," she said to Doug, who was now stretched out on the sofa with the Sunday *New York Times*. She heard Pearl in the next room, scratching at the dining room table. Good and sharp, Pearl was saying. I have them good and sharp. My claws are so pretty. I'm shedding. Why doesn't somebody comb me?

"I've let you down," Doug said suddenly. Marcia tensed. "I don't mean just with Emma, I mean generally." They had not spoken of that incident since the night of Pearl's revelation.

"No, you haven't," Marcia said.

"I have. Maybe we should have had a kid. I don't know."

"You know I don't want kids now. Anyway, we can't afford it yet."

"That isn't the only reason," Doug said, staring at the dining room entrance, where Pearl now sat, licking a paw, silent for once. "You know how possessive Siamese cats are. If we had a kid, Pearl would hate it. The kid would have to listen to mean remarks all day. He'd probably be neurotic."

Pearl gazed at them calmly. Her eyes seemed to glow.

"Maybe we should get rid of her," Doug went on.

"Oh, no. You're just mad at her still. Anyway, she loves you."

"No, she doesn't. She doesn't love anyone."

Pet me, Pearl said. Somebody better scratch me behind the ears, and do it nicely.

"We have chickens today," Mr. Anton said as Marcia entered the store. "I'll be getting beef in next week." He leaned against the counter, glancing at the clock on the wall; it was almost closing time. "Jeannie's coming back on Tuesday. Things'll be normal again."

"I suppose," Marcia said. "You'll probably be seeing me on Saturdays from now on. I finally found a job. Nothing special, just office work." She paused. "Doesn't it make you feel funny?" She waved a hand at the chickens.

"It did at first. But you have to look at it this way. First of all, chickens are stupid. I guess nobody really knew how stupid until they could hear them thinking. And cows—well, it's like my supplier said. No one's going to hurt some nice animal, but a lot of them don't have nice things to say about people, and some of them sound like real troublemakers. You know who's going to get the ax, so to speak. It's a good thing they don't know we can hear them." Mr. Anton lowered his voice. "And the pigs. Think they're better than we are, that's what they say. Sitting around in a pen all day, and thinking they're better. They'll be sorry."

As Marcia walked home with her chicken and eggs, the street seemed quieter that evening. The birds still babbled: My eggs are warm. The wind lifts me, and carries me to my love. The wires hum under my feet. I am strong, my nest is sound, I want a mate. A squirrel darted up a tree. Tuck them away, tuck them away. I have many acorns in my secret place. Save, save, save. I am prepared.

She did not hear the neighborhood pets. Some were inside; others were all too evident. She passed the bodies of two gray cats, then detoured around a dead mutt. Her eyes stung. We've always killed animals, she thought. Why should this be different?

Louise Novak was standing by her dead cocker spaniel, crying. "Louise?" Marcia said as she approached the child. Louise looked up, sniffing. Marcia gazed at the spaniel, remembering that the dog had liked her.

"Dad killed her," the girl said. "Mrs. Jones overheard her and told everybody Dad hits Mom. Dad said she liked Mom and me best, he heard her think it. He said she hated him and chewed his slippers on purpose and she wanted to tear out his throat because he's mean. I wish she had. I hate him. I hope he dies."

When Marcia reached her own house, she saw the car in the driveway; Doug was home. She heard him moving around upstairs as she unpacked her groceries and put them away. Pearl came into the kitchen and meowed, then scampered to the door, still meowing. I want to go outside. Why doesn't she let me out? I want to stalk birds, I want to play.

Pearl was so unaware, so insistent, so perfect in her otherness. You'd better be careful, Marcia thought violently. You'd better keep your mind quiet when our friends are here if you know what's good for you, or you'll stay in the cellar. And you'd better watch what you think about me. Appalled, she suddenly realized that under the right circumstances, she could dash the cat's brains out against the wall.

I want to go outside.

"Pearl," Marcia said, leaning over the cat. "Pearl, listen to me. Try to understand. I know you can't, but try anyway. You can't go outside, it's dangerous. You have to stay here. You have to stay inside for your own good. I know what's best. You have to stay inside from now on."

Jack Schaefer

CAT NIPPED

Corporal Clint Buckner ambled slowly across the flat, baked surface of what would someday be the parade ground of Fort McKay. He carried a stubby cavalry carbine in the crook of his left elbow and patted the stock affectionately with his right hand as he walked. The hot Kansas sun beat full strength upon him and upon the double row of tents that flanked one side of the level space and upon the three sod-walled structures that stretched at a right angle to mark another side. The sun beat with equal untiring fervor upon the sweating bodies of Sergeant Peattie and a crew of half-naked privates piling strips of sod one on another for the walls of the first of the structures that would line the third side.

Corporal Clint ambled in a slow curve to pass near Sergeant Peattie and his swearing crew. He paused to yawn and wipe imaginary dust from the carbine and ambled on. The dripping privates stopped their work to watch him move past.

"Ain't he the brave hunter, toting that big gun."

"Takes nerve to go after those critters like he does."

"Yep. Turrible dangerous when wounded."

Chuckles and a climbing guffaw disturbed the afternoon quiet. Corporal Clint paid no attention to them. "Envy makes a mighty strong poison," he remarked to no one in particular. He ambled on to the doorway of the middle of the three sod-walled structures and into the shaded interior.

Outside the sun beat down with steady glare. Inside Corporal Clint widened his eyes to look through the relatively cool dimness. He stood in a semblance of attention and raised his right hand in a limp salute. Angled across from him in a corner, Lieutenant Henley, acting commissary officer, was perched on a stool using an upturned packing box as a desk. Lieutenant Henley waggled a hand in what could have been a languid salute or a mere greeting and returned to pencil figuring on a piece of wrapping paper. Corporal Clint perched himself on another stool with his back to the wall where he could look along the rough ground-floored aisle between two long piles of grain in bags. He set the carbine across his knees.

Partway down the aisle between the grain bags a prairie mouse crept out and into the open and darted back and crept out again. Corporal Clint raised the carbine and aimed with casual ease and fired. There was a smudge on the ground where the mouse had been. Over in his corner Lieutenant Henley looked up. Corporal Clint nodded at him. Lieutenant Henley reached with his pencil and made a mark beside many other marks on a piece of paper tacked to the side of his box desk. He sighed and returned to his figuring. Corporal Clint took out of a pocket a linen cartridge holding its lead ball and powder and reloaded the carbine. He inspected the percussion cap. He set the carbine on his knees and watched the aisle in quiet content.

Outside the sun beat down upon the laboring soldiers. Inside was shaded silence punctured only by the occasional sharp blast of the carbine and the sighs and some soft new anguished grunts from Lieutenant Henley. Corporal Clint smiled drowsily to himself. A mouse slipped into view. Corporal Clint raised the carbine.

"Stop that infernal racket!"

Corporal Clint jumped to his feet. He snapped to attention. Off in his corner Lieutenant Henley did the same. Captain McKay stood in the doorway, mopping his face and peering into the dimness.

"How's a man to get a report written or even take a nap wondering when that damn thing's going off again?" Captain McKay waved Corporal Clint aside and sat on the stool by the wall and stretched out his legs. "An infernal nuisance."

"You're right, sir." Lieutenant Henley came forward with his paper in his hand. "And useless, sir. Utterly and completely useless."

"Yes?"

"Well, sir, I've been doing some figuring." Lieutenant Henley's voice was weighty with overtones of awe. "According to that animal book, these damn mice have four to ten young ones at a time, and it only takes them six weeks to have them. Worse than that, they start breeding soon as they're six weeks old." Lieutenant Henley sighed and stared down in somber fascination at his paper. "Well, sir, you take a middle figure for that litter number to be on the safe side, and you just say only half each litter is females, and you say again only half those females live to breeding age, and all the same starting with just one pair after ten generations you've got close to half a million of those damn mice ruining my commissary, and all of them busy breeding when they're not eating, and they're averaging about a bag of grain a day already and making holes in all the bags. They're multiplying fifty times faster than Buckner here could kill them if he was triplets and every one of him as good a shot."

Captain McKay mopped his face again. "A formidable enemy, the way you put it."

"Beg pardon, sir, but it's no joke." Lieutenant Henley waggled his piece of paper. "We'll run short of feed for the horses, and they're getting into our own provisions. We could try wooden bins, but we can't get any good wood out on this damned prairie, and they'd gnaw through it anyway. I just don't know what to do."

"Cats," said Corporal Clint.

Captain McKay slumped in his chair and drummed fingers on the onetime kitchen table that was his desk. From behind the hanging canvas partition that marked off his one-room living quarters in the same sod-walled building came a soft melodic humming and other small bustling noises as his wife moved about engaged in some incomprehensible feminine activity. The humming annoyed him. Two months they had been out here on the empty prairie, creating an Army post out of next to nothing with supplies always short and no new appropriation to draw on for things needed, and he didn't even have decent quarters for her yet because he was an old-line Army fool who believed in taking good care of his men first, and still she was cheerful and could hum silly tunes and never once complain. By rights she ought to complain. And because she wouldn't, he couldn't, not even in the bosom, so to speak, of his own family and had to go on pretending to be a noble soul who enjoyed hardship for the sake of duty nobly done.

His fingers stopped drumming, and he looked down again at the canceled requisition that had been returned in the fortnightly mail. Clipped to it was a note in vigorous handwriting: "Mac, lucky I caught this before it went any higher.

Cats! You're starting a post out there, not a blooming menagerie. Next thing you'll be asking for slippers and dressing gowns and a squad of nursemaids."

The chair squeaked as he shifted his weight. "Nursemaids," he muttered. "I'll nursemaid that jackass when I see him again. Even if he does outrank me."

The finger drumming began again. It stopped short as Captain McKay realized he was keeping time with the humming from behind the partition. He stood up and strode to the doorway and looked out where his sweating sod crews were raising the walls of the second barracks. "Buckner!" he bellowed. He saw the solid, chunky figure of Corporal Clint Buckner turn and start toward him, and he swung back to his table desk.

The side edge of the canvas partition folded back, and the cheerful face of Mrs. McKay appeared around it. "You be nice to that boy. He found me some more flowers this morning."

"Boy?" said Captain McKay. "He's seen thirty years if a day. Spent most of them doing things a boy wouldn't. Or shouldn't. I don't mean picking flowers."

Sweat gleamed on the broad face and dripped from the broad chin and rolled in little streams down the bare peeling chest of Corporal Clint as he came to attention before the table desk. Not even the heat had wilted the jaunty manner that often stirred in Captain McKay brief memories of his own cocksure youth. "Rest," said Captain McKay, and Corporal Clint relaxed all over and began to appreciate the shaded interior of the room.

Captain McKay clasped his hands behind his head with his elbows flung wide. He noted that the canvas hung undisturbed, but there was no humming behind it. He noted too the wary what's-coming-now look on Corporal Clint's face. "Buckner," he said. "How many times have you been busted and had to earn that stripe all over again?"

"Not so often, sir. Only about four times, sir."

"And how many times have you been in line for a sergeancy and missed it for some damnfoolishness or other?"

Corporal Clint had the tone pegged now. His face exploded in a grin. "Reckon I've lost count on that, sir. But I'll
make it yet."

"Maybe," said Captain McKay. "At least I'm giving you
a chance. I'm giving you ten days and fifteen dollars and
telling you to go find me some cats. Go easy on the money.
It's coming out of my own pocket. My guess is there ain't a
cat yet in the whole of Kansas Territory. But it was your
notion, and now you're stuck with it. You bring me some cats,
and the other stripe's yours."

Corporal Clint Buckner woke with the first light of dawn
through the open doorway of the dugout. He lay on a thin
matting of straw on the dirt floor of this one place that offered
any accommodations at all for thirty miles in either direction
along the wagon trace outside. He was not alone. His host,
a beard-matted trader, was snoring two feet away. A pair of
lank and odorous mule skinners lay like logs on the other side
of the doorway. And the straw had a moving multitude of its
own inhabitants.

Corporal Clint sat up and ruffled bits of straw out of his
hair. Four of his ten days and a large part of the fifteen dollars
were gone. It was time to start looking for cats in earnest. He
had covered considerable territory already and made casual
inquiries, but there had been no pressure in the search. Two
whole days he had wasted in the one settlement within a
hundred miles of the post. Well, not exactly wasted. The
settlement boasted no cat, but it did boast a pert waitress at
the false-fronted building called a hotel. She had slapped him
the first time he kissed her. She had forgotten to slap the
second time. He might have been there yet if her husband had
not come home with a wagonload of potatoes and turnips and

a positive itch to lambaste anyone interested in her. Corporal Clint had no aversion to fighting, anyplace and anytime, but it was against his principles to fight husbands.

Outside by the well he stripped himself bare and sloshed himself thoroughly with several buckets of water. While his skin dried in the early-morning air he conducted a careful search through his clothes to eliminate any visitors from the straw. "Wouldn't want to kidnap any of these critters," he said. "Now if they were only cats . . ."

Dressed again, he caught his horse in the small-pole corral by the dugout and saddled and started off. He was traveling light in boots and pants and shirt and hat. His saddle roll consisted of a blanket, a razor, and an empty grain bag with a few holes punched near the top. He had a vague notion of carrying any cats he might collect in the bag. His armament consisted of a standard cavalry pistol in a snap-shut holster on his left hip and the cherished carbine in a saddle scabbard. He had a long day's route mapped in his mind to cover the far-scattered squatters' roosts and ranch stations within a wide radius.

The welcome slight coolness of evening found Corporal Clint Buckner atop a long rolling ridge that gave him a view of several hundred square miles of catless Kansas. He was a tired and downcast man. As usual the more tired and downcast he was, the more determined he became. "Legwork won't do it," he said. "Like hunting a needle in a hell of a big haystack without even knowing a needle's there. This calls for heavy thinking."

He dismounted and let the horse graze while he studied the problem. There were several villages of friendly Indians within reaching distance, but Indians didn't have cats. They likely wouldn't even know what a cat was. Only white settlers who might bring them from back East would ever have cats. At that, only a few would do it. Cats weren't good travelers like dogs. They had to be carried in the wagons and were a nuisance. They wandered off and were left behind or got lost or some bigger animals made meals of them. But settlers offered the only possible chance. New settlers, those fresh out from back East a ways.

In the cool of the dark Corporal Clint picketed his horse. He was ten miles farther south near the deepening road ruts of the main route of the emigrant wagon trains heading farther west to pick up the Santa Fe Trail. He lay quiet, rolled in his blankets, and watched the nearly full moon rise over the left-hand ridge. "Just one of the scratching little brutes," he said, "and I'll make the old man give me that stripe."

Refreshed and jaunty in the morning sun, Corporal Clint rode along beside the wagon ruts. As he rode he hummed a small wordless tune. He had breakfast with an emigrant family, exchanging advice on the best route ahead for his food and edging around at last to the subject in hand. "Cats?" said the man. "Why sure, we had one. Coyote got it two days back."

Corporal Clint rode on, jauntier than before. "On the right track now," he said. He began humming again, and after a while his small tune had words.

> *I'm hunting a feline critter*
> *Some people call a cat.*
> *To me any day it's a sergeant's pay—*
> *A new feather in my hat.*

Ten hours, seventy miles, three wagon trains, and two ranch stations later, no longer jaunty, Corporal Clint dismounted by a small stream and unsaddled before he led the horse to the water. There were several hours of daylight left, but the horse was done for the day. He could have pushed it farther, but he had the true cavalryman's respect for his mount. He fastened the picket rope and sat on a slight rise near the stream and chewed on the sandwiches he had collected at his last stop. "There ain't a cat between here and Missouri," he said. "Wonder if a gelded skunk might do."

He finished the sandwiches and plucked a blade of grass and chewed it long and thoughtfully. Far to the east along the rutted trail a small dust cloud rose and grew and drifted in the freshening breeze. It came closer, always renewed, and beneath it and moving in it were men on horseback and ox teams straining into yokes to pull a motley collection of wagons. They came closer and swung past in an arc to line up and stop along the bank of the stream.

Corporal Clint chewed on his grass blade and watched the wagons swing past. The third wagon was driven by a faded woman in a faded sunbonnet, and beside her on the seat sat a brighter, sharper-colored copy with no sunbonnet to cramp a tumbled glory of dark-brown hair. Corporal Clint forgot to chew and stared at this second woman. "Man alive," he said, "that's a mighty attractive sight." He leaned forward and stared some more. "Yes, sir," he said. "Without any argufying or equivocating whatsomever, that's the most attractive sight I ever sighted." The woman had seen him on his knoll and had turned to look at him as the wagon swung past. Curled in her lap was a cat.

Corporal Clint Buckner was helpful to have around. He helped the man unyoke the third wagon and water the oxen and picket them along with the man's horse by some good grass. He was expert at finding buffalo chips for the fire in places overlooked by previous overnight campers. And he was a contagious and shrewd talker. By the time cooking smells were drifting around, he had adequate information in hand. The man and the faded woman, his wife, were headed for California. The other woman was the wife's sister. Her name was Ellen. The cat belonged to her, and it was a damn nuisance too. The man didn't think much of this sister business. She was too independent and she thought she knew all there was to know and she made too much fuss over animals and she was another mouth to feed, but his wife had nagged him into letting her come along.

Corporal Clint squatted on his heels and sniffed the cooking smells. "Why sure, ma'am," he said to the faded woman, "I've only had four meals so far today so of course I'll join you. Ain't often I get me real woman's cooking."

Corporal Clint squatted on his heels by the stream bank and watched the sister rinsing off the dishes. "Miss Ellen," he said, "that cat must be a trouble to you on a jaunt like this. If you're so minded, I'd do you the favor of taking it off your hands. Give it a nice home at my quarters."

Corporal Clint leaned against a wagon wheel and looked down at Miss Ellen on a stool plying a needle with knowing skill. "Tell you what," he said, "I always was seven kinds a fool. I'll give you a dollar for that cat."

Corporal Clint stood straight and solid and indignant and glared at Miss Ellen shaking out blankets before making up beds under the wagon. He calculated what remained in his pocket. "Miss Ellen," he said, "you're the obstinatest female I ever met. That cat's just a scrawny, mangy, piebald sort of thing. But I'll give you four dollars and thirty-seven cents for it."

Miss Ellen faced him, not as solid but just as indignant. "Mr. Soldier. That's a good healthy cat, and you're a mangy sort of thing to say it isn't. I've told you and told you it's not for sale. It's my cat. It stays with me. It goes where I go. Now you go do some soldiering and stop bothering me."

Corporal Clint lay sleepless in his blanket on his knoll and watched the almost full moon climb the sky. "Could sneak down there now they're asleep," he said. "Nab the critter, leave the money, make some tracks." The moon climbed higher. "No," he said. "Can't do that to a woman." He lay on one side for a while and then on the other, and the ground seemed uncommonly hard. "If I'm going to get places in this damned Army," he said, "I got to get started soon. I need that stripe." The moon arched overhead and started its downward sweep, and still his eyes remained open. "So it goes where she goes," he said. "Got to keep that in mind." He squirmed on the ground and sat up and hunted under the blanket and removed a small stone and lay quiet again. "Awful lot to ask of a man," he said, "just to get hold of a cat." The moon dropped toward the horizon, and he began figuring the time he had left. Four days. One would be needed for the return to the post. Three days. Nights too. It would work out about right. In that time, the way the train was headed, it would be close to a meeting with the regular mail wagon bound for the post. "Shucks," he said. "She's unattached and she's a woman. That's plenty of time. Even got me a full moon coming on schedule."

In the early light of morning Miss Ellen held fast to the handle of a bucket of water as Corporal Clint Buckner tried to take it from her. "I'm quite capable of carrying this myself. And if you say one word about my cat, I'll dump this water right over your grinning head."

"Cat?" said Corporal Clint. "Oh, you mean that pet of yours. Shucks, ma'am, I was only pretending to be interested in that cat trying to please you, you're so fond of it. Took one look at you coming along in that wagon and haven't been able to think of a thing else ever since but trying to please you."

Corporal Clint Buckner was very helpful to have around. He was on hand wherever help was needed along the wagon line, particularly in the neighborhood of the third wagon. Neither heat nor dust dimmed his cheerfulness. He knew the best camping places. He knew every kink in the trail and a cutoff that saved ten miles. He rode away across the prairie and out of sight, and Miss Ellen watched him go with a speculative look in her eyes. He rode back with the carcass of an antelope over the withers of his horse, and Miss Ellen watched him come back with a half smile on her lips and found her hands fussing with her hair. Corporal Clint knew his way around in many ways. Walking with her in the moonlight, he wasted no time talking about cats.

In the relative cool of approaching evening, Corporal Clint stood by the unyoked wagon and watched Miss Ellen and her sister making antelope stew. He felt a familiar warning prickling on his skin and looked down the arc of bedded wagons and saw two men coming toward him, the two men, youngish and healthy and hefty in the shoulders, who herded the milk cows and spare oxen that tagged the train. He had the notion from the way they had looked at him now and again that their opinion of him was not flattering. They were looking at him now, and their forward tread was full of purpose.

"Soldier," said the first one, "me and Bert been talking about you. We been watching you. We don't like it. We decided a couple weeks back Miss Ellen was going to have one of us and she'd have to pick which when we get where we're going. We decided now it's time you—"

"Oh-h-h-h," said Miss Ellen. "I guess I have something to say about that."

No one paid any attention to her, not even Corporal Clint. He was inspecting the two men, and his eyes were beginning to brighten.

"That's right," said Bert. "We just don't like it. Three days you been hanging around Miss Ellen. Last night was my night and night before was Jeb's, but when we come looking she wasn't around. She was gallivanting off with you somewheres. We decided you better start traveling."

"Well, well," said Corporal Clint. "Ain't it too bad I don't feel any traveling urge."

"We decided mebbe you wouldn't," said Bert. "We decided we'd just have to give it to you."

They stepped forward. Corporal Clint stepped to meet them. With a grin on his face and a gleam of joy in his eyes, Corporal Clint moved into battle. He bent low and drove his broad head like a cannonball into Bert's middle and straightened and swung to work on Jeb with experienced fists. Bert rolled on the ground and groaned.

"Oh-h-h-h," said Miss Ellen, and ran to bend over Bert, "you poor man. Did he break your ribs?"

Corporal Clint heard. He saw. His blows began to go wild. They missed Jeb entirely or when they hit they no longer carried a powerful jolt. He winced when Jeb struck him and began to retreat. Jeb rushed at him, hot with encouragement, and Bert struggled to his feet and gulped in air and plunged to join Jeb. Together they battered Corporal Clint. The air hummed with sweeping fists. Corporal Clint went down. He groaned. He staggered to his feet. He went down again. His groan was a plaintive and appealing sound. His body twitched and was still.

"Oh-h-h-h," said Miss Ellen. She stood beside his prone body and smacked at Bert and Jeb with her words. "You cowards! Two of you beating him!"

Bert and Jeb stepped backward. "Why, Miss Ellen," said Jeb. "We just decided—"

"Who cares what you decided?" said Miss Ellen. "I hate the sight of both of you. You get away from here and back with those cows, which is just about all you're fit to associate with." As Bert and Jeb retired in confusion she ran to the wagon and dipped a cloth in the water bucket and ran back to raise Corporal Clint's limp head with one hand and wipe off his bruised dusty face with the other. Corporal Clint opened his eyes. "You have such nice hands," he said, and groaned again, a small satisfied groan, and closed his eyes.

Half an hour later, limping painfully, Corporal Clint edged around the wagon. Out of sight behind it, he strode off toward the rear of the line of wagons. The limp disappeared, and he strode with a purposeful stride. He found Bert and Jeb squatted by a fire downing third cups of coffee in sullen discouragement. "Stand up, boys," he said. "We'll take up now where we left off." With the same grin on his bruised face and gleam of joy in his half-closed eyes, Corporal Clint moved into battle. Seven minutes later he looked down upon Bert and Jeb reclining dazed and much more discouraged on the ground. "Take a bit of advice," he said. "Don't go deciding to interfere with the Army again." He strode back the way he had come behind the line of wagons, and as he went the limp began once more and became more pronounced with each step, and as he limped he caroled his small tune to himself with new words.

> *I found me a feline critter—*
> *A lady's personal pet.*
> *Goes where she goes but I'm one knows*
> *It won't be hard to get.*

Walking with Miss Ellen in the moonlight, he endured his limp with gallant fortitude. It forced him to lean some on her for support and to put an arm over her shoulders.

The light mail wagon rolled steadily over the prairie. Fifty yards ahead the escort, two privates and a lance corporal, trotted steadily forward and with them, happy at freedom from constant sitting on a board seat, trotted the regular driver astride Corporal Clint Buckner's horse. In the wagon, jaunty and cheerful with the reins in his hands, sat Corporal Clint; and behind him, between the mailbag and a box, was a woman's trunk; and beside him sat Miss Ellen; and curled in her lap was the cat.

The miles slipped away under the wheels. "Clint," said Miss Ellen, "my head's been in such a whirl I didn't think before. Is there a preacher at the post?"

"Preacher?" said Corporal Clint. "Whatever for?"

"Why, to marry us, silly."

"Shucks," said Corporal Clint. "We don't need a preacher. The old man, that's the captain, he's got authority to do the job right and even better."

"A military ceremony!" said Miss Ellen. "That'll be fun. Will they cross swords for us?"

"Sabers," said Corporal Clint. "I ain't a commissioned officer so it won't be too fancy."

More miles slipped away. "Clint," said Miss Ellen, "you're a sergeant, aren't you? You said so. But there's only one stripe on your sleeve."

"Well, I am," said Corporal Clint, not quite as jaunty as before. "In a manner of speaking I am. I mean I will be when I get back there."

"Oh," said Miss Ellen. "You're being promoted you mean. I knew you'd be the kind of man who gets promotions. What did you do to get this one?"

"Shucks," said Corporal Clint, "nothing much. Just a little special duty." He began to notice that it was a hot and dusty day.

They stopped for a midday meal and to rest the horses. Corporal Clint strutted some, giving orders because he was the ranking man present, but his voice lacked its usual confident clip. He chewed in a strange silence, very thoughtful. The cat wandered about forty feet away, intent on its own individual business. Corporal Clint leaped to his feet and raced to grab it and bring it back. He smiled weakly at Miss Ellen. "Dangerous country," he said. "Coyotes and things around."

They drove forward again, and Corporal Clint was restless on the wagon seat. Miss Ellen did not notice. She had missed most of her sleep the night before, and the slight swaying of the wagon as it rolled easily along the trace among the grass tufts made her drowsy. She pulled his right arm about her and snuggled close and rested her head, half dozing, on his shoulder. Corporal Clint could feel her hair blowing softly against his cheek in the breeze of their movement and his shirt suddenly felt too small around his chest and this was very nice hair brushing his cheek and he knew he should be pleased, but he was too bothered by troublesome thoughts to appreciate the pleasure.

The miles dropped away beneath the hooves and the wheels, and they came to a shallow stream and splashed into it. The front wheel on Corporal Clint's side hit a stone and rose up on it tilting the wagon. Miss Ellen slid on the seat squealing and clutching at him, and the cat tumbled out of her lap into the water. Corporal Clint yanked on the reins and dropped them and scrambled past Miss Ellen to follow the cat. He landed on all fours in the eight inches of water, scrabbled about in it, and rose dripping with the cat in his arms.

"Good grief!" said Miss Ellen. "You didn't even bother about me but just that cat."

"Might have been a pool over on this side," said Corporal Clint, trying to smile at her and failing. "Might have been real deep water."

"Silly," said Miss Ellen. "Maybe cats don't like water, but they can swim all right if they have to. Well, I suppose it's nice you worrying so about that cat just because I like it so. I hope you don't catch the sniffles now."

"It ain't sniffles I'm worried about catching," said Corporal Clint.

The afternoon sun was low on the left as the mail wagon topped the last swell of the prairie that gave a clear view of the beginnings of Fort McKay in the distance. "That's it," said Corporal Clint Buckner with little of a prospective bridegroom's joy in his voice. His eyes brightened. "Maybe I'd better get on my horse and hurry on in ahead to sort of prepare the way some."

"And leave me?" said Miss Ellen. "I think we should

drive in together. I want to see how surprised everyone is, too. And don't worry what I'll think about how you behave. I know you have to salute and stand at attention and things like that."

The escort dropped respectfully to the rear to tail the wagon in. Corporal Clint's face grew pale as he saw they had been sighted coming and the entire personnel of the post was assembling for a good view. It grew paler as he saw that Captain McKay, contrary to custom at this hour, was not in his quarters but was standing outside with Mrs. McKay beside him. Corporal Clint sighed. Then he straightened on the seat and snapped back his shoulders and cocked his head at a jaunty angle. He urged the team into a faster trot. He pulled up close to Captain McKay with a flourish and jumped to the ground. His salute was a gesture of swift and precise perfection. "Reporting for duty, sir. Right on the tenth day, sir. Brought a young lady with me, sir, who has done me the honor of consenting to become my wife, sir. With your permission, of course, sir. I'm asking for same now, sir. And to perform the ceremony yourself, sir. As soon as—"

"But—" said Captain McKay. "But—but—"

"Awfully sudden, sir," said Corporal Clint. "But it had to be that way. Begging your pardon, sir, but I can report later. Bring her around for official introduction later too, sir. Really ought to be fixing her some quarters right away, sir. It's been a long drive. And dusty. She'll want to rest first, sir, and clean up some before a formal meeting. If you'll just let me have a tent, sir, I can fix—"

"But—" said Captain McKay. "But—but I sent you out to get some cats."

"Oh-h-h-h-h-h," said Miss Ellen.

"I told you I'd report later, sir." Corporal Clint took another breath. "Explain everything then, sir. I've done my duty. Done the best I could, sir. Things kind of happened and turned out this way. All for the best all around, sir. If you'll just let me have a tent—"

"Shut up!" bellowed Captain McKay. "I don't know what particular breed of devilment you've pulled this time, but I know it's all of a piece with past behavior. Send you out with orders to find some cats, and you come back bringing another woman to this godforsaken place that ain't fit—"

"But she's got a cat, sir," said Corporal Clint.

"Oh-h-h-h," said Miss Ellen. "So that's why you were so interested in my cat! And jumping after it all the time without caring what happened to me! Talking about marrying just to trick me into coming here so maybe you could steal it!"

"I did not," said Corporal Clint. "That's not right. That's—"

"I hate you," said Miss Ellen. "I just plain utterly despise you. Taking me away from the only folks I had and making it all sound so nice when it isn't at all. I wouldn't marry you now even if—well, I just wouldn't—I wouldn't—" Suddenly Miss Ellen was crying and she was ashamed to be crying in front of a group of startled and embarrassed men and she put her head down in her arms and the cat slipped out of her lap and retreated over the seat into the rear of the wagon, and she was sitting there with her shoulders shaking.

"Humph!" snorted Mrs. McKay. "A fine mess you men've made now. But then you always do. Where a woman's concerned anyway. Yelling at each other. Blathering about cats. A nice lovely girl like that too." She marched to the wagon and cooed soft reassurances at Miss Ellen and helped her down from the seat. In a silence made ominous by the expression on Captain McKay's face she led Miss Ellen into the captain's quarters. They disappeared from sight.

"Buckner," said Captain McKay. His tone was mild and deadly. "You have committed so damn many offenses under the military code from the moment you started yapping at me before I gave you permission to speak that I won't even try to list them now. God only knows what devilish things you've been doing while you were gone, but I intend to find out. You're under arrest. Go to your quarters and stay there till I decide what to do with you. While you're there improve your time taking that stripe off your sleeve."

Captain McKay wiped his forehead and turned to go inside and face Mrs. McKay and Miss Ellen. Surrounded by his fellows and a babble of jeering and commiserating and even envious voices, Corporal Clint moved toward the double row of tents. The mail escort rode forward, and one of them dismounted and climbed to the wagon seat to drive it over by the stable. "Wait a moment," said Lieutenant Henley, pushing out from the shade of one of the sod-walled buildings. He leaned over the backboard of the wagon and reached inside and lifted out the cat.

Private Clint Buckner sat on a three-legged stool in the end tent of the front row facing the stretch of level ground that would someday be the parade ground and stared out into the morning sun. Somehow it was hotter under the canvas than it would have been outside under the open sun with a sod crew. The heat was personal, oppressive, made so by the silence, the solitude of that particular corner of the post, and his complete ignorance of what was happening in Captain McKay's quarters and adjacent areas.

He twisted on his stool to get a better view. Across the way there was a flurry of unusual activity. Sergeant Peattie appeared with a squad of fast-stepping privates carrying various things, and walking beside him, pert and chipper with her dark-brown hair a tumbled glory about her head, was Miss Ellen. Private Clint could see that Sergeant Peattie was unusually neat and natty and was strutting to good effect and barking orders with obvious relish. The squad stopped and began to erect a tent almost exactly opposite the one in which Private Clint sat in his solitude and close to the bend in the lazy, almost dried-up little river that ran alongside the post. The tent went up quickly and was pegged tight. Into it went a cot, a chair, a washstand made of a box set on end with a cloth covering the open side, and Miss Ellen's trunk.

The squad was gone. Even Sergeant Peattie, who had lingered long, was gone. The flaps of the newly erected tent were closed. "Can't any more than shoot me," said Private Clint. He crawled under the rear canvas of his tent and set off on a wide circuit, bent low and crawling at times, taking advantage of all possible cover. He came up behind Miss Ellen's tent. He lifted its rear canvas and poked his head under. "Good morning, ma'am."

Miss Ellen was busy at her trunk. She jumped around, startled. She stared at the broad face peering up turtlewise. "Oh, it's you," she said.

"It's me, all right," said Private Clint. He crawled the rest of the way under and perched himself on the chair. "I'm mighty peeved too. If you'd only had sense enough to keep your yap shut—"

"Mr. Buckner," said Miss Ellen, "all I have to do is yell, and you'll be—"

"Go ahead and yell," said Private Clint. "Another charge or two won't mean much to me now. I want to know what the hell—and I won't ask pardon for that either—is going on over here."

"Why, Mr. Buckner," said Miss Ellen, very sweetly. "I don't figure you have any right to know, but I'll tell you. Everybody's being so nice to me. That Lieutenant Henley's taking good care of my cat, and he says it's just a marvelous mouser. And this tent is all my own and I'm to have a better place soon as more buildings are up and it'll be fixed real nice and I'm to be the officers' laundress and have my meals with the McKays and get right good pay too."

Private Clint groaned. He tried to make his voice plaintive. "But what about me?"

"You?" said Miss Ellen. "I don't know as that's any concern of mine. I have myself to worry about, seeing as you got me in such a fix. I think I'm doing right well." Miss Ellen reached up and fluffed her hair. "Maybe you've not noticed, being a man, but that Sergeant Peattie is a fine-looking man himself."

"Peattie," moaned Private Clint. "You watch out for him. I've been on leaves with him, and I'm telling you—"

"He's told me plenty about you," said Miss Ellen. "Now I remember what he's told me I think it's time you crawled out of here and stayed away."

"Shucks," said Private Clint. "Peattie always did stretch things too far. How about you remembering those nights when the moon—"

"I will not!" Miss Ellen stamped one foot and glared at him. "You get out of here now, or I really will yell!"

"Damn woman," muttered Private Clint, as he crawled under the canvas. "Always being so damn womanish." The last he saw before he let the canvas drop and departed on his return circuit was Miss Ellen standing straight and glaring at him and prettier than he'd remembered her all through the previous night. What he did not see and what Mrs. McKay did see five minutes later, as she pushed through the tent flaps with her arms laden with blankets and a mirror, was Miss Ellen slumped on the chair and crying.

Captain McKay stomped into his office hot and dusty from his afternoon jaunt to inspect his work crews at their labors. For an instant he thought he had been hearing voices from behind the canvas partition as he entered, but now there was no sound. He listened. A soft melodic humming began and he relaxed. His wife indulged in that silly humming only when she was alone. He sat behind his table desk and wiped dust from his face. The canvas partition folded back at the front edge, and Mrs. McKay's face appeared around it followed by the rest of her.

"Mac," she said, "you've left that Buckner boy sweating in that tent and wondering what you're going to do all last night and most of today. Don't you think it's time you had him over here to speak up for himself?"

"Speak up?" said Captain McKay. "He spoke up so damn much yesterday I've a mind to let him squat over there the rest of the summer. If we were back anywhere near civilization and he behaved like that and I didn't have his hide, there's plenty other officers'd think I was losing my grip."

Mrs. McKay simply looked at her husband and smiled a small smile. "Oh, I know," he said. "We're way out here the end of nowhere, and I'm top dog and I can do about anything I damn well please. So I'm just letting him sit there awhile meditating on his sins. It'll do him good."

"Mac," said Mrs. McKay, "he's the only one out here, yourself included, ever thought to find me flowers. He's talked a girl you've been making sheep's eyes at yourself into coming here to marry him, and now he's talked himself under arrest and into having her think mighty small of him. Sometimes I think you're not the same man I married twenty-too-many years ago." The canvas partition folded back again, and Mrs. McKay disappeared behind it.

Captain McKay sat still, drumming his fingers and remembering many things. He rose and went to the doorway and out a short distance. "Buckner!" he bellowed across the level space and remembered bellowing that same name in that same voice when he and his command were pinned down in small scattered groups in a dry streambed by many times their own number of hostile Indians and he needed a man who might be just reckless enough and tough enough to get through with a message for reinforcements. The thought flashed through his mind that likely he'd be bellowing that same name again when the settlers his post and others were supposed to protect began coming in real numbers to populate the Territory and the Indians got worried again about losing their lands and made trouble. He returned and sat again behind his table desk and made himself look stern and official.

Private Clint Buckner stood before him with that what's-coming-now look on his face.

"Buckner," said Captain McKay, "how much of my fifteen dollars have you got left?"

"Four dollars and thirty-seven cents, sir."

Captain McKay thumped a fist on the table. "Better'n ten dollars gone, and you didn't spend a nickel on cats. I've heard the girl's story. By rights I ought to skin you alive and hang your hide out to dry. Maybe I will yet. First I want you to tell me how you got yourself in such a fool fix."

"Well, sir," said Private Clint, "you wanted cats. I couldn't find cats. Well, sir, I found one and it was attached to that Miss Ellen woman and she wouldn't sell it. I figured the only way to get it here was get her here. I figured the only way to get her here was to marry her. You're a man, sir. You know how it is. It seemed a kind of good idea at the time."

"Damned if I do know how it is," said Captain McKay. "It's never crossed my mind to marry a woman to get a cat."

"That's only how it started, sir. More I saw of her the more I figured it was a good idea all by itself. She's a mighty attractive woman, sir."

"In a sort of way," said Captain McKay, conscious of Mrs. McKay behind the partition. "But she says it's plain you've been interested mostly in that cat all the time. Says you paid more attention to it coming here than to her. Says you were willing to about knock her out of the wagon to save that cat from a little water."

"That's all backward," said Private Clint. "That cat gives me a pain just thinking of it. You see, sir, when we headed here I got to thinking. I got to thinking what a real chunk of woman she is. Nerve enough to leave that wagon train and the only folks she knew and go to a place she didn't know a thing about and take a chance on a cross-branded Army mule like me. That's my kind of woman, sir. I got to thinking the only way I'd ever keep up with her and take care of her the way I ought was being a sergeant. That's the cat. I had to keep it safe. You promised me if I—"

"So-o-o-o," said Captain McKay. "A hell of a soldier you are. Conducted your campaign without thinking through to the finish. Forgot till too late how your fine talk would sound to her when she found out about the cat. Walked right into what I'd call a verbal ambush. Now you've lost out all around. Lost the girl. Lost the sergeancy. I distinctly told you cats. Plural. You brought just one."

The partition folded back and around it came Mrs. McKay. Behind her and moving up beside her came Miss Ellen. Miss Ellen's head was held high, and her eyes were bright. "Captain McKay," she said, "that cat is cats." Miss Ellen blushed very prettily and looked at Private Clint and looked away and blushed even more prettily. "That cat had an—well, an—affair with another cat back in Springfield when we came through. It won't be long now. She always has four or five at a time."

Captain McKay looked at Miss Ellen blushing so prettily. He looked at Private Clint Buckner, who was looking at Miss Ellen with his head at a jaunty angle and a grin on his broad face. He looked at Mrs. McKay, who was looking at him with that expectant expression that meant he had better do something and it had better be the right thing. He cleared his throat. "Sergeant Buckner, you will report back here directly after mess in the neatest uniform you can beg, borrow, or steal around this post. You may regard the fifteen dollars as a wedding present. The ceremony will be at seven o'clock."

Joan Aiken

THE CAT WHO LIVED IN A DRAINPIPE

Three hundred years ago, in the times when men wore swords and rode on horses, when ladies carried fans and traveled in carriages, when ships had sails and kings lived in castles, and you could buy a large loaf of bread for a penny, there lived three cats in Venice.

Venice is a very peculiar town, built on about a hundred islands. The streets in between the houses are canals full of water. Only in the narrowest alleys and lanes can you walk on dry ground. If you want to go across town you take a gondola. If a housewife wants to visit her neighbor on the other side of the street, she has to row herself over, unless there is a bridge by her house. Children and cats in Venice learn to swim almost as soon as they learn to walk.

The three cats I am going to tell you about were called Nero, Sandro, and Seppi.

Nero was large and pitch black and very tough indeed. His master was a chimney sweep called Benno Fosco. Nero helped with the sweeping. In Venice, chimneys are swept from above. The sweep, standing on the roof, lets down a long bunch of twigs like a witch's broom to knock out the soot. Nero and his master climbed all over the roofs of Venice with their brooms and their bags full of soot. If a chimney was narrow or very choked up, Nero would go down first, at top speed, like a diver, boring out the soot with his sharp claws and his powerful paws and sweeping it loose behind him with his strong, whiplike tail.

It was lucky that Nero was black, so that the soot didn't show on his fur; he was always absolutely wadded with soot and left a cloud of it behind him as he walked about. And if his master rubbed behind his ears, out came another black cloud. No one, apart from Benno Fosco, would ever have dared to stroke Nero; he might have bitten the finger off anybody who tried. When the chimney sweep poled his gondola along the canals, loaded with sacks of soot, Nero sat on one of the bags, right at the front, looking like a big fat figurehead carved out of coal. Mostly he stayed silent, but every once in a while he let out a single low, threatening howl: *Ow-wow-ow-ow-ow!* It meant, Does anybody feel like a fight? And when he did so, the other cats along the waterside, sitting on windowsills or doorsteps or on bridges or other boats, would half close their eyes, shrug, and keep quite quiet until he had gone by. Nobody ever felt inclined to fight with Nero.

Sandro was quite a different kind of cat. His long, soft fur was a dark-orange color, like a French marigold. His expression was always calm and sleepy and very refined; he spent most of his days dozing on a red velvet cushion in the boudoir of his mistress, who was a princess and lived in a palace in one of the grandest streets. Two or three times a day, the princess used to comb Sandro with a silver comb. While doing so she would exclaim admiringly, *"Bello* Sandro! *Bello gatto!* Beautiful cat!" Sandro never paid the least attention to this, but merely went on dozing harder than ever, with his nose pushed well in under his tail. The only exercise he took during the hours of daylight was an occasional short spell of washing. But at night, when his mistress, the Princess Cappella, was asleep, he went out over the roofs of Venice.

Seppi, the third cat, was quite different again from either of the others. For a start, he was much smaller. Seppi belonged to nobody; he had been born in a worm-eaten fish basket, and he lived in a broken drainpipe. His mother, unfortunately, had fallen off a fishing boat and been drowned when he was a kitten; from that day on, Seppi never grew any bigger. He lived on fish heads and moldy scraps of macaroni stolen from garbage heaps. He was an ugly little cat, black and white in patches of various sizes, with one black paw and three white, a black mask across his white face, and a saddle of black from shoulders to tail. One ear was black with a white lining, and one white with a black tip; one eye was yellow, and one blue. Also, he had suffered from a mishap to his tail; most of it was missing, leaving only a short black stump. It made him look like a rabbit and ruined his balance. Where other cats could leap gracefully onto narrow ledges or walk easily along slender rails, Seppi had to concentrate with all his might or he was liable to overshoot and topple off edges. But he practiced at balancing most patiently, and when he did fall he always landed lightly; he was so skinny that he weighed little more than a duster. Every day he clambered gaily and dangerously all over the roofs and walls and pinnacles and boats and bridges of Venice; he was always hungry but he was always hopeful, too, and full of energy and curiosity. People laughed at him and shouted *"Pulcinello"* as he went trotting by on his own business, because, in his black mask, he looked so like a clown.

These three cats, Nero, Sandro, and Seppi, were not precisely friends. Nero was too tough to need friends, and Sandro too lazy. And both were inclined to look down their noses at Seppi, who was such a common little gutter cat and so much younger and smaller as well.

But one bond joined all three of them together, and that was music. They were all passionately fond of it. Regularly, every Friday evening, they assembled together for a singing session. They always met in the same place, on a wooden humpbacked bridge over a quiet backwater. And there, all night, in all weather except snow, they would hold their concert, until the first light of the rising sun began to dapple the canal water like pink lettuce leaves.

This was why Nero and Sandro were prepared to tolerate Seppi and overlook his clownlike appearance and vulgar ways and lack of tail. In spite of his being so small, he had a remarkably loud voice, and furthermore he could sing higher up the scale than any other cat in Venice.

Their program of singing was always the same. Nero began, because his voice was the deepest. Squatting on the top step of the bridge, like a big shapeless black lump, with elbows and whiskers sticking out sideways, he would slowly let out four or five howls, all on the same deep, gritty, throbbing bass note, like an old mill wheel creaking: *How, row, row, row, row.*

Then there would be a long, silent pause, until Sandro was ready to sing his part of the trio, which was a slow, sorrowful, wailing tenor cry, not unlike the hoot of a ship's siren a great way off in the fog: *Harayyyyyyyyyyyyyy?*

Afterward, all three cats would sit silent and motionless, without even the twitch of a whisker, for so great a stretch of time that any listener might be fooled into thinking that they had finished their concert and gone home to bed. But not a bit of it. All of a sudden little Seppi would let out such an ear-piercingly shrill scream—*Freeeeeeeeeeeee!*—that birds, even at dead of night, would wake and twitter in protest under the eaves of nearby houses, dogs would bark for two miles around, while any person walking rather close to a canal in that district would almost certainly be so startled that he fell into the water. Even Sandro and Nero never became completely accustomed to Seppi's shriek; each time, after he had sung his part, they would gaze at him almost respectfully for a few moments.

Then they would repeat the recital, always in the same order, with Nero singing first and Seppi coming in at the end, and long pauses in between the solo parts. At the very end, there would be a short chorus, with all singing together.

Very occasionally, a strange cat might make an attempt to join their group, but neither Sandro nor Nero would dream of permitting this. Sandro would let out a terrifying hiss, and Nero would shoot from his place on the top step and give the impertinent candidate such a clip on the ear with a sooty paw that he would fly for his life and think himself lucky to escape with his ears and tail.

In this way, the concerts were held every Friday night. Half the cats of Venice came to listen and sat in admiring silence, at a respectful distance.

Then, at sunrise, the three singers would silently part and go their various ways: Nero flitting over the rooftops to the first job of the day; Seppi trotting off through a network of narrow lanes and alleys, where he might hope to find a fish tail or a couple of inches of cast-off spaghetti; Sandro gracefully waving his golden tail and summoning a boat to take him back to the palace where he lived. All the gondoliers who plied their boats for hire along the Venetian canals knew the Princess Cappella and her cat; Sandro never had the least trouble in finding a gondola to take him home. Any boatman who picked him up knew that a fee of three golden ducats would be paid without question by the butler who opened the door.

So matters went on for many months.

But one Friday evening in a cold November, when Sandro and Nero reached the bridge at their usual hour, they were surprised to see that Seppi was not there. Usually he was first at the meeting place, having nothing to do apart from hunting for scraps in the gutters, whereas Nero might be kept late sweeping a chimney, and Sandro might have been obliged to accompany his mistress on a round of calls.

"Where can the little wretch have got to?" Sandro said impatiently, after they had waited for ten minutes. He shivered, for an icy wind was blowing. "I wish he'd hurry up. There's nothing to beat music for warming you."

"Shall we start without him?" suggested Nero.

"No, it would be hopeless without the treble part. I do trust the little fool hasn't been kicked into a canal and drowned."

"More likely got into a fight with someone bigger than himself and had his head bitten off," said Nero uneasily. "Now I come to think about it, I haven't seen him around the streets for the last few days."

"No, it's all right. Here he comes," said Sandro in relief, noticing a small black-and-white shape slip along the top of a wall.

Seppi trotted up the steps to join his fellow singers. But he did not seem quite his usual, carefree self. He offered no explanation as to why he was late, he made no apologies, even when Nero growled at him and Sandro let out a reproving hiss, but sat in silence, with his feet apart and mouth open, staring up dreamily and absentmindedly at the small, frozen-looking moon that floated overhead. Furthermore, when it came to his turn to sing, he waited so long that both his companions began to wonder anxiously if he had lost his voice. And when he did at last let out his screech, it was nothing like so loud and shattering as usual; in fact, it was quite a soft, plaintive note, not much louder than the cry of a gull, and both Nero and Sandro were quite disgusted by it.

"Come on, sing up, you good-for-nothing!" said Nero, giving him a box on the ear. "What kind of a noise is *that?* A newborn kitten would be better. Why, a person could hardly hear it across the canal."

"Are you sick?" inquired Sandro, more sympathetically.

"No, no," murmured Seppi in a vague manner, still staring at the moon.

"Well, then, kindly pull yourself together!" said Nero sharply.

Afterward, Seppi did pull himself together and sang even better than usual, so well, in fact, that dogs barked all the way to the village of Mestre, and the other two forgot his strange behavior.

But, next week, they had cause to remember it again, for he arrived even later than on the previous Friday and in a most peculiar state, with his whiskers dangling downward, faraway eyes narrowed to slits, and a layer of dust and cobwebs all over his fur.

Moreover, when it came to his turn to sing, all he could let out was a faint squeak, hardly louder than the noise made by a bat.

"Look here, this is useless!" said Nero in disgust. "Come on, you'll have to tell us what's up. Where have you been all week? I haven't seen you since last Friday. Where are you spending your time these days?"

"Yes, speak up, Seppi," added Sandro. "You owe it to us to tell us what's happened. After all, we taught you all the music you know."

At that, Seppi was suddenly galvanized; his faraway look vanished, his stump of a tail and scanty whiskers bristled, and he burst into speech.

"Music?" he said. "Oh, my dear partners, you think we are producing good music here? You think our trio makes the best music in Venice? Just come with me. I'll take you where you can hear something that will make you realize we don't know the first thing about music!"

At this, Nero and Sandro exchanged glances. The little fellow must have gone crazy, their eyes and ears and whiskers suggested. Sandro elegantly shrugged his tail. Oh, well, we'll have to humor him. Perhaps we can get him out of this nonsensical fit somehow. Otherwise, we'd better start looking for another treble. Too bad.

Anyway, they followed him.

Seppi bolted down the balustrade of the bridge and along the path beside the canal. Then he led the way at a gallop through twisting alleys, across paved squares, over bridges, along quaysides, until they had come to a much grander and richer part of the town.

Here Seppi went upward—up onto a gate, along a wall, onto a roof, and from there in a long leap across an alley onto a higher roof.

"Why are you bringing us here?" said Nero. "I know this house. It belongs to a wealthy paper manufacturer. I've often swept the chimneys. Once the mistress gave me a whole bowlful of fresh sardines."

"Yes, yes, I daresay. Come along," said Seppi inattentively, and he led them up and up, toward an attic window. "Now come up here and keep quiet and listen!"

The window was a kind of dormer, right in the middle of the roof. All three cats perched on the sill, which was very dusty. It was only a few feet above the level of the flat roof (which was lucky, for Seppi was in such an excited state that he kept losing his balance and toppling off the edge). "Now listen, listen!" he begged again, breathlessly.

Nero and Sandro peered through the window, to see what had made their young colleague so excited. They were looking down into a smallish attic containing nothing save a chair, a box, and a music stand. On the box lay an oboe. On the chair sat a young man, who was tuning a violin, and a minute or two after they had settled on the sill he began to play it.

As he played, Nero's and Sandro's eyes became larger and larger, rounder and rounder. Presently Nero surreptitiously wiped a tear off his black nose with the back of his paw. Sandro was soon so overcome by emotion that he had to bury his face in his bushy, golden tail. As for Seppi, his blue eye and his yellow one were shining like a sapphire and a topaz respectively.

"There!" he whispered during a pause. "Did you ever hear anything as beautiful as that? Ever in your *life?*"

Speechlessly they shook their heads. They were quite choked with wonder and awe, both at the skill of the player and the magic of the music.

"There!" said Seppi again, when the player had finished his piece. "What did I tell you? Now do you see why I have been a bit absentminded lately? I've spent the whole of every day just sitting on this windowsill, listening to him play."

"Who is the young man?" inquired Sandro graciously, when he had recovered himself a little.

"I know him," said Nero. "He is the paper manufacturer's son. His name is Tommaso. Once, when I had gone down the chimney and come out into a big saloon downstairs, I heard his father say to him, 'Tommaso, my son, music is a fine thing, but why don't you ever go out and amuse yourself like the other young men? Why spend all your days playing your fiddle up there in the attic?' And the mother said to her husband, 'Oh, leave the boy alone, Antonio! If he wants to play his fiddle and his oboe, that's a harmless hobby for a young man, and not at all expensive.' "

Now the young man began to play again, on the oboe this time, and the tunes he played were so supremely beautiful that Sandro was soon heaving with silent sobs, thinking of his childhood, while Nero had to run twice around the dormer to recover himself. Both of them thanked Seppi from the bottom of their hearts for having given them such a musical treat.

From that time on, there were no more concerts on the bridge. Not Friday night only, but every evening of the week was spent by the three partners perched on the dusty sill, listening wide-eyed and openmouthed to the music made by young Tommaso in his attic. Their own music making was entirely abandoned; all the cats in Venice wondered what had become of the famous trio and grieved at their loss. Indeed, another trio of cats had the impudence to take over the wooden bridge, but their singing was so inferior that the whole audience joined together to chase them off, and from that time on, Friday nights in that quarter were no different from any other. The people in the houses round about were not sorry, but the cat population thought it a sad loss.

During daylight, of course, Nero and Sandro were obliged to return to their usual occupations, which they did most reluctantly. Benno Fosco soon began to grumble that Nero's chimney sweeping was becoming very hasty and careless; the Princess Cappella complained that her pet's fur was disgracefully dusty and neglected; little Seppi gave such scanty attention to hunting for scraps of food that he grew as thin as a withered leaf. He stayed on the windowsill all day long unless young Tommaso went out for a short airing. When he did so, Seppi would hastily scramble down from the roof and try to follow him, either slipping along behind through the lanes and squares or nipping on board his gondola, where, perched in some cranny, he would watch the young man with unblinking love and admiration.

Oh, he often thought sadly to himself, how happy I would be if only I could belong to him, as Sandro does to the princess. How proud I would be to sit on the prow of his boat as it glided along the canal. Or he would imagine lying on a blue velvet cushion in a warm room, listening to his master play for hours. Surely life could hold no greater happiness than that.

Still, he thought, I might as well put such ideas out of my head. He could have the handsomest cat in Venice. He'd never look at an ugly little cat like me.

In fact, once or twice, young Tommaso had noticed Seppi stowed in a corner of his gondola and had called to the gondolier, "Is that cat yours?"

"No, sir, that's little Seppi. He belongs nowhere. He's nobody's cat."

"How did he get on board?"

The boatman would shrug.

"Well, throw him off; he's probably full of fleas!"

Seppi was quite resigned to being thrown off the boat if discovered and would simply return to the attic windowsill and wait for Tommaso to come back.

Due to this habit of following the young man and listening to his conversation, Seppi was better informed about the family's affairs than the other two partners.

Two or three months later, there came a violent quarrel between Tommaso and his father, which ended in the young man's rushing up to the attic and slamming the door. The father hardly ever climbed above the first floor, where the grand reception rooms were, but on this occasion he came storming up after his son.

"If that's your last word," he shouted through the door, "you can just stay in the attic till you change your mind." And he locked the door and pocketed the key.

Tommaso made no reply.

"I shall tell the servants not to let you have any food or drink until you get this ridiculous notion out of your head!" shouted old Antonio furiously.

Tommaso answered nothing.

"And you needn't think you can talk your mother around, for I'm taking her off to stay with Auntie Gabriella in the country!" roared the old man, and he stamped away downstairs.

"What's all that about?" said Sandro to Seppi (for it was evening, and all three cats were there). "What has young Tommaso done that's so upset the old man?"

"He has fallen in love with a girl at one of the orphanages. He wants to marry her."

(There were four big orphanages in Venice, where the orphans were all taught music and learned to sing most beautifully.)

"Dio mio!" said Nero. "What possessed him to do that? I thought the orphans were all bowlegged or one-eyed."

"Not this one," said Seppi. "I've seen Tommaso meet her. She is very pretty. And she has a fine singing voice. Her name is Margherita."

"Then why won't his father let Tommaso marry her?"

"He wants his son to marry some rich girl."

"Humph," said Sandro. "I daresay Tommaso will give in when he begins to feel really hungry."

"If he had any gumption he'd escape over the roof," said Nero.

"He could never do it," said Seppi. "A cat could, but not a human being."

It was true that the house was extremely high; the roof commanded a beautiful view over half of Venice, but there was no way down, except for cats. Next morning young Tommaso found that out for himself; he climbed out his window, walked around the roof inspecting its possibilities, and then, shrugging, returned to the attic, where he spent the day composing and playing the most heartrending tunes.

"The parents have gone off to the country," reported Seppi, when Sandro and Nero arrived that evening. "And they took all the servants with them except for a very bad-tempered steward, who has orders not to allow Tommaso any food until he writes a letter to his father promising to stop thinking about the girl."

Indeed, at that moment, they heard the steward, whose name was Michele, banging on the attic door. "Will you write to your father and say you have changed your mind?"

"Never!" shouted the young man, and he blew a defiant blast on his oboe.

"Then you get no supper," said Michele, and they heard his footsteps retreating down the stairs.

Two days went by.

"This is becoming serious," said Sandro. "The young man is growing pale and thin. Human beings have to eat a lot in order to survive. Suppose he should die? No more music!"

Even Nero looked grave, and little Seppi nearly fell off the windowsill at such a dreadful idea. During the next day, with terrible difficulty because of his poor balance, he lugged up two large fish heads onto the roof and laid them hopefully on the windowsill. But the prisoner inside did not seem to notice them. After another night, Tommaso just lay all day on his cloak, which was spread on the floor; he seemed to be very weak and did not play on his violin, though he occasionally blew a few notes on his oboe.

"A terrible thing has happened!" reported Seppi agitatedly, when Sandro and Nero arrived on the following evening.

"What now?"

"That steward, Michele, he got mixed up in a fight with some sailors on the quayside. I was watching from the garden wall. A stone hit him on the head, and he was carried off as if he were dead."

"So now nobody in Venice knows that the poor young man is starving in the attic?" said Sandro.

"*Zio mio!* That's bad," said Nero.

"It's up to us to do something about him," said Seppi.

"But what?" said Sandro.

All three sat racking their brains.

"He needs food," said Nero, after a lot of thought.

"He didn't see the fish heads I brought him," said Seppi sadly.

"Fish heads are no use," said Sandro with scorn. "Human beings don't eat that kind of stuff."

There was another long, worried silence.

"If only we could get through the window," said Seppi.

But it was shut tight. All their poking and prying had no effect. And the young man was lying with his back to them, without moving, as if he were very weak indeed.

At last Seppi said, looking rather embarrassed, "I think I have had an idea."

"Well, what is it?" said Nero. "Come on, speak up."

"Well," Seppi said, more and more bashful as the other two waited expectantly, "I have a—a sort of a friend; he—he occupies the other end of the drainpipe where I live."

"Who is this person?"

Nero and Sandro exchanged looks and shrugs. Evidently it was some frightfully low connection, though what alley cat could be lower down the social scale than Seppi, it was hard to imagine.

"His name is Umberto," muttered Seppi, blushing under his fur.

"Never heard of him. I thought I knew all the cats in Venice," said Nero.

"Umberto isn't—isn't exactly a cat."

"Well? What is he?"

"He's—he's a—a m-mouse."

"What!" Nero and Sandro nearly fell off the sill in their outrage and disapproval.

"A highly intelligent mouse, of course," Seppi went on hastily, gabbling in his anxiety. "He saved my life once, when I had a fishbone stuck in my throat. He pulled it out."

"Well?" demanded Nero after another awful silence. "What is your idea in regard to this *mouse?*"

"Don't you see?" Seppi picked up courage a little. "Mice can get *into* places. If I brought Umberto here—but you would have to promise to—to respect his advisory position— he could probably nibble a way into the attic. And he could carry in food."

"What sort of food could *he* take?" said Sandro scornfully.

Seppi had been thinking hard about this.

"Well, cheese. Peas. Things that a mouse can carry."

"Humph," said Nero. "Yes. It's a possibility, I will admit. Anyway, there's no use discussing what he could carry until we have met this character and he has surveyed the situation. Could you fetch him here, Seppi?"

"I could try."

"Trying is not good enough. I had better come with you," said Sandro. "You have such a wretched sense of balance; it would be disastrous if you dropped this person on your way here. I'm sure he's the only mouse in Venice who has ever got into conversation with a cat."

"All right, come along if you think so," agreed Seppi doubtfully. "But you will be careful with him, won't you?"

"Honor of a Cappella. I've often carried out the kitchen cat's kittens when they get into my mistress's boudoir. I know all about handling."

Seppi was so worried about Tommaso that he wasn't particularly embarrassed at taking Sandro to his humble home. His mind was occupied with the problem of what food could be transported to the attic. Eggs? Could mice carry eggs? Carrots? Meatballs?

Umberto was a large, stocky brown mouse with flashing black eyes and a gray muzzle, whiskers, and tail, for he was fairly advanced in years. Seppi had already told him about the poor young man's plight, so he was not greatly astonished when the two cats arrived at his end of the drainpipe and asked if he would come with them, though he did not look altogether happy at the prospect of being carried there in Sandro's mouth.

However, Sandro proved to be a careful and reliable bearer; in record time he carried Umberto back over the walls and rooftops as delicately as if he had had a peacock's egg between his jaws. Umberto certainly had a more comfortable ride than he would have if Seppi had carried him by the scruff of his neck, though Seppi did wonder, when they arrived at the attic windowsill, if Umberto's whiskers had not gone a shade or two whiter.

Nevertheless, the minute he was set down, the mouse began to bustle about the windowsill, surveying its possibilities in a thoroughly professional manner.

"Why, this will be quite easy," he said. "In fact, there is already a mousehole through the wooden window frame; it has been blocked with putty and scraps of paper, but I can clear that out in fifteen minutes."

And he began briskly nibbling with his razor-sharp teeth and scooping out the debris with his tiny but strong and skillful paws.

The other three sat watching and wishing they could do something helpful.

"Why don't you fetch some food while I do this?" Umberto suggested, when he came out of his tunnel for a mouthful of fresh air.

This seemed a good idea. Sandro and Nero left at once. But Seppi said that he would remain behind and help.

"When you have made the hole just a little bigger, I can poke in my paw and bring out the loose stuff."

In ten minutes Nero and Sandro returned, Nero with a hunk of parmesan cheese, Sandro carrying half a long, thin loaf of bread. They had stolen these things from a trattoria at the end of the street.

"Excellent," said Umberto, who was gaining more confidence as he became used to the situation. "Now if Seppi can push in his paw once more, I think it will be possible to push the rest of the barrier through into the attic."

Seppi thrust his paw in up to the shoulder and managed to shift the rest of the stopping; then Umberto ran through the tunnel.

"All clear," he reported, coming back. "And the young man is asleep, not dead; he's breathing, but his eyes are shut."

Meanwhile, the others had been nibbling off small scraps of cheese and bread of a suitable size to be taken in through the hole. Umberto carried some of them in and laid them beside the young man. His report was unpromising, however.

"He doesn't seem to want to wake up and eat them. Human beings are so sluggish! If you put delicious, strong-smelling cheese beside a sleeping mouse, he would be awake in a moment."

"Could you lay a crumb or two on his mouth?" suggested Seppi.

Umberto tried.

"No good," he came back to say presently. "The young man just brushes them off with his hand. And his head is as hot as a fire. I think he has a fever."

"When my mistress had a fever," said Sandro, "she ate a lot of fruit. Oranges and melons."

"Melons! How are we going to carry *melons* up here?" said Nero irritably.

"I have an idea!" said Seppi. "Grapes! And I know where there are some, too. Down below, at the back of this house, there is a big glass room—sometimes I come up that way over its roof—and inside there is a vine covered with grapes. Umberto, couldn't you go down inside the house and fetch some, or ask the house mice to help? There must be plenty inside somewhere. Every house in Venice is full of mice."

"I will see if it can be done," said Umberto. And he disappeared back through the tunnel. Presently he pushed his head out to announce that it was possible to squeeze under the attic door and he intended to go on a journey of exploration. He vanished again and did not return for a long time.

By now the night was nearly past. Roosters were crowing in backyards, and all the domes and pinnacles of Venice were beginning to turn pink. Nero and Sandro reluctantly went off to their day's duties.

"But we'll come back this evening," they promised.

"Bring some food when you come," begged Seppi. "Or some drink."

"*Drink!* How do you expect us to do that?"

But then Nero reflected. "My master has a leather wine bottle that's not too big. I might be able to carry it. But how shall we get it into the attic? It's far too large to go through that hole."

"Perhaps Umberto can make the hole bigger before you come back. Or I can. I'll work at it all day."

After they had gone, Seppi turned to a plan of his own. Umberto's opening of the passage had slightly loosened the bottom left-hand windowpane. Seppi pushed his paw into the mousehole and worked it from side to side, shoving with his shoulder against the loose pane, which rattled and shifted and gave, little by little. But it was slow, hard, tiring work; he wished that Umberto would come back and help by nibbling away the putty around the edge of the pane. Seppi tried to do this himself, but his teeth were not the right shape. He went back to pushing and poking. After a couple more hours of this —all of a sudden, triumph!—the pane fell inward, onto the floor, with a tinkling crash.

It was a very small pane, however. Seppi wondered if he would be able to squeeze through the square hole that it had left. I shall look a real fool if I get stuck halfway, he thought, and tried his whiskers for size. They fitted exactly. Holding his breath, Seppi wriggled through. He could just do so, due to his extra thinness from the past few days of anxiety.

At last he was in the attic, where he had so often longed to be! It's lucky I'm small, he reflected; neither Nero nor Sandro could have done it.

He crept across the floor to where Tommaso lay on the cloak and sniffed the young man all over. Alive, thank goodness! But Umberto was right; Tommaso was certainly sick. His hands and forehead were burning hot, his lips were dry and cracked, and he tossed from side to side, muttering in his feverish dream: *"Mamma!* Please don't punish me. I played that last piece too fast, I must play it again slower. Margherita, why won't you come to see me? Please look this way. . . ."

Seppi was greatly distressed at being able to do so little for his hero. He licked Tommaso's forehead all over several times, in hopes of cooling it a little; he fetched in some more of the bread and cheese from outside. But it was plain that the young man was too seriously ill to benefit from this kind of food.

At last, to his great relief, Seppi heard a soft snuffling and scraping from the other side of the attic door and turned in time to see Umberto squeeze underneath, rolling in front of him a large green grape. He was followed by a second mouse —a third—a fourth—a fifth. Each of them had brought a grape. More and more mice came pouring in, until the attic floor was quite covered with mice, and grapes were rolling about everywhere.

"Oh, *bravo, bravo!* Well done, my dear, dear friend!" exclaimed Seppi joyfully. "Now if only we can get the young man to eat one of the grapes . . ."

Easier said than done, however. Seppi tried dropping the grapes onto Tommaso's mouth. But, like the bread and cheese crumbs, they only rolled off. "And, in any case, he might choke if one went into his throat," pointed out Umberto. "Like you with the fishbone, Seppi."

At last they solved the problem. Working together, two of the mice, one seated on Tommaso's collar and one on his cheekbone, managed to squeeze a grape so that its juice ran into the corner of the patient's open mouth.

"He swallowed!" cried Seppi. "I saw his throat move. Quickly! Another grape!"

In no time they had a relay system working. Grapes were passed from paw to paw, as fast as drops of rain running down a railing. When, fairly soon, the two grape squeezers became exhausted, with aching paws and heaving chests, they were replaced by two others. Mice rushed to and fro, under the door, down the stairs to the hothouse, where the vine grew. The patient swallowed and swallowed, always with his eyes shut.

Finally he gave a deep sigh and shut his mouth tight, so that the juice from the last grape ran over his chin. Then he turned over, burying his face in his folded arm; two of the mouse squeezers narrowly avoided being squashed.

"I think he has had enough for now," said Umberto. "Sick people should not have much at a time. But I believe the grapes have done good."

It was true that the young man was breathing more easily. His head was not so hot, and he had stopped talking in his sleep. The mice ran all over him sympathetically.

"*Poverino!* Poor young man. It is a shame. His parents should not treat him so. Such a handsome young fellow, too!"

"I expect they did not mean him to die," Seppi said. "They believe the steward is here to keep an eye on him."

"But he is not! He has never come back. Downstairs the house is quite empty."

"Is there any food about?"

"Some. Not a lot. What should we bring up?"

"Anything you can carry."

So, during the rest of the day, there was a continuous come-and-go of mice, up and down the stairs, and under the attic door, with all the food they could find and carry: nuts, olives, dried cherries, beans, Brussels sprouts, grains of rice, more grapes, small pieces of carrot, of artichoke, of cheese, of dried fish.

Seppi sat by the young man, lovingly licking and relicking his forehead all day, over and over, until his tongue became quite tired and dry. Twice more Tommaso half woke and was given more grape juice each time by relays of helpful mice.

After dark, Nero and Sandro returned. They were staggering with fatigue. Between them, taking it in turns, they had carried up a heavy leather bottle.

"*Dio mio!*" Nero said. "It will be days before my neck muscles recover from carrying that thing. But I think we can just squeeze it through the hole. What a lucky thing that you managed to get that pane out."

Nero and Sandro pushed; Seppi gripped the neck of the flask and pulled. At last it fell through onto the floor.

"What's in it? Wine?"

"No, much better," said Sandro. "*Teriaca!* My mistress got it from a witch."

Teriaca was a kind of medicine much used in Venice at that time. It was made from cinnamon, pepper, fennel, rose leaves, amber, gum arabic, opium, and many other herbs and spices. It was supposed to cure everything except the plague.

"How are we going to get the cork out?"

The mice were equal to that. They soon had the cork nibbled away.

Now came a difficulty, though. Even Seppi and the mice together were not strong enough to hoist up the bottle to Tommaso's mouth, and there was a great danger, as they pushed and pulled, that all the precious contents would be spilled. Nero and Sandro, watching through the window, shouted advice but couldn't get in to help; the hole was too small for either of them to climb through. "Prop his head on the violin. No, on the oboe!" But this proved impossible.

"Well, we'll have to use drastic measures," Seppi announced, and, ordering the mice to keep the bottle tipped upward as close to the young man's face as possible, he bit Tommaso's hand sharply.

Roused by the sudden pain, the young man opened his eyes and saw the bottle right in front of them.

"I'm dreaming, dreaming," he murmured, but he raised himself on one elbow, grasped the bottle, and drank off its powerful-smelling contents in one long swallow. Then he fell back again and shut his eyes.

"Bravo, bravo!" cried the mice. "Now he will be better! The *teriaca* will cure him! All we need do is keep him fed, and soon we shall be hearing his beautiful music again.

"And now his large excellency the Great Black Cat is here, perhaps your honor wouldn't mind coming down to the kitchen and taking the lid off the big iron pot there. We know it is full of cooked spaghetti, which the steward made before he went away, but the lid is too heavy for us to shift. Your Magnificence will be able to do it easily."

Nero was rather affronted at being given orders by the mice, although they had been very polite about it. He stared at them sharply to make sure they were not poking fun at him.

"How do you suggest I get into the kitchen?" he said coldly.

"Why, *ebbene,* down the chimney of course! *Il signore* Nero knows better than anyone in Venice how to do *that.* The fire is out—since many days."

"Yes, that does seem a good idea, Nero," Sandro remarked. "And while you are down in the kitchen you might find other kinds of food that the mice can't reach."

"You won't be *unkind* to any of the mice while you are

down there, will you?" Seppi said anxiously. "They are working so hard to save Tommaso."

Nero promised to restrain himself and went off to the chimney stack, which was at the other side of the roof. They heard a heaving and thumping, then nothing more. A considerable time passed.

Sandro began to worry. "I do hope he has not got stuck in the chimney. After all, it is different when his master is there with brushes and ropes."

But presently mice began to emerge from under the door, dragging immense lengths of spaghetti that they had hauled all the way up the stairs from the kitchen. Soon a large, pale pile of it was coiled up in one corner of the attic. From some scuffles and a few curses on the other side of the door, it could be guessed that Nero was helping in this operation but was finding it hard to cooperate with the mice.

After a while he reappeared outside the window, dragging a bunch of very sooty dried sausages, which he pushed through the hole.

"There wasn't much else in the kitchen," he reported. "I daresay the family took most of the food with them when they went to the country. We'll have to arrange for a supply of food from outside."

Since the prisoner was now well supplied for the moment, however, with enough to last him at least for a couple of days, and since everybody was tired out, the mice limped off to their quarters downstairs, and Nero and Sandro prepared to go home. Seppi said that he would spend the night with the patient. Umberto asked, rather diffidently, if someone could take him home, as it was rather a long journey and he was not certain of the way.

"My dear Umberto! Of course I shall see you back to your door," Sandro said graciously.

In consequence of which, an amazed late-night gondolier, poling his craft home along the Grand Canal, found himself beckoned to the quayside by a negligent wave of Sandro's golden tail. "And, would you credit it, there was a *mouse* riding on the cat's back!" he reported later to his wife. "And they *both* got off at the Cappella palace."

"Ernesto, you've had too much chianti again," said his wife, turning over sleepily in bed.

Luckily the drainpipe shared by Seppi and Umberto was only a couple of blocks from the Cappella palace. Sandro carried Umberto to his door as promised, and then went home himself for a well-earned day's sleep. Nero was already curled up on a soot sack in his master's boat, taking a cat nap. But Seppi sat up for the rest of the night, watching the sleeping Tommaso and observing with joy, as dawn approached, that the young man's breathing became slower and easier, his brow was cool, his hands were damp, and the fever had left him. At last, satisfied that the patient would recover, Seppi curled up in a ball, comfortably jammed against Tommaso's chest, and they slept together.

They woke together, too, for Tommaso, halfway through the morning, suddenly sat up with a strangled shout, dislodging Seppi, who bounced onto his feet with his fur on end.

"What—what am I doing here?" said the young man confusedly. "I dreamed—I was dreaming I had been alone for days and days. I was starving to death. Was it true? Good heavens," he added, looking around him at all the little heaps of olives and grapes, the rows of carrots and beans, the tastefully arranged little patterns of cherries and chestnuts, of rice and peas, and the pale heap of spaghetti. "Who brought all this? Did Michele?"

"Prrrt," said Seppi.

"Or did you?" said Tommaso, looking at him closely. "How did *you* find your way in here? I know you. You're the little fellow who's always trying to steal a ride on my gondola. Well, I'm happy to have your company now, I can tell you. You are kindly welcome to share my breakfast."

Seppi did not wish to do this, but watched with huge satisfaction as the young man made a good meal of spaghetti and olives, grapes and chestnuts and sausages.

Presently some of the house mice arrived to ask if more supplies were needed yet; they brought with them small lumps of fresh *stracchino* cheese.

"Some friends from outside had heard of the young gentleman's situation, and they sent this in, as they live in a dairy. They wondered if he could use it."

Tommaso watched in utter amazement as the procession of mice rolled pieces of cheese across the floor and Seppi supervised their arrangement on an artichoke leaf.

Then a gull tapped at the window. "Beg pardon, I understand that the young fellow who lives here and plays the violin is in need of a bit of fruit?"

About fifty gulls swooped past, each dropping an orange or a grapefruit onto the roof.

Next a whole flock of pigeons arrived, each bearing some delicacy: a small cake, a shrimp, a sardine.

"We picked these up in the street market," one of them told Seppi. "There's a rumor going around among all the mice of the town that the young musician here is starving. We couldn't have that. Everybody loves his playing."

And a convocation of swans flew by, each bearing an oyster. "With best wishes for the young gentleman's recovery."

And a procession of rats came toiling over the rooftops from a spaghetti factory; Tommaso had enough spaghetti to last him a year, piled up on the roof.

"Seppi," he said in amazement, "you seem to have the whole town organized."

Seppi modestly busied himself in washing his stump of tail; he felt that it was unfair he should receive all the credit.

Three or four days passed in this manner, a week, two

weeks. Sandro and Nero returned every evening. But Seppi stayed with Tommaso daylong and nightlong; by day he watched contentedly as Tommaso nibbled at his provisions and slowly grew stronger; by night they both slept curled up together under Tommaso's cloak.

At the end of the first week, Tommaso was sufficiently recovered to begin playing a few tunes on his oboe. And at that, Seppi was flooded by such happiness that he hardly knew how to contain himself. To be able to sit, hour after hour, on the musician's cloak, listening to his marvelously beautiful music! What other cat in the world could possibly have such good fortune?

On the fifteenth day a gull flew over, shouting, "The parents are coming! They are coming along the canal in a gondola!"

Soon there was a confused noise downstairs, of doors opening, bumps and thumps, and loud voices exclaiming in horror.

Then heavy steps running up the stairs. The mice all bolted for cover.

And suddenly the door flew open, after a rattling of key in lock, and in burst Tommaso's father and mother. Their faces were as white as *stracchino* cheese. Plainly they expected to find their son stretched out dead on the floor.

"My son, my son!"

"My darling child!"

"Oh, my dear boy!"

"*Dio mio,* he is safe, he is alive! Heaven be thanked."

They embraced Tommaso over and over. "Oh, my dear child! By what merciful providence are you still with us?" said his father. "Where is Michele? What happened? We had told him to let you out after four days, even if you did not change your mind. And we meant to come back at the end of a week, but your mother fell ill in the country, and we could not leave until yesterday. And we had heard nothing from Michele. What has happened? We found the house empty and all the fires out. *Who* has been feeding you all this time?"

"Quite evidently the blessed saints have been looking after the boy," said his mother, gazing around, with the tears pouring down her face. "Now do you see, Antonio, that he is something special, and that if he wants to marry a girl called Margherita from the orphanage—who, I daresay, is a perfectly nice little thing—he should be allowed to do so?"

"Oh, very well," agreed old Antonio, who, in fact, was so glad to find his dear son still alive that he would have allowed him to marry a mermaid, if one had been at hand. "But was it really the blessed saints who were looking after you, my dear Tommaso?"

"No, Father. It was an ugly little cat with no tail called Seppi."

"A *cat?* Where is he?" cried the mother. "He shall sit on a gold cushion till the end of his days."

But Seppi, scared by all the noise and excitement, had darted in nervous haste out through the window hole, thanking his stars that he had eaten only very politely and sparingly of Tommaso's provisions and was still thin enough to squeeze through. No sign of either him or the mice remained—only a room piled high with olives and chestnuts and cheese.

Tommaso's parents practically carried him downstairs; they wanted to feast him on all the finest delicacies in Venice, but he said he was really full up and could eat nothing more just then. So, instead, they sent a note to the orphanage, asking for the hand of Margherita Rimondi for their son and heir. It was arranged that the young couple should be married two weeks from that day.

A couple of days later, Tommaso's mother said to him, "What is the matter, my son? You look thoughtful. Aren't you quite happy?"

"Well, yes, I am, Mother, happy as the day is long. But

I wish I could find that little cat. I wish he hadn't disappeared. It was really he who saved my life."

"Are you sure you didn't dream him in the fever, my son?"

"Oh, I do hope I didn't!" said Tommaso. But then he added, "No, I'm sure I didn't dream him, for I used to find him hiding in my gondola before all this happened."

"Well, then, it should be possible to find him."

In the meantime, where *was* Seppi?

Back in his drainpipe. He had fled to his only refuge, feeling sure that, now the young man's family had returned and all was forgiven, nobody would even spare a thought for a dirty little alley cat with most of his tail missing.

Day after day Seppi stayed crouching in the pipe, damp and melancholy, not even bothering to step outside for a breath of fresh air.

"You really ought to take a bit of exercise, you know," said Umberto disapprovingly from the other end of the pipe. Seppi merely grunted in reply. He was thinking, When Tommaso is married, he might move away from Venice. I may never see him anymore, never hear him play again.

He was very miserable.

And then, one day, he heard a gondola swishing along the canal outside his drainpipe, and he heard Nero's deep bass bellow, "Seppi! Come out of there! Everybody is looking for you!"

Seppi put his head out of the pipe. There was Benno Fosco's boat, full of black sacks, and Nero, sooty, stately, and commanding.

"Come on! Hurry up! Tommaso is getting married to-morrow, and he wants all the friends who helped him when he was a prisoner to join in his wedding procession, and you especially."

"Oh, he won't miss *me,*" said Seppi, pulling his head back in again.

"What rubbish! Why, he's had notices put up all over Venice. Wanted to find: Small black-and-white cat with one blue eye, one yellow, and half a tail."

"Really?"

"He wants you to live in his house!"

"Wh-what?"

"And you might just as well," said Nero kindly. "I think it's an excellent scheme. After all, Sandro and I have good homes of our own, but what have you got? A drainpipe! What kind of an establishment is that? Hurry up! Benno can't wait about all day. We've got six customers to take care of."

It was an unforgettable wedding. Gulls and pigeons flew over the bridal gondola. Swans drifted after it. Mice lined the quayside and bridges. And all the cats of Venice were there —perched on sills, on doorsteps, on steps, on skiffs and ferries, on hulls and prows. So many cats together were never seen before or since.

Seppi went to live with Tommaso and Margherita. He slept on a blue velvet cushion. He became brilliantly clean, his white patches like silk and his black like ebony. But he never grew any bigger. He played with all the six children of Tommaso and Margherita as they came along, and his nine lives extended on and on, until they seemed more like ninety-nine. He was happier than any other cat in Italy, for, alone of all the household, he was allowed into the musician's workroom and could listen to every note that his master—who became a famous composer—ever played.

(But on one night a week, Seppi went out over the roofs and sang in a concert with Sandro and Nero. All the Venetian cats were delighted to have their favorite trio back, and indeed the three became so well known that cats traveled from Milan and even Rome to hear them.)

Several years later Tommaso, now very famous indeed, was invited to visit the duke of Bavaria. And while on this visit, one day in the street, he ran into a man who went chalk-white at the sight of him, fell on his knees, and stammered, "It's n-n-never the young master? Praise be to all the holy saints! I thought you were dead!"

He was Michele, the steward.

He told how he had been knocked unconscious in a street fight and woke to find himself on a ship, where he had been dumped by someone who thought he was a sailor. The ship was already halfway to Africa.

"And when I thought of how you had been left—all alone in the house—oh, I nearly went mad! A week had gone by. I thought you must be dead already. I never dared go back to Venice. I've been in terrible grief all my days, thinking about you and how your father and mother must have felt when they returned. Oh, forgive me, forgive me!"

"Forgive? It was not your fault!" said Tommaso. "Quick! Jump on a horse and hurry back to Venice! You were only doing what you had been ordered."

"I was to let you out after four days!"

"So you would have. You didn't mean to leave me shut up in the attic. But anyway what a good thing you did! For without that, I should never have married. And I would never have found my Seppi!"

NOTE: *Tommaso Albinoni, son of a wealthy paper manufacturer, lived in Venice from 1671 to 1750, wrote beautiful music, married Margherita Rimondi, and had six children. There is no record of his having a cat. But he probably did. Venice is full of cats.*

Terry and Carol Carr

SOME ARE BORN CATS

 aybe he's an alien shape-changing spy from Arcturus," Freddie said.

"What does that mean?" asked the girl.

Freddie shrugged. "Maybe he's not a cat at all. He could be some kind of alien creature that came to Earth to spy on us. He could be hiding in the shape of a cat while he studies us and sends back reports to Arcturus or someplace."

She looked at the cat, whose black body lay draped across the top of the television set, white muzzle on white paws, wide green eyes open and staring at them. The boy and the girl lay on her bed, surrounded by schoolbooks.

"You're probably right," she said. "He gives me the creeps."

The girl's name was Alyson, and it was her room. She and Freddie spent a lot of their time together, though it wasn't a real Thing between them. Nothing official, nor even unofficial. They'd started the evening doing homework together, but now they were watching "Creature Features," with the sound turned down.

"He always does that," Alyson said. "He gets up on the television set whenever there's a scary movie on, and he drapes his tail down the side like that and just *stares* at me. I'm watching a vampire movie, and I happen to glance up and there he is, looking at me. He never blinks, even. It really freaks me out sometimes."

The cat sat up suddenly, blinking. It yawned and began an elaborate washing of its face. White paws, white chest, white face, and the rest of him was raven black. With only the television screen illuminating the room, he seemed to float in the darkness. On the screen now was a commercial for campers; a man who looked Oriental was telling them that campers were the best way to see America.

"What kind of a name is Gilgamesh?" Freddie asked. "That's his name, isn't it?"

"It's ancient Babylonian or something like that," Alyson told him. "He was kind of a god; there's a whole long story about him. I just liked the name, and he looked so scraggly and helpless when he adopted us, I thought maybe he could use a fancy name. But most of the time I just call him Gil anyway."

"Is George short for anything?" the boy asked. George was her other cat, a placid Siamese. George was in some other part of the house.

"No, he's just George. He looks so elegant, I didn't think he needed a very special name."

"Gilgamesh, you ought to pay more attention to

George," the boy said. "He's a *real* cat; he acts like a cat would really act. You don't see *him* sitting on top of horror shows and acting weird."

"George gets up on the television set too, but he just goes to sleep," Alyson said.

The cat, Gilgamesh, blinked at them and slowly lay down again, spreading himself carefully across the top of the TV set. He didn't look at them.

"Do you mean Gil could be just hypnotizing us to think he's a cat?" Alyson asked. "Or do you suppose he took over the body of a real cat when he arrived here on Earth?"

"Either way," Freddie said. "It's how he acts that's the tipoff. He doesn't act like a cat would. Hey, Gil, you really ought to study George—he knows what it's all about."

Gilgamesh lay still, eyes closed. They watched the movie, and after it, the late news. An announcer jokingly reported that strange lights had been seen in the skies over Watsonville, and he asked the TV weatherman if he could explain them. The weatherman said, "We may have a new wave of flying saucers moving in from the Pacific." Everybody in the studio laughed.

Gilgamesh jumped off the television set and left the room.

Freddie's Saturday morning began at eight o'clock with the "World News Roundup of the Week." He opened one eye cautiously and saw an on-the-spot reporter interviewing the families of three sky divers whose parachutes had failed to open.

Freddie was about to go downstairs for breakfast when the one woman reporter in the group smilingly announced that Friday night, at 11:45 P.M., forty-two people had called the studio to report a flying-saucer sighting. One man, the owner of a fish store, referred to "a school of saucers." The news team laughed, but Freddie's heartbeat quickened.

It took him twenty minutes to get through to Alyson, and when she picked up the phone, he was caught unprepared, with a mouthful of English muffin.

"Hello? Hello?"

"Mmgfghmf."

"Hello? Who *is* this?"

"Chrglfmhph."

"Oh, my goodness! Mom! I think it's one of those obscene calls!" She sounded deliriously happy. But she hung up.

Freddie swallowed and dialed again.

"Boy, am I glad it's you," Alyson said. "Listen, you've got to come right over—it's been one incredible thing after another ever since you left last night. First, the saucers—did you hear about them?—and then Gil freaking out, then a real creepy obscene telephone call."

"Hold it, hold it," Freddie said. "I'll meet you back of the house in five minutes."

When he got there, Alyson was lying stomach down on the lawn, chewing a blade of grass. She looked only slightly more calm than she sounded.

"Freddie," she said almost tragically. "How much do you know?"

"About as much as the next guy."

"No, seriously—I mean about the saucers last night. Did you see them?"

"I was asleep. Did you?"

"*See* them! I practically *touched* them." She looked deep into his eyes. "But Freddie, that's not the important part."

"What is? What?"

"Gilgamesh. I seriously believe he's having a nervous breakdown. I hate to think of what else it could be." She got up. "Wait right here. I want you to see this."

Freddie waited, a collage of living-color images dancing in his head: enemy sky divers, a massacred school of flying saucers, shape-changing spies from Arcturus. . . .

Alyson came back holding a limp Gilgamesh over her arm.

"He was in the litter pan," she said significantly. "He was covering it up."

"Covering what up?"

"His doo-doo, silly."

Freddie winced. There were moments when he wished Alyson were a bit more liberated.

Gilgamesh settled down to Alyson's lap and purred frantically.

"He has *never,* not once before, covered it up," she insisted. "He always gets out of the box when he's finished and scratches on the floor near it. George comes along eventually and does it for him."

Gilgamesh licked one paw and applied it to his right ear. It was a highly adorable action, one that never failed to please. He did it twice more—lick, tilt head, rub; lick, tilt head, rub —then stopped and looked at Freddie out of the corner of his eye.

"You see what I mean?" Alyson said. "Do you know what that look means?"

"He's asking for approval," said Freddie. "No doubt about it. He wants to know if he did it right."

"Exactly!"

Gilgamesh tucked his head between his white paws and closed his eyes.

"He feels that he's a failure," Alyson interpreted.

"Right."

Gilgamesh turned over on his back, let his legs flop, and began to purr. His body trembled like a lawn mower standing still.

Freddie nodded. "Overdone. Everything he does is self-conscious."

"And you know when he's not self-conscious? When he's staring. But he doesn't look like a cat then, either."

"What did he do last night, when the saucers were here?"

Alyson sat up straight; Gilgamesh looked at her suspiciously.

"He positively freaked," she said. "He took one look and his tail bushed out and he arched his back. . . ."

"That's not so freaky. Any kind of cat would do that."

"I know . . . it's what comes next." She paused dramatically. "In the middle of this bushy-tailed fit, he stopped dead in his tracks, shook his head, and trotted into the house to find George. Gil woke him up and chased him onto the porch. Then you know what he did? He put a paw on George's shoulder, like they were old buddies. And you know how George is—he just went along with it; he'll groove on anything. But it was so weird. George wanted to leave, but Gil kept him there by washing him. George can't resist a wash—he's too busy grooving to do it himself—so he stayed till the saucers took off."

Freddie picked up Alyson's half-chewed blade of grass and put it in his mouth. "You think that Gil, for reasons of his own, manipulated George into watching saucers with him?"

Gilgamesh stopped being a lawn mower long enough to bat listlessly at a bumblebee. Then he looked at Alyson slyly and resumed his purring.

"That's exactly what I think. What do you think?"

Freddie thought about it for a while, gazing idly at Gilgamesh. The cat avoided his eyes.

"Why would he want George to watch flying saucers with him?" Freddie asked.

Alyson shrugged elaborately, tossing her hair and looking at the clear blue of the sky. "I don't know. Flying saucers are spaceships, aren't they? Maybe Gilgamesh came here in one of them."

"But why would he want George to look at one?"

"I'll tell you what," said Alyson. "Why don't you ask Gilgamesh about that?"

Freddie glanced again at the cat; Gilgamesh was lying preternaturally still, as though asleep, yet too rigid to be truly asleep. Playing 'possum, Freddie thought. Listening.

"Hey, Gil," he said softly. "Why did you want George to see the flying saucers?"

Gilgamesh made no acknowledgment that he had heard. But Freddie noticed that his tail twitched.

"Come on, Gil, you can tell *me*," he coaxed. "I'm from Procyon, myself."

Gilgamesh sat bolt upright, eyes wide and shocked. Then he seemed to recollect himself, and he swatted at a nonexistent bee, chased his tail in a circle, and ran off around the corner of the house.

"You nearly got him that time," Alyson said. "That line about being from Procyon blew his mind."

"Next time we tie him to a chair and hang a naked light bulb over his head," Freddie said.

After school Monday, Freddie stopped off at the public library and did a little research. They kept files of the daily newspapers there, and Freddie spent several hours checking through the papers for the last several months for mentions of flying saucers or anything else unusual.

That evening, in Alyson's room, Freddie said, "Let's skip the French vocabulary for a while. When did you get Gilgamesh?"

Alyson had George on her lap; the placid Siamese lay like a dead weight except for his low-grade purr. Alyson said, "Three weeks ago. Gil just wandered into the kitchen, and we thought he was a stray—I mean, he couldn't have belonged to anybody, because he was so dirty and thin, and anyway, he didn't have a collar."

"Three weeks ago," Freddie said. "What day, exactly?"

She frowned, thinking back. "Mmm . . . it was a Tuesday. Three weeks ago tomorrow, then."

"That figures," Freddie said. "Alyson, do you know what happened the day before Gilgamesh just walked into your life?"

She stared wonderingly at him for a moment, then something lit in her eyes. "That was the night the sky was so loud!"

"Yes," said Freddie.

Alyson sat up on the bed, shedding both George and the books from her lap in her excitement. "And then that Tuesday we asked Mr. Newcomb in science class what had caused it, and he just said a lot of weird stuff that didn't mean anything, remember? Like he really didn't know, but he was a teacher, and he thought he had to be able to explain everything."

"Right," said Freddie. "An unexplainable scientific phenomenon in the skies, and the next day Gilgamesh just happened to show up on your doorstep. I'll bet there were flying saucers that night, too, only nobody saw them."

George sleepily climbed back onto the bed and settled down in Alyson's lap again. She idly scratched his ear, and he licked her hand, then closed his eyes and went to sleep again.

"You think it was flying saucers that made all those weird noises in the sky?" Alyson asked.

"Sure," he said. "Probably. Especially if that was the night before Gilgamesh got here. I wonder what his mission is?"

"What?" said Alyson.

"I wonder why he's here, on Earth. Do you think they're really planning to invade us?"

"Who?" she asked. "You mean people from flying saucers? Oh, Freddie, cool it. I mean a joke's a joke, and Gilgamesh *is* pretty creepy, but he's only a little black-and-white cat. He's not some invader from Mars!"

"Arcturus," Freddie said. "Or maybe it's really Procyon; maybe that's why he was so startled when I said that yesterday."

"Freddie! He's a *cat!*"

"You think so?" Freddie asked. "Let me show you something about your innocent little stray cat."

He got off the bed and silently went to the door of the bedroom. Grasping the knob gently, he suddenly threw the door open wide.

Standing right outside the door was Gilgamesh. The black-and-white cat leaped backward, then quickly recovered himself and walked calmly into the room, as though he had just been on his way in when the door opened. But Freddie saw that his tail was fully bushed out.

"You still think he's a cat?" Freddie asked.

"Freddie, he's just a little weird, that's all—"

"*Weird?* This cat's so weird he's probably got seven hearts and an extra brain in his back! Alyson, this is no ordinary cat!"

Gilgamesh jumped up on the bed, studied how George was lying, and arranged himself in a comparable position next to Alyson. She petted him for a moment, and he began to purr his odd high-pitched purr.

"You think he's just a cat?" Freddie asked. "He sounds like a cricket."

"Freddie, are you serious?" Alyson said. Freddie nodded. He'd done his research at the library, and he was sure something strange was going on.

"Well, then," said Alyson. "I know what we can do. We'll take him to my brother and see if he's really a cat or not."

"Your brother? But he's a chiropractor."

Alyson smiled. "But he has an X-ray machine. We'll *see* if Gilgamesh really has those extra hearts and all."

On her lap, George continued to purr. Next to her, Gilgamesh seemed to have developed a tic in the side of his face, but he continued to lie still.

Alyson's brother, the chiropractor, had his office in the Watsonville Shopping Center, next door to the Watsonville Bowling Alley. His receptionist told them to wait in the anteroom, the doctor would be with them in a moment.

Alyson and Freddie sat down on a black sofa, with the carrying case between them. From inside the case came pitiful mews and occasional thrashings about. From inside the office came sounds of pitiful cries and the high notes of Beethoven's Fifth. Somebody made a strike next door; the carrying case flew a foot into the air. Freddie transferred it to his lap and held it steady.

A young man with longish brown hair and a white jacket opened the door.

"Hey sister, hi Freddie. What's happening?"

Alyson pointed to the carrying case. "This is the patient I told you about, Bob."

"Okay. Let's go in and take a look."

He opened the case. Gilgamesh had curled himself into a tight ball of fur, his face pressed against the corner. When the doctor lifted him out, Freddie saw that the cat's eyes were clenched shut.

"I've never seen him so terrified," Alyson said. "Weird, freaky, yes, but never this scared."

"I still don't understand why you didn't take him to a vet if you think he's sick," her brother said.

Alyson grinned ingratiatingly. "You're cheaper."

"Hmpf."

All this time the doctor had been holding the rigid Gilgamesh in the air. As soon as he put him down on the examining table, the cat opened his eyes to twice their normal size, shot a bushy tail straight up, and dashed under the table. He cowered there, face between paws. Alyson's brother crawled under the table, but the cat scrambled to the opposite side of the room and hid behind a rubber plant. Two green eyes peeked through the leaves.

"I think stronger measures are indicated," the doctor said. He opened a drawer and removed a hypodermic needle and a small glass bottle.

Freddie and Alyson approached the rubber plant from each end, then grabbed.

Freddie lifted the cat onto the examining table. Gilgamesh froze, every muscle rigid—but his eyes darted dramatically around the room, looking for escape.

The doctor gave him the shot, and within seconds he was a boneless pussycat who submitted docilely to the indignities of being X-rayed in eight different positions.

Ten minutes later Alyson's brother announced the results: no abnormalities; Gilgamesh was a perfectly healthy cat.

"Does he have any extra hearts?" Alyson said. "Anything funny about his back?"

"He's completely normal," said her brother. "Doesn't even have any extra toes." He saw the worried expression on her face. "Wasn't that what you wanted to find out?"

"Sure," said Alyson. "Thanks a lot. I'm really relieved."

"Me, too," said Freddie. "Very."

Neither of them looked it.

"Lousy job," said Gilgamesh.

They turned to look at him, mouths open. The cat's mouth was closed. He was vibrating like a lawn mower again, purring softly.

Freddie looked at the doctor. "Did someone just say something?"

"Somebody just said, 'Lousy job,'" said the doctor. "I thought it was your cat. I must be losing my mind. Alyson?" She looked to be in shock. "Did you hear anything?"

"No. I didn't hear him say 'Lousy job' or anything like that." Still in a daze, she went over to the cat and stroked him on the head. Then she bent down and whispered something in his ear.

"Just haven't got the knack," said Gilgamesh. "Crash course." He smiled, closed his eyes, and fell asleep. But there was no doubt that it was he who had spoken.

Freddie, who had just got over the first wave of disbelief, said, "What was in that injection, anyway?"

"Sodium pentothal. Very small dose. I think I'd better sit down." The doctor staggered to the nearest chair, almost missing it.

"Hey, Alyson?" the doctor said.

"Huh?"

"Maybe you'd better tell me why you really brought your cat in here."

"Well," said Alyson.

"Come on, little sister, give," he said.

Alyson looked at the floor and mumbled, "Freddie thinks he's a spy from outer space."

"From Arcturus," said Freddie.

"Procyon," said Gilgamesh. He yawned and rolled onto his side.

"Wait a minute," said the doctor. "Wait a minute, I want to get something straight." But he just stared at the cat, at Freddie, at Alyson.

Freddie took advantage of the silence. "Gilgamesh, you were just talking, weren't you?"

"Lemme sleep," Gilgamesh mumbled.

"What's your game, Gil?" Freddie asked him. "Are you spying on us? You're really some shapeless amoebalike being that can rearrange its protoplasm at will, aren't you? Are your people planning to invade Earth? When will the first strike hit? Come on, *talk!*"

"Lemme sleep," Gilgamesh said.

Freddie picked up the cat and held him directly under the fluorescent light of the examining table. Gilgamesh winced and squirmed, feebly.

"Talk!" Freddie commanded. "Tell us the invasion plans."

"No invasion," Gilgamesh whined. "Lemme down. No fair drugging me."

"Are you from Procyon?" Freddie asked him.

"Are you from Killarney?" the cat sang, rather drunkenly. "Studied old radio broadcasts, sorry. Sure, from Procyon. Tried to act like a cat but couldn't get the hang of it. Never can remember what to do with my tail."

"What are you doing on Earth?" Freddie demanded.

"Chasing a runaway," the cat mumbled. "Antisocial renegade, classified for work camps. Jumped bail and ran. Tracked him to Earth, but he's been passing as a native."

"As a *human being?*" Alyson cried.

"As a cat. It's George. Cute li'l George, soft and lazy, lies in the sun all day. Irresponsible behavior. Antisocial. Never gets anything done. Got to bring him back, put him in a work camp."

"Wait a minute," Freddie broke in. "You mean you came to Earth to find an escaped prisoner? And George is it? You mean you're a *cop?*"

"Peace officer," Gilgamesh protested, trying to sit up straight. "Law and order. Loyalty to the egg and arisian pie. Only George *did* escape, so I had to track him down. I always get my amoeba."

Alyson's brother dazedly punched his intercom button. "Miss Blanchard, you'd better cancel the rest of my appointments," he said dully.

"But you *can't* take George away from me!" Alyson cried. "He's my *cat!*"

"Just a third-class amoeba," Gilgamesh sniffed. "Hard to control, though. More trouble than he's worth."

"Then leave him here!" Alyson said. "If he's a fugitive, he's safe with me! I'll give him sanctuary. I'll sign parole papers for him. I'll be responsible—"

Gilgamesh eyed her blearily. "Do you know what you're saying, lady?"

"Of course I know what I'm saying! George is my cat, and I love him—I guess you wouldn't know what that means. George stays with me, no matter what. You go away. Go back to your star."

"Listen, Alyson, maybe you should think about this. . . ." Freddie began.

"Shaddup, kid," said Gilgamesh. "I'll tell you, George was never anything to us but a headache. Won't work, just wants to lie around looking decorative. If you want him, lady, you got him."

There was a silence. Freddie noticed that Alyson's brother seemed to be giggling softly to himself.

After long moments, Alyson asked, "Don't I have to sign something?"

"Nah, lady," said Gilgamesh. "We're not barbarians. I've got your voice recorded in my head. George is all yours, and good riddance. He was a blot on the proud record of the Procyon Co-Prosperity Sphere." Gilgamesh got to his feet and marched rigidly to the window of the office. He turned and eyed them greenly.

"Listen, you tell George one thing for me. Tell him he's dumb lucky he happened to hide out as a cat. He can be lazy and decorative here, but I just want you to know one thing: there's no such thing as a decorative amoeba. An amoeba works, or out he goes!"

Gilgamesh disappeared out the window.

On the way back to Alyson's house, Freddie did his best to contain himself, but as they approached her door, he broke their silence. "I told you so, Alyson."

"Told me what?" Alyson opened the door and led him up the stairs to her room.

"That the cat was an alien. A shape-changer, a spy hiding out here on Earth."

"Pooh," she said. "You thought he was from Arcturus. Do you know how far Arcturus is from Procyon?"

They went into her room. "Very far?" Freddie asked.

"Oh, *boy!*" Alyson said. "Very *far!*" She shook her head disgustedly.

George was lying in the middle of the bed, surrounded by schoolbooks. He opened one eye as the two of them tramped into the room, then closed it again and contented himself with a soft purr.

Alyson sat on the side of the bed and rubbed George's belly. "Sweet George," she said. "Beautiful little pussycat."

"Listen, Alyson," said Freddie, "maybe you ought to think about George a little bit. I mean, you're responsible for him now—"

"He's my cat," Alyson said firmly.

"Yeah, well, sort of," Freddie said. "Not really, of course, because really he's an alien shape-changing amoeba from Procyon. And worse than that, remember what Gilgamesh said, he's a runaway. He's a dropout from interstellar society. Who knows, maybe he even uses drugs!"

Alyson rested a level gaze on Freddie, a patient, forgiving look. "Freddie," she said softly, "some of us are born cats, and some of us achieve catness."

"What?"

"Well, look, if *you* were an amoeba from Procyon and you were sent off to the work camps, wouldn't you rather come to Earth and be a cat and lie around all day sunning yourself and getting scratched behind the ears? I mean, it just makes *sense*. It proves George is *sane!*"

"It proves he's lazy," Freddie muttered.

George opened his eyes just a slit and looked at Freddie —a look of contented wonder. Then he closed his eyes again and began to purr.

Italo Calvino

AUTUMN

THE GARDEN OF STUBBORN CATS

The city of cats and the city of men exist one inside the other, but they are not the same city. Few cats recall the time when there was no distinction: the streets and squares of men were also streets and squares of cats, and the lawns, courtyards, balconies, and fountains; you lived in a broad and various space. But for several generations now domestic felines have been prisoners of an uninhabitable city; the streets are uninterruptedly overrun by the mortal traffic of cat-crushing automobiles; in every square foot of terrain where once a garden extended or a vacant lot or the ruins of an old demolition, now condominiums loom up, welfare housing, brand-new skyscrapers; every entrance is crammed with parked cars; the courtyards, one by one, have been roofed by reinforced concrete and transformed into garages or movie houses or storerooms or workshops. And where a rolling plateau of low roofs once extended, copings, terraces, water tanks, balconies, skylights, corrugated-iron sheds, now one general superstructure rises wherever structures can rise; the intermediate differences in height, between the low ground of the street and the supernal heaven of the penthouses, disappear; the cat of a recent litter seeks in vain the itinerary of its fathers, the point from which to make the soft leap from balustrade to cornice to drainpipe, or for the quick climb on the roof tiles.

But in this vertical city, in this compressed city where all voids tend to fill up and every block of cement tends to mingle with other blocks of cement, a kind of countercity opens, a negative city, that consists of empty slices between wall and wall, of the minimal distances ordained by the building regulations between two constructions, between the rear of one construction and the rear of the next; it is a city of cavities, wells, air conduits, driveways, inner yards, accesses to basements, like a network of dry canals on a planet of stucco and tar, and it is through this network, grazing the walls, that the ancient cat population still scurries.

On occasion, to pass the time, Marcovaldo would follow a cat. It was during the work break, between noon and three, when all the personnel except Marcovaldo went home to eat, and he—who brought his lunch in his bag—laid his place among the packing cases in the warehouse, chewed his snack, smoked a half cigar, and wandered around, alone and idle, waiting for work to resume. In those hours, a cat that peeped in at a window was always welcome company, and a guide for new explorations. He had made friends with a tabby, well fed, a blue ribbon around its neck, surely living with some well-to-do family. This tabby shared with Marcovaldo the habit of an afternoon stroll right after lunch; and naturally a friendship sprang up.

Following his tabby friend, Marcovaldo had started looking at places as if through the round eyes of a cat and even if these places were the usual environs of his firm he saw them in a different light, as settings for cattish stories, with connections practicable only by light, velvety paws. Though from the outside the neighborhood seemed poor in cats, every day on his rounds Marcovaldo made the acquaintance of some new face, and a meow, a hiss, a stiffening of fur on an arched back was enough for him to sense ties and intrigues and rivalries among them. At those moments he thought he had already penetrated the secrecy of the felines' society; and then he felt himself scrutinized by pupils that became slits, under the surveillance of the antennae of taut whiskers, and all the cats around him sat impassive as sphinxes, the pink triangle of their noses convergent on the black triangles of their lips, and the only things that moved were the tips of the ears, with a vibrant jerk like radar. They reached the end of a narrow passage, between squalid blank walls; and, looking around, Marcovaldo saw that the cats that had led him this far had vanished, all of them together, no telling in which direction, even his tabby friend, and they had left him alone. Their realm had territories, ceremonies, customs that it was not yet granted to him to discover.

On the other hand, from the cat city there opened unsuspected peepholes onto the city of men; and one day the same tabby led him to discover the great Biarritz Restaurant.

Anyone wishing to see the Biarritz Restaurant had only to assume the posture of a cat, that is, proceed on all fours. Cat and man, in this fashion, walked around a kind of dome, at whose foot some low, rectangular little windows opened. Following the tabby's example, Marcovaldo looked down. They were transoms through which the luxurious hall received air and light. To the sound of Gypsy violins, partridges and quails swirled by on silver dishes balanced by the white-gloved fingers of waiters in tailcoats. Or, more precisely, above the partridges and quails the dishes whirled, and above the dishes the white gloves, and poised on the waiters' patent-leather shoes, the gleaming parquet floor, from which hung dwarf potted palms and tablecloths and crystal and buckets like bells with the champagne bottle for their clapper: everything was turned upside down because Marcovaldo, for fear of being seen, wouldn't stick his head inside the window and confined himself to looking at the reversed reflection of the room in the tilted pane.

But it was not so much the windows of the dining room as those of the kitchens that interested the cat: looking through the former you saw, distant and somehow transfigured, what in the kitchens presented itself—quite concrete and within paw's reach—as a plucked bird or a fresh fish. And it was toward the kitchens, in fact, that the tabby wanted to lead Marcovaldo, either through a gesture of altruistic friendship or else because it counted on the man's help for one of its raids. Marcovaldo, however, was reluctant to leave his belvedere over the main room, first as he was fascinated by the luxury of the place, and then because something down there had riveted his attention. To such an extent that, overcoming his fear of being seen, he kept peeking in, with his head in the transom.

In the midst of the room, directly under that pane, there was a little glass fish tank, a kind of aquarium, where some fat trout were swimming. A special customer approached, a man with a shiny bald pate, black suit, black beard. An old waiter in tailcoat followed him, carrying a little net as if he were going to catch butterflies. The gentleman in black looked at the trout with a grave, intent air; then he raised one hand and with a slow, solemn gesture singled out a fish. The waiter dipped the net into the tank, pursued the appointed trout, captured it, headed for the kitchens, holding out in front of him, like a lance, the net in which the fish wriggled. The gentleman in black, solemn as magistrate who has handed down a capital sentence, went to take his seat and wait for the return of the trout, sautéed *à la meunière.*

If I found a way to drop a line from up here and make one of those trout bite, Marcovaldo thought, I couldn't be accused of theft; at worst, of fishing in an unauthorized place. And ignoring the meows that called him toward the kitchens, he went to collect his fishing tackle.

Nobody in the crowded dining room of the Biarritz saw the long, fine line, armed with hook and bait, as it slowly dropped into the tank. The fish saw the bait, and flung themselves on it. In the fray one trout managed to bite the worm, and immediately it began to rise, rise, emerge from the water, a silvery flash, it darted up high, over the laid tables and the trolleys of hors d'oeuvres, over the blue flames of the crêpes Suzette, until it vanished into the heavens of the transom.

Marcovaldo had yanked the rod with the brisk snap of the expert fisherman, so the fish landed behind his back. The trout had barely touched the ground when the cat sprang. What little life the trout still had was lost between the tabby's teeth. Marcovaldo, who had abandoned his line at that moment to run and grab the fish, saw it snatched from under his nose, hook and all. He was quick to put one foot on the rod, but the snatch had been so strong that the rod was all the man had left, while the tabby ran off with the fish, pulling the line after it. Treacherous kitty! It had vanished.

But this time it wouldn't escape him; there was that long line trailing after him and showing the way he had taken. Though he had lost sight of the cat, Marcovaldo followed the end of the line; there it was, running along a wall; it climbed a parapet, wound through a doorway, was swallowed up by a basement. . . . Marcovaldo, venturing into more and more cattish places, climbed roofs, straddled railings, always managed to catch a glimpse—perhaps only a second before it disappeared—of that moving trace that indicated the thief's path.

Now the line played out down a sidewalk, in the midst of the traffic, and Marcovaldo, running after it, almost managed to grab it. He flung himself down on his belly; there, he grabbed it! He managed to seize one end of the line before it slipped between the bars of a gate.

Beyond a half-rusted gate and two bits of wall buried under climbing plants, there was a little rank garden, with a small, abandoned-looking building at the far end of it. A carpet of dry leaves covered the path, and dry leaves lay everywhere under the boughs of the two plane trees, forming actually some little mounds in the yard. A layer of leaves was yellowing in the green water of a pool. Enormous buildings rose all around, skyscrapers with thousands of windows, like so many eyes trained disapprovingly on that little square patch with two trees, a few tiles, and all those yellow leaves, surviving right in the middle of an area of great traffic.

And in this garden, perched on the capitals and balustrades, lying on the dry leaves of the flower beds, climbing on the trunks of the trees or on the drainpipes, motionless on their four paws, their tails making a question mark, seated to wash their faces, there were tiger cats, black cats, white cats, calico cats, tabbies, Angoras, Persians, house cats and stray cats, perfumed cats and mangy cats. Marcovaldo realized he had finally reached the heart of the cats' realm, their secret island. And, in his emotion, he almost forgot his fish.

It had remained, that fish, hanging by the line from the branch of a tree, out of reach of the cats' leaps; it must have dropped from its kidnapper's mouth at some clumsy movement, perhaps as it was defended from the others, or perhaps displayed as an extraordinary prize. The line had got tangled, and Marcovaldo, tug as he would, couldn't manage to yank it loose. A furious battle had meanwhile been joined among the cats, to reach that unreachable fish, or rather, to win the right to try and reach it. Each wanted to prevent the others from leaping; they hurled themselves on one another, they tangled in midair, they rolled around clutching each other, and finally a general war broke out in a whirl of dry, crackling leaves.

After many futile yanks, Marcovaldo now felt the line was free, but he took care not to pull it: the trout would have fallen right in the midst of that infuriated scrimmage of felines.

It was at this moment that, from the top of the walls of the gardens, a strange rain began to fall: fishbones, heads, tails, even bits of lung and lights. Immediately the cats' attention was distracted from the suspended trout and they flung themselves on the new delicacies. To Marcovaldo, this seemed the right moment to pull the line and regain his fish. But, before he had time to act, from a blind of the little villa, two yellow, skinny hands darted out: one was brandishing scissors; the other, a frying pan. The hand with the scissors was raised above the trout, the hand with the frying pan was thrust under it. The scissors cut the line, the trout fell into the pan; hands, scissors, and pan withdrew, the blind closed—all in the space of a second. Marcovaldo was totally bewildered.

"Are you also a cat lover?" A voice at his back made him turn round. He was surrounded by little old women, some of them ancient, wearing old-fashioned hats on their heads; others, younger, but with the look of spinsters; and all were carrying in their hands or their bags packages of leftover meat or fish, and some even had little pans of milk. "Will you help me throw this package over the fence, for those poor creatures?"

All the ladies, cat lovers, gathered at this hour around the garden of dry leaves to take food to their protégés.

"Can you tell me why they are all here, these cats?" Marcovaldo inquired.

"Where else could they go? This garden is all they have

left! Cats come here from other neighborhoods, too, from miles and miles around. . . ."

"And birds, as well," another lady added. "They're forced to live by the hundreds and hundreds on these few trees. . . ."

"And the frogs, they're all in that pool, and at night they never stop croaking. . . . You can hear them even on the eighth floor of the buildings around here."

"Who does this villa belong to anyway?" Marcovaldo asked. Now, outside the gate, there weren't just the cat-loving ladies but also other people: the man from the gas pump opposite, the apprentices from a mechanic's shop, the postman, the grocer, some passersby. And none of them, men and women, had to be asked twice; all wanted to have their say, as always when a mysterious and controversial subject comes up.

"It belongs to a marchesa. She lives there, but you never see her. . . ."

"She's been offered millions and millions, by developers, for this little patch of land, but she won't sell. . . ."

"What would she do with millions, an old woman all alone in the world? She wants to hold on to her house, even if it's falling to pieces, rather than be forced to move. . . ."

"It's the only undeveloped bit of land in the downtown area. . . . Its value goes up every year. . . . They've made her offers—"

"Offers! That's not all. Threats, intimidation, persecution . . . you don't know the half of it! Those contractors!"

"But she holds out. She's held out for years. . . ."

"She's a saint. Without her, where would those poor animals go?"

"A lot she cares about the animals, the old miser! Have you ever seen her give them anything to eat?"

"How can she feed the cats when she doesn't have food for herself? She's the last descendant of a ruined family!"

"She hates cats. I've seen her chasing them and hitting them with an umbrella!"

"Because they were tearing up her flower beds!"

"What flower beds? I've never seen anything in this garden but a great crop of weeds!"

Marcovaldo realized that with regard to the old marchesa opinions were sharply divided: some saw her as an angelic being, others as an egoist and a miser.

"It's the same with the birds; she never gives them a crumb!"

"She gives them hospitality. Isn't that plenty?"

"Like she gives the mosquitoes, you mean. They all come from here, from that pool. In the summertime the mosquitoes eat us alive, and it's all the fault of that marchesa!"

"And the mice? This villa is a mine of mice. Under the dead leaves they have their burrows, and at night they come out. . . ."

"As far as the mice go, the cats take care of them. . . ."

"Oh, you and your cats! If we had to rely on them. . . ."

"Why? Have you got something to say against cats?"

Here the discussion degenerated into a general quarrel.

"The authorities should do something: confiscate the villa!" one man cried.

"What gives them the right?" another protested.

"In a modern neighborhood like ours, a mouse nest like this . . . it should be forbidden. . . ."

"Why, I picked my apartment precisely becuase it over-looked this little bit of green. . . ."

"Green, hell! Think of the fine skyscraper they could build here!"

Marcovaldo would have liked to add something of his own, but he couldn't get a word in. Finally, all in one breath, he exclaimed: "The marchesa stole a trout from me!"

The unexpected news supplied fresh ammunition to the old woman's enemies, but her defenders exploited it as proof of the indigence to which the unfortunate noblewoman was reduced. Both sides agreed that Marcovaldo should go and knock at her door to demand an explanation.

It wasn't clear whether the gate was locked or unlocked; in any case, it opened, after a push, with a mournful creak. Marcovaldo picked his way among the leaves and cats, climbed the steps to the porch, knocked hard at the entrance.

At a window (the very one where the frying pan had appeared), the blind was raised slightly and in one corner a round, pale blue eye was seen, and a clump of hair dyed an undefinable color, and a dry skinny hand. A voice was heard, asking: "Who is it? Who's at the door?" the words accompanied by a cloud smelling of fried oil.

"It's me, Marchesa. The trout man," Marcovaldo explained. "I don't mean to trouble you. I only wanted to tell you, in case you didn't know, that the trout was stolen from me, by that cat, and I'm the one who caught it. In fact the line—"

"Those cats! It's always those cats . . . ," the marchesa said from behind the shutter, with a shrill, somewhat nasal voice. "All my troubles come from the cats! Nobody knows what I go through! Prisoner night and day of those horrid beasts! And with all the refuse people throw over the walls, to spite me!"

"But my trout . . ."

"Your trout! What am I supposed to know about your trout!" The marchesa's voice became almost a scream, as if she wanted to drown out the sizzle of the oil in the pan, which came through the window along with the aroma of fried fish. "How can I make sense of anything, with all the stuff that rains into my house?"

"I understand, but did you take the trout or didn't you?"

"When I think of all the damage I suffer because of the cats! Ah, fine state of affairs! I'm not responsible for anything! I can't tell you what I've lost! Thanks to those cats, who've occupied house and garden for years! My life at the mercy of those animals! Go and find the owners! Make them pay damages! Damages? A whole life destroyed! A prisoner here, unable to move a step!"

"Excuse me for asking: but who's forcing you to stay?"

From the crack in the blind there appeared sometimes a round, pale blue eye, sometimes a mouth with two protruding teeth; for a moment the whole face was visible, and to Marcovaldo it seemed, bewilderingly, the face of a cat.

"They keep me prisoner, they do, those cats! Oh, I'd be glad to leave! What wouldn't I give for a little apartment all my own, in a nice clean modern building! But I can't go out. . . . They follow me, they block my path, they trip me up!" The voice became a whisper, as if to confide a secret. "They're afraid I'll sell the lot. . . . They won't leave me. . . . won't allow me. . . . When the builders come to offer me a contract, you should see them, those cats! They get in the way, pull out their claws; they even chased a lawyer off! Once I had the contract right here, I was about to sign it, and they dived in through the window, knocked over the inkwell, tore up all the pages. . . ."

All of a sudden Marcovaldo remembered the time, the shipping department, the boss. He tiptoed off over the dried leaves, as the voice continued to come through the slats of the blind, enfolded in that cloud apparently from the oil of a frying pan. "They even scratched me. . . . I still have the scar. . . . All alone here at the mercy of these demons. . . ."

Winter came. A blossoming of white flakes decked the branches and capitals and the cats' tails. Under the snow, the dry leaves dissolved into mush. The cats were rarely seen, the cat lovers even less; the packages of fishbones were consigned only to cats who came to the door. Nobody, for quite a while, had seen anything of the marchesa. No smoke came now from the chimneypot of the villa.

One snowy day, the garden was again full of cats, who

had returned as if it were spring, and they were meowing as if on a moonlight night. The neighbors realized that something had happened; they went and knocked at the marchesa's door. She didn't answer: she was dead.

In the spring, instead of the garden, there was a huge building site that a contractor had set up. The steam shovels dug down to great depths to make room for the foundations, cement poured into the iron armatures, a very high crane passed beams to the workmen who were making the scaffoldings. But how could they get on with their work? Cats walked along all the planks, they made bricks fall and upset buckets of mortar, they fought in the midst of the piles of sand. When you started to raise an armature, you found a cat perched on the top of it, hissing fiercely. More treacherous pusses climbed onto the masons' backs as if to purr, and there was no getting rid of them. And the birds continued making their nests in all the trestles, the cab of the crane looked like an aviary. . . . And you couldn't dip up a bucket of water that wasn't full of frogs, croaking and hopping. . . .

Translated by William Weaver